JUSTICE ACCUSED

JUSTICE ACCUSED

ANTISLAVERY AND THE JUDICIAL PROCESS

Robert M. Cover

New Haven and London
Yale University Press
1975

Copyright © 1975 by Yale University.
All rights reserved. This book may not be
reproduced, in whole or in part, in any form
(except by reviewers for the public press),
without written permission from the publishers.
Library of Congress catalog card number: 74-19573
International standard book number: 0-300-01789-8

Designed by Sally Sullivan
and set in Times Roman type.
Printed in the United States of America by
Vail-Ballou Press, Inc., Binghamton, N.Y.

Published in Great Britain, Europe, and Africa by
Yale University Press, Ltd., London.
Distributed in Latin America by Kaiman & Polon,
Inc., New York City; in Australasia and Southeast
Asia by John Wiley & Sons Australasia Pty. Ltd.,
Sydney; in India by UBS Publishers' Distributors Pvt.,
Ltd., Delhi; in Japan by John Weatherhill, Inc., Tokyo.

To my parents
Martha and Jacob L. Cover
with gratitude and love

Justice cools the fierce glow
of moral passion by making
it pass through reflection.

Shalom Spiegel,
Amos v. Amatziah

CONTENTS

PART II: RULES, ROLES, AND REBELS: NATURE'S PLACE DISPUTED

PART III: THE MORAL-FORMAL DILEMMA

ACKNOWLEDGMENTS

In 1968 I wrote a short polemic against what I characterized as judicial complicity in the crimes of Vietnam. In that piece I compared judicial involvement in the war with judicial acquiescence in the injustices of Negro slavery. Several of my colleagues at the Columbia Law School seemed more upset at the rather facile judgments passed upon the revered and honored dead for their part in slavery than at the attack upon the sitting bench for its part in Vietnam. From that reaction came the determination to write this book. I am grateful to those colleagues for alerting me to all the complexities of the process of complicity that forms the subject matter of this work.

A great many colleagues have read all or parts of this work at various stages in its development. Professors Louis Henkin and Abraham Sofaer of the Columbia Law School read a very early, hazy draft of some of these ideas. Their thoughtful criticism was most helpful. At a much later stage, Carol Weisbrod, Jerrold Guben, Professors Leon Lipson, Joseph Goldstein, Jan Deutsch, Arthur Leff, Owen Fiss, W. Michael Reisman, Barbara Underwood, and Guido Calabresi of the Yale Law School were most generous of their time and ideas in reading and commenting upon this text. I am also indebted to Professor David B. Davis of the Yale University History Department for his most helpful reading of large sections of this work. Needless to say, I take full responsibility for the failings and inadequacies of the book.

I have benefited from the generous institutional support of the Columbia Law School, under Dean Michael Sovern, and of the Yale Law School, under Dean Abraham Goldstein. The Columbia Law Library, under Edwin Schuck, and the Yale Law Library, under Arthur Charpentier, have provided generous and ready help on numerous occasions with respect to materials far outside the normal bounds of a law library's interests.

My deepest debt is to Professor Joseph Lukinsky of the Jewish Theological Seminary who first opened my eyes to the complexity of moral choice.

I am grateful for the help of Mrs. Geraldine Formica and of Mrs. Mimi Strassner in preparation of the manuscript.

I have had the good fortune to work with a helpful and most perceptive editor; my thanks also to Jane Isay of the Yale University Press.

Works are but vanities without a life into which they fit. I owe more than gratitude to Diane, and more recently to Avi, who share and create that life with me.

All citation to legal materials except for books and treatises is in accord with the forms suggested or required in the Harvard Law Review et al., *A Uniform System of Citation* (11th ed., 1967, published by the Harvard Law Review Association).

PRELUDE: Of Creon and Captain Vere

1

Antigone's star has shown brightly through the millennia. The archetype for civil disobedience has claimed a constellation of first-magnitude emulators. The disobedient—whether Antigone, Luther, Gandhi, King, or Bonhoeffer—exerts a powerful force upon us. The singular act, the risk, the dramatic appeal to a juster justice, all contribute to the high drama of the moment and the power of the actor's role. No wonder, then, that such men and women are celebrated in literature and history. No wonder that a great psychiatrist like Erikson, upon embarking on a venture in history and biography, chose Luther and Gandhi as his first subjects.[1]

Yet, in a curious way, to focus upon the disobedient and the process of disobedience is to accept the perspective of the established order. It is a concession that it is the man who appeals beyond law that is in need of explanation. With the sole exception of Nazi atrocities, the phenomenon of complicity in oppressive legal systems (oppressive from the actor's own perspective) has seldom been studied.* Thus, Creon is present only as a foil for Antigone, not himself the object of the artist's study of human character. In *Antigone* note the curious one-dimensional character of the King. How he comes to

* Complicity with the Nazi regime has been the object of much study. But at least the transatlantic emphasis has been an analysis of responsibility on the command and policy initiative level in a genocidal situation. Some attempts have been made to associate legal positivism—especially in its Kelsenian form—with the atrocities. H. L. A. Hart has vigorously and convincingly argued that positivism has no necessary relationship to such amoral and immoral judicial conduct. Indeed, he has demonstrated how the English positivists, and most especially Bentham, urged the analytical distinction between law as it is and law as it ought to be and stressed the human origins of law in order to be able to effectively measure the law against an external standard for reform purposes. (In Bentham's case the external standard was, of course, utility. But one need not accept the utilitarian basis of morality to accept the necessity of the analytical distinction.) See, e.g., H. L. A. Hart, "Positivism and the Separation of Law and Morals," 71 *Harvard Law Review* 593 (1958). While I argue within that a thoroughgoing legal positivism was one of the many factors that determined the complicity of the antislavery judge in the system of law that he himself considered immoral, it is but one such factor. Moreover, I shall also argue that the same jurisprudential perspective contributed to the most radical of the opposition viewpoints with regard to slave law. See, Chapter 9, infra.

make his law and at what cost in psychic terms is not treated at all. Indeed, Creon's first conflict is not between right and law, but between his son and his pride. And even in the midst of that conflict he betrays his singular obtuseness to the complexity of the situation he created by crying filial impiety and anarchy in one breath. He is astounded by the possibility of Haemon's sympathy to an affront to authority. Much of the simplicity of Creon lies in the choice of a tyrant as model for legal system. The making of law and its applications are wholly confined to a single will unconstrained by any but the most personal of considerations such as the feelings and actions of a son.

Melville's Captain Vere in *Billy Budd* is one of the few examples of an attempt to portray the conflict patterns of Creon or Creon's minions in a context more nearly resembling the choice situations of judges in modern legal systems. Billy Budd, radical innocence personified, is overwhelmed by a charge of fomenting mutiny, falsely levied against him by the first mate Claggart. Claggart seems to personify dark and evil forces. Struck dumb by the slanderous charges, Billy strikes out and kills the mate with a single blow. Captain Vere must instruct a drumhead court on the law of the Mutiny Act as it is to be applied to Billy Budd—in some most fundamental sense "innocent," though perpetrator of the act of killing the first mate.[2] In what must be, for the legal scholar, the high point of the novella, Vere articulates the "scruples" of the three officers (and his own) and rejects them.

> How can we adjudge to summary and shameful death a fellow creature innocent before God, and whom we feel to be so?—Does that state it aright? You sign sad assent. Well, I too feel that, the full force of that. It is Nature. But do these buttons that we wear attest that our allegiance is to Nature? No, to the King.

And, but a few paragraphs farther on, Vere asks the three whether "occupying the position we do, private conscience should not yield to that imperial one formulated in the code under which alone we officially proceed." [3]

In Vere's words we have a positivist's condensation of a legal system's formal character. Five aspects of that formalism may be discerned and specified: First, there is explicit recognition of the role character of the judges—a consciousness of the formal element. It is a uniform, not nature, that defines obligation. Second, law is distinguished from both the transcendent and the personal sources of obligation. The law is neither nature nor conscience. Third, the law is embodied in a readily identifiable source which governs transactions and occurrences of the sort under consideration: here an imperial code of which the Mutiny Act is a part. Fourth, the will behind the law is vague, uncertain, but *clearly not* that of the judges. It is here "imperial will" which, in (either eighteenth- or) nineteenth-century terms as applied to England, is not very easy to describe except through a constitutional law treatise. But, in any event, it is not the will of Vere and his three officers. Fifth, a corollary of the fourth point, the judge is not responsible for the content of the law but for its straightforward application.

> For that law and the rigor of it, we are not responsible. Our vowed responsibility is in this: That however pitilessly that law may operate in any instances, we nevertheless adhere to it and administer it.[4]

These five elements are part of Vere's arguments. But *Billy Budd* is a literary work and much that is most interesting about Vere is not in what he says but in what he is, in overtones of character. For example, we have intimations from the outset of a personality committed to fearful symmetries. His nickname, derived from Marvell's lines

> Under the discipline severe
> Of Fairfax and the starry Vere

suggests an impersonal and unrelaxed severity. And his intellectual bent, too, reinforces this suggestion of rigidity. He eschewed innovations "disinterestedly" and because they seemed "insusceptible of embodiment in lasting institutions." And he lacked "companionable quality." A man emerges who is disposed to approach life institutionally, to avoid the personal realm even where it perhaps ought to hold sway, to be inflexibly honest, righteous, and duty bound.[5]

It is this man who, seeing and appreciating Budd's violent act, exclaimed, "Struck dead by an angel of God! Yet the angel must hang." And, characteristically, it is Vere who assumes the responsibility of conveying the dread verdict to the accused. Melville's speculations on that "interview" are revealing. He stresses the likelihood that Vere revealed his own full part in the "trial." He goes on to speculate that Vere might well have assumed a paternal stance in the manner of Abraham embracing Isaac "on the brink of resolutely offering him up in obedience to the exacting behest." [6] Such a religious conviction of duty characterizes our man. Neither conventional morality, pity, nor personal agony could bend him from a stern duty. But in Vere's case the master is not God but the King. And the King is but a symbol for a social order.

Righteous men, indeed, suffer the agonies of their righteousness. Captain Vere betrayed just such agony in leaving his meeting with Billy Budd. But there is no indication that Vere suffered the agony of doubt about his course. When Billy died uttering "God Bless Captain Vere," there is no intimation that the Captain sensed any irony (whether intended or not) in the parting benediction. If Captain Vere is Abraham, he is the biblical version, not Kierkegaard's shadow poised achingly at the chasm.

Melville has been astonishingly successful in making his readers ask dreadful questions of Vere and his behavior. What deep urge leads a man to condemn unworldly beauty and innocence? To embrace, personally, the opportunity to do an impersonal, distasteful task? How reconcile the flash of recognition of "the angel must die" and the seizing of the opportunity to act Abraham, with declared protestations, unquestionably sincere, that only plain and clear duty overcomes his sense of the victim's cosmic innocence? We have so many doubts about a man who hears and obeys the voice of the Master so quickly, and our doubts are compounded when it is a harsh social system that becomes the Lord.

I venture to suggest that Melville had a model for Captain Vere that may bring us very close to our main story. Melville's father-in-law was Chief Justice Lemuel Shaw of the Massachusetts Supreme Judicial Court. A firm, unbending man of stern integrity, Shaw dominated the Massachusetts judicial system very much as Captain Vere ran his ship. The Chief Justice was a noted, strong opponent to slavery and expressed his opposition privately, in print, and in appropriate judicial opinions. [7] Yet, in the great causes célèbres involving fugitive slaves, Shaw came down hard for an unflinching application of the harsh and summary law. The effort cost Shaw untold personal agony. He was villified by abolitionists. I cannot claim that Vere is Lemuel Shaw (though he might be), for there is no direct evidence. I can only say that it would be remarkable that in portraying a man caught in the horrible conflict between duty and conscience, between role and morality, between nature and positive law, Melville would be untouched by the figure of his father-in-law in the *Sims Case,* the Latimer affair, or the Burns controversy.[8] We know Melville's predilection to the ship as microcosm for the social order. He used the device quite plainly with respect to slavery in *Benito Cereno.*

The fugitive slave was very Budd-like, though he was as black as Billy was blonde. The Mutiny Act admitted of none of the usual defenses, extenuations, or mitigations. If the physical act was that of the defendant, he was guilty. The Fugitive Slave Act similarly excluded most customary sorts of defenses. The alleged fugitive could not even plead that he was not legally a slave so long as he was the person *alleged* to be a fugitive. The drumhead court was a special and summary proceeding; so was the fugitive rendition process. In both proceedings the fatal judgment was carried out immediately. There was no appeal.[9]

More important, Billy's fatal flaw was his innocent dumbness. He struck because he could not speak. So, under the Fugitive Slave Acts, the alleged fugitive had no right to speak. And, as a rule, slaves had no capacity to testify against their masters or whites, generally. Billy Budd partakes of the slave, generalized. He was seized, impressed, from the ship *Rights of Man* and taken abroad the *Bellipotent.*[10] Aboard the *Bellipotent* the Mutiny Act and Captain Vere held sway. The Mutiny Act was justified because of its necessity for the order demanded on a ship in time of war. So the laws of slavery, often equally harsh and unbending, were justified as necessary for the social order in antebellum America. Moreover, the institution itself was said to have its origin in war.

But most persuasive is Vere and his dilemma—the subject matter of this book. For, if there was a single sort of case in which judges during Melville's lifetime struggled with the moral-formal dilemma, it was slave cases. In these cases, time and again, the judiciary paraded its helplessness before the law; lamented harsh results; intimated that in a more perfect world, or at the end of days, a better law would emerge, but almost uniformly, marched to the music, steeled themselves, and hung Billy Budd.

Of course, *Billy Budd,* like any great work of literature, exists on many levels. I would not deny the theology in the work, nor the clash of elemental good and elemental evil in Budd and Claggart. But the novella is also about a judgment, within a social system, and about the man who, dimly perceiving the great and abstract forces at work, bears responsibility for that judgment. It is about starry-eyed Vere and Lemuel Shaw.

2

The rest of this book is not about literature, but about Lemuel Shaw and many judges like him. It is the story of earnest, well-meaning pillars of legal respectability and of their collaboration in a system of oppression—Negro slavery. I have chosen to analyze at length only the dilemma of the antislavery judge—the man who would, in some sense, have agreed with my characterization of slavery as oppression. It was he who confronted Vere's dilemma, the choice between the demands of role and the voice of conscience. And it was he who contributed so much to the force of legitimacy that law may provide, for he plainly acted out of impersonal duty.

In a static and simplistic model of law, the judge caught between law and morality has only four choices. He may apply the law against his conscience. He may apply conscience and be faithless to the law. He may resign. Or he may cheat: He may state that the law is not what he believes it to be and, thus preserve an appearance (to others) of conformity of law and morality. Once we assume a more realistic model of law and of the judicial process, these four positions become only poles setting limits to a complex field of action and motive. For in a dynamic model, law is always becoming. And the judge has a legitimate role in determining what it is that the law will become. The flux in law means also that the law's content is frequently unclear. We must speak of direction and of weight as well as of position. Moreover, this frequent lack of clarity makes possible "ameliorist" solutions. The judge may introduce his own sense of what "ought to be" interstitially, where no "hard" law yet exists. And, he may do so without committing the law to broad doctrinal advances (or retreats).

In a given historical context the way in which judges are likely to respond to the moral-formal dilemma is going to be determined by a wide variety of intellectual and institutional variables. Judges, more than most men, are conscious of the baggage of the past. Thus, the traditions that they inherit will be important. For both slavery and the judicial role in antebellum America the judge had a library of works that influenced the idiom in which he thought. The nature of that intellectual tradition is my first inquiry. I shall examine the natural law tradition on slavery as it stood in the late eighteenth century. I shall then explore the actual uses of principled preferences for liberty in the first thirty or forty years of the nineteenth century. This exploration will delineate the areas of accepted usage of preference for liberty in judicial opinion and the areas where the judge could move the law in the direction of freedom. I shall then explore the sorts of demands that were made upon the judiciary to go beyond those accepted areas and the judicial refusal to do so. That refusal will be traced on the cognitive level to carefully formulated ideas about the judicial function that are themselves the products of a heritage of conflict over the values that ought to govern judging. The dialectical context for the judge's response was not constant, and it is necessary to examine responses to many demands varying, in part, with the ideology of the lawyers and the movements they represented.

Finally, I shall confront directly the question of personality. With Captain Vere we have the sense that it is not logic alone that leads him to his response. So, with Lemuel Shaw, John McLean, Joseph Story, and others, we must inquire into the internal forces that produced an almost uniform response of role fidelity. The theory of cognitive dissonance provides a suggestive framework for integrating the uniform response, the personalities of these men, and the professional and intellectual milieu in which they worked.

Make no mistake. The judges we shall examine really squirmed; were intensely uncomfortable in hanging Billy Budd. But they did the job. Like Vere, they were Creon's faithful minions. We must understand them—as much as Antigone—if we are to understand the processes of injustice.

CHAPTER ONE: The Intellectual Tradition:
Slavery, Natural Law, and Judicial Positivism
in the Eighteenth Century

When, in 1781, Levi Lincoln argued for the freedom of the Negro
Quock Walker, he asked, "Is it not a law of nature that all men are
equal and free?" [1] In a later branch of the same case, in 1783, Chief
Justice Cushing's charge to a jury characterized slavery as unfavorable to "the natural rights of mankind." [2] Seventy-five years after
the Quock Walker case, T. R. R. Cobb's treatise, *The Law of Negro
Slavery,* was published. Some three hundred pages, heavily annotated, packed with authorities, are devoted to refuting the proposition
that slavery, or Negro slavery, is contrary to the law of nature.[3]

In the very same year, 1858, John Codman Hurd published his
two-volume treatise, *The Law of Freedom and Bondage in the United
States.* Hurd wrote more than one hundred pages investigating
whether natural law propositions with respect to slavery have any
place within a legal system.[4] During the three-quarters of a century
between the Quock Walker cases and the treatises of Hurd and Cobb,
judges had chosen the language of natural law to express their moral
doubts about the institution of slavery in literally hundreds of cases.
It would not be too far-fetched to view the story of the American judiciary's articulated struggle with slavery as a set of variations upon
this theme from natural law. The variations involved elaborate coun-
terpoint as well as dense harmonies. But almost all were constructed
on or in response to a simple proposition: Slavery is contrary to natural law. It is no wonder that both the underlying moral proposition
and the language chosen to express it would be subject to analysis
and criticism. For, although the natural law tradition was but a part of
a structure of ideology and was by no means the only determinant of
the judge's thought and action, yet, as the component of ideology
most reflective of moral doubts about slavery, it assumes priority for
examination. That the institution of slavery is immoral or that it
creates grave moral difficulties could have been stated in a variety of
ways. The consistent recourse to "natural law," "natural right," or

"natural justice" to convey that sense suggests a common tradition of some strength and a set of connotations for the term "natural" which extends beyond mere approbation. It is the ambiguity, the vague richness of the language of natural law, that made it so convenient, yet threatening, a tool for expressing moral doubt and concern about slave law.

As David Davis has so thoroughly demonstrated in *The Problem of Slavery in Western Culture,* the institution of slavery and the idiom of natural law have a common intellectual history of over 2,000 years. But a 2,000 year continuity of phrasing in no way implies continuity of conception. There is a process of accretion whereby a phrase picks up at least some small part of the contextual richness of its use over time. Certainly, the life of language, even less than the life of law, has been logic. Consequently, if we wish to understand the late eighteenth- and nineteenth-century American jurist in his use of natural law, a brief excursion into the past is necessary. But, we ought not forget that the more immediate sources leave the freshest and deepest trails upon the mind. Thus, it is more important that we understand Blackstone than Aristotle, Otis than Aquinas, Montesquieu than Justinian. For, if the eighteenth century is a confused amalgam of classical traditions, it is more helpful to appreciate the contours of the confusion than to isolate the pure classical threads of which it was woven.

The Natural Law Tradition

In the 1780's the language of natural law came easily. The use of the idiom with respect to slavery was overdetermined. Both the rhetoric of the revolution, and many basic sources for legal education raised natural law and natural rights questions about slavery. Levi Lincoln and Judge Cushing picked up a phrase that could in some sense be attributed to such disparate sources as Blackstone, Montesquieu, Mansfield, Coke, Pufendorf, Grotius, Rutherforth, Paine, Jefferson, or Otis.

The Lawyer's Library

A lawyer's education in mid-eighteenth-century America might include anything from haphazard perusal of random English works during the busy days of a clerk-apprenticeship, to formal study at the Inns of Court in England. For the well-educated American who stayed at home, the study of law included a large dose of "natural" law along with English common law, a bit of civil law, and equity. Judge William Smith of New York, in outlining a course for legal education, provided for all of these elements. And a glance at the legal education of such luminaries as Jefferson and John Adams reinforces these conclusions.[5]

The gentleman lawyer confronted the natural law tradition explicitly and in a more or less structured way. Just as there were sources of the common law—Coke's *Institutes,* Wood, Hale, Hawkins, various reports, and other treatises—so there were sources of natural law—the Bible, philosophy, but most directly Grotius, Pufendorf, Rutherforth, and to a lesser extent Burlamaqui. Natural law was studied not as a source for rules of decision, but as a source for the larger principles which underlie the rules or at least ought to do so. Natural law was fundamental law in this quite literal "foundational" sense.

In his study of natural law, the eighteenth-century lawyer happened on a perplexing array of discussions of the institution of slavery. If he were of a bookish turn, given to garnishing his work with classical references, he would have encountered the Aristotelian justification of slavery in terms of the "natural" slave. He would, more dramatically, have met the perplexing treatment of slavery in Justinian's *Institutes*. There, slavery is declared to be contrary to natural law, a creature either of civil law or of the law of nations.[6] Moreover, this lack of foundation in natural law is unique. While the *Institutes* recognize many legal phenomena with a basis in the law of one country—Rome, alone—but without a reflection in natural law, only slavery is also said to have a basis in the *ius gentium*—the shared law of nations belonging to all mankind—while yet without a basis in *ius naturale*—the law of nature.[7]

The significance of this divergence for the Roman law system is open to question. Some have asserted that such natural law flourishes are the work of the rhetoricians uncritically incorporated within the Roman corpus. In any event, we may be sure that the divergence of *ius naturale* and *ius gentium* did not have revolutionary overtones for the Roman. The law of nature was not meant to be a mandate for Spartacus. At the most, the natural law position of slavery was an admission of the imperfection of society. Indeed, the Roman tradition may be viewed as not going even that far. For the statement about slavery's natural law position is really a theory of origins, not a moral thermometer. The basis for slavery in the law of nations was the acquisition of captives in war—a justification for slavery that would still be offered in the nineteenth century.[8] The Roman law justified slavery on the theory that the captive in war was spared from death by the captor. Anything short of death was an exercise of a lesser included power by the victor.

Coupled with this discussion of the origins and jurisprudential status of slavery in the *Institutes,* a discussion well within the ambit of the American's intellectual world, was a strange multitude of rules about the master-slave relationship. While the natural law doubts and the justification for slavery were reflected in a host of more modern and more English works, the detailed rules of the Roman law were very different from the day-to-day slave law the eighteenth-century Anglo-American lawyer encountered. If the Roman law of slavery had any force at all, it was on the "fundamental" level of ultimate rationale, not on the transactional level calling for rules of decision.*

More extensive or more up-to-date discussions of natural law and slavery were constantly before the gentleman lawyer or student as he studied or scanned his library. The foundation of a legal education was Coke—at least until Blackstone appeared in 1769. The *Institutes* were written before chattel slavery became an important English colonial institution. But, as in many works of that period, servitude is discussed in the context of villenage. Coke reiterates the civilian learning on servitude:

> How villeinage or servitude began and for what cause? . . . The condition of villeines from freedom into bondage, of ancient time grew by constitutions of nations, and not by the law of nature. . . .[9]

* There were, however, a few very important practical rules borrowed from the Roman and civil law sources: e.g., "Partus Sequitur Ventrem" (Offspring follows the mother). North American slave codes did involve some borrowing from the islands with a concomitant Spanish legacy, but the distinctive elements of a "romanism" were not involved. The code borrowing did not carry with it a full civil law heritage—for example, Los Siete Partidas has no Anglo-American application. Nor did borrowing carry with it the interpretive structures for using the codes. What did get passed through was the tendency to "codify" slave law and certain particular techniques of slave control that tended to be local and not characteristic of the Roman tradition.

Both in his choice of idiom—''not by the law of nature''—and in the concomitant implicit disapproval of servitude, Coke is following a well-trod trail of English legal sources. Fortescue, whom Coke cites, similarly, even more forcefully, condemned servitude and praised the English law of villenage as an improvement on the civil law.[10]

It is strange, however, that English treatises did not adapt to the growing importance of chattel slavery in the colonies in the 150 years following Coke. A standard work like Wood's *Institutes,* published well after Negro slavery had become a kingpin of the colonial economy and long after the Royal African Company had begun to flourish, had not a word about ''modern'' slavery. Viner's *Abridgment* had a relevant entry ''Negroes'' that summarized a few cases like *Smith v. Brown and Cooper*—cases that suggest that domestic English law knows no slavery, but that the law of Empire tolerates slavery in the colonies. Such cases clearly stated the obvious by the time Viner reached America in the 1750's.[11]

Before Blackstone's appearance on the scene, the most apposite discussions of slavery in the colonial lawyer's library were to be found in the works of the civilians: Grotius, Pufendorf, Montesquieu.[12] Grotius and Pufendorf elaborate on classical civilian positions on slavery. It is an institution unknown to nature, but not by virtue of that fact to be condemned. In Rutherforth's *Institutes of Natural Law,* self-styled ''the substance of a course of lectures on Grotius *de jure belli et pacis''*—a work well-known to the colonists—the distinction is made: Slavery, Rutherforth states, is not a natural relation, but it ''may be introduced consistently with the law of nature.'' [13]

In Pufendorf the discussion of slavery is considerably more developed. Pufendorf takes issue with the Aristotelian notion of a natural slave. Indeed, he derives the proposition that servitude is not natural from the natural equality of men which he earlier endeavors to establish.[14]

Pufendorf's more extensive discussion of slavery in Book VI of his work is properly understood as part and parcel of the anti-Hobbesian polemical purposes of the book. The author writes no brief against slavery. His purpose, rather, is to justify the institution without recourse to Hobbes's characterization of the state of nature.

His task is to derive slavery through variations on consensual themes, from a natural state of equal liberty. As might be expected, Pufendorf begins with civil bondage. For, in such cases one may imagine a *quid pro quo* for servitude, merely in sustenance.[15] But, the traditional derivation of slavery from captivity in war is too arbitrary for Pufendorf. He asserts that mere subjugation and captivity, since it involves no consensual act, cannot give rise to an obligation to serve. Indeed, the captive, held only by force, is privileged to run away or kill his captor. His only restraint is superior force. Pufendorf cringed from the implications of an institution with no bonds of obligation, so he took analysis of captivity one step further. Along with Hobbes, he concluded that it is the captor's agreement to unchain the slave, to permit him some of the security and benefits of normal life, which is the consideration for the slave's promise to serve.

> The obligation, therefore, of a Slave of War towards his master, doth not spring from the bare saving his life, nor deferring his death; but is built on his exemption from chains and imprisonment.

The most significant of Pufendorf's quarrels with Hobbes concerns the degree of absoluteness inherent in the master's authority. Here slavery is a model for autocratic government, generally. Pufendorf is concerned, therefore, to challenge the reasoning that the initial, consensual, submission having been made, the authority of the master stops only at the death of the slave. He asserts that the submission "only proves thus much, that the slave ought not to complain, whatever work is enjoined him by his master, provided it lie within the compass of his strength. . . ." [16]

A major shift in the emphasis of work on slavery occurs from the publication of *The Spirit of the Laws* of Montesquieu.[17] Montesquieu was certainly well-known to the colonists. *The Spirit of the Laws* marks a great departure from the traditional natural law theorists with respect to slavery, as with other issues. The formal analysis of slavery from assumptions made about abstract or mythical natural states is gone. The analysis begins with the question of slavery's place in a contemporary polity. The institution is rejected as "in its own nature bad." Its evil is measured by the impact on both master and slave.

When Montesquieu comes to address the arguments about slavery in the ancient and natural law writers, he does so by way of inquiry into the justifications for the institution. He rejects both civil bondage and captivity in war as adequate bases. Civil bondage is rejected because

> To sell one's freedom is so repugnant to all reason as can scarcely be supposed in any man. . . . The same (civil) law annuls all iniquitous contracts; surely then it affords redress in a contract where the grievance is most enormous.[18]

As to the basis of slavery in war, Montesquieu, like Vattel, denies the power of the victor to take the life of a captive in ordinary circumstances, thus destroying the greater power from which the lesser is normally derived.

Montesquieu marks a departure as well in his specific discussion of slavery of Negroes in the Americas. He sarcastically derides arguments justifying Negro slavery on the basis of racial characteristics:

> It is impossible for us to suppose these creatures to be men, because allowing them to be men, a suspicion would follow that we ourselves are not Christians.

The limited justification for slavery allowed by Montesquieu relates to necessary use of slaves in hot climates where no civilization can exist except insofar as men are forced to work. But this rationale serves mainly as a bridge to the question of how slaves ought to be treated.[19]

For a man like Jefferson, a kindred spirit of enlightenment, Montesquieu's influence was immediate and telling, but for the colonies as a whole, the full impact of Montesquieu's thought upon slavery would not be felt until merged with the rhetoric of revolution, on the one hand, and with the English legalisms of Blackstone, on the other. From around 1750, works concerned with English law could no longer ignore Negro slavery. Even a treatise on the laws of England and Scotland, in 1751, compared English and civil law on slavery. The issue of Negro slavery in the colonies was sufficiently important to warrant explication of the dichotomy between the law of England and of the colonies.[20] Still more important was Viner's *Abridgment*, noted above (see note 11).

In terms of impact, however, Viner was but a passing breeze. The natural law learning with respect to slavery stood very much in balance when Blackstone appeared. The older works denied slavery's origin in nature but, essentially, held it to have been "introduced" consistently with nature. Montesquieu had riddled the justifications for the "introduction" of slavery but *The Spirit of the Laws* was not really a part of the English canon. Nor had Montesquieu coupled the natural law position of slavery with the common law of England.

Many of the commentators on the intellectual history of slavery have noted Blackstone's debt to Montesquieu with respect to the discussion of slavery. So obvious is the debt—direct and extensive quotation—that it has obscured the particular contribution of Blackstone, a contribution that explains the acceptance and influence of the *Commentaries* on this issue. It was Blackstone's blessing and curse to almost uniformly find coincidence of common law and natural law. It was this tendency that so infuriated Bentham and led him to expose the reactionary, apologetic function of natural law in the *Commentaries*.[21] This tendency also accounts for Jefferson's suspicions about Blackstone.[22] But the coincidence had great appeal. For it merged the nation's pride in its native law—a pride that focused on the tradition of recourse to "law" against authority—with the appeal to universal moral truths. In the colonies, where men were seeking ways to loyally appeal beyond the Crown, the merger had particular force.[23]

Blackstone not only served as publicist for the ideas of Montesquieu, which stripped slavery of its justifications in natural law; he joined to that universalist condemnation the assertion that the common law of England embodied these great principles of freedom and had done so for ages.

> And this spirit of liberty is so deeply implanted in our constitution, and rooted even in our very soil, that a slave or a negro, the moment he lands in England, falls under the protection of the laws; and so far becomes a freeman.[24]

And, again, after asserting that "it is repugnant to reason, and the principles of natural law, that such a state [slavery] should subsist anywhere"[25]—proving his point with Montesquieu's rejections of the classic argument—Blackstone reiterates: "Upon these principles the Law of England abhors, and will not endure the existence of, slavery within this nation."[26]

The early editions of Blackstone (pre-1772) had only uncertain authority to rely on as to the position of slavery in the common law. Blackstone cites only *Smith v. Brown and Cooper*.[27] In that case, decided in 1705, Lord Holt held that a plaintiff could not plead in an *"indebitatus assumpsit"* that he had sold the defendant a Negro. Holt held, one "may be a villein in England but not a slave." Nevertheless, the plaintiff was permitted to amend his declaration to assert that though the sale took place in England, the Negro was in Virginia and by the laws of Virginia a Negro may be a slave. In other words, *Smith v. Brown and Cooper* already set up the dichotomy of common law and colonial law. Common law, in accord with nature, rejected slavery, though colonial law fostered it.

It is impossible to overemphasize the impact of Blackstone on legal education in America. After 1770 every American lawyer and many another "gentleman" began his study of legal and political institutions with the *Commentaries*. Blackstone's work was not only the primer, it was the organizing matrix for learning law.[28] Consequently, on the eve of the Revolution, American lawyers found a long and perplexing tradition of natural law on slavery focused by Blackstone into a much more explicit attack on the institution in moral terms. No one could avoid the influence of Blackstone. Even Jefferson, distrusting the commentator's politics, had to concede that the work excelled in its lucid, almost too easy, exposition of the common law. Nevertheless, it might have been argued that Blackstone wrote on slavery with only uncertain authority. That defect was cured by Lord Mansfield in 1772.

The antecedents of *Somerset's Case* are quite complex. Not doctrinally but ideologically and institutionally. Professor David Davis is currently demonstrating just how complicated the background is. However, for purposes of our analysis, it is enough to speak of the report of *Somerset's Case,* which reached America before the Revolution, the report in *Lofft's Reports,* later reproduced in *Howell's State Trials*.

Somerset was a Negro, a slave in Virginia, who was brought to England by his master in 1769. He deserted his master, was apprehended in 1771, and was locked aboard ship for a voyage to Jamaica. In early 1772, Lord Mansfield ordered that Somerset be discharged. There has been scholarly controversy over the words he used in his order. However, it is clear that the words that reached American eyes included:

> the state of slavery is of such a nature, that it is incapable of being introduced on any reasons . . . but only by positive law.
> . . . It is so odious, that nothing can be suffered to support it, but positive law.

Mansfield is explicit about the limited impact of his holding. He does not say that slavery cannot be legal; he does say, explicitly, that an obligation of service or the incidents of a sale may be given extraterritorial effect in England. However, the act of restraint itself is "so high an act of dominion" that it must have a positive law basis in the law of the country "wherein it is used." [29]

Somerset's Case vindicated Blackstone. As reported by Lofft, it combined strong moral condemnation of slavery with an explicit holding that the (internal) common law of England knew no such relationship. But *Somerset's Case* also held that there was nothing necessary or inevitable about the law's harmony with nature. Where positive law sanctioned slavery, Mansfield explicitly conceded the supremacy of such positive law. For the colonies *Somerset's Case* added Mansfield's prestige to Blackstone's in portraying a troublesome moral gap. Slave law is morally wrong, but it can exist. For America, then, where positive law provided for slavery, the natural law idiom became a way of expressing the disparity between law and morality. It told of what law should be, but wasn't. Even where the idiom was used in refusing to strike down slavery, it was a reproach to the positive law which authorized, legitimized, or facilitated the institution.

Of course, propositions of natural law or natural justice had an accepted, nonrevolutionary role to play in eighteenth-century American jurisprudence. The law to the colonists was perceived not as a "seamless web," but as a patchwork quilt of distinct "laws." The "common law" was the most important of these, but the law administered by admiralty courts, equity, the law of nations and, in an attenuated sense, the law of nature, were also part of the quilt. It was to be expected that any given one of the many legal traditions might have little or nothing to say about a particular issue. Thus, one would not expect to look to common law sources for principles of trust administration, nor to equity for a determination of title to land. In the colonies, where the legal sources also included the King's prerogative, often enough expressed through rulings of the privy council, the multiplicity of sources of law did not necessarily produce so complex a structure of independent courts, each with its own jurisdictional limits. The courts that did exist could not, however, avoid inheriting some degree of the thought processes by which the law of the Empire was seen to manifest itself through distinct kinds of traditions.

Each of the laws, which together made up the law of England, was, in theory, governed by principles that determined its role with respect to the others. For instance, admiralty "was restricted to things 'done upon the sea' and not 'within the bodies of the counties.' " Natural law, unlike the "common law," "equity," "admiralty," or "ecclesiastical law" never had a distinct court in which it held sway. Yet, by analysis of the way in which "natural law" is used by the colonial courts, one may find that it too had a distinct, determined place within a multiform system of laws.[30]

In general, natural law was applied when no appropriate English system of law provided an applicable rule for a given case. It was residual law because it consisted not of rules of decision, but of the raw principles from which they are formed. Moreover, it was closely identified with civil and Roman law. One might expect to find natural law used with respect to colonial institutions that were not reflections of English ones. Slavery was one such institution. There are examples, however, in other areas as well.

Thus, in Virginia in the 1730's, one finds the colony willing, apparently, to grant lands—that, under ordinary English rules, escheat —to members of the decedent's family not heirs at law. However, in one case two members of the family, one a brother of the half-blood, the other an aunt of the half-blood, both sought the grant. Counsel argued vehemently on civil law and natural law principles that the nearer kin in degree (the brother of the half-blood) should take. It was appropriate to argue from natural justice because there were no peculiarly English law sources in point.*

---

* *Edmondson v. Tabb,* 2 Virginia Colonial Decisions (Barradall's Reports) B 359 (1741?), wherein it was argued, at B 361: "Judges are bound by an oath to determine according to law [.] Yet where a matter is left at large to the will of the Prince or of those who act under him [in this context, the court.] I humbly conceive the Law of Nature and Reason is the best Guide to foll[ow]."

Natural law was similarly used in an important Virginia slave case on the eve of the Revolution. The issue in *Robin v. Hardaway* was whether a presumption of slavery attached to certain Indians. Counsel for both parties argued from natural law sources, not because they wished to attack slavery as contrary to all right or justice, but because the principles most directly in point would be likely to be found in Pufendorf not in Coke; in Grotius, not in Wood, Hale, or Hawkins. From the civil law and natural law sources, counsel argued that slavery is justifiable only as a result of conquest in a just war. Randolph, argued for the slave, that the seventeenth-century wars of conquest in which some Virginia Indians were enslaved could not qualify as "just" wars. Without the natural law framework, the nature of the Indian wars could not have been a material issue in the case.[31]

But, cases such as *Robin v. Hardaway* were not all that common. They were important as they seemed to call for the searching out of basic principle. But the natural law tradition was more important for what it said about law than for what it said as law.

The Rhetoric of Revolution

Almost a decade before *Somerset's Case,* while Blackstone delivered his Vinerian lectures at Oxford, James Otis proclaimed the "Rights of the British Colonies" in Boston.[32] The simultaneousness of these two events, equally portentous for the future of American political theory, emphasizes the currency of a common natural law trend as to slavery. For Otis, too, noted slavery as a jarring inconsistency with the rights of man:

> Nothing better can be said in favor of a trade that is the most shocking violation of the law of nature, has a direct tendency to diminish the idea of the inestimable value of liberty, and makes every dealer in it a tyrant from the director of an African company to the petty chapman in needles and pins on the unhappy coast.[33]

In the assertions of Otis, we see two trends, one looking with Blackstone backward to a common antislavery source, to Montesquieu. For Otis, too, uses Montesquieu as authority, citing, in particular, Montesquieu's satiric rejection of the racial argument for slavery. Otis, however, also anticipates an antislavery extension of the argument in a way that would have been foreign to Blackstone's nature. That slavery corrupts, that the institution renders those involved with it tyrants, is not the sort of conclusion that Blackstone would readily reach from the mere lack of basis for slavery in natural law. Otis leaps from a natural law statement to assessment of responsibility. And his conclusions as to responsibility implicate broadly. The assertion of individual responsibility reaching deeply, beyond the leaders of society to all who reap at the expense of the slave, would be typical of a line of thought continuing through the Reverend Hopkins to the abolitionists. Moreover, such an attack is so broad that it very nearly implies the rejection of such moral excuses as superior orders or formal limitations. Otis bears the seed of the tradition that will hold the judge, too, personally responsible for his place in the society of slavery.

Otis did not set out to write a tract against slavery, nor did he attack the institution except as an aside in his major work. But it is by no means an uncharacteristic aside. Bernard Bailyn, the most acute student of the prerevolutionary pamphlet literature has concluded that attacks on slavery, coupled to the growing demand for freedom from the "slavery" of the British rule, "[b]y 1774 . . . had become a commonplace in the pamphlet literature of the northern and middle colonies." [34] Indeed, both proponents and opponents of the growing radicalism in colonial rhetoric noted the incongruity of slaveholding to such vigorous assertions of the natural right to liberty.[35] This was a retort to which the colonists were sensitive. Indeed, it may account, to some small extent, for the rather general assertion that slavery was foisted on the colonies by the Crown—an excuse that found its way into preliminary drafts of the Declaration of Independence as one of the crimes of the King.[36]

The application of revolutionary natural rights doctrine to slavery, however, was by no means simply a reaction to Tory and British critics. Both the public utterances and private musings of the vanguard of revolutionary thought bear out the widespread misgivings with respect to slavery, misgivings that constitute not reaction to criticism so much as reflexive acts of men who took their ideology seriously. Thus, we find Patrick Henry in 1773 writing to Robert Pleasants, a Quaker in the front ranks of antislavery thought of the time,

Is it not amazing that at a time when the rights of humanity are defined and understood, in a country . . . fond of liberty, that . . . we find men . . . adopting a principle as repugnant to humanity as it is . . . destructive to liberty.[37]

Tom Paine's career bears the same imprint. His first public writing in America was a short but strong natural law attack on slavery. One of his last public acts in the New World was the writing of the preamble to Pennsylvania's Act for Emancipation in 1780.[38] This last act is significant not only because Paine wrote the powerful natural rights declaration, but even more because he was chosen to write it: ample testimony to the fact that contemporaries perceived slavery as subject to the revolutionary natural rights ideology.

The overflow effect of revolutionary rhetoric on slavery was not confined to pamphlets nor to men prominent in the cause of independence. Negroes, themselves, were sensitive to the implications of the white man's ideology. In 1777, Massachusetts blacks appealed to the colonists' natural law in petitioning for freedom.[39] And many contemporaries were aware that the plea for independence sounded hollow in the mouths of slaveholders. The Reverend Samuel Hopkins, in his series of remarkable pleas for emancipation, noted that blacks could not help but know that their own plight justified rebellion more than the plight of their masters.*

John Adams noted that during the decade preceding the Revolution, in law suits trying a Negro's right to freedom, Massachusetts juries were universally inclined to decide for liberty. Although his own notes on slave cases during that period do not fully bear out Adams's later recollection, it seems clear that there was some public pressure fc. freedom arising from the rhetorical inconsistencies of the period's politics.[40]

Thus, the "natural law" idiom, by 1780, had assumed motiva-

---

* "The present [1776] situation of our public affairs and our struggle for liberty, and the abundant conversation this occasions in all company, while the poor Negroes look on and hear what an aversion we have to slavery and how much liberty is prized . . . that slavery is more to be dreaded than death . . . this, I say, necessarily leads them to attend their own wretched situation more than otherwise they could." From the Reverend Samuel Hopkins, *A Dialogue Concerning the Slavery of the Africans . . .* , reprinted in *Works of Samuel Hopkins, D. D.* (Boston: Doctrinal Tract and Book Society, 1852), 2 : 547 ff. Quotation is on p. 570. The original pamphlet was published in 1776. Other similar remarks are to be found in the *Dialogue* and in *A Discourse Upon the Slave Trade* and *The Slave Trade and Slavery,* also by Hopkins.

tional as well as speculative force as to slavery. The lawyer's library was a repository of political philosophy gently probing, doubting, but usually apologizing for slavery. The lawyer's own political milieu was one in which "natural rights" had justified a harsh war and had led to breaking sacred political bonds. The same natural rights were fast becoming the rock on which new polities were to be founded. Both the Revolution and Constitution were the outgrowth of the practical determination to realize natural rights.

Because of the practical import of the revolutionary rhetoric, words and phrases that were not too uncomfortable in the library, began to itch madly. If legal sources characterized slavery as against nature, then revolutionary ideology suggested that something be done about it. Obviously, I do not mean to imply that Americans were incapable of justifying slavery, nor do I suggest that the work of Revolution itself did not have a heavy dose of practical expedience about it. Nevertheless, with these qualifications it still remains true that natural law and slavery had come to have uncomfortable and motivational import for the first generation of independent Americans.

Doctrinal Opposition to Natural Law

While the natural law idiom reached its zenith in America on the crest of the approaching Revolution, it was subjected to intense and hostile philosophical scrutiny in England. As will be shown in the next section, Blackstone himself exhibited striking ambivalence because of that intellectual milieu. Despite the fact that he was not wholly immune from enlightenment advances, however, the commentator resisted the onslaught on nature.

The three English thinkers who attacked natural law thinking most articulately and with greatest portent for postrevolutionary America were David Hume, Jeremy Bentham, and Edmund Burke. The ascendancy of the ideas of these three men in American thought is largely a story of the nineteenth century. But Hume and Burke, at least, enjoyed an attentive American audience before 1800.[41] It is not my intention to add to the already voluminous literature on the political and legal philosophy of these three giants, but only to suggest a few of the English developments that marked a countertrend to the natural law current of the American scene.

Hume is the cornerstone for the English edifice dedicated to the revolt against nature. In his philosophical radicalism, his clear-eyed rejection of verbal totemism, he is Bentham's acknowledged predecessor and master.[42] In his deep historicism, he antedates and presages Burke. In his *Enquiry Concerning the Principles of Morals*, first published in 1751, Hume begins with the intention of demonstrating not only that part of the "merit" of justice lies in its utility, but that therein lies its *sole* origin and merit. Hume begins by showing "justice" to be irrelevant in a society that knows no scarcity, just as it seems irrelevant or less relevant to nonscarce goods within society (e.g., water and air—with a neat reference to Genesis to show reversal of water and land in biblical context). At the other extreme, Hume argues, justice is equally irrelevant in cases of extreme necessity. Even absent plenty or plague justice is a virtue only for its utility, and its usefulness exists only insofar as we presuppose a society of roughly equal beings.[43] Hume distinguishes the virtue of kindness from that of justice. Kindness, notes Hume, may characterize our relations with animals or with inferior races. Thus, though by no means conceding the factual premise of the racial inferiority of Asians, Hume argues that accepting the premise *arguendo,* the treatment of Indians, though unkind, is not unjust. The function of justice is the performance of distributive tasks with a measure of peace. The acknowledgment by Hume that the definition of what is just should proceed from the actual unequal states of men rather than from some presumed anterior "natural" state of substantial equality marks an enormous gap between him and Pufendorf.

Hume not only sets up an alternative model to natural justice, but he also vigorously attacks the weaknesses in the formulation of the "natural" model. He seizes on the imprecision of "nature":

> The word natural is commonly taken in so many senses, and is of so loose a signification, that it seems vain to dispute whether justice be natural or not.[44]

The attack on nature was not confined to technical philosophical works. Hume's most popular pieces were the *Political Discourses* and, in those essays, he pursued analogous lines of attack.

Hume's critique was picked up and elaborated by Jeremy Bentham in 1776 with the publication of the *Fragment on Government*. The

Fragment may be read as an essay on the inadequacy of the designation "natural," at least as used by Blackstone. The ambiguity of the word in Blackstone, the facile resort to nature to purportedly explain the bases for political obligation, the ethical standards by which law is to be measured, and the origins of the state infuriated Bentham. Unless natural law is to be construed as simply an unclear and inelegant way of reformulating principles of utility, Bentham argued

> I see no remedy but that the natural tendency of such doctrine is to impel a man, by the force of conscience, to rise up in arms against any law whatever that he happens not to like.[45]

Of course, Bentham understood that Blackstone intended no such result. Indeed, he understood full well that Blackstone's affinity for the phrase was the result of a contrary turn of mind—the happy facility for finding the common law and natural law so closely in harmony. Thus, it was a crutch supporting obedience and rejecting reform. Because Bentham saw how well the ambiguity of nature could be turned equally to revolutionary and reactionary purposes, he concluded that the terms were literally meaningless. In his famous phrase, that natural rights were "nonsense", natural and imprescriptible rights, "nonsense on stilts." [46]

Of the eighteenth-century English thinkers, it is Burke who characteristically brings the discussion to practical applications. Burke is not so passionately concerned with precision or with truth. He measures natural law by its workability as a political idiom. By this standard, Burke claimed that the vocabulary and syntax of natural law were too impoverished to adequately reflect the reality of moral choices in political society. The current idiom of natural law "are all extremes; and in proportion as they are metaphysically true they are morally and politically false." For choices in governments are of a different sort:

> The rights of men in governments are their advantages; and these are often in balances between differences of good, in compromises sometimes between good and evil, and sometimes between evil and evil.[47]

In 1775 one would be more likely to come upon James Burgh's radical applications of natural law than Hume's rejection of it in

American revolutionary literature. And, certainly, few had taken an interest in applying the rejection of natural law principles to slavery. But the impact of these ideas was not long in coming. Burke had a worthy American emulator in John Adams, and we shall see in the next chapter Adams's very pragmatic second thoughts about slavery and natural law. Hume and Burke were read in America from before the Revolution, though, of course, the *Reflections on the Revolution in France* did not appear until 1790. By the last decade in the eighteenth century, the current of skeptical political thought represented by these two giants began to draw a more attentive audience in America. Bentham was not known at all in America until the turn of the century, and, then, his influence, though against the natural law grain, was by no means in the same direction as that of Hume and Burke. Both skeptical conservatism and rationalistic reform, however, rejected natural law as relevant or meaningful in the formulation of social policy through law. That rejection was well under way by the late eighteenth century.

Positivism and Higher Law

Like so many great primers in the social studies, Blackstone owed at least part of his success to a cultivated ambiguity about crucial and controversial issues. Nowhere was that ambiguity more apparent in the *Commentaries* than with respect to the import of natural law. On the one hand, Blackstone could assert that any human law in conflict with natural law was absolutely void. Yet, this invalidity turned out to be of questionable significance, as Blackstone squarely addressed the question of whether any court may reject an unreasonable or unjust act of Parliament and concluded

> I know of no power in the ordinary forms of the Constitution, that is vested with the authority to control it [Parliament].[48]

It is possible, of course, to reconcile these points. Blackstone seemed to make the higher law assertion in the context of the obligations of legislators and citizens. No law maker ought to transgress natural law and no citizen had a moral obligation to obey law contrary to natural law. But, judicial obligation was of a different character and was to be determined by constitutional principles—the allocation of power

between courts and Parliament. Thus, Blackstone was a constitutional
positivist who yet retained a large place for natural law in terms of
personal obligation outside that constitutional structure.[49]

The eighteenth century already fully realized the implications both
of Blackstone's natural law theory of obligation and of his constitutional positivism. Grenville Sharp attacked Blackstone vigorously for
the constitutional positivism, asserting that it was ungodly and dangerous to the liberties of Englishmen. Bentham, as we have seen, attacked Blackstone equally vigorously for the natural law basis of
obligation.[50] The ideas of Hume and Burke also contributed to the
Benthamite attack on Blackstone. If "natural right" or "natural law"
is inherently too insusceptible of gradation and differentiation, then
Bentham's perceived danger of the identification of "natural law"
with personal preference is persuasive. In his more popular *Political
Essays,* Hume had made almost the identical point in demonstrating
that the social contract idea was but a servant of political ideology,
malleable enough to serve extreme monarchist and revolutionary in
turn.[51]

Blackstone's ambivalence was neatly summed up in his oft-quoted
definition of "Law":

> A rule of civil conduct prescribed by the supreme power in a
> state commanding what is right, and prohibiting what is
> wrong.[52]

How much of law is "power?" How much right and wrong? That
ambivalence was certainly shared by many American readers. They
had many more and graver doubts about the doctrine of absolute parliamentary supremacy. True, those doubts were not so much jurisprudential as constitutional. Equally true, the thrust of their constitutional argument led to greater authority for local legislatures rather
than for the courts. Nevertheless, one reason often given for opposing
the plenary power of Parliament was that its application to unrepre-
sented colonists violated the rights (either natural or English) of those
men. For such a purpose, that side of Blackstone that saw law in
conflict with nature as void, was ideal.

It was, however, in the task of "constituting" the states and the
federal union that eighteenth-century Americans disclosed how
deeply ran their constitutional positivism and how sharply they per-

ceived its implications for the judiciary. Some of the intellectual stalwarts of rebellion, like James Otis, actually came to associate principles of natural law and natural equity with positive law—to assert that what is right is therefore law.[53] But those giants who managed the awesome transition from revolutionaries to "constitutionaries"—men like Adams and Jefferson; Dickinson and Wilson; Jay, Madison, Hamilton, and, in a sense, Mason and Henry—were seldom, if ever, guilty of confusing law with natural right. These men, before 1776, used nature to take the measure of law and to judge their own obligations of obedience, but not as a source for rules of decision. And after the Revolution they either supported or opposed constitutions on the assumption that it was the will of men—"the people," but in actual convention, not as an abstraction—that would determine explicit, precise, and articulated allocations of delegated power and its corresponding limits.[54]

The most telling aspect of the American variant of constitutional positivism was the enthusiasm for written constitutions—the almost compulsive mania for rendering the allocation of power explicit. And the opponents of various constitutions—especially the Anti-Federalists—were not less compulsive about this but more so. They usually stood in opposition because of the failure to make limits and bounds of power explicit enough.[55] This phenomenon of explicit, written constitutional limits on authority had special implications for the judiciary. In the *Federalist,* No. 78, Hamilton pinpointed a number of these implications. First, he noted that with a written constitution there is explicit law, with a sovereign source, limiting the scope of legislative and executive authority. Consequently, that explicit and positive law is, like any other source of law, incumbent upon the judge. If there be conflict between that constitutional law and a statute, the judge must rule according to the "prior" and "higher" source—the Constitution. But Hamilton does not stop with the implication of judicial review. Judicial review is tolerable because judges themselves are limited. The very instrument that affords them their power is also their master. For the judge may not properly act of his own "will." His function is one of "judgment" among the indicia of the various "wills" of others.[56]

Neither Hamilton nor his contemporaries were naive enough to believe that the judge would always act as a will-less judgment ma-

chine. In the *Federalist,* No. 22, Hamilton charges that one of the
deficiencies in the Articles was the lack of a federal judiciary.[57] And
the reason this was such a serious deficiency was the tendency of the
several state judiciaries to produce many distinct interpretations of
laws and treaties. Such variation is the product of differences in will
and judgment. Moreover, in No. 78, Hamilton explicitly concedes
that a judge might substitute will for judgment and abuse his office.
The *Federalist*'s answer to this possibility is the very practical one
that with neither sword nor purse the capacity for such a willful judge
to cause damage is quite limited. Of course, most judges are not expected to abuse the office, and a conscientious execution of the
judge's job involves self-limitation to explicit constitutional and legal
authority, i.e., to positive law.

To this point I have stressed the sense in which a written constitution is positive law and fidelity to its self-declared supremacy, a form
of legal positivism. But, one should not forget that the particular
processes by which such a constitution comes to be supreme positive
law have a natural law and natural rights base for many of its proponents. Whatever a descriptive jurisprudence might have to say about
the matter, many Americans of the 1780's and 1790's thought that
the Constitution could rightfully elicit men's fidelity because it had
about it something of a social compact. The American experience
was seen by one school of constitutional interpretation as having removed some noticeable blemishes on Locke. In Chapter 8 I treat this
view at greater length. The abstract notion of social compact came to
be identified with the particulars of this concrete constitutional compact, and the natural law obligations of a man to a common social life
came to be associated with his obligations to the particular common
social life for which the Constitution established the Rule of Recognition. Thus, the basis was laid for a natural law obligation to obey the
particular positive law generated by the United States Constitution—a
view that was reinforced by the identity of the constitutional compact
with the social contract itself.[58]

The Conflict Pattern

The preceding sections are but a thumbnail sketch of quite complicated ideological and doctrinal lines. However, they should suffice to

establish the eighteenth-century background for a pattern of moral-formal conflict. In the natural law tradition on slavery, the judge inherited a device for expressing the gap between the law as it is and the law as it ought to be. The words, themselves, had been used variously over the centuries: sometimes to articulate the necessary imperfection of human institutions; sometimes as a theory of origins; often as a quest for what ought to be. In the late eighteenth century that varied tradition on slavery merged with the rhetoric of revolution and gave the idiom a sound of urgency. Because "nature" was being invoked as a call for action on one front, it became more difficult to justify its relegation to a purely speculative device in a related area.

The judge's natural law heritage was not mere rhetoric, speculation, and polemic. While the day-to-day work of slave law rarely turned on the "natural law" of slavery, there were exceptions. *Somerset's Case* and, less directly, *Blackstone* intimate grave significance for natural law in conflict-of-laws cases—cases where a court must decide on the extraterritorial effect to be given a master-slave relationship created by the law of a foreign sovereignty. And the case of *Robin v. Hardaway* suggested that at the borderland of slavery, where neither statute nor custom provided guidance, recourse to first principles might be appropriate.

But the judge also inherited a tradition binding him to the explicit sources of law. Constitutions were the highest examples of such explicit law. In their written form they justified judicial review precisely because they were positive law. The notion that out beyond lay a higher law to which the judge *qua* judge was responsible was never a part of the mainstream of American jurisprudence.

Above all, the tradition of positivism meant the judge ought to be will-less. Responsible judging has no element of the personal preferences of the magistrate. For that reason, the philosophical attacks on natural law are quite important. For, just as the new American judiciary was about to begin its struggle with slave law, the viability of the common heritage for expressing the gap between law as it is and law as it should be, was under fire. As a result, judicial recourse to "natural law," which had its legitimate though limited role, was to sound less and less like an appeal to commonly accepted sources for principle and more and more like a party slogan. For Hume and Bentham had laid the foundation for rejecting any such appeal on the

ground that, meaningless in itself, nature could signify whatever the
speaker wanted it to. Gradually, from 1780 to the eve of the Civil
War, the natural law condemnation of slavery came to mean not a
common cultural tradition but a personal (or at least, party) preference. Indeed, I shall show in the following chapter that the ways in
which judges used principled preferences for liberty in judicial work
depended to a great degree on the extent to which they operated in an
intellectual milieu that accepted the natural law tradition on slavery
described above: Slavery has no source in right, and the ultimate end
(*telos*) of the law ought to be liberty.

PART I

NATURE TAMED

Let us begin by discussing the way
in which the speaker should make use of
laws. . . . It is clear that, if the
written law is adverse to our case, he
must appeal to the universal law, and
to the principles of equity as representing a higher order of justice. . . .
The speaker may observe, too, that a
given law conflicts with another, approved,
law, or even contradicts itself; . . .
Again, he should note if a law is ambiguous,
so that he may turn it and see which construction lends itself to justice, which to
expediency.

Aristotle, *Rhetoric*

CHAPTER TWO: Natural Right in Legislation

Introduction

Too often scholars and critics have studied natural law in legal and political thought only in its most spectacular forms. The contours of natural law as part of the rhetoric of revolution from 1765 to 1780 has been analyzed and dissected time and again.[1] Similarly, the relationship of judicial review to "higher law" theories has been studied from a number of perspectives. Scholars like Gough and Corwin have traced the roots of judicial review to earlier notions of fundamental law, which are in turn linked to the ongoing natural law tradition.[2] Analysts of certain episodes of Supreme Court activism have also purported to find in the natural law tradition the basis for the Court's lawmaking.[3] And natural law is always trotted out when the ideology of civil disobedience or resistance is at issue, either philosophically or historically.[4] The standard "histories" of natural law in American political thought thus skip blithely from detailed consideration of the revolutionary period to the abolitionists, with a brief stopover, if judicially minded, for perusal of the early contracts clause cases.[5] Recent work on slavery and on revolutionary rhetoric has qualified these conclusions only by stressing that for a short period of fifteen to twenty-five years following the Revolution serious efforts were made to apply the content of natural law to legislation on slavery.[6] That period saw the "first emancipation" in which all the states north of Delaware began the process of liberation, while the upper south considered emancipation seriously and, in some cases, acted to facilitate private manumission.[7] With some justification, this phenomenon has been labeled a carry-over or fallout effect of the revolutionary impulse. It may well have been the recent revolutionary use of "natural law" and "rights" that provided the urgency, the motivational component, in applying natural law to slavery.*

* This conclusion is buttressed by the almost universal recourse to July 4 as the effective date for emancipatory legislation. I do not, however, wish to imply that the application of natural law to slavery enlisted anything approaching universal acquiescence.

33

It is useful, however, to approach the place of natural law in a legal system more cautiously. For nature had a place in the jurisprudence of the late eighteenth and early nineteenth centuries that, properly defined, was scarcely a subject of controversy. And it is in these noncontroversial uses of natural law—against the revolutionary background—that we perceive the sprouts of a dilemma of conscience.

Throughout the sixty year period following the Revolution, most judges and lawyers would have conceded the sense and validity of the pair of statements: (1) natural law has a place in our legal system; and (2) slavery is no creature of natural law, but of municipal law in conflict with natural law. What the "place" of natural law was in the legal system admits of no easy answer. I shall argue in this chapter that, minimally, its "place" gave rise to no constitutional confusion with respect to slavery; that the courts uniformly recognized a hierarchy of sources of law for application in which "natural law" was subordinate to constitutions, statutes, and well-settled precedent. This hierarchy was clearly established and unambiguously articulated by the courts. The reason for natural law's subordinate place was a thoroughgoing positivism concerning the origin of "law." Law was perceived as operative and valid because of a human constituent process and by virtue of valid lawmaking processes in pursuance of that Constitution. It was the will of men that gave law its force. But men look to various sources for the content of their law. And one very important kind of source is that which declares what is right and just. Most of the jurists of this period felt comfortable designating this tradition as "natural law" and finding it in books and maxims that were self-styled statements of the law of nature. This body of principles and rules was conceived of as "existing," though without authority, apart from its incorporation, by virtue of men's wills, in the "law" of a particular state. Natural law was, indeed, a subject for study by the lawyer or law student because it was helpful in understanding the principles underlying so much of a rational legal system. It was also one potential source for formulating new rules or modifying old ones.

While the understanding of "law" as a sovereign act clearly mandated the subordination of natural law to constitutions and statutes, it nevertheless left open the question of whether these instruments of sovereignty might choose to incorporate a natural law principle. Even as thoroughgoing a positivist as Austin conceded that the law of nature had a place in the "science of legislation." [8] It ought not to be surprising, therefore, to find disputants over legislation affecting slavery referring to natural law propositions. But, while just about everyone would have conceded "nature" a place in the legislative process, no one would have maintained its exclusivity and many would have denied its primacy as a basis for legislative choice.

While "nature" struggled for expression in legislative deliberation, it assumed, more quietly, a gently transmuted tone in judicial work. A principled preference for liberty was often articulated and applied in very imprecise and cautious terms. In the judge's eclectic groping for canons of construction and principles of exegesis in his work with statutes, in his search for a common law process, both adequately flexible and sufficiently certain; in his struggle to adjust conflicting rules and principles of diverse sovereign entities, he often spoke of the preference for liberty or the natural right of freedom or the undesirability of slavery. His warrant for making and applying these judgments was taken to be an "abstract" principle of natural law. I must stress, however, that almost all of these interesting and often important applications of natural law and preferences for liberty were subject to the usual hierarchy of sources for law: constitutions, statutes, and well-settled precedent.

Part I of this book considers the uses of principled preference for liberty by the judiciary from 1780 to the early 1840's. By and large the cases considered here were decided without the additional complications of an organized, ideologically oriented bar. Few of these cases were accompanied by the presence or threat of civil disobedience or resistance. Many of these cases were decided in a doctrinal context, which left open the potential for at least partial convergence of law and antislavery morality. It is necessary to understand how judges used the preference for liberty in such relatively low-tension situations, before we proceed, in Part II, to the explosive mixture of doctrinal divergence and radical advocacy and resistance. The very persistence of the language of natural law, even within the circumscribed areas to be considered in this section, had the effect of publicly proclaiming the gap between law as it was and law as it should have been. To speak of slavery as against natural law, even if the legal consequences of the statement were few and undramatic, was to admit the moral blemish on the legal system.

Legislation: Natural Right and Social Expedience

In 1791, James Wilson wrote

Government, in my humble opinion, should be formed to secure
and to enlarge the exercise of the natural rights of its members.*

Wilson wrote these words as part of a rejoinder to Burke's very
recent *Reflections on the Revolution in France*. And Wilson had
been, by this time, a participant in all of the down-to-earth give-and-
take of constitutional politics. He had been active in the Convention,
itself. Perhaps even more important, he was the Constitution's leading proponent in Pennsylvania. Wilson was a justice on the United
States Supreme Court when he delivered his *Lectures on Law*. So, it
was neither the lack of a sophisticated, skeptical perspective on "natural law," nor the lack of experience in daily political strife, that
produced so straightforward a reliance on nature as the proper end of
civil government. Like most of his contemporaries, Wilson was comfortable with this manner of expressing the ultimate ends of law. Accordingly, when writing of slavery, Wilson gravitated easily to repeating Blackstone's conclusion that the state of slavery in any social
system violates the law of nature.

While such a conclusion sufficed for a treatise, it did not constitute
a legislative program. The legislative process may derive its desiderata from nature, but execution of policy requires adjustment of and
accommodation to various interests. No reader of the *Federalist* can
fail to discern just how thoroughly that generation was concerned
with wholesome and public process for neutralizing the potentially

* Bird Wilson, ed., *The Works of the Honourable James Wilson* (Philadelphia: Lorenzo
Press, printed for Bronson and Chaucey, 1804), 2 : 466. Chapter 12 of vol. 2 is almost exclusively devoted to refuting Burke's critique of the idiom of natural right. Similar statements
about the ends of government and of law may be found in almost all early American legal
writers. See, e.g., Zephania Swift, *A System of the Laws of the State of Connecticut* (Windam,
Conn.: Printed by John Byrne for the author, 1795–96), 1 : 73. I do not mean to imply that this
teleological use of nature was a major preoccupation of American legal thought. It was, rather,
a commonly accepted, hardly thought-about, background concept. The early American works
are, in the manner of the more familiar *Federalist,* preoccupied with the distribution of authority. Thus, if there be a single theoretical concept of overriding import it is that of sovereignty.
Americans were devoted to breaking down the English (Blackstonian) concept of sovereignty
and replacing it with both an abstract, residual sovereignty in the "people" and an operational,
practical mechanism of limited power in government officialdom.

disastrous, but, natural, pursuit of self-interest. The juxtaposition of a strong impulse to emancipatory solutions, perceived as emanating from natural law, and recognition of the multiplicity of interests that legitimately constitute factors in the legislative quest for expedient solutions may be studied in an exchange of letters between two of the young Republic's foremost legal minds: St. George Tucker and John Adams.*

St. George Tucker became Professor of Law at William and Mary in 1792. The enterprise of teaching the common law as part of a general college curriculum was new. In fact, only Blackstone in the Vinerian Chair at Oxford, and George Wythe at William and Mary had preceded Tucker. It is no wonder that Tucker gravitated to the use of the *Commentaries* as a teaching tool. But, Tucker found Blackstone inadequate on many issues. Not only were the *Commentaries* out of date as to English law, but the Revolution and the colonial experience had wrought important changes in the private law of Virginia and the United States. As to public law, the *Commentaries* were not only inaccurate, they were dangerous. Throughout the decade of his teaching career, Tucker endeavored to provide the student with a commentary on the *Commentaries,* a refutation of Blackstone's political theory and a supplement to his law. This endeavor culminated with Tucker's edition of *Blackstone* in 1803. More than 1,000 textual footnotes updated the law, and more than 800 pages of appendices, consisting of essays, refuted or supplemented the *Commentaries* on major issues.[9]

In the teaching of Virginia law, one of the major gaps left by the *Commentaries* was with respect to slavery. Tucker's position on slavery was close to that of Blackstone. The wholehearted condemnation of the institution on natural law grounds found a sympathetic reader.[10] But, Blackstone wrote of slavery smugly, savoring the coincidence of the common law and natural law on this point. Tucker had to teach in a slave society. Whether on account of his own prior incli-

---

* St. George Tucker of Virginia was a relatively important legal scholar and judge from the early 1790's through 1811. His biography has yet to be written, though there is a "memoir." Mary Haldane Coleman, *St. George Tucker, Citizen of No Mean City* (Richmond, Va.: Dietz Press, 1938). Tucker's edition of *Blackstone* is, to the author's mind, the most interesting and original of American legal works (excluding the *Federalist*) from the Revolution to Story's *Conflicts.* See my review article of Tucker's *Blackstone,* 70 *Columbia Law Review* 1475 (1970).

nations or as a result of his attention to his pedagogic duties, by the mid-1790's Tucker had begun to collect materials for a major study of the institution of slavery. The study was to be a policy paper, not a history. From the result of the study, first published in 1796 and later reprinted in *Blackstone,* we know how thoroughly Tucker came to accept the natural law condemnation of slavery, how completely he associated the theoretical justifications of the Revolution with the demand for emancipation:

> For our bill of rights, declares, "that all men are, by nature *equally free,* . . ." This is, indeed, no more than a recognition of the first principles of the law of nature. . . . It would be hard to reconcile reducing the negroes to a state of slavery to these principles, unless we first degrade them below the rank of human beings . . . but surely it is time we should admit the evidence of moral truth, and learn to regard them as our fellow men. . . .[11]

Already in 1795, Tucker had decided on a plea for emancipation as the framework of his essay. He began to collect material on the workings of successful attempts at emancipation in the North. The statutory framework of Pennsylvania was readily available. The process by which Massachusetts had come to report no slaves in the 1790 census, however, was decidedly murky. Tucker wrote to Jeremy Belknap, corresponding secretary for the new Massachusetts Historical Society, for information. He wanted to know not only about the legal stroke that emancipated the slaves, but also about the shape of the institution before the emancipation, and the nature of the "Negro problem" that followed upon it. In the course of collecting answers for Tucker, Belknap corresponded with a number of important Massachusetts public figures and lawyers, among them John Adams.[12]

The nature of Tucker's inquiries demonstrate his attention to the kind of practical considerations evident in the Pennsylvania Act: How are Negroes to be supported? What is the relationship of emancipation to the Poor Laws? What dislocations are to be expected? Is there to be protection for the very old or very young black? But, despite the evidence that Tucker considered more than the bare demand of natural right for freedom, there is, in the course of his correspondence with Belknap a curious passage—perhaps the understandable lapse of a man whose fondest dream seemed destined for miscarriage. In considering the plight of the slave, the horrors of slavery, and the self-evident natural right to freedom, Tucker wrote that he sometimes felt the proper course was *"fiat justitia, ruat coelum"* (let justice be done, though the Heavens fall).[13] If this stray phrase stood for Tucker's general attitude, it would, indeed, reveal a most unusual legal mind. However, even understood as an isolated phrase, perhaps at most a temperamental tendency, the phrase is significant for the response it evoked from Belknap's correspondents, most notably John Adams. Adams fully justified himself as an inheritor of the political thought of Burke and Hume. He wrote to Belknap:

> If I should agree with him in his maxim, "Fiat justitia ruat coelum" the question would still remain, what is justice? Justice to the Negroes would require that they should not be abandoned by their masters and turned loose upon a world in which they have no capacity to procure even a subsistence. What would become of the old? the young? the infirm? Justice to the world, too, would forbid that such numbers should be turned out to live by violence, by theft, or fraud.

In short, justice is not natural; it is a concept whose very meaning is given only in societal contexts.[14]

James Sullivan, a prominent Boston jurist, replied to Tucker in a similar vein. He conceived of the magnitude of slavery in Virginia and its importance to her economic institutions as insurmountable obstacles to any immediate abolition. Sullivan neatly pointed out that in the one instance in history of so grand an emancipation, the exodus from Egypt:

> It was necessary, not only to open the sea, . . . but more necessary to close it again in order to prevent their return. Even then, though a spontaneous supply of bread from Heaven supported the camp . . . so incapable were the men who had been bred in a state of slavery . . . that it was necessary to waste them all in the wilderness.

Sullivan concluded that the key to any successful emancipation lay in its gradualness.[15]

Tucker certainly took Adams's and Sullivan's qualifications to heart. Though the essay he wrote began by asserting that the oppression of the black slave by Americans had been "ten thousand times more cruel than the utmost extremity of those grievances and oppressions of which we [the colonists] complained," and though he was fully aware that those grievances of the colonists had led to war, he proposed a plan of gradual emancipation that would have taken 105 years to free the last slave held in Virginia during which time most of Virginia's Negro population would have remained enslaved. In formulating this plan, Tucker articulated at some length the justification for prolonging so horrible a wrong. True, natural right is the starting point for legislation:

> From this view of our jurisprudence respecting slaves, we are unavoidably led to remark how frequently the laws of nature have been set aside in favor of institutions, the pure result of prejudice, usurpation and tyranny.[16]

But even prejudice, usurpation, and tyranny establish expectations that in the course of time must be respected. Moreover, they establish interests that must be expected to demand and fight for a measure of recognition. Thus, Tucker acknowledged that his plan "savors strongly of prejudice," but, he claimed, any plan for emancipation must either "encounter or accomodate itself" to prejudice.

> Under such an arrangement [a prolonged period of transition from slavery with denial of civil rights to Negroes] we might reasonably hope, that time would either remove from us a race of men, whom we wish not to incorporate with us, or obliterate those prejudices, which now form an obstacle to such incorporation.[17]

Of course, Tucker badly underestimated the power of the forces with which he had to contend. Moreover, he characteristically overrated the power of reason in enlightening men. When he sent his modest proposal to the legislature of Virginia, it was barely considered and was ultimately tabled without the grace of a formal rejection. His surprise and disappointment are evident from a later letter to Belknap:

> Nobody I believe had read it; nobody could explain its contents. Nobody was prepared to meet the blind fury of the ene-

mies of freedom. . . . Actual suffering will one day perhaps open the oppressor's eyes.*

Both the natural law impulse to abolish slavery and the very practical form in which implementation was attempted were characteristic of Tucker and of his age. It is well to remember that even the Declaration of Independence made no mean concession to the dictates of prudence as a process for evaluating the competitive claims of stability as against the claim of natural rights. No contradiction was sensed in both attributing the ends of law and politics to "nature" and pursuing those ends with due regard for established interests.

* "Letters and Documents Relating to Slavery in Massachusetts," *Collections of the Massachusetts Historical Society,* 5th Ser., 3 (1877), 427–28. [Hereafter cited as *Belknap, Letters and Documents.*] Tucker's plan was first generally described in a letter to Belknap. It was set forth in detail with supporting arguments in a classic pamphlet in 1796. The full text of that pamphlet became Note H in the 1803 *Blackstone.* St. George Tucker, *Blackstone's Commentaries with Notes of Reference to the Constitution and Laws of the Federal Government of the United States and of the Commonwealth of Virginia,* 5 Vols. (Philadelphia: William Young Birch and Abraham Small, 1803), Vol. 2, Appendix, p. 31. [Hereafter cited as *Tucker's Blackstone.*] Tucker's plan called for an act that would provide that all *females* born after the effective date be born free, but that they be required to serve for twenty-eight years. Their freedom would be transmitted to all their descendants, male and female. However, all such children born to a mother still under an obligation of service, would inherit the obligation to serve for a like period (twenty-eight years). Tucker's detailed calculations, available in Note H, indicated that it would be over a hundred years before all blacks would be free during which time, between two-thirds and three-fourths of the black population would labor under at least temporary servitude.

CHAPTER THREE: Judicial Construction of a Natural Law Text: The "Free and Equal" Clauses

If the legislative musings of a man both firmly antislavery and at home with the natural rights idiom led to a scheme recognizing conflicting interests and policies to the tune of projecting a hundred year transition period of enslavement, then we ought not to wonder at judicial attention to the same multiplicity of interests and policies in treatment of constitutions and statutes. For these judges were often participants or close observers of the process of creating the instruments they construed. Moreover, they subscribed to a jurisprudence in which the judicial role was, in Hamilton's words, one of "judgment" not "will," [1] or in Swift's words, one of "expounding" not "framing" law. [2] Since it is the will of others that they expound, and since that will, with regard to slavery, recognized a number of conflicting interests, judicial work ought to reflect the same patchwork of compromise and adjustment. Yet, as Zephania Swift wrote

> The science of law is grounded on certain first principles. These have been introduced by the statutes of the legislature, or have been derived from the dictates of reason, and the science of morals. On this basis, our courts have erected an artificial fabrick of jurisprudence, . . . and a deviation from any fundamental principle deranges the whole superstructure. A judge therefore . . . must take into view the whole system of law, and make his decision conformable to the general principles on which it is founded. [3]

These general principles might include natural law and would certainly do so when explicitly incorporated into the organic law of the state. The twin desires—to found the New Jerusalem on the rock of reason and right and to make this foundation explicit and binding—led to the Declarations of Rights in most of the state constitutions. I am concerned here with one very common and important phrase in those declarations: the "free and equal clause."

42

In 1776 Virginia declared that "all men are by nature equally free." Similar language found its way to the constitutions of Pennsylvania (1776), Vermont (1777), New Hampshire (1784), Massachusetts (1780), Connecticut (1818), and New Jersey (1844).[4] Such a clause had obvious potential applications to the institution of slavery, and in some of those states judges were called upon to determine just what the effect of the clause would be. The concern here is with the method and assumptions of the judge in doing this work. In Vermont the task was easy, for the instrument itself called for the end of slavery as a consequence of the free and equal clause.[5] In the other states, however, the judges' task was not so straightforward. A series of cases beginning in 1781 and stretching to 1845 construed these provisions in a variety of contexts.

Massachusetts

In 1778 Massachusetts rejected a proposed constitution. The returns of the various towns have been preserved and provide a unique record of the dynamics of a state constitutional controversy from the revolutionary period.[6] The 1778 proposal provided a very limited basis for suffrage and this was the primary cause of its defeat. Yet, at least a recurring theme in the negative returns is the absence of a Declaration of Rights from the Constitution. Such a Declaration of Rights would be presumed to include a free and equal clause—as had the several declarations enacted in 1776. Moreover, a few towns also noted the condonation of Negro slavery in the 1778 proposal. Article V of that proposal had implicitly recognized the possibility of slavery by limiting the suffrage first to men who were free. The article also discriminated against nonwhites, denying Negroes, Indians, and mulattoes the suffrage even if they qualified in terms of status and property. To Article V the town of Westminster replied

> . . . the following articles appear to us Exceptionable viz—Article 5th which deprives a part of the humane Race of their Natural Rights, . . . Which in our opinion no power on Earth has a Just Right to Doe.[7]

The return of the town of Sutton is stronger still and more detailed in its objections. After first characterizing the offending article as "wear[ing] a very gross complexion of Slavery," the town went on to characterize the Massachusetts proposal as a continuation of the great sin of the slave trade and kidnapping, "adding to the already accumulated load of guilt" of those crimes. Sutton concludes its objections with a concrete proposal:

> We therefore think that we ought to have an article expressive of what the State is to consist of. And to Say in express terms that every Person within the State 21 years of age Shall have a Sole absolute Property in himself and all his earnings having an exclusive right to make all manner contracts. . . .*

The constitution proposed after the defeat of 1778, ratified in 1780, extended the suffrage and began with a Declaration of Rights. Article I now read:

> All men are born free and equal, and have certain natural, essential, and unalienable rights; among which may be reckoned the right of enjoying and defending their lives and liberties; that of acquiring, possessing, and protecting property. . . .[8]

The constitution did not contain any explicit emancipation clause or any authorization of legislation effecting emancipation. It was to be expected, therefore, that the question of slavery in Massachusetts would depend on judicial construction of a Declaration of Rights that affirmed liberty as a natural right in the usual, general terms.

The long-standing tradition has it that the Massachusetts courts declared slavery unconstitutional, as violative of the state free and equal clause, in the *Quock Walker* cases. That tradition has become a historian's perennial football [9] because of certain ambiguities in the records and, I think, because of the rather different senses of "unconstitutionality" that eighteenth-, nineteenth-, and twentieth-century minds have brought to the materials.

In 1795, Jeremy Belknap responded to St. George Tucker's question about how Massachusetts abolished Negro slavery in the following terms:

---

* Robert Taylor, ed., *Massachusetts, Colony to Commonwealth: Documents on the Formation of the Constitution 1775–1780* (Chapel Hill: University of North Carolina Press, 1961), pp. 68–69. Additional confirmation of the view that Article I may have been intended to abolish slavery is the tradition that Judge John Lowell, who wrote the Article, so intended. *Proceedings of the Massachusetts Historical Society* (Boston: Massachusetts Historical Society, 1874), 13 : 299–300.

The general answer is, that slavery hath been abolished here by publick opinion; which began to be established about thirty years ago.[10]

Belknap goes on to relate various unsuccessful legislative efforts and inconclusive judicial decisions prior to the constitution of 1780. He then writes that

In 1781, at the court in Worcestor county, an indictment was found against a white man for assaulting, beating, and imprisoning a black. He was tried at the Supreme Judicial Court in 1783. His defence was, that the black was his slave, and that the beating, etc. was the necessary restraint and correction of the master. This was answered by citing the aforesaid clause in the declaration of rights. The judges and jury were of opinion that he had no right to beat or imprison the negro. He was found guilty, and fined forty shillings. This decision was a mortal wound to slavery in Massachusetts.[11]

James Sullivan also indicated his belief that the Worcester cases ended slavery in Massachusetts.[12] Despite this virtually contemporaneous evidence and repeated assertions by Massachusetts courts that the Worcester cases ended slavery, the matter has not been at rest since 1866. In that year the publication, under the auspices of the New York Historical Society, of Moore's *Notes on the History of Slavery in Massachusetts* began a war of the historical societies in which the Massachusettsians came out second best. However, Moore's thesis—that slavery in Massachusetts had a legal sanction before 1780, that the institution probably persisted to some small extent after 1781, and that Massachusetts involvement in the slave trade continued shamefully well after *Quock Walker*—does not affect the general perception of the Worcester cases as the authoritative construction of the 1780 Bill of Rights' free and equal clause.

Much of the ambiguity about the effect of these cases inheres in the fact that in Massachusetts, at this time, all judicial cases including appeals were tried before a jury. Thus, we have records of the argument of counsel and of the charge to the jury, but no extensive judicial opinion. The second source of ambiguity lies in the misapplication of later notions of judicial review to as yet imperfectly formed judicial institutions. The mechanism by which *Quock Walker* led to slavery's abolition was very probably not the treating of a judicial opinion as abolition by fiat, but the public acquiescence in an interpretation of a constitutional phrase combined with the reinforcement of a tendency among Negroes to simply act as free. Belknap suggests as much. For our purposes here, however, the mechanisms of transforming legal pronouncement to social reality is less important than the principles of interpretation and construction of a natural rights phrase.

In 1781, Quock Walker, allegedly a slave of Jennison, ran away to work for a neighbor, Caldwell. For simplicity I shall hereafter refer to Walker as the Negro to Jennison as the master and to Caldwell as the employer. The master recaptured his Negro and beat him. The Negro sued the master for assault. In turn, the master sued the employer for enticing a servant. In both cases the determinative issue was whether the Negro was free. If Walker was free, then the master would be liable to him on account of the beating, and the employer would not be liable to the master for enticing. At the Court of Common Pleas two juries rendered inconsistent verdicts in the two causes, holding the master liable for beating Walker, but holding also that the employer was liable to the master for enticing his slave. One might add parenthetically that from 1765 on Massachusetts juries had become somewhat notorious for finding in favor of slaves in actions, in the nature of trespass, brought to test whether the slave was legally enslaved or free. This syndrome may account to some extent for the inconsistent verdicts. At any rate, appeals were taken from both cases to the Superior Court of Judicature—then a circuit court. At the same time an indictment was brought against the master for assault. Probably by arrangement, the indictment was not prosecuted after the master dropped his appeal. The employer's appeal was then to be construed as determinative. The verdict in that case, *Jennison v. Caldwell,* on appeal was in favor of the employer, removing all inconsistency. After a year the master attempted to relitigate the issue in a different forum by petitioning the legislature for a special bill. In retaliation for that petition, the indictment was reinstated against him and tried before the Supreme Judicial Court sitting with a full bench and jury. The defendant was convicted.

There are two main sources that have been preserved for the basis of the verdicts in these three cases. One is the brief or notes of Levi

Lincoln, counsel for the employer, Caldwell in *Jennison v. Cald-well*.[13] From this brief we know the nature of the argument of counsel on both sides. It has been argued that the charge of Justice Sargent in the *Caldwell* case on appeal largely followed the argument of Lincoln. Furthermore, in the criminal case of *Commonwealth v. Jennison,* there are two sources for the supposed charge to the jury of Chief Justice Cushing. While the two sources differ in some respects, they are in fundamental agreement as to the points that will be made below.[14] The text used here is that preferred, and largely quoted, by J. D. Cushing in his 1961 article on "The Cushing Court and the Abolition of Slavery in Massachusetts."

The brief of Levi Lincoln is remarkable for its lack of reliance on the constitutional text. In part this strategy was dictated by the fact that he was arguing before a jury and could, perhaps, hope for great success with a more pure natural rights argument. Moreover, implicit in Lincoln's brief is the concession from the opposition that Article I of the constitution may be taken to prospectively emancipate Negroes born after the ratification of the instrument. If the only issue of constitutional construction between the two sides was the prospectivity of Article I's emancipatory effect, then Lincoln could hardly be blamed for steering the jury's mind to the broader ground of nature. In fact, Levi Lincoln more or less conceded that the slavery of Quock Walker could be viewed either as constitutional or unconstitutional. However, he argued that it was clearly a deprivation of preexisting natural rights, a violation of natural law and of the law of God. Lincoln threatened the jury with the argument that on the last day we would all be tried before one common judge and that there the Quock Walker case would be retried and the verdict of the jury tried along with it:

> It will then be tried by the laws of reason and revelation, Is not a law of nature that all men are equal and free. Is not the laws of nature the laws of God. Is not the law of God, then, against slavery.[15]

If the constitution be construed as authorizing enslavement, then there is a conflict and the jury must choose between the law of God and the law of the state. Lincoln advises choosing in favor of the law of God, since disobedience of men's laws can but destroy the body while disobeying the law of God may damn the soul. Coming, as it does, on the heels of the Revolution, Counsel's rhetoric is not very surprising.

Nevertheless, Cushing's charge to the jury in the related *Commonwealth v. Jennison* two years later stands in marked contrast to that rhetoric. The judge unequivocally sides with the slave, directing a verdict of guilty with the words: "The Deft. must be found guilty as the facts charged are not controverted." But Cushing reaches this conclusion by reading Article I as *granting* rights incompatible with the continued existence of slavery.

> In short, without resorting to implication in constructing the constitution, slavery is in my judgment as effectively abolished as it can be by the granting of rights and privileges wholly incompatible and repugnant to its existence.[16]

For Cushing there is no doubt but that the natural right to freedom, which is acknowledged as preexisting, would not suffice of itself as a rule of decision. It is the act of positive law, of incorporating the content of that law of nature into the constitution that renders it effective in Massachusetts. Yet, once finding a positive law base for the natural law proposition, Cushing apparently construes the natural law phrase as if it has a life and content of its own. I say "apparently" because from a short charge to a jury, it is difficult to derive too much in the way of legal philosophy. Yet, with that qualification, it should be noted that nowhere does Cushing think it necessary to assert, much less prove, that the framers of the Constitution or the ratifiers intended to abolish Negro slavery with Article I. Indeed, the only reference to the framers is that sentiments favorable to human rights of the revolutionary era led them to declare that all men are free and equal and that all have a natural right to liberty. The meaning of the free and equal clause is taken to exclude Negro slavery. It is not entirely clear whether the court assumed the purpose of the framers to have been emancipation or whether it believed their intention to be irrelevant except insofar as it was to incorporate the natural law favoring liberty.

In terms of the impact that the Quock Walker cases had on contemporaries, the Tucker-Belknap correspondence provides some clues. Most of Belknap's Massachusetts correspondents agreed that it was the Massachusetts Declaration of Rights of 1780 that had abolished slavery in the state, as interpreted by the courts in 1781 or 1783 (Quock Walker). Nevertheless, some, including John Adams, either didn't know of the cases or thought them irrelevant to the process by which slavery ended in Massachusetts. One correspondent clearly assumed Quock Walker to have abolished slavery but considered it a misconstruction of the constitution by which many men were deprived of their property. Finally, the most detailed reference to the case is from the letter of James Sullivan, a member of the constitutional convention that penned Article I, and a judge of some repute. He makes no remarks as to the validity of the construction given Article I, implicitly approving it. Belknap himself, in summing up the replies in his answer to Tucker's initial queries, attributes to the Quock Walker cases the effect of having construed the constitution of 1780 as emancipating the slaves. Moreover, he contrasts the Massachusetts action with the result reached as to construction of the New Hampshire free and equal clause. There, too, the language was read as applicable to Negro slavery, but was given prospective effect only. Belknap barely conceals his distaste for the limitation in the New Hampshire construction.[17]

I would not want to speculate too freely about the mind of Chief Justice William Cushing, about whom we know very little. But it is desirable to outline the circumstances in which he rendered his jury charge. For, certain tentative hypotheses about judicial behavior in such instances will be advanced in Chapter 13. Massachusetts in 1783 presented a pattern of doctrinal convergence for the legal and moral norms of slavery. The new state constitution could be read as authorizing the end of slavery without doing violence either to its language or to what was known of the intentions of its framers. Moreover, public ópinion supported such a reading of the constitution. And a line of decisions going back to the 1760's showed juries increasingly hostile to legal claims and defenses based on the master-slave relationship. Dislocation caused by the *Quock Walker* decision was minimal. The economy of the Commonwealth was more heavily tied to the trade than to domestic slavery within Massachusetts. Negroes were wandering off, acting as if they were free, in any event. And most masters lacked either the inclination or the power to enforce any legal rights of dominion they might have.[18]

We do not know how consciously and explicitly Cushing and Sargent took these factors into account in giving their jury charges. Cushing's brief reference to sentiments favorable to human liberty might be construed as such a recognition. In any event, free from direct and indirect evidence of contrary intentions; unfettered by the organized opposition of conflicting pressure groups; bulwarked with slight but real enough indications of a prior trend toward freedom, the Massachusetts judiciary could give "free and equal" a straightforward but far-reaching construction that ended slavery in the Commonwealth.

Virginia *

Virginia's free and equal clause was proclaimed at the outset of the Revolution. No one then thought Virginia had emancipated her quarter-million slaves. Jefferson, in his *Notes on the State of Virginia,* penned some of the most famous lines of his era on Negro slavery. But there is not a word that might indicate that he thought Virginia had already embarked on the venture of emancipation.[19] In 1782, 1792, and 1806 very significant legislation on slavery was passed in Virginia with no one suggesting that the institution had already been done away with.[20] Yet, we have already seen that St. George Tucker considered slavery morally and logically inconsistent with this Declaration of Rights. The words of the free and equal clause against the unmistakable reality and importance of slavery in Virginia presented in starkest form the question of whether judges act according to large principles or specific intentions—whether the judge refers to the will and intent of men in authoritative positions or

---

* The judicial treatment of the Virginia "free and equal" clause, considered in this section, was not next after Massachusetts in point of time. New Hampshire's free and equal clause may have been interpreted to give a right to freedom to all Negroes born after its passage, though no case has come down to us. See Arthur Zilversmit, *The First Emancipation* (Chicago: University of Chicago Press, 1967), p. 117 and sources cited therein, especially Belknap's view of the matter in "Tucker's Queries," *Collections of the Massachusetts Historical Society,* 1st Ser., 4 (1795) : 204.

More important, an attempt was made to secure judicial interpretation of the Pennsylvania free and equal clause as forbidding the limited servitude explicitly permitted under the Pennsylvania gradual emancipation statute. This antislavery offensive apparently failed in 1798 in a case, *Flora v. Graisberry,* no report of which has yet been found. A detailed account of that case, were one available, would enrich the present narrative considerably. See Zilversmit, pp. 204–205.

to the apparent "meaning" of the words the men choose. For, in Virginia the question was not what, if anything, had the framers meant to do about slavery? Everyone knew they meant to leave it alone. The question was, whether they had done something without knowing or intending it; whether the words of natural law, once "declared," have a life of their own. It was St. George Tucker, now a judge on the Court of Appeals, who ultimately ruled in the remarkable case *Hudgins v. Wright* [21] that even where broad declarations of natural right are incorporated into the organic law of the state, judges act according to the designs of the men who framed the instrument, not according to the logic of the principle they articulate. However confused Tucker's speculative jurisprudence might have been with regard to natural law, in the realm of judicial action he unhesitatingly and surefootedly stood on the grounds of legislative intent and the location of policy-making in the popular branch of government.

Hudgins v. Wright was decided in 1806. An Indian family, held to servitude by one Hudgins, was about to be transported from the state. They sued for freedom in the Richmond District Court of Chancery where the venerable George Wythe presided. Wythe was a prominent opponent of slavery and one of the great figures of the Virginia bench—at that time the leading legal community in America. Wythe's opinion in the *Hudgins* case has not been preserved, and, astonishingly, his part in the case is not even mentioned by his biographer. [22] Nevertheless, from the appellate court opinion and arguments we can reconstruct the tenor of the decision. Wythe apparently held in favor of the Indian plaintiffs on two alternative grounds. First, he held that upon viewing three generations of the family before him they appeared physically to range from Indian to white and showed no Negroid features. Thus, the family was presumptively free, and the defendant failed to overcome this presumption with direct evidence of descent from a slave mother. Alternatively, Wythe reasoned that all men were presumptively free in Virginia in consequence of the 1776 Declaration of Rights. Again the presumption was not overcome in this case. [23]

When Wythe proclaimed this astounding presumption, the state of Virginia was on the threshold of what Winthrop Jordan labeled the "first step on the slippery slope that led to Appomattox." [24] For

Virginia had led the South in 1782 in opening the doors to private manumission. In 1806 she closed that door by requiring newly freed blacks to leave the state within one year. This reversal of what had become a commitment to gradual vitiation of slavery was the end product of long legislative debate in which at least one lawmaker conceded that the restrictive measure he favored ran counter to the natural rights of man. It was at this critical juncture that Jefferson wrote of his despair that an early end to slavery could be achieved.[25] George Wythe, at the end of a long and honorable role, must have sensed some of the same despair.

Wythe's last years had been preoccupied with the problem of slavery. Thirty years earlier he had, with Jefferson, considered incorporating a plan for emancipation in the law-revision for which they, with Edmund Pendleton, were responsible.[26] Now, in 1803, an old man, he made his last will and provided that Michael Brown, his black former slave protégé, was to be beneficiary of much of his estate. Moreover, Thomas Jefferson was appointed Brown's guardian. Michael Brown was Wythe's private experiment with regard to the capacities of black men. It was an experiment that ended tragically, with the murder of Wythe and of Michael Brown by the old man's nephew who was to inherit Brown's share should the Negro predecease him.[27]

It is not at all clear how the events of this troublesome period influenced or were influenced by Wythe's opinion in *Hudgins*. The Chancellor might have been trying to wind up his judicial affairs, as he wound up his personal affairs, with a noble experiment to promote freedom. As a man approaches eighty, he has either acquired or run out of patience. Alternatively, Wythe may have assumed that he was making a gratuitous gesture. Since there was an alternative ground to his decision that was sufficient and well within the racial ideology of the day, we cannot tell precisely what the significance of a general presumption of freedom might have been. Could it be rebutted by evidence as to racial characteristics or only by evidence as to status of the maternal line? If the presumption were rebuttable by racial characteristics alone it was simply a euphemism for a denial of a presumption of freedom to blacks. Enough of speculation. Poor Wythe didn't leave us his own words.

Hudgins v. Wright was appealed to the Virginia Supreme Court of

Appeals. There the decision was affirmed on the racial ground with express disapproval of Wythe's alternative, far-reaching presumption.[28] It was St. George Tucker who wrote the most thorough of the opinions of the court. It must have cost Tucker something to have written the opinion. Wythe, his teacher and his predecessor at William and Mary, had just been murdered partly as a consequence of his forthright private action on slavery. Only three years earlier, Tucker's own work, the *Blackstone,* had trumpeted his moral opposition to slavery. He had first-hand knowledge of the efficacy of a judicial stroke in ending slavery in Massachusetts. Yet Tucker was firmly convinced that the human agencies that had framed the Declaration of Rights had done so "with a cautious eye" toward slavery— that they had meant to leave the institution undisturbed. Thus, Tucker concluded

> . . . I do not concur with the Chancellor in his reasoning on the operation of the first clause of the Bill of Rights, which was notoriously framed with a cautious eye to this subject, and was meant to embrace the case of free citizens, or aliens only; and not by a side wind to overturn the rights of property. . . .[29]

Tucker held that the presumption of freedom attached to Indians not because of any force of the Bill of Rights but because of the circumstances of Indian enslavement, which were very limited in time and scope. Thus, the fact of being an Indian is somewhat probative of freedom. Similarly, yet more forcefully, the presumption attaches to whites. As to Negroes, however, it is notorious that most were brought as slaves and are the descendants of slaves on the maternal line. Consequently, no presumption of freedom rationally attaches as to them.[30]

Wythe's remarkable effort to derive logically from natural rights principles incorporated within the organic law of the state—the virtual emancipation of many thousands of slaves—represents the extreme application of the Massachusetts methods. The application was extreme because it was attempted in a context of more than two decades of clear acceptance of slavery as an integral part of Virginia's institutions after the passage of the Declaration of Rights. In effect, Wythe said that by these words Virginia dealt a mortal blow to Negro slavery without being aware of it. The facts of the history of Virginia made it necessary to face squarely the extent to which natural law phrases, incorporated within the positive law of the state, were to have meaning and effect apart from the intent of the men who wrote and approved them. Tucker and the Court of Appeals brought the phrase back to be viewed in the light of the "cautious eye" of the framer. So read, there was no evidence of intent to free the slaves.

Tucker's opinion in *Hudgins* is short, straightforward, and businesslike, with no internal evidence that its author was himself opposed to slavery. There is no explicit disclaimer of responsibility for the result nor is there an attempt to portray the judicial role as a mechanistic one. I note the absence of such factors because they appear with such frequency in the opinions of other, later antislavery judges in other situations. There were many attributes of the context of *Hudgins v. Wright* and of Tucker's life that marked the case off from those other opinions, described in Chapters 7, 10, and 11. First, Tucker was an active political fighter for emancipation. He did not have to feel that in rejecting broad judicial pronouncements, he was giving up the ghost. He was personally involved in the struggle on the legislative front and on the general educational level. The involvement in the moral struggle in other areas would likely reduce the guilt of nonfurtherance of liberty judicially. Second, while rejecting a universal presumption of freedom, Tucker was reinforcing a libertarian rule as to Indians. He could take some comfort in a victory on the limited front and hope for its spread to black slaves through other means. Moreover, the application of the libertarian presumption to Indians could be achieved without violence to a neutral jurisprudence. Third, Tucker need not have felt, in 1806, that the South's (and Virginia's) commitment to slavery was irrevocable. True, in hindsight, it seems that the turning point had already been reached. However, Tucker had only recently tentatively suggested that the vast expanse of the Louisiana Territory be considered for Negro settlement.[31] So long as options remained open, Tucker could plausibly feel that a judicial stroke was an inappropriate means to abolition. Finally, Tucker was, as we have seen from his initial plan, aware of the many competing interests to liberty. He, himself, before formulating his proposal, had listed the factors that distinguished Virginia's "Negro problem" from that of Massachusetts. Consequently, we may suppose that Tucker continued to believe that the dislocations to be expected from any sudden stroke in Virginia were too fearful to be encouraged. Only legislation could incorporate the accommodations to property and safety necessary to an emancipation scheme. Thus, it is almost certainly policy as well as positivism that leads Tucker to his conclusions.

The opinion in *Hudgins v. Wright* does not say all of the above. But, we may plausibly account for the brevity of the case through assuming that much of this contextual sensitivity was understood and accepted by all the participants in the legal proceedings. The counsel for the plaintiff (the Indians) were not interested in emancipating Virginia's slaves. They were perfectly content to win their case on the narrower, racial grounds. It seems likely that Wythe had seized on a makeweight rhetorical flourish of counsel to impose a revolutionary step from above. Before Tucker and the Court of Appeals, this argument was not pressed. St. George Tucker, in disclaiming the Declaration of Rights, confronted not a movement, but only the ghost of George Wythe.

New Jersey *

In 1844 New Jersey ratified a new constitution with a free and equal clause. The New Jersey cases of *State v. Post* and *State v. Van Buren* were decided in 1845.[32] Although these cases reached the same general conclusion about the proper effect of a free and equal clause as *Hudgins v. Wright,* the context in which it was reached and the approach of the New Jersey Supreme Court to the language of natural law were quite different. In mid-century New Jersey, slavery was not an important economic fact of life. In 1804 the state had adopted a scheme for gradual emancipation. By 1845 there were only an estimated seven hundred slaves left. Perhaps as many as 50 percent of these seven hundred Negroes were over fifty-five. For these older slaves it is at least conceivable that the security supposedly guaranteed by the Act was as valuable as a few years of freedom. The aboli-

---

* Between *Hudgins* and the New Jersey experience, the "free and equal" clause of Connecticut was also construed judicially. In *Jackson v. Bullock,* 12 Conn. 39 (1837), the Connecticut Supreme Court rejected a claim that the free and equal clause operated to free a Negro passing through the state, preferring to base its holding for freedom on the gradual emancipation statute of 1784. The free and equal clause was not the major argument for the Negro and is considered almost in passing by the court.

tion of slavery in New Jersey in 1845 would only have accelerated, by a few years, the end of the process started forty years earlier. Also important was the fact that by the 1840's the abolitionist crusade had become pervasive in American political life. The *Post* and *Van Buren* cases were a part of that crusade. Advocacy in these cases was highly ideological: It was undertaken for purposes of the movement—to dramatize the inconsistency of slavery with underlying principles of a democratic state. And the advocacy was a crucible for utopian theories of constitutional law (of which the free and equal clause argument was the only plausible one).[33]

Almost immediately after ratification of the 1844 constitution, suit was brought on behalf of two kinds of black plaintiffs. One case sought freedom for a slave born prior to the gradual emancipation act of 1804 and thus not freed by that law. A second suit asserted the unconstitutionality of even the limited servitude for years imposed, by the 1804 act, on the first generation of freed blacks. These cases were engineered and argued by Alvan Stewart, a New York abolitionist of idiosyncratic views who was prominent among antislavery utopian constitutional theorists. Stewart's career as legal theorist culminated with the publication of a tract asserting the unconstitutionality of slavery under the federal Constitution. He argued that the "peculiar institution" violated the due process clause of the United States Constitution. This position was steadfastly held despite a recent Supreme Court decision holding the Fifth Amendment inapplicable as a restraint on state action, and despite the four clauses of the Constitution, which, by any candid construction, at least acknowledged the lawful existence of slavery in some states.[34]

In the New Jersey cases Stewart argued that the servitude of the petitioners violated the due process clause, the republican form of government clause, and the privileges and immunities clause of the federal Constitution. He also argued that natural law, in and of itself, required the court to free the bondsmen. But, it was the more recent constitutional incorporation of the natural law language of "free and equal," that seemed most promising.

Finding themselves the target for a barrage of radical antislavery legal theory, Judges Nevius and Randolph of the New Jersey Supreme Court were a bit taken aback by the nature of the arguments before them. Judge Nevius remarked "that much of the argument seemed rather addressed to the feelings than to the legal intelligence of the court." [35] In their opinions, the judges simply ignored the tenuous arguments based on a natural right to liberty, and the still more flimsy arguments from the United States Constitution, and treated the case as one of interpretation of the new state constitutional provision.

The most marked difference between the New Jersey court and the Massachusetts court sixty-five years previous to it, was that the New Jersey court in no sense thought it obvious that a free and equal clause had a potential application to Negro slavery. In 1844 there seemed to be a tendency to see such a clause as a preamble, a theoretical dissertation on the origins of government or of society, but not as a principle or standard relevant to legal or political decisions in an ongoing state. As Judge Nevius wrote,

> In framing this fundamental law, the convention set out with the general proposition, that men in their social state are free to adopt their own form of government . . . [and] never designed to apply this language to man in his private, individual or domestic capacity. [36]

In his concurring opinion, Judge Randolph even more explicitly asserted

> Yet strictly speaking, it is but a preamble, setting forth the reasons or the principles on which the following instrument is based; . . . they seem to make a kind of preface of general abstract principles for the whole. . . . [37]

These sentiments were a far cry indeed from the firm position of Massachusetts' Chief Judge Cushing in 1783 that a free and equal clause establishes the state on a base inconsistent with slavery and compels the adherence of the courts to the first principles of government.

Nor was the New Jersey court ignorant of the history of Massachusetts' implementation of its free and equal clause. Stewart argued from the Massachusetts cases. The actual text of Cushing's charge to the jury was not available in 1844, but in two subsequent Massachusetts reported cases, first Chief Judge Parsons and then his successor Lemuel Shaw had alluded to the manner of the abolition of slavery in Massachusetts. The New Jersey court carefully considered and rejected the Massachusetts approach. Judge Nevius of New Jersey thought the result wrong in principle and explicable primarily by virtue of the strength of "the humane spirit of abolitionism which prevailed in that state." Moreover, he suspected Lemuel Shaw of having been unable to overcome his firm antislavery principles.* Nevius, here, appears a bit confused, apparently unable to understand from the limited later references what had taken place in Massachusetts. Certainly Shaw was only repeating a well-established tradition. If there is anything revealing in this bad history of the New Jersey judges, it is the pains that were taken to disassociate themselves from a "humane spirit of abolitionism," which supposedly animated a judiciary of far greater capacity than their own.

The primary and most convincing of the arguments of the court for ignoring the free and equal clause was that a gradual scheme for emancipation was already in the process of rendering the matter moot. An entire legislative scheme is not to be judicially overturned on the basis of "certain general phrases of abstract natural right" without hard evidence of intent to abolish slavery.[38] Indeed, since the end was in sight, the New Jersey court seemed puzzled by the fervor of Alvan Stewart's attack. Thus, like Tucker in Virginia, the New Jersey judges were positivists and felt constrained to look to the purposes of the framers rather than to the supposed logic of the vague phrases of natural law. However, they displayed a far more explicit and vigorous distaste for even potential application of such phrases. Tucker had asserted that the Virginia framers *did not* mean to affect slavery. Nevius and Randolph went much farther. Such natural rights language is viewed as *generally* inoperative, theoretical, abstract, without any implications in courts of law. "The humane spirit of abolitionism" has appropriated such phrases, but they do not belong in a court of law; when so introduced, they are addressed to "feelings."

---

* 20 N.J.L., pp. 376–77: "It is no matter of surprise that Chief Justice Shaw, entertaining the opinions he did upon this question of slavery, should have found it repugnant to the spirit of their Constitution." This passage is interesting confirmation not only of Shaw's antislavery views, but of his repute for those views. See Chapter 13, infra. Nevius's views of the Massachusetts bench are most interesting. He seems to think it a breach of judicial duty to succumb to a public demand for "benevolence," though he excuses the Massachusetts courts since he acknowledges that even men of integrity may fail to "escape" the influence of such public opinion.

The tone is quite rigid: "Legal intelligence" is divorced from "feelings." "Humane abolitionism" renders suspect even the words of an admitted giant like Lemuel Shaw.*

This tone is not the holding of the cases. There is a sufficient rationale for denial of relief merely in the absence of any intent on the part of the framers to accelerate the end of slavery. But it is precisely tone and attitude that distinguishes these cases from *Hudgins v. Wright*. The difference may be attributable to a host of factors, but four stand out as particularly significant.

First, in Virginia the question of intent seemed dispositive for reasons both of jurisprudence and policy. After all, one shouldn't significantly alter the dominant labor system and an important category of property on the basis of a phrase with little or no thought for the purposes of those who adopted it. Yet the shape of slavery in New Jersey was such that emancipation might plausibly fall within the ambit of judicial lawmaking. If positivism would lead to the same conclusions as *Hudgins,* policy need not. It may have thus appeared necessary to say more than that the framers did not intend the end of slavery. Second, constitution-making in 1844 was a far cry from constitution-making in the revolutionary era. Even as late as 1806 men were still discovering what had been wrought by words in those early constitutions. A state had been created and no one could "intend" all the consequences of the instruments of its creation. By contrast, the constitution of 1844 was not the "creation" of New Jersey. Like other state constitutional changes in the mid-nineteenth century (Rhode Island excepted), the purposes were specific cosmetic or technical changes. Whether so articulated or not, a sensitive judge could not help but approach the construction of such an instrument more narrowly.

Third, the presence of a forceful advocate, representing not so much a group of blacks seeking freedom as an ideological, natural law position of utopian constitutionalism, made it necessary to con-

---

* There is more than a hint of "the lady doth protest too much" in these opinions. Both Nevius and Randolph trot out the rather mechanistic view of the judicial function. Both disclaim responsibility for the result and externalize responsibility—placing it on the legislature. There is much less of this disclaiming in *Hudgins*. This phenomenon is considered at much greater length in Chapter 13 in cases where a still higher level of anguish and externalization is reached.

sider at greater length the place of a Declaration of Rights in the doctrinal order. While Tucker had to address only Wythe's memory, the New Jersey judges, Nevius and Randolph, had to respond to Stewart and to an entire school of constitutional utopians whom he represented. The response was not only to belittle the broad implications that Stewart would have drawn from "free and equal" but also to downgrade the potential for any implications whatsoever from such language.

Finally, though the New Jersey cases presented a potential for heightened conflict in the shape of the advocacy, they presented a less troubling moral problem for the judges because of the doctrinal pattern of convergence of law and morality. If there was a gap at the particular time of 1845 it was a gap that was closing. The Act of 1804, working itself out, would end slavery in but a few more years. Thus, the impulse to close the gap, if there was any, was lessened. One need not act if everything will end well anyway. (Significantly, only the abolitionists saw that there was urgent reason to act on the injustice being done to the transitional generation. If it is a matter of "rights," how does a court ignore the "rights" of those before it on the ground that their children are guaranteed such rights in the future?) In this very important respect, the *Post* and *Van Buren* cases differed from fugitive slave cases of the same period.

The free and equal clause cases demonstrate thoroughgoing judicial positivism and contextual sensitivity. With the possible exception of the *Quock Walker* cases they show the nineteenth-century judges unwilling to be sucked into an open-ended exploration of the natural rights of slaves unless explicitly authorized by "law." And by "law" was meant not simply words in instruments. It was the fabric of purposes and motives associated with the men who wrote them. Even when men proclaimed and declared "natural" rights, it was not the natural but the human fabric that gave it its shape and import.

But within the area of this positivism, important differences emerged. Under the circumstances of Massachusetts in 1783, one could readily assume a purpose of emancipation: at least by emphasizing some strands of history rather than others. By contrast, in New Jersey in 1845, amidst a campaign of utopian constitutionalism that threatened legal formalism with its daring use of words out of context, a court would equally easily assume the purpose of "free and equal" to have been mere rhetoric. For Tucker the inapplicability of "free and equal" to Negro slavery was judicially clear but morally paradoxical. For he made no bones about the general significance of a Declaration of Rights. Tucker had grappled with the clause, but as legislator and teacher, not as a judge.

The task of construing broad constitutional language is a perennial invitation to judicial lawmaking. Any vague phrase, over time, comes to have little significance except through its history of applications. If the American judiciary asserted the limits of its role and referred to human purposes with regard to such inviting, broad language as "free and equal," it is hardly surprising to find a comparable positivist jurisprudence at work in the interpretation of statutes. Yet, it would not be accurate to assert that the natural law tradition with regard to slavery had no place in this process. It could have a role to play in at least three forms. First, in some instances the purpose of the statute, itself, could be viewed as the furtherance of the natural right to freedom. In such cases the court may further these ends without conflict with positivist principles. Second, whatever the larger purposes of the statutory scheme, there is likely to be a gray area of applications not determined by a fair reading of the statute itself. In such instances the court could assert a principled preference for liberty as one of those larger principles of law which are the basic stuff out of which rules of decision are formed. Finally, the court can assert a sort of bend-over-backward principle by which there is an obligation to achieve a profreedom result unless there is very specific, concrete positive law that prevents it. In the examples of interpretation that follow, all three forms of reference to the right of freedom will occur, but it is the first and second forms that predominate. The third variation was seldom used and, as time went on, explicitly disowned.

Gradual Emancipation in Pennsylvania

The Pennsylvania Act of 1780 was a prototype for all the gradual emancipation statutes that followed on its heels. The basic structure was elegantly simple. Everyone born after July 4, 1780, was to be born free. Persons already slaves before that date would owe service for life. The children of these servants for life would inherit an obligation of service for twenty-eight years.[1]

For all its simplicity, the execution of this statutory scheme depended on a regulatory mechanism that was quite ambitious for the late eighteenth century: registration. In order to ascertain whether a person was born before or after July 4, 1780, it was necessary that births be registered and that those persons already born into servitude also be registered. A servant for life had to be registered within four months after July 4, 1780. Servants for years had to be registered as they were born. Courts were constantly called upon to determine whether various defects in registration rendered the alleged servant free.[2]

The simplicity of the act also masked important omissions. Astonishingly, the act was not explicit as to the status of children born to a servant for twenty-eight years during the period of service. Did this generation, too, inherit an obligation to serve? Was the parents' master obligated for the child's support? * This critical issue would also be determined by the judges.

The first case to reach the Pennsylvania Supreme Court, *Respublica v. Negro Betsey,* 1789, was a registration case, noteworthy for what it revealed of judicial method and assumptions. At stake was the question of whether failure to register a slave born prior to July 4, 1780, operated only to relieve her of servitude for life (servitude until age twenty-eight remaining), or whether it operated to relieve her of any obligation whatsoever.[3]

Counsel for both master and servant and all the judges seemed agreed that the general interpretive framework to be applied was positivist and neutral.

> The intention of the legislature is to govern in the construction
> of this act, which, as well as in all other legislative acts, in
> doubtful cases, must be construed according to the reason and

---

* The act provided only that "Every Negro and Mulatto child, born within this State after the passing of this act . . . *(who would in case this act had not been made, have been born a servant for years, or life, or a slave)* shall be deemed to be, and shall be . . . the servant of such person . . . who would . . . have been entitled to the service of such child, until such child shall attain unto the age of twenty-eight years . . ." (Act of 1780, § 4). This language may easily be construed as passing on an indefinite chain of limited servitude. Or, it can be interpreted as applying only to one generation. For resolution of this issue, see p. 66.

sense of the lawmakers . . . to be collected by considering the frame and design of the whole.[4]

One judge, Atlee, thought that given the general emancipatory purposes of the statute and the ringing natural rights preamble, "Such a construction as will secure freedom to them, . . . will, I think, *agree best with the design of the legislature* [italics added]." [5] Thus, because of supposed legislative incorporation of and motivation by the libertarian principles, courts should construe the act to secure freedom. Judge Rush agreed as to the larger purposes of the act and as to the implications for judicial construction. In an enigmatic short opinion, a third judge, Bryan, concluded, "Upon a clause of so obscure a kind [the clause relied on by the master's counsel], I would not wish to press an argument against liberty." [6] Here there is a hint that it is not only legislative intent, but a general disfavoring of antilibertarian construction that is involved. Not only is the substance of these quotations noteworthy, but the very fact that each of the four judges chose to consider the nature of their interpretive principles suggests a hidden agenda, a discomfort with the problem at hand.

As the statutory scheme worked itself out, the neutral principles of interpretation became more explicit. Chief Judge William Tilghman came to dominate the court. Tilghman was a most tepid variant of the antislavery judge. He did consider slavery as an economically inferior system and remarked, in 1818, that its introduction was to be "lamented." On the Missouri question, he timidly noted a desire to see the institution "mitigated and, if possible, extinguished." Yet Tilghman, through no compulsion of either legal or social form, owned slaves in Maryland. In 1811 he began gradually emancipating those slaves. In short, Tilghman was a timid opponent of slavery amidst circumstances that (unlike those of Tucker or Wythe) demanded no great courage.[7]

Tilghman was Chief Justice of the Pennsylvania Supreme Court from 1806 until 1827. As early as 1810, he rejected the common argument that registration requirements should be strictly construed, that "The most strict conformity with the Act should be required in favor of liberty." Thus, where the public records appeared contradictory, there would be no automatic result in favor of liberty.*

---

* *Commonwealth v. Blaine*, 4 Binney 186 (Pa. Sup. Ct., 1811). In *Blaine* the registry showed an entry of June 26, 1807, recording a birth on January 2, 1808. Because of the

Rather, parole evidence would be admissable to determine the relevant information.

After almost a decade of judicial experience, Tilghman, in two cases, expressed his view of the registration provisions of the Act of 1780 and their proper construction in a more expansive way.[8] He saw the act, not so much as a freedom-favoring measure, but as an adjustment of conflicting interests. If the ultimate end is one of freedom, it is equally significant that the means chosen affords substantial recognition of masters' property rights. Thus, it is impermissable in cases that pose a question of the proper balance between those interests to resort to a principle of construction that favors one over the other. Moreover, Tilghman reveals his own substantial agreement with the legislative recognition of the masters' qualified property rights. Tilghman's conclusion about registration was

> The act creates a forfeiture of property in case of a defective registry, and therefore, where there appears to have been an intent to comply honestly with all its directions, the construction should be liberal in favour of the master. This is the spirit in which it has hitherto been considered. So that to adopt a different mode of construction now; to extend the statute, *by equity,* in favour of freedom, and against the right of property, would be to depart unwarrantably from former decisions.[9]

Careful perusal of Tilghman's registration opinions reveals no unwarranted perversion of the act to favor either master or slave. But the broad area of doubt—where the defect could, but need not, be considered serious enough to warrant the sanction of liberating the servant—was very large.[10] The great John B. Gibson, upon his ascension to the court, implied his disagreement with the long line of cases, holding that certain formalities could be excused. While indisposed to overrule these cases, he announced his intention to go no farther than the court had already gone in permitting deviation from

---

manifest contradiction, John Gibson, arguing for the Negro, asserted that the only remedy was freedom for his client. Tilghman held that fraud was inconceivable. Almost certainly the error was simply one in the year of the birth. The owner so testified. At that time an owner had six months to register a birth, so the registration would be good. Gibson, who later joined the Supreme Court and ultimately succeeded Tilghman as Chief Judge, argued that any technically tenable construction should be adopted in favor of liberty. As a judge he would continue to dissent from what he considered undue laxness in registration cases, but he never articulated quite so broad a principle of preference for liberty from the bench.

the strict statutory requirements of registration.* Gibson did not espouse an alternative interpretive framework. He certainly did not depart from the formal principles of legislative intent. He simply thought unqualified language authorized a stern, unqualified construction. Yet, it is conceivable that his own views on slavery led him to construe the registration provision as more stern and demanding on the master, just as Tilghman's experience as a "benevolent" slave-holder produced a view more sympathetic to "good faith" failures to comply with the letter of the law.

It was entirely reasonable to construe the registration provisions of the Act of 1780 as an adjustment of competing interests as to any specific case of conflict between servant and master. The fact that the act ultimately furthered liberty could not easily serve to decide such cases. However, even William Tilghman could understand that some issues of construction were of a different sort. As noted above, the act did not explicitly answer the question of whether the child of a servant for twenty-eight years, born during the period of servitude, would himself be obligated to serve for a period of years. Tilghman correctly discerned the distinction between this issue and the registration cases:

> If the argument in favor of servitude be correct the legislature of Pa., though it abolished slavery for life, established a kind of slavery, a servitude until the age of 28 years, which may continue from generation to generation to the end of the world. This would be so contrary to the general spirit of the act of assembly, and of the time when it was passed, that it requires clear expressions to prove it.

Finding no such clear expression, Tilghman held that no person could be subject to this servitude save one whose mother was a servant for life or slave at the time of his birth.[11]

---

* See the concurring opinion of Gibson in *Wilson v. Belinda,* 3 S & R 396 (Pa. Sup. Ct., 1817), p. 400. Gibson viewed an Act of 1788, amending the Act of 1780 and rendering its registration provisions more explicit, as "exclusively for the benefit of the servant registered. . . ." Gibson therefore stated: "In every case of a registry . . . I, for one, shall hold the master to a strict and formal execution for every thing enjoined, except where express decisions of this court may have established a contrary construction. . . . I should think I took an unwarrantable liberty with the expressions of the legislature, were I to carry the construction further against the slave than the decisions have already done." Gibson also dissented without elaboration in some registration cases. See, e.g., *Commonwealth v. Vance,* 15 S & R 36 (Pa. Sup. Ct., 1826), p. 39.

William Tilghman steadfastly refused to, in his own words, "strain the law" to achieve a result of freedom. He absolutely refused to consider the preference for liberty as a general principle of construction and interpretation. Yet, he could readily perceive the larger purposes of freedom in the design of legislation and act to further that design. His "neutral principles" can best be summed up in his own remarkable phrase: "I know that freedom is to be favored, but we have no right to favor it at the expense of property." [12] Without a principled preference for liberty in the registration cases, he could at least discern the ultimately libertarian principles of the legislature that had authored the act.

Private Manumission

Virginia [13]

Prior to 1782, manumission of slaves within Virginia, without special act of the legislature, was forbidden. The Quakers, led by Robert Pleasants, mounted a campaign of correspondence to major liberal Virginians to change that law. In 1782 these efforts were successful. The Act of 1782 provided:

> That it shall hereafter be lawful for any person by his or her last will and testament, or by any other instrument in writing, under his or her hand and seal attested and proved in the county court by two witnesses, or acknowledged by the party in the court of the county where he or she resides, to emancipate and set free his or her slaves, or any of them. . . .[14]

This act remained the basis for manumission in Virginia until the Civil War, though it was severely qualified by the Act of 1806 requiring freed Negroes to leave the state within twelve months or upon reaching their majority.[15]

Though straightforward and explicit, setting forth a precise and clearly defined method of exercising a capacity created by the law, this act was ambiguous in purport and motive, creating grave problems for construction whenever courts confronted cases that fell outside the literal language of the act. Undoubtedly, for many of the moving forces behind the original statute, this act was meant to be only first step in the gradual vitiation of slavery in Virginia. They hoped that the combined force of private manumission, prohibitions against importation, and public distaste for slavery would lead to withering away of the institution. The cotton gin was still eleven years away, and almost everybody seemed agreed that prohibitions against importation ought to be strictly enforced. The hope for a relatively painless end to slavery was not quixotic. Quakers and others knew that the key to public acceptance of emancipation was public tolerance of the free black. In a real sense, therefore, the private manumission law was a trial balloon. The free black population would increase and with it the opportunity to test public reaction to such a class.[16]

Not all of the support for the Act of 1782 came from those who imperfectly programmed an ultimate emancipation. There were many who simply felt that the property rights of a master ought to extend to the power of liberating his property if he so chose. Just as men could gratuitously fulfill charitable impulses by leaving or giving property to churches or other worthy causes, so they ought to be able to fulfill an impulse to a humane broadening of the area of liberty. However, the power to fulfill such gratuitous impulses was always limited by the rights of those with a claim of justice to such property as slaves. Creditors' rights were superior to those of a beneficiary of a gratuitous transfer. So, in the Act of 1782, as in all other private manumission statutes, the rights of those with a claim against the master or his estate were superior to the interests of slaves who were to be emancipated.[17]

In construing this apparently simple statute, courts could choose from a variety of interpretive principles. Clearly, they ought to effectuate legislative intent. However, as stated, the larger purposes of the act were not clear. Was this simply tolerance for whim or an invitation to the end of slavery? The courts could also choose to appeal to the normal principles of construction for the instruments of gratuitous transfers: wills and trusts. Thus, the intent of the testator or settlor was an important touchstone. Appeal to such principles carried with it the question of whether and how the normal limits on the capacity of a testator or settlor would be effectuated. Were there public policy limitations? Did the Rule against Perpetuities apply? How should formalities be treated? Finally, the court could appeal to the principled preference for liberty.

At the outset, in the first cases under the act decided at the turn of the century, the Virginia court made eclectic use of equitable, common law and statutory devices all informed by and infused with a favorable attitude toward manumission. This hospitable attitude seems, in part, the product of a principled preference for liberty, in part the product of a sympathy with the Quaker-dominated antislavery upper class. Robert Pleasants's dilemma of conscience was perhaps more real to these judges than his slaves' desires for freedom. In any event, the early attitude did not last long. Later judges came to implicitly and explicitly reject the earlier cases and—most important—the interpretive principles on which they rested.

The first of the Virginia cases was *Pleasants v. Pleasants,* decided in 1799. The case involved the devise of John Pleasants (father of Robert) and of his eldest son. It was a significant case for three reasons. It involved the leading Quaker family in the state; it construed an instrument affecting the freedom of literally hundreds of Negroes; and it afforded an opportunity to explore the foundations and purposes of the Manumission Act.[18]

John Pleasants died before passage of the Act of 1782. He provided in his will that his slaves "shall be free if they chose it when they arrive at the age of thirty years, and the laws of the land will admit them to be set free. . . ." He provided further that should the laws not so permit, the slaves were to be bequeathed to various members of the family subject to the condition that they allow the slaves to be set free "if the laws of the land would admit of it." The *Pleasants* litigation was instituted by John's son, Robert, as executor under his father's will. Robert sought to enforce the slaves' rights to freedom as against various legatees and their successors in interest who had refused to free the Negroes after the Act of 1782.*

---

* *Pleasants v. Pleasants,* 6 Va. (2 Call), 319 (1799), 334–340. There is an interesting procedural side to *Pleasants v. Pleasants* that reinforces the conclusion that the court picked and chose from among principles to achieve a libertarian result. One might ask how it came to be that Robert Pleasants was able to sue on behalf of all the potential beneficiaries under his father's and brother's wills. True, Robert had been appointed executor under those instruments, but ordinarily his office would have ceased with distribution of the property to various legatees and trustees. Indeed, this very question arose again some twenty-five years later in North Carolina. There, in *Pride v. Pulliam,* 4 Hawks (N.C., 1825), the Supreme Court of North Carolina held that when slaves "were delivered over to representatives by the consent of their executor, the trust would seem to cease in the latter, and attach to the former" (*Pride,* p. 60). But the *Pleasants* court took an extraordinary, almost twentieth-century approach to the procedural issue. Since Robert Pleasants's petition did set forth the issues, since it obviated the necessity of a multitude of suits, since it seemed, in short, the most straightforward way to get

From a legal standpoint, Pleasants's will presented a number of difficulties. Most important, when executed and when probated, the will could not legally operate to free these slaves, for manumission was prohibited. Thus, if it were to have effect at all, the will would have to be construed as creating a trust with the legatees as trustees who would be under a duty to effectuate the freedom of the slaves "if the laws allow." Such an appointment, however, presented two problems. First, if construed to affect unborn generations of blacks, it would violate the rule against perpetuities. The "Rule," as stated in the roughly contemporaneous Dane's *Abridgment,* provided:

> that all . . . executory interests whatever, including executory devises, must . . . cease to become contingent, and become vested within a life or lives in being, . . . with a mother's pregnancy and the child's minority added; this rule applies not only to inheritances in lands, . . . but to personal estate and chattels real.[19]

The contingency contemplated in the Pleasants will was the passage of a statute or some other change in Virginia law that would permit manumission. There was no certainty, then, that the interest in freedom provided for in the will would vest within lives in being plus twenty-one years nine months, at least as to the interest in freedom of remote generations. Second, perpetuities aside, the question remained whether the 1782 Act would operate to posthumously ratify a settlor's act for which no capacity existed at the time of his death. For the judge of this time, that issue hinged on the nature of manumission. If manumission is only "tolerated," then there is certainly no good reason to give effect to a dead man's wishes, which could not have been effectuated at the time of his death. However, if manumission is

---

the substantive matter before the court, it would be entertained despite the judges' bewilderment as to the exact source of the authority for so acting: "On mature consideration, I am of opinion, that the suit in Chancery cannot be sustained upon the ground of the appellee's claim as heir at law to take the slaves for the condition broken, it being the practice of the court to relieve against forfeitures and not to aid or enforce them. Neither will his claim, as executor, have that effect; because, having long since assented to the several legacies and bequests of these people, he had fully executed his power over the subject. At the same time, these characters furnish a commendable reason for his stating the case of these paupers to the court; and it ought to be heard and decided upon, without a rigid attention to strict legal forms, since it can be done, without material injury to the other parties" (p. 350).

favored, then the removal of the disability may be analogized to any remote contingency for which a testator may provide.

The *Pleasants* case was first heard by Chancellor George Wythe. Wythe, not surprisingly, ruled in favor of the slaves, requiring the legatees and their successors to do their duty under the instrument. He went still farther and ordered an accounting of the Negroes' profits for the period of their wrongful enslavement. On appeal, the Supreme Court of Appeals upheld Wythe on most major points, but reversed as to the accountings.[20] Each of the judges wrote a separate opinion.

Judge Spencer Roane thought that if an analogy to ordinary property and trust principles would arguably suffice to validate the Negroes' interests, then the result "will hold with increased force, when the case is considered in its true point of view, as one which involves human liberty." Thus, the preference for liberty is an explicit principle of construction, a necessary part of the reasoning *a minori ad majus.* This preference goes hand-in-hand with a reading of the animus of the statute as not simple toleration, but a "policy of authorizing or *encouraging* emancipation." [21] Pendleton and Carrington, the other two judges, agreed that the major goal ought to be effectuating the object of the testator and of the Negroes. They, too, read the act to be applied to retroactively ratify Pleasants's will.[22]

The judges were equally expansive in dealing with the Rule against Perpetuities. Roane stated his respect for the public policy behind the Rule—the refusal to let the disposition of property be governed too long by the dead—however, he doubted "whether the doctrine of perpetuities is applicable to cases in which human liberty is challenged." The policy of freedom is of greater weight.[23] Carrington agreed that devises respecting liberty are not subject to the limitations on those respecting chattel interests. And Pendleton thought, "That it would be too rigid to apply that rule, with all its consequences, to the present case." [24]

The *Pleasants* case was the product of judicial sympathy with the Pleasants family and with their aspirations; of a vision of the Act of 1782 as reflective of a state policy favoring manumission; and of a sense of residual law favoring freedom. Liberty is to be pursued where law is unformed.

The *Pleasants* case was extended four years later in *Charles v.*

Hunnicutt.[25] The *Charles* case presented an even more difficult issue for the court. The Quaker testator, Gloister Hunnicutt, died in 1781 leaving a will that provided

> that the following negroes should be manumitted on or before the first month next 1782. . . . I give the above named Negroes to the monthly meeting, of which I am a member, to be manumitted by such members of the said meeting, as the meeting shall appoint.[26]

This provision differed significantly from *Pleasants* in that it purported not to direct a manumission when the laws should allow, but to direct a manumission on a date certain; which date, unfortunately, was prior to the effective date of the Act of 1782.

The *Pleasants* case was relied on by the plaintiff, one of the named Negroes, in suing for his freedom. His counsel, the reporter Call, and Taylor asserted that *Pleasants* stood for application of the broad proposition that "subsequent statutes will embrace anterior dispositions made with a view to the existence of future laws." [27] The opposition claimed that *Pleasants,* by its own terms, explicitly distinguished the case of a bequest that purported to make a manumission when it was not permitted by law.

St. George Tucker read the language of the will as not being an immediate act of manumission, but rather the settling of a trust. Accordingly, the trust instrument should be read to effectuate the settlor's intent "and that such intention be construed, if it be possible, not to be repugnant to the law, or the policy of the law." [28] He construed the will as if it had been written like that of Pleasants, supplying the phrase "if the laws allow." Roane embraced a similar reading. The president of the court, Peter Lyons, brought the preference for liberty to the fore:

> Devises in favor of charities, and particularly those in favor of liberty, ought to be liberally expounded: and upon the present occasion, it is fair to infer, that the testator meant that the deed of manumission should not take place, until an act of assembly, to authorize it, should pass . . .[29]

As in the case of *Pleasants,* the court also deemed it advisable to take a very flexible view of procedure. The plaintiff had sued for his freedom in an action at law. There was some doubt as to whether the common law court ought to apply rules and standards involving the obligations of the "Quakers meeting" as trustee as against the claim of an executor of the estate, or whether such relief would be available only in a Court of Equity. Roane argued strongly that "The courts of law will rather stand in the place of courts of equity in relation to the principles of their decision." [30] Roane thought that even the more rigid of common law judges "would have approved that system in relation to the case before us: a case involving human liberty." [31]

I would not want to make too much of the phrases favoring liberty in these opinions. Certainly, I am not asserting that such principles were invariably applied even by the same judges in somewhat different cases. Roane, for example, in the term following *Charles v. Hunnicutt,* wrote in a much different vein when the conflicting interests were those of slave and creditor.

> In considering this case, I cannot for a moment, forget (whatever my sentiments may be on the abstract questions discussed before us), that slaves are a species of property recognized and guaranteed by our laws. The most this court can do, in the case, is, to extend to the appellees (Negroes) all the consideration and favour which is compatible with the rights of property.[32]

Spencer Roane had before him a choice of principles—and he could choose one for a Quaker will and the other for a "defrauded" creditor. The residual "natural law" determined no choice in favor of freedom, but it permitted one.[33]

Moreover, Roane and St. George Tucker were capable of procedural and remedial creativity to accommodate even such conflicting legitimate claims of creditors and manumitted slaves. In *Patty v. Colin,* Tucker's decree and Roane's concurring opinion provided that if possible, where there was inadequate nonhuman property to satisfy creditors, manumitted slaves should be hired out for a term to satisfy the estate's debts rather than be sold or seized. Roane combines this remedial twist with a general principle of procedural flexibility in favor of manumitted slaves.*

* *Patty v. Colin,* 11 Va. (1 Hen. & M.) 519 (1807). "The Spirit of the decisions of this Court in relation to suits for freedom, while it neither abandons the rules of evidence, nor the rules of law as applying to property, with a becoming liberality respects the merit of the claim,

By 1821 decisions in the area of conflict of laws already foretold a decisive shift in the attitude and technique of the Virginia court.[34] In 1824, in *Maria v. Surbaugh* [35] that shift manifested itself in a private manumission case with the disclaimer that principles of interpretation favoring liberty have any place in decisions on private emancipation. Parenthetically, the case resolved a relatively important question that might have gone either way against the Negroes claiming freedom.

In *Maria* the court held that an instrument providing for the manumission of a slave upon her reaching a specific age would not have the effect of rendering free, children born to her between the effective date of the instrument and her attainment of the given age. Spencer Roane had reached the opposite conclusion in *Pleasants* and on natural rights grounds, though the rest of that court had chosen other inconclusive reasoning.[36] Even more significant than the result, for purposes of this analysis, is Judge Green's perception of the interpretive process:

> in deciding upon questions of liberty and slavery, . . . it is the duty of the Court, uninfluenced by considerations of humanity on the one hand, or of policy (except so far as the policy of the law appears to extend) on the other, to ascertain and pronounce what the law is: leaving it to the legislature, . . . to deal . . . with a subject involving . . . such important moral and political considerations.[37]

If any doubt might have remained about an explicit rejection of earlier standards, they were certainly dispelled by the court in *Gregory v. Baugh* in 1831:

> But all who have examined the earlier cases in our books, must admit, that our judges (from the purest motives, I am sure) did, *in favorem libertatis,* sometimes relax, rather too much, the rules of law. . . . Of this, the court in later times, has been so

---

and the general imbecility of the claimants. On this ground it is, that parties of this description are not confined to the rigid rules of proceeding, and that their claims are not repudiated by the court, as long as a *possible chance* exists, that they can meet with a successful issue. Instances of the former kind are numerous; and, of the latter, it will be seen in the case of *Abby v. Woodly* . . . that this court only determined against the paupers in the *last* resort, and after every possible source of redemption should be found to have failed.'' (p. 528; italics in the original).

sensible, that it has felt the propriety of gradually returning to the legal standard, and of treating these precisely like any other questions of property.[38]

North Carolina [39]

In North Carolina legislative policy with respect to manumission was clear. Until 1830 manumission was forbidden except for meritorious service as determined by an appropriate court. This strict policy against private emancipation, its roots in the colonial period, was reasserted in 1777, 1796, and 1801 in the face of determined pressure by the important Quaker minority.[40] However, it turns out to be almost as difficult to stamp out private virtue as it is to stamp out private vice. In 1781, the North Carolina Yearly Meeting declared that slaveholding was a grievous sin, and in 1782 it directed monthly meetings to "endeavor to convince them [friends who continued to hold slaves] of the iniquity thereof." [41] Caught between the law and the position of the Yearly Meeting, the individual Quaker sought devices to rid himself of his moral burden. Many hundreds emigrated from the Carolinas and formed an antislavery hard core in the Western Reserve of Ohio and elsewhere. But for those who remained the problem persisted. A degree of accommodation was achieved simply through political influence. The Friends were concentrated in certain counties where they often constituted the single most powerful political force in the area. In such counties, there is some evidence that the county courts applied the "meritorious service" standard loosely to facilitate Quaker manumissions. However, as Quaker emigration continued, their statewide influence waned. Reprisals were taken against them. In 1818, jurisdiction over manumission was taken from the county courts and vested in the circuit, superior courts. The constituency of those courts was regional or state wide. The Quaker plight had little impact on them.[42]

Even before the shift in jurisdiction, the Friends turned to other devices for ridding themselves of sin. It must be stressed that despite Quaker sympathy for the general anti-slavery cause and a large degree of overlap between the Friends and the North Carolina Antislavery Society, the official positions of the Society of Friends were concerned with the capacity to achieve personal, moral salvation. The Quakers' sins were the motivating factors, not the bondage of the slave. Thus, the Quakers agitated and struggled for a Virginia-type accommodation to manumission, rather than for emancipation.

For years Quakers had used the trustee device in a manner analogous to that upheld in Virginia in *Pleasants v. Pleasants*. Slaves were bequeathed to a trustee who was to emancipate them when the laws should allow.[43] Depending on the exact form of the bequest and the exercise of the trustee's discretion, the trust could be performed in one of three ways. The slaves could be taken from North Carolina and formally freed in the manner permitted by some sister state; the slaves could be held in North Carolina while manumission for meritorious service was sought from the appropriate court; or the slaves could be benevolently held by the trustee hoping for a statutory change in North Carolina law. As the "meritorious service" option came under increasing attack, the Friends moved to enlarge the scope of the third option. Suppose the trust be administered by the Society itself or subject to its supervision; suppose further that the Society seize the opportunity for education of its wards and preparation for freedom; suppose finally that the Society exercise its power of dominion in such a manner as to permit the Negroes a wide degree of freedom, earning power, and choice as to whether they be emancipated outside the state? Such a scheme would amount to an island of quasifreedom created by private transactions.

The Quakers turned to William Gaston, a leading North Carolina lawyer of known libertarian sympathies, for help in the construction of such a scheme. Gaston drew up a form instrument for transferring slaves to the trustees of the Society of Friends. That instrument was used from 1807 through the 1820's.[44]

The problem which the Quaker trusteeship scheme presented to the North Carolina Supreme Court was the converse of that presented to the Virginia Court of Appeals. In North Carolina a statutory scheme largely hostile to manumission did not explicitly outlaw the Quaker trusteeship, while in Virginia a statutory scheme largely hospitable to manumission did not explicitly ratify preexisting private bequests in favor of freedom. The North Carolina Supreme Court considered the Quaker trusteeship scheme in *Trustees v. Dickenson* (1829).[45] The majority of the court construed the legislation as evincing a policy against creation of a free Negro class. They refused to legitimate the aspirations of Quakers for humane extrication from the sin of slaveholding and perceived themselves instruments of legislative policy:

> But if a sense of religious obligation dictates to a Society the ex-
> ercise of an enlarged benevolence, which however virtuous and
> just in the abstract, the policy of the law, founded on the duty of
> self-preservation, has forbidden, it irresistibly follows that a
> transfer of property so directed, must be void.[46]

The dissenter, Judge Hall, did not deny the authority of the legislature to determine policy, but he thought no specific determination
covered this case: ". . . if on account of our unfortunate connection
with slavery, these sentiments [of the Quakers] tend to a mistaken
policy, if self-preservation impels us to a different and contrary
course, that course should be pointed out by the legislature. . . ."[47]
Since Hall considered the case one for which no unambiguous legislative expression was available, he thought the court ought to make a
value choice.

> If we take a step into the moral world and contemplate the un-
> biased principles of our nature, we will discover for the exercise
> of our discretion a wide range between humanity and cruelty.
> . . .[48]

Trustees v. Dickenson is one of the first of a long line of North
Carolina cases in which the competing factions of this court would
articulate their positions on slavery in terms of the broadest possible
principles. Natural right would be opposed to self-preservation. In
those cases, Judge Thomas Ruffin would become the most eloquent
spokesman for a doctrine of stern necessity, requiring an unflinching,
conscious disregard of natural justice.* Ruffin, who joined the su-

---

* Thomas Ruffin presents a fascinating figure with regard to slavery. Ruffin's opinion in
State v. Mann, 13 N. Car. (2 Devereux) 263 (1829), has both attracted and repulsed commentators for over a century. In *Mann* Ruffin, for the court, held that the intentional wounding of a
hired slave by the hirer could not constitute a crime. In reaching this conclusion Ruffin articulated better than any other judge the position that the master-slave relationship is a creature of
force and force alone and that the law must reflect the cruel origins of the relationship: "With
slavery it is far otherwise. The end is the profit of the master, his security and the public safety;
the subject, one doomed in his own person, and his posterity, to live without knowledge, and
without the capacity to make anything his own, and to toil that another may reap the fruits.
What moral consideration shall be addressed to such a being, to convince him what, it is impossible but that the most stupid must feel and know can never be true—that be this to labour upon
a principle of natural duty, or for the sake of his own personal happiness. Such services can
only be expected from one who has no will of his own; who surrenders his will in implicit
obedience is the consequence only of uncontrolled authority over the body. There is nothing
else which can operate to produce the effect. The power of the master must be absolute, to
render the submission of the slave perfect" [*State v. Mann,* 13 N. Car. (2 Dev.) 263, 266
(1829)]. Harriet Beecher Stowe, in the *Key to Uncle Tom's Cabin* (Boston: J. D. Jewett, 1853),

preme bench only in 1830, was the presiding trial judge who held against the Quakers in *Dickenson*. Counsel for the Quakers was William Gaston, the man who had conceived the trust device almost twenty years earlier. Gaston would later be elevated to the state supreme court and would author some of the most eloquent of the liberal opinions on slavery, relying heavily on "humanity" and natural right.[49]

It must be understood that neither Gaston nor Ruffin (nor, indeed, Nash, Taylor, Hall, or other North Carolina judges) departed from the positivist formal assumptions of the day. All looked to legislative enactments and policy as controlling. But they did differ on the place of values in the gray areas of doubt. And that difference colored their view of what legislative purposes really were. Ruffin conceived of slavery as necessitating a thorough suppression of the humane and liberal values. He was extraordinary (really very much like Holmes) in his eagerness to confront the reality of the unpleasant iron fist beneath the law's polite, neutral language. Ruffin's unusual refusal to clothe an exploitative and brutal relationship with the trappings of anything save power and force led him to infer a legislative policy of the utmost brutality from the mere existence of slavery. So long as the continued existence of slavery was an unquestioned legislative policy, there could logically be no place for a principled preference for either liberty or kindness in the law's operation. By contrast Gaston and Hall were quite willing to use a principled preference for liberty or for "humanity" where legislative policy was unclear. While they would hardly have sanctioned a serious inroad upon slavery through such a device, they considered residual and interstitial preference for freedom to be wholly consistent with a viable slavery.

Much of the above analysis reflects dicta in cases that had nothing

---

found Ruffin a fascinating figure. She was appalled at the legal system's capacity to reduce a man of intellect and insight to a tool for oppression: "No one can read this decision, [*Mann*] so fine and clear in expression, so dignified and solemn in its earnestness, and so dreadful in its results, without feeling at once deep respect for the man and horror for the system. The man, judging him from this short specimen, which is all the author knows, has one of that high order of minds, which looks straight through all verbiage and sophistry to the heart of every subject which it encounters. He has, too, that noble scorn of dissimulation, that straightforward determination not to call a bad thing by a good name, even when most popular and reputable and legal, which it is to be wished could be more frequently seen, both in our Northern and Southern States. There is but one sole regret; and that is that such a man, with such a mind, should have been merely an *expositor*, and not a *reform* of law." (Stowe, pp. 78–79).

to do with the issue of manumission,[50] but Quaker trusteeship cases, which followed *Dickenson,* also reflected these general approaches. An Act of 1830 permitted manumission, provided that the freed blacks leave the state within ninety days. Ruffin, now on the Supreme Court, continued to find testamentary trusts in favor of the Quakers void. In 1833 he held out the safety of the community—a natural law principle in its own right—against the natural right to liberty:

> Qualified emancipation . . . stands upon the same ground as a bequest for that purpose . . . . It cannot be supported in a court of justice. A stern necessity arising out of the safety of the commonwealth forbids it.[51]

And, by the late 1840's Ruffin's brethren were not only in full agreement; they were also overtly impatient with the now seemingly endless line of cases coming before the court with minor variations on the Quaker theme.[52]

Only Judge Hall, who had dissented in *Dickenson,* deviated from the Court's prohibition on "qualified emancipation." Both in *Dickenson* and in the later case of *Stevens v. Ely,*[53] he took the view that it was tenable to refuse to read the prohibition on emancipation so expansively as to void bequests that, on their face, were valid.

Judge Gaston, whose antislavery views were well-known did not dissent in any of the "qualified emancipation" cases (though he also never wrote an opinion in any of these cases). It may be that he simply felt the law clearly settled by precedent by the time he joined the Court in 1834. He did, however, write the leading opinion holding that a bequest for emancipation outside the state was not forbidden and should be liberally construed.[54] Such a devise was both in furtherance of Gaston's view of public policy, and to be favored as a charitable bequest.

Summary

From the three above statutory schemes, chosen for this study, a pattern emerges that seems to have been reflected in other states and in other doctrinal areas as well. First, there was a broad consensus on how the work of interpretation was to proceed. The critical factor was the intent of the legislature. However, judges who actually did the work of construction of texts could not naively assume that such specific intent would always be clear. The second point of substantial agreement, then, was that where purpose or intent failed to illuminate a specific question, the larger goals of the legislative scheme, taken as a whole, would govern. While, as a matter of principle, this canon of construction was admitted by all, its application was, at times, equally difficult. For Ruffin, North Carolina's larger legislative purposes seemed to be the perpetuation of a secure master-slave relationship, with the emphasis on security. For Hall or Gaston, the goal of the legislative structure was presumed to be maximization of the sphere of liberal and humane treatment consistent with the perpetuation of slavery. In Virginia, for Roane, Tucker, or Lyons the manumission scheme represented a step toward libertarian ends. For Green, twenty years later, the restrictive rather than the libertarian strands were emphasized, and emancipation became essentially a sop thrown to a few humane, perhaps misguided, slaveholders.

So long as the larger purposes of legislation were deemed to coincide with the natural right of freedom, then use of the principle of construction *in favorem libertatis* was easy. The moment the end of the legislative scheme was taken to be either expressly counterlibertarian (the majority view of North Carolina manumission) or to be the balancing of libertarian and other principles (Tilghman's view of the registration provisions in Pennsylvania), then the construction in favor of liberty could be introduced only as a presumption that operated of its own force and despite the purposes of the legislature. Such a principle of construction was never actually used, though Hall in North Carolina and Gibson in Pennsylvania were very loathe to find clear evidence of counterlibertarian intent.

The judicial work in these cases of statutory construction also reveals a degree of contextual sensitivity that was more operational than doctrinal. That is, judges decided cases with a high level of awareness for facts and factors not necessarily incorporated into their pronouncements on their principles of construction. In the North Carolina Quaker cases the court often suggested that the objective of the Quaker trusteeship scheme was evasion of the prohibition on freeing slaves and permitting them to remain within the state. Unlike Judge Hall, the majority of the court was convinced, from what it knew of the Quakers and their practices, that they could assume and take judicial cognizance of an intent to subvert the law's policy. In Virginia, the court's movement from a generous to a restrictive reading of identical statutory language was accompanied by the movement of the society as a whole to a greater commitment to slavery, and most important, to greater antipathy to free blacks. It was certainly natural to understand the Negro Removal Act of 1806 as a cue to construe the Manumission Act of 1782 a bit less expansively. It is interesting that in *Patty v. Colin* and other cases arising immediately after the Act of 1806, the old judges, Tucker, Roane, Lyons, seemed not to have fully absorbed this cue. In those early cases, where the Act of 1806 was not, in terms, applicable, its antilibertarian spirit was not carried over to interpretation of the 1782 statute. By 1824, however, any judge could understand that the deeper sense of legislative purpose—that sense of purpose that is understood as pervading not only a clause or an act, but a whole institution—had shifted and was no longer represented by the original goals of the Manumission Act of 1782, but by those of the Removal Act of 1806.

Despite the broad area of agreement on formal principles, antislavery morality did make a difference. John Gibson opposed slavery in a way that William Tilghman did not; Tucker and Roane were qualified opponents, Jeffersonian doubters about slavery, in a way that Green was not; Hall and Gaston were receptive to ameliorist half-way libertarian ventures, while Thomas Ruffin decidely was not. Because formal principles do not decide all cases, because there remained areas of doubt as to what the legislature intended, how to characterize the broader spirit of legislation, or which of the cues of context were more significant, there remained a fair ground for difference of opinion between men of equally good faith but unequal libertarian convictions. This area of difference was not terribly large when compared to the area of agreement. It was not a difference about the structure of the judicial role nor about the ultimate roots of slavery in law. Yet, had Gibson rather than Tilghman prevailed on the Pennsylvania registration cases, it would have meant freedom for dozens, perhaps hundreds, of servants. Had Hall rather than Ruffin prevailed on the Quaker trusteeships, it would have meant many hundreds, perhaps thousands, of quasifree blacks in North Carolina; had the Tucker-Roane jurisprudence persisted in Virginia, additional hundreds of slaves would have been freed. No claim can be made that the ultimate American tragedies—slavery for millions, Civil War, racism—would have been averted or truncated through such statutory construction. The area for libertarian principles of interpretation, given the broad agreement on basic formal principles, was relatively narrow. Yet, even that small area contained a threatening principle. For if liberty ought to be favored even there, then it was a reproach to the elaborate legal structures that ousted liberty of its presumptive spot elsewhere. Only a thoroughgoing *neutral* positivism of the sort proclaimed by Judge Green of Virginia would suffice to remove this reproach.

We have seen the limited bases for judicial application of principles favoring liberty in construction of statutes and constitutions. Even where explicit natural rights language was used, it was construed in terms of the purposes and intention of the human agencies who framed the instrument. Where no explicit natural rights language was to be found, the courts might still indulge in interstitial preference for liberty but not in the face of clear manifestations of a contrary legislative policy. When, as was not uncommon, a difference of opinion occurred as to the appropriateness of application of principled preference for liberty, judges chose between neutral and liberty-skewed canons. A Judge Ruffin might take personal responsibility for what he considered to be the inexorable logic of a slave system's necessity; a Judge Hall would opt for an exercise of discretion in favor of "humanity."

General Principles of Choice, Law, and Sovereignty

When the transactions before a court have multistate dimensions, when the parties are of different states or the relevant occurrences transpired in different states, or the consequences will be directly felt in different states, then the court must choose its rules of decision from among the potentially different rules of law of the various relevant jurisdictions. This process, "choice of law," is one of the main branches of the area of law known as "conflict of laws" or as "private international law." [1]

In conflict-of-laws cases expressions of the natural law favoring liberty were stronger and more frequent than in the cases considered until now. But, the order and frequency of the expression should not blind us to the fact that the place of natural law was not, in principle, any different in conflicts cases than in other areas of law.

By the nineteenth century it was already generally accepted that conflicts law was the law of the forum state with respect to transactions and occurrences with multistate dimensions and that application of the content of foreign law was only by authority of the law of the forum state. As Kent asserted in his *Commentaries:*

> There is no doubt of the truth of the general proposition, that the laws of a country have not binding force beyond its own territorial limits; and their authority is admitted in other states, not *ex proprio vigore,* but *ex comitate.* Every independent community will judge for itself, how far the *comitas inter communitates* is to be permitted to interfere with its domestic interests and policy.[2]

This general principle is traced by Story, in the leading American treatise on the subject,[3] back to Huber and Boullenois. Story unequivocally accepts the proposition

> That whatever force and obligation the laws of one country have in another, depends solely upon the laws, and municipal regulations of the latter, that is to say, upon its own proper jurisprudence and polity . . .[4]

and he unhesitatingly rejects the suggestion "of some jurists" that application of foreign law "is not so much a matter of comity, or courtesy, as of paramount moral duty." [5] Writing in 1834, Story could assert with ample authority that these theories of Huber had already prevailed in English and American case law.

On a theoretical level, then, choice of law presented no challenge to a positivist view of law and of sovereignty. The authority for "lawmaking," for creating rules of decision, is plenary in the polity of the forum court whether or not there are multistate dimensions. However, when such multistate dimensions are present, the forum court may, and ordinarily will, look to the law of another state for the content of its rule of decision. But this practice is one of comity, not compulsion.

Such a view of the choice of law process may be jurisprudentially sound and consistent. However, it does not answer the practical question: How does a court know when to comply with the ordinary practice of comity and when to refrain? Principles and rules of choice-of-law begin to answer such questions. While these principles are themselves not obligatory on any sovereign state, they constitute a body of law, like international law or common law—not without ambiguity and difficulty—but ordinarily applied where relevant. The sources for these choice-of-law principles were (and are) primarily case law and treatises. Certainly, where constitutions or statutes troubled to prescribe a conflict-of-laws rule, the dominant positivist view of both legislation and of conflict-of-laws made such a rule dispositive. However, choice-of-law had long been an area of legislative neglect and of judicial cultivation. Out of habit, history, and a sense of expertise, this field was peculiarly that of the judge.

Principles of choice-of-law are one level of abstraction above those that decide cases. A choice-of-law rule is a rule telling the judge how to choose the rule that will decide the case. Modern conflicts theorists refer to the level of case-deciding rules as "local law." They refer to a legal system's totality of rules, including both its choice principles and its local law, as "whole law." For Joseph Story, Chancellor Kent, or any reasonably educated lawyer of the antebellum period it was crystal clear that, when Massachusetts applied New York law in construing a New York contract between New York and Massachusetts parties, it did so by virtue of the authority of Massachusetts law. In modern language, the whole law of Massachusetts (including its choice principles) directed the decision maker to the local law of New York for the content of the rule of decision. In the idiom of Kent or Story, the law of Massachusetts admits the New York rule by reason of comity.

Since choice-of-law principles are designed to determine fairly which of conflicting local law rules are to govern, it was deemed necessary to construct those choice-of-law rules out of the universals of jurisprudence underlying all law. Thus, not of its own force or as a higher law theory, natural law came into the picture. It was incorporated into the choice process by courts of sovereign states in search of an appeal to a set of principles that would accommodate both their own and other local rules. By and large, these principles of nature afforded recognition and legitimacy to legal relations created by or under the laws of other states. However, in rare cases, where the relations created by the other polity were deemed inconsistent with nature, then recognition would be withheld. The two primary examples of such withholding of extraterritorial effect and legitimacy were slavery and polygamous marriage. Story, for example, wrote that

> Personal disqualifications not arising from the law of nature, but from the principles of the customary or positive law of a foreign country . . . are not generally regarded in other countries, where the like disqualifications do not exist.[6]

Slavery was his primary illustration for this principle.

Since the authority to make law in a "conflicts situation" is conceded to be unqualified in the forum state, it is clear that the power to respect that state's self-interest and favored policies is present and will, in important enough situations, be exercised. Therefore, no description of choice-of-law process can fail to recognize that public policy of the forum state will, in fact, be a limit on the recognition and effectuation of extraterritorial legal relations. When public policy coincided with natural law it could not be clear which, if either, of the two bases for not affording comity were necessary or sufficient. For example, under Story's conflicts jurisprudence, a free state may be said to have both a public policy and a natural law basis for refusing to give extraterritorial effect to a master-slave relationship created by the law of some other jurisdiction. Is it nature or policy that determines the rule? The ambiguity of theory was equally evident in case law. Clarification might come, of course, with the "reverse fact situation." What extraterritorial effect would a slave state give to the law of a free state that resulted in freeing a slave?

Before addressing the cases that considered these and related questions, a word about the peculiar position of the judge in these cases is in order. In the choice-of-law situation, the judge had little explicit evidence of the policy or will of the legislature or of the people. He had the sole responsibility for determining whether there was a state public policy for or against slavery—whether the state interest in slavery or freedom was stronger than its interests in adherence to principles of comity among states. The judge had a body of law to guide him, but it was case law, not statute. The degree of freedom in dealing with case law was commonly accepted as much broader than that afforded by legislation. On a reasoned basis, a judge could discard precedent, either through explicit rejection or by "distinguishing" earlier cases. Where the judicial responsibility for lawmaking was so broad there was, as we might expect, far greater scope for judicial recourse to the moral principles underlying law and slavery.

Early American Cases

Story's starting point for analysis of slavery in his treatise was *Somerset's Case*. He might, of course, have gone farther back. The contemporaneous English treatise on conflicts, Burge's *Colonial and Foreign Laws,* purported to trace the conflicts rule in favor of freedom to continental sources of the early sixteenth century.[7] But *Somerset's Case* was the determinative English precedent; not that the precedent was free of difficulty.

Lord Mansfield had been called on to decide whether extraterritorial effect would be given to the laws of Virginia affording a master the right to detain, imprison, and transport his slave. The local law of England would prohibit such acts. Could these acts, because they were lawful by the local law of Virginia—the domicile of master and slave—be performed in England? The Chief Justice ruled that "So high an act of dominion must be recognized by the law of the country where it is used." [8] By fixing on this language, *Somerset's Case* may be read very narrowly: The lawfulness of an act of restraint, and imprisonment, is determined by the local law of the state in which it transpires *(lex loci iniuriae)*. Only those excuses or justifications valid under the local law (e.g., parental restraint of minor child) will be upheld.

A very different reading of *Somerset's Case* may emerge by focusing on the statement that "It [slavery] is so odious that nothing can be suffered to support it but positive law." [9] Leaving aside the question of whether Mansfield ever said this, the statement appears applicable not only to restraint, the tort of imprisonment, but to the entire relationship of slavery and to its incidents. The language that reached America as the text of Lord Mansfield supported the conclusion that a slave became free upon setting foot in a free jurisdiction.

The broad language in *Somerset's Case* was more important for its ideological than for its practical effect. Not only was the slaveholder denied extraterritorial protection for his slave property, he was denied it on the ground that appeal to natural law and right reason revealed the odious character of the master-slave relation. The reasoning of *Somerset* was a reproach, a constant reminder to the judge who read it, of the disparity between slave law and the moral principles un-

derlying a decent legal order. It is not at all surprising, therefore, that
the constitution of the Confederate States of America—which by and
large tracked the United States Constitution word for word—
specifically overruled the doctrine of *Somerset's Case*.[10] This was an
ideological gesture, since the practical problem of passage through
southern states with slaves was hardly an immediate issue given the
makeup of the Confederacy.

The reception of *Somerset's Case* in the United States was peculiar. On the one hand, American courts continued to repeat and pass
on the high-sounding ideologically provocative language. Nevertheless, in application of the rule, the courts were quite sensitive to
subtle distinctions and were always prepared to recognize the supremacy of any form of "positive law." The dictum of Mansfield was a
cheap way of expressing moral uneasiness with slavery, but distaste
would not interfere with conscientious performance of judicial duty.

During the critical decade of the 1780's, it was almost axiomatic
that the operation of normal "international" reciprocity would not
lead to the recognition by one state of the slave property of another.
Madison argued forcibly at the Virginia ratifying convention that the
Fugitive Slave Clause was a boon to Virginia because without it es-
caped slaves would not be returned.* And Pennsylvania incorporated
a specific authorization for congressmen to hold slaves for the period
of their tenure at the capital, then Philadelphia.[11] The implication of
the special immunity for congressmen seemed to be that without such
a special statutory provision the common law and the Pennsylvania
Act of 1780 would operate to free such a slave. Against this background, the early cases struggled with variations in the basic problem.

In 1799 attorneys before the Maryland Court of Appeals in *Mahoney v. Ashton* asserted a broad reading of *Somerset's Case*. They

---

* Jonathan Elliot, *Debates on the Federal Constitution*, 2nd ed. (Philadelphia: J. B. Lippincott Co., 1836), 3 : 453: "At present, if any slave elopes to any of those states where slaves are
free, he becomes emancipated by their laws; for the laws of the States are uncharitable to one
another in this respect." It is arguable that Madison was simply misstating the "common law,"
at least in so far as he held the laws of the free states to work a total emancipation to all purposes. However, it is more likely that he appealed to a very logical broad reading of *Somerset's
Case* that had already become current. I take his term "uncharitable" to mean that they do not
ordinarily afford a basis for comity.

represented a woman who claimed that her maternal ancestor had been brought into England. She asserted that Maryland, though a slave state, ought to give recognition to free status so acquired. The lower court agreed:

> For the rule is undoubted, that courts of justice will notice the laws of other countries, and enforce them, where a principle like the present is agitated, if they are not repugnant to justice or to our own civil institutions.[12]

But the Court of Appeals reversed the judgment of the General Court. Its reasoning indicates that it was neither Story nor the 1830's that introduced positivism into the conflict of laws:

> acting as a court of an independent country, . . . and bound to decide according to the laws of this state . . . By a positive law of this state in 1715, then the province of Maryland, the relation of master and slave is recognized . . . and all Negro and other slaves, then imported, or thereafter to be imported . . . are declared to be slaves . . .

Conceding the authority of England to govern the extent of dominion and the status itself in England,

> [Y]et upon bringing An Joice into this state . . . the relation of master and slave continued . . . *as authorized by the laws of this state* [italics added].[13]

Even more striking both in its articulate positivism and in its appeal to nature for the content of a choice-of-law rule is a pair of opinions by Judge Woodward of Michigan in *Denison v. Tucker* and *Pattinson v. Whitaker*.[14] Woodward wrote in the backcountry frontier of Michigan Territory in 1807. His learned and sophisticated opinions reveal how pervasive the impact of *Somerset's Case* had become. In *Denison,* Judge Woodward confronted a claim of freedom on habeas corpus by Negroes who had apparently been held as lawful slaves in "Upper Canada" prior to the Statute of the Province of Upper Canada of 1793, providing for gradual emancipation. The masters had brought their slaves into Wayne County, which was disputed but conceded to be part of Michigan by the Jay and Grenville Treaty of 1794. The masters claimed the benefit of a provision of the 1794 Jay-

Grenville Treaty: "All Settlers and Traders shall continue to enjoy unmolested all their property of every kind." [15] The slaves' counsel argued from the Northwest Ordinance, forbidding slavery, and from the general principles of conflict of laws, that Michigan ought not to recognize the master's interest created by Canadian law. The court at once asserted that the issue was "novel," "important," and "difficult." Woodward relied primarily on construction of the treaty provisions, rather than choice-of-law principles. For, the Constitution itself provides for treaties as a source of positive law. And positive law

> may regulate the nature and tenure of property in a manner that contravenes the just and inalienable rights of human Nature. . . . and force can alone redress an evil, which, where *it* is incompetent must be submitted to as irremediable.[16]

Woodward explicitly rejects the possibility of judicial officers effectuating natural law in the face of positive enactments.

> . . . [M]agistrates . . . are the creatures of civilized society. . . . Deriving their powers and rights from this source they must necessarily be regulated by the obvious condition of the trust, an implicit obedience to the known will of the nation or society delegating it.[17]

Woodward went on to interpret the treaty as including slaves within the term "property of all kind," since the history of Michigan and of Upper Canada showed lawfully preexisting slavery at the date of the treaty. As a result, he ruled that the Canadian master's claim would be upheld.

However, in the companion case, *Pattinson,* Woodward considered the issue of a fugitive from Upper Canada. The treaty provision relating to "settlers and traders" was not applicable. The petitioner (master) sought to invoke the general rule of international law that one nation will return property that accidently strays from another. Judge Woodward pointed out that this general principle of international law may not be invoked in the case of property in man, since such property is a creature only of statute and any such statute "is itself unjust, and in Contravention of the rights of human nature." *Somerset's Case* is cited as authority for this proposition.[18]

Woodward departed from the commonplace in his analysis of

whether to adopt Lord Mansfield's rule for Michigan. He started by asserting that the principle of *Somerset's Case* was a just principle in harmony with natural law. But he went on to ask what a contrary principle might mean:

> A human being escaping from chains of tyranny could find no place in the whole earth to rest. Go where he would the power and the arm of the tyrant would still reach him.

Thus, to refuse to accept *Somerset's Case* as a general rule of international law would be to universalize slavery.[19]

Woodward next addressed the question of whether the United States having recognized slavery within its boundaries, and having provided for the rendition of the fugitive domestically, ought do the same for a master of foreign nationality. He was obviously troubled by the inconsistency.

> This enquiry will tend to show how dangerous it is to admit even the Smallest degree of injustice and oppression into a free government. It tends to demonstrate that Nothing Can be Stable that is not just, that nothing can be morally harmonious and beautifull that is not perfectly Consistent with rectitude.[20]

Fortunately though, troubled as he was by the inconsistency, Woodward could easily fall back on the distinction between the international and interstate contexts. In the international scene, such matters are a question of favor and of reciprocity. No statutory base exists for the former, nor a factual basis for the latter. Great Britain's own conduct in refusing rendition of American slaves and military deserters is conclusive against her subjects seeking such favors from the United States.

The *Pattinson* case grounded the content of the choice-of-law rule firmly in natural law, while *Denison* showed that a positive law (treaty) provision would nonetheless be afforded supremacy over nature. Such positive law may manifest itself in ways other than legislation. Certainly, a treaty is such an act of sovereignty. But, in the absence of an affirmative act of law-making such as a treaty, it is the court's responsibility to determine the appropriate conflicts rule. Asserting that *Somerset's Case* is the English rule on the subject, Woodward continued: "it only remains to enquire whether the same principle is to be received here." Woodward chose the "common law" rule because "The principle is certainly a just principle. . . ." [21]

In 1810 the Massachusetts Supreme Court had occasion to consider another variation on the *Somerset* theme. Lord Mansfield had confined his holding to the case where the point at issue was actual restraint of a man. But the problem of slavery could arise in choice of law situations where the actual point at issue was a purely commercial one.

In *Greenwood v. Curtis* [22] a contract had been made by which the defendant was to have delivered slaves and African coin at Rio Pangos, Africa, in return for a shipload of commodities. Only a small part of the slaves were delivered and the plaintiff ultimately sued for the money equivalent of the slaves not delivered. The majority of the court, in an opinion by Chief Justice Parsons, upheld the action on the contract. Parsons stressed that the nondelivery of the slaves meant that the plaintiff was, in essence, suing for payment for a supply of perfectly upright goods. Presumably, the result might have been different if there had been nonpayment upon delivery of slaves.

Judge Sedgwick filed a dissent.[23] He thought that if the original agreement, itself, was wholly void, it would not support what amounts to a subsequent agreement to take money instead of slaves for the goods. Sedgwick's decision hinged, therefore, on the enforceability of a contract for the transatlantic shipment of slaves. Sedgwick's principle was that "where a contract is immoral, or . . . malum in se, a discussion about any lex loci is nugatory." As to whether such a contract is fundamentally immoral, Sedgwick had no doubt.

> Can we seriously ask whether, for the gratification of our unlicensed avarice, we may rightfully reduce to bondage beings who in their material form and essential character (whatever our supercilious arrogance may suggest to the contrary) bear equally with ourselves the impress of Divinity and are equally entitled to all the rights of humanity.*

* *Greenwood v. Curtis,* 6 Mass. 358 (1810), pp. 365–66. Sedgwick also met the argument for comity in these terms: "No foreign nation can justly require, and no civility demands, that judges should thus become the panders of iniquity."

The majority in *Greenwood* never went quite this far, even in its dictum, though there is a characterization of the trade as immoral and the suggestion that were compensation for slaves being sued upon instead of nondelivery of slaves, the case might go the other way. Story, in the *Treatise on Conflicts* appears to disapprove the majority holding in *Greenwood v. Curtis* and considers the case within the general rule that a contract for an immoral or vicious purpose will not be enforced by the forum even if legal by the law of the place of contract or by the law of the state where it was to be performed.[24]

I have dwelt at some length upon *Pattinson, Denison,* and *Greenwood* in part because they are little known judicial expressions that deserve more attention. For they are among the earliest of extended American analyses of *Somerset* and of its implications. Woodward and Parsons were clear-eyed jurisprudentially and refused to blur the distinctions between right and law. But natural right was, to them, a source for rules of decision in the absence of positive law, and such natural right, per Woodward, is unequivocally against slavery. Even in recognizing masters' rights under the Jay-Grenville Treaty, Woodward managed to write a small dissertation on the evils of slavery. In this sense, with *Somerset's Case* always in the background, every conflicts case was a potential ideological rebuke. *Greenwood* reinforced this point. For, in a sense, one point of dispute between majority and dissent was whether the slave trade was just very bad, or so very bad as to pollute all contracts made with respect to it.

Public Policy and Natural Right

The early pattern of *Mahoney,* of *Pattinson* and *Denison,* and of *Greenwood* continued well into the century. That pattern mandated (1) judicial subordination to explicit or clearly implied expressions of legislative will; (2) judicial responsibility for the content of choice-of-law rules where legislation was silent; (3) a tendency for judges to speak of eternal principles of right—the natural law on slavery in fixing the content of their choice principles; and (4) a concomitant tendency to reinforce their decisions by speaking of state policy in determining choice principles. In the free states the application of the latter two phenomena led to the same conclusions, while in the South they required a delicate process of adjustment. The Northern cases should be considered first.

In 1836, Chief Justice Lemuel Shaw of Massachusetts assumed the law to be "established . . . that the moment that the master carries his slave into a country where domestic slavery is not permitted, he becomes free." But when Shaw was presented with facts squarely forcing the issue, he found no Massachusetts precedent directly on point. His 1836 decision in *Commonwealth v. Aves* held that even a temporary sojourner in Massachusetts is not entitled to restrain another person, though he be lawfully enslaved by the law of the domicile.[25]

Shaw's opinion is ambiguous about the basis for his choice. Slavery is presumed to be contrary to natural law, but Shaw disavows any deduction from that proposition as to its place in either municipal law or the law of nations. Indeed, citing Justice Marshall's judgment in *The Antelope,* Shaw concedes slavery and the trade to be lawful under international law. Yet, despite the disavowal, we find the following passage:

> . . . though by the laws of a foreign state . . . a person may acquire a property in a slave, such acquisition, being contrary to natural right, and effected by the local law, is dependent upon such local law for its existence and efficacy, and being contrary to the fundamental laws of this state, such general right of property cannot be exercised or recognized here.

Is it the fact that slavery is "contrary to the fundamental laws of this state" or the fact that it is "contrary to natural right" that is determinative? Is "natural right" in these cases superfluous rhetoric? The mere absence of law confirming slavery would not, without the proposition on natural right, suffice to prohibit restraint within Massachusetts. For, ordinarily, states out of comity will enforce foreign rights. Because of the natural rights argument, the state interest in comity is presumed to be attenuated. Fundamental positive law is also necessary, for if slavery were known in Massachusetts, it might recognize out-of-state slave relations even without a basis in natural law and morality.

It is where natural right diverges from state policy that the ambiguity of *Aves* and *Somerset's Case* present real problems for the judge.

A judge sitting in Kentucky, Louisiana, Missouri, or Virginia could not assume that both fundamental positive law of his state and natural right would support his decision. The South had its own more difficult variant on the facts of *Somerset's Case:* the question of the effect of residence or sojourn in a free state on a Negro, a slave by the law of the Southern state, who is brought back to a slave state after such residence or travel. The case of the *Slave Grace,*[26] the English decision that decided this very question in favor of the resumption of slave status, was not decided until 1826, by which time a number of Southern states had already confronted the issue.

In *Rankin v. Lydia,*[27] the Kentucky Court of Appeals staked out what was to be the dominant Southern position until the 1850's. The court decided that a fixed residence (even without domicile) in a free state suffices to work an emancipation of the slave. Even if the slave is brought back to the slave state, without any judgment in his favor, the slave state is bound to respect the right to freedom that becomes vested by virtue of the residence in the nonslave territory. The case of the temporary sojourner is distinguished. He retains his right to travel through free territory with his slaves. The slave state will recognize no such vested freedom in them. *Rankin v. Lydia* echoes *Somerset's Case.* The first step in the court's reasoning was to find that, by the law in force in the territory of Indiana (where Lydia was brought and where she resided as a child for seven years before being sold back to Kentucky), Lydia acquired freedom, though she had an obligation there for service for years. This step was based on the language of the Northwest Ordinance.

The court, then, had to deal with two contentions of the master. The first was that the right to freedom as a consequence of bringing of a slave into Indiana is a penal statute and should not be enforced in Kentucky. The second contention was that the institutions of Kentucky include Negro slavery, so that the policy of the state is furthered by not permitting the municipal law of another jurisdiction to interfere with the ownership of the slave. The penalty argument was rejected by the court with the statement that

> freedom is the natural right of man, although it may not be his birthright. . . . If these rights are once vested in Indiana or any other portion of the United States, can it be compatible with the

spirit of our confederated government to deny their existence in any other part.[28]

Thus, the court rejected the proposition that free law is owed no greater comity than slave law. The argument that slavery might reattach upon resuming residence within Kentucky was treated as an insult by the court. For the court took as established that slavery, being contrary to natural right, can only be created by positive law. The acceptance of the natural law premise by the Kentucky court led it to concede extraterritorial effect to status determined by the positive law of Indiana, which would not be conceded in a free state to the status determined by the law of Kentucky. The courts of a free state are presumed to rightfully set free a Negro brought into the free state so long as it is not simply a temporary sojourn. They may do this because slavery is the product only of municipal law and is contrary to the law of nature. Of course, they must so hold when, as in the case of Indiana, there is also legislation that forbids slavery. However, in a slave state such acts of the free state are to be given effect, not out of simple comity—since no reciprocal recognition of slave status is expected—but because the fact that freedom is in harmony with the law of nature mandates at least specific municipal authority for reenslavement. In the Kentucky court's view, we find again the idea of a preexisting natural law in favor of freedom that is always subject to the superior authority of the sovereign, but that governs for want of the exercise of such authority.*

In Louisiana, as Helen Catterall has shown in great detail,[29] the state Supreme Court was even more firm in extending extraterritorial effect to the status acquired by residence in a free state.[30] Indeed, at least as to a free foreign nation, there is some evidence that a brief sojourn would suffice to vest a right to freedom.[31] Only a statute in 1846 put an end to this line of cases in Louisiana. Even that statute was read with an eye to the past policy of the court. It was given only prospective effect, not applied to the case of a slave claiming free-

---

* *Rankin v. Lydia,* 9 Ky. (2 A. K. Marsh.) 467 (1820), p. 472: "She was not the slave of the purchaser while he remained in Indiana . . . and is it to be seriously contended that so soon as he transported her to the Kentucky shore, the noxious atmosphere of this State, without any express law for the purpose, clamped upon her newly forged chains of slavery, after the old ones were destroyed." Note the allusion to the old maxim of the "free air" of England through its opposite "noxious atmosphere."

dom after the act on the basis of residence in free territory before the act.[32] Nevertheless, in the Louisiana cases there is little talk of natural law as a basis for conflict-of-laws principles. In part, we may presume a tacit understanding and acceptance of those principles. However, the absence of the language of natural law may be largely explained by the fact that as a civil law jurisdiction, the Louisiana courts did not borrow from the language and argument of *Somerset's Case*. Rather, they tended to introduce notions of right and justice through the principle: everything which may properly be done *in favorem libertatis* should be done.[33]

Both by legislation and by judicial decision, the Southern approach described above was generally reversed in the last ten or fifteen years before the Civil War.[34] However, even in the period before 1830, the approach of Louisiana, Missouri, and Kentucky was by no means unchallenged. The Virginia cases are somewhat unrevealing, but the single extensive judicial statement on the subject takes an approach that ignores completely the impact of *Somerset's Case* and of natural law and is suggestive of a totally different framework. In *Griffith v. Fanny*,[35] decided in 1820, the Virginia court achieved, with almost no discussion, the result of *Rankin v. Lydia*. A slave sold into Ohio, returned after residence in Ohio to Virginia, was to be granted freedom, apparently by force of respect for the effect of the Ohio constitution, which had effectively emancipated her in Ohio. Exactly one year later, the court decided against the slave petitioning for freedom in a very similar case, *Lewis v. Fullerton*.[36] The slave claimed that she had been sent out to work in Ohio. There, she also succeeded in claiming her freedom upon a writ of habeas corpus. Moreover, in return for entering into an indenture for two years, the master executed, in Ohio, a deed of manumission. The Virginia court rejected all these bases for freedom, holding that temporary presence in Ohio, though it might suffice for a jurisdictional basis for Ohio to declare the slave free for Ohio purposes, does not give Ohio the power to bind Virginia to recognize the freedom so conferred. Moreover, given the temporary nature of the Ohio residence, and given the rather hasty proceedings in habeas corpus, the Virginia court declined to exercise its discretion to give effect either to the Ohio act or to its proceedings. The court chose to characterize the case not primarily as a "conflicts" situation, but as a problem of enforcement of the manu-

mission and Negro removal laws. It should be noted that if sojourn in
a sister (free) state creates free status, which is afforded full recognition in Virginia, then by transporting a slave into a free state and then
back to Virginia, an emancipation may be worked by operation of
law. Thus, the provisions of the manumission laws requiring the
owner to give security against the Negro's becoming a public charge,
and the Act of 1806 requiring the manumitted Negro to leave within
twelve months, would be obviated. The Ohio deed of manumission
was rejected as not in compliance with the Manumission Act of
Virginia, which determined the exclusive procedures by which a
valid emancipation may be effected. Unquestionably, the natural law
as to freedom played no part in *Lewis v. Fullerton*. The conflict-of-
laws theory implicit in the decision is one in which the courts effectuate the primary interests of the state. But the Virginia court did not
see the state policy determination as simply a choice between favoring slavery or freedom. They considered Virginia policy to be an explicit stand against uncontrolled manumission. To give full effect to
the Ohio transactions would be to permit an emancipation without the
basic protections required of analogous Virginia transactions. If
Lewis v. Fullerton had been decided in favor of freedom, it might
have provided authority for widespread evasion of these manumission
requirements. The court would not take responsibility for such a
result.

It should be noted that in none of the cases discussed in this section
did the court purport to apply a personal or factional moral proposition against slavery. Rather, the tradition of *Somerset's Case* gave institutional recognition to antislavery morality, incorporating that view
of natural law as a common law and conflict-of-laws principle. When
the judge referred to that natural law, he felt, as securely as judges
ever do with case law, that he was appealing to a common, identifiable source for doctrine. Eve T. R. R. Cobb, amidst an elaborate attempt to prove that the law of nature authorizes slavery, was constrained to admit that the proposition that slavery was against natural
law "has been almost universally adopted by courts and jurists."

But just as this natural law was a creature of juridical works, so its
sphere of operation was juridically limited. The conflicts cases are
important because they demonstrate the judicial cognizance and obeisance to those limits even where explicit directives from other law-

making branches were usually absent. The Virginia court's attention to the policy elements of the manumission and removal laws was not an uncommon phenomenon. In Louisiana, the courts gave similar consideration to such policies though they concluded on factual grounds that the threat was minimal.

CHAPTER SIX: Perspectives from International Law

International law, even more than "conflicts," has a long history of identification with the law of nature. Many of the prominent discussions of slavery's place within the law of nature, noted in Chapter 1, are contained within books that are predominantly works of international law. Yet the law of nations, with its affinity for the law of nature, operates by virtue of its being incorporated within the law of a sovereign state. It is not in force by its own authority (*ex proprio vigore*) but by authority of some sovereign entity. As early as 1784, we have a suggestion of judicial recognition of this critical jurisprudential point in one of the first applications of international law in the new republic:

> This is a case of first impression in the U.S. It must be determined on the principles of the laws of nations, *which form part of the municipal law of Pennsylvania.* . . . This law [of nations], in its full extent, is part of the law of this State, and is to be collected from the practice of different Nations, and the authority of writers.[1]

The content of international law, like the content of choice-of-law rules must, however, if it is to be workable, share something of both principle and practice. If the foundation of the rules governing relations among nations has nothing about it save a reflection of what is done by nations, there is a circularity: What is, is lawful. Some recourse must be made to more or less agreed upon principles of what ought to be: the law of nature. Yet, given the fact that international law must depend for its *authority* on the incorporation into the "municipal" law of real states, it cannot be utopian. The practices of nations must be reflected in the content of the law. The tension between international law as hopelessly utopian and as mere apologetics is a real one today and was felt forcibly in the applications of this field to slavery and to the slave trade.*

---

* The slave trade and international law is a fascinating and complex subject that deserves a full treatment. Here, I suggest only that two minor motifs in that complex history—the question of identity of natural and international law as to the characterization of the trade as piracy and

100

Slave Trade and Piracy

Justice Story came closest to asserting a utopian identity of the law of nature and the law of nations. In 1822 in the case *La Jeune Eugenie,* Story, on circuit, was confronted with the question of whether the peacetime search and subsequent seizure of a slaver flying the French flag could be upheld in the prize action brought by the American ship.[2] Story held that a seizure of this sort could be justified only in the case of a pirate. That is, an American naval vessel had the right to search a suspected pirate with or without probable cause. Should the search prove justified by the outcome—evidence that the suspected vessel was a pirate—the seizure would be good. However, should the vessel prove not to be a pirate, the searchers would have acted at their own risk. The validity of the seizure in the instant case, therefore, turned on whether a slaver might be characterized as a pirate by the law of nations. Story began his analysis with the strongest possible condemnation of the slave trade:

> It begins in corruption, and plunder, and kidnapping. . . . It desolates whole villages and provinces. . . . It breaks down all the ties of parent, and children. . . . It manacles the inoffensive females and the starving infants. It forces the brave to untimely death in defence of their humble homes. . . . It stirs up the worst passions of the human soul, darkening the spirit of revenge, sharpening the greediness of avarice, brutalizing the selfish, envenoming the cruel, famishing the weak, and crushing to death the broken-hearted. This is but the beginning of the evils.[3]

The boldness of Story's opinion, however, lies not in its vigorous condemnation of the slave trade, but in the Justice's firm linkage of this moral perception to the law of nations:

---

the question of the effect to be given slave mutinies—reinforced already extant ideological trends in highly charged circumstances. Any proper study of the subject as a whole must begin with the British Parliamentary Papers. For some recent literature that touches on the problem of slavery and international law—or at least on the diplomacy of slavery—see Leslie Bethell, *The Abolition of the Brazilian Slave Trade* (Cambridge: The University Press, 1970); Philip Curtin, *The Atlantic Slave Trade, A Census* (Madison, Wis.: University of Wisconsin Press, 1969). Still most useful for the Anglo-American diplomatic front is Hugh Soulsby, *The Right of Search and the Slave Trade in Anglo-American Relations 1814–1862* (Baltimore: Johns Hopkins Press, 1933), though Bethell's work places the English endeavors in a more comprehensive picture.

But I think it may be unequivocally affirmed, that every doctrine, that may be deduced . . . from . . . the nature of moral
obligation, may theoretically be said to exist in the law of nations; and unless it be relaxed and waived by the consent of nations, which may be evidenced by their general practice and customs, it may be enforced by a court of justice, whenever it arises
in judgment.[4]

Story concluded that only when the flag of the ship permits the trade
under its domestic law, can the slaver claim any status other than
pirate. As France did not permit the trade, the seizure of *La Jeune
Eugenie* was upheld.*

Only three years after Story's bold opinion, Chief Justice Marshall
wrote for the Supreme Court in *The Antelope*.[5] He affirmed, in pertinent part, the decision of Justice Johnson on circuit. Johnson had
reached a result, in an analogous case, directly opposed to that
reached by Story. Marshall, like Story, found slavery contrary to natural law: "That every man has a natural right to the fruits of his own
labor, is generally admitted. . . ."[6] But Marshall saw international
law, no less than domestic law, in conflict with natural law on the
issue of slavery. The obligation of a court is to look to the practices
of nations as the source of law. Resort to such a standard unfortunately led to the result "in favor of the legality of the trade."[7]
Marshall and Story agreed however, that insofar as the law of nations
legitimated slavery and its incidents, a gap between law and morality
existed.

In fact, Story and Marshall differed more upon emphasis than substance. Story had conceded that the presumptive identity of the law of
nations and nature may be refuted by the actual practice of nations.
Marshall simply began with the practice of nations. With respect to
the application of these principles to the slave trade, the facts of the
international scene in the 1820's renders a firm conclusion difficult.
The United States and Great Britain had outlawed the trade for their
citizens and for ships flying their flags. Most of the European trading
nations had followed suit. But these steps were comparatively recent
in 1822. Only twenty years earlier every major trading nation permit-

* 26 F. Cas. 846. Story, however, finding the source of *La Jeune Eugenie's* crime in international law, did not give relief to the libelants. Rather, he decided that the French government
should be given the ship for proceedings under French law.

ted the trade. Nor was the reform as yet complete. The practice of nations, then, provided no sure guide. It is in precisely such cases that
the somewhat different emphases in the approaches of Marshall and
Story might be expected to lead to different results. The differences
in result in the two cases can also be explained, however, in terms of
the changed domestic political environment over three short years.

In *La Jeune Eugenie* and *The Antelope,* the American courts struggled with the difficult issues of visitation and search of foreign vessels in time of peace.[8] British warships had once claimed such a right
with respect to the slave trade. But in 1817, in the case *Le Louis,* the
enormous weight of Sir William Scott and of the British admiralty
courts was committed against the right of search.[9] The refusal of the
admiralty courts to authorize peacetime search left the British crusade
against the trade diplomatic and political solutions. But these attempts, too, proved inadequate. Great Britain formulated a general
scheme of bilateral treaties with maritime nations, providing for a
zone of reciprocal right of search and for courts of mixed commission
to try and condemn ships allegedly engaged in the slave trade.[10]
However, this scheme was unacceptable to the United States. In
1818, the United States, per Secretary of State John Quincy Adams,
rejected British overtures.[11] American hesitancy to accept right of
search was certainly attributable in large part to the fear of British
abuse, a fear that was rendered plausible by the expansive treatment
of the belligerent's right to search, which England had used throughout the Napoleonic Wars, and by the recurrent thorn of impressment.
The British proposal was also rejected on the ground that trial of
American nationals by courts of mixed commission was probably unconstitutional. Even admitting the moral horror of the slave trade, the
United States could not concede a principle of search at sea in peacetime, "a violation of [the] natural right to pursue unmolested . . .
peaceful commercial intercourse." [12]

From 1818 through 1824 the forces in the United States seeking
some more effectual design for cooperation with England against the
trade, looked to the possibility of accord in branding the illegal trade
as piracy.* Such a characterization would probably have the effect of

* In 1820 Congress declared the trade piracy, though the act related only to those who
engaged in the trade under the American flag [Act of May 15, 1820, Chap. 113, § 4, 5, 3 St.
600 (1820)]. In March 1823 the House of Representatives adopted a resolution calling on the

permitting a peacetime search at sea should the result prove the vessel to have been a slaver, but it would not concede, as a general matter, the right to search or visit an innocent vessel to determine whether she be a slaver or not. The searcher would be acting at his own risk, so this method would be less effectual than the British scheme. On the other hand, the Americans would acquire a concession on the general rights of vessels, which was extremely important in the context of the immediate post-Napoleonic years.

Story's decision in *La Jeune Eugenie* should be understood in terms of the maneuverings then under way to make the piracy characterization the cure-all for the impasse between Great Britain and the United States. Story may have been doing nothing less than attempting to create the characterization judicially by derivation from the law of nature.[13] Between *La Jeune Eugenie* and *The Antelope,* however, much had happened on the political scene. Exchanges of letters between Secretary of State Adams and British ministers Castlereagh and Canning finally led to a proposed convention by Great Britain, which, proceeded from the piracy characterization; provided for only a limited right of search; contained express safeguards against impressment; and used no courts of mixed commission. The convention was rejected by the Senate of the United States.[14] It was in the context of that recent course of events that *The Antelope* was decided in 1825. While Story could justify his judicial aggressiveness in terms of forwarding a process still in flux in 1822, by 1825 a similar judicial stroke would have meant doing what the Senate had explicitly refused to do. This difference might well account for Story's acquiescence in the Supreme Court decision in *The Antelope.* If my un-

---

President to negotiate with maritime powers to abolish the trade and have it declared piracy under the law of nations. (Soulsby, *Right of Search and the Slave Trade,* pp. 26–27.) See Thomas Hart Benton, *Abridgment of the Debates of Congress* (New York: D. Appleton and Co., 1858–61), 7 : 455–56 for text of resolution. The text of the debate, pp. 456–59, suggests several juridical positions on the slave trade and piracy. Representative Charles Mercer of Virginia, sponsor of the resolution, stated in the course of the debate: "I am aware, sir, that technical objections have been urged, and sneers have been indulged against the legal accuracy of the application of the term piracy to this offence. Such criticism has no sound reason to sustain it. The law of nations is in part natural; in part conventional. . . . . The consent of nations may make piracy of any offence upon the high seas. . . . . is there no analogy between the African slave trade, and the offence of piracy which would warrant the proposed classification of the former crime under the latter title?" (p. 467). The resolution passed 131 to 9. The currency of the pirate idea only a couple of months after the decision of *La Jeune Eugenie* is thus established.

derstanding of these two cases is correct, what emerges is the conclusion that first, natural law was a potential source for international law, which would be subordinated to constitutions, statutes, and the practice of nations. Second, as with interpretation of statutes, courts would exhibit a contextual sensitivity. It is not only what the legislature has said on a subject, but also what it has intimated by nonaction or by action in related areas that must be taken into account. In short, use of the natural law characterization of the slave trade was itself an act of judicial lawmaking, recognized as such, and, therefore, subject to the many cautions and limits that were so pervasive in the judicial process.

Mutinies and the Right of Revolution

I have spoken so far of a domesticated natural law: a tame, legalistic reflection of the driving impulse of the American Revolution. But the domesticated and the wild creatures both trace their ancestry honestly, to the prerevolutionary sources. The coexistence of the two rather different offspring uneasily persisted, for they served different functions. The same man could appreciate the limits to which natural law must be subject in the formulation of rules of decision by the judiciary while holding the identical substantive doctrines sufficient basis for acts of revolution. For example, Justice Joseph Story knew well the accepted limits to the judicial function. Yet, Story in his *Commentaries on the Constitution,* hypothesized a state of affairs in which the various departments of government instead of checking one another "concur in a gross usurpation." He hypothesized that the normal remedies—legislative change or constitutional amendment—would be unavailing should the oppressed group be a minority. In such a case, asserts Story,

> If there be any remedy at all . . . it is a remedy never provided for by human institutions. It is by a resort to the ultimate right of all human beings in extreme cases to resist oppression, and to apply force against ruinous injustice.[15]

The moral right was asserted here, side by side with the denial of the possibility of institutional reflection of that right.

Yet men hesitate to frankly acknowledge that their own acts are contrary to what they believe to be first principles of morality. It is rare to find a man ready to concede that a revolution with himself as the target would be just. Jefferson's enigmatic phrase that he "trembled" when he remembered that God is just has become a deserving classic because it is so atypical of the insights of a master class and of those who serve it.* The coexistence of slavery, of a doctrine holding slavery contrary to natural right, and of a doctrine holding that in extreme cases of the denial of natural right the oppressed class may resort to revolution is unstable.† In the states that came to be thought of as "free" the instability was resolved by the elimination of slavery, though the tension persisted in different form because of the part played by the federal union in supporting, recognizing, or acknowledging the slavery of the South. In the deep South the tension was resolved for many through a frank disclaimer of the preference for liberty, or, more commonly, through the creation of an exception to these natural laws for the Negro.[16] But, for much of the nation, prejudice against the black was not sufficient to warrant his being excluded, in theory, from the rights of man. There, the instability of the doctrines of natural right and slavery were least satisfactorily resolved. It was resolved by setting up "necessity" as a polar coun-

---

* "Indeed, I tremble for my country when I reflect that God is just; that his justice cannot sleep forever; that considering numbers, nature and natural means only, a revolution of the wheel of fortune, an exchange of situation is among possible events; that it may become probable by supernatural interference! The Almighty has no attribute which can take side with us in such a contest." Thomas Jefferson, *Notes on the State of Virginia* (New York: Harper Torchbooks, 1964), p. 156. One is tempted to read something into the bifurcation of Jefferson's discussion of slavery in the *Notes*. In his chapter on the "Administration of Justice," Jefferson discusses slavery extensively. But the discussion is a racist, tentative justification for the institution. In his chapter on "Particular Customs and Manners," the strong language quoted above appears. Could it be that some habit of thought turned Jefferson from his more radical critique while discussing slavery as a legal issue? Jefferson on slavery is, of course, an enormous subject. See Winthrop Jordan, *White over Black* (Chapel Hill: University of North Carolina Press, 1968), pp. 429–81.

† The argument that the oppressed may justly resort to revolution is not the same as the argument that sympathetic men may resort to revolution on behalf of the oppressed. For a sensitive treatment of these and other distinctions see Michael Waltzer, *Obligations* (Cambridge, Mass.: Harvard University Press, 1970). The distinction was well recognized by antislavery thinkers. The political rights of the white friends of the slave imposed obligations to refrain from certain acts of insurgency. See, e.g., Richard Dana's distinction in his defense of Charles Davis, *Report of the Proceedings at the Examination of Charles G. Davis Esq., on a Charge of Aiding and Abetting in the Rescue of a Fugitive Slave* (Boston, 1851). "We are not subjects of a monarchy, which has put laws upon us that we have no hand in making. I do not hesitate to say, here, that, if the act of 1850 had been imposed upon us, a subject people, by a monarchy, we should have rebelled as one man" (p. 27). Of course, Dana's logic led straight to justification of revolution for *slaves*.

terweight to natural right. To the maxim *fiat justitia* the torn master responded *salus populi suprema lex est.*

This model of a tug-of-war between the demands of justice and the dictates of necessity was very much in the minds of jurists who took the slavery issue seriously. Even St. George Tucker answered his own use of the very words *fiat justitia.* Admitting the potentially disastrous consequences either of immediate emancipation or of insurrection, Tucker called upon the notion of necessity:

> The claims of nature, it will be said are stronger than those which arise from social institutions only. I admit it, but nature also dictates to us to provide for our own safety, and authorizes all *necessary* measures for that purpose [italics in original].[17]

The argument from necessity and the claim of a natural right of revolution share a number of characteristics and reinforce one another. With respect to the legal system, both are frankly metalegal in character. They serve to justify law or to justify its undoing, but they are not themselves principles for rules of decision. Also, both claims assume an antithesis of interest between master and slave. It is the master's necessity that is claimed or the slave's right of revolution. Finally, both arguments make sense only in the context of the continuation of the slave system. The end of slavery puts the end to the necessity of revolution (on that account) and, of course, to the necessity for harsh measures of slave discipline to assure safety. Moreover, clearly the two arguments form an escalating dialectical spiral. The possibility of revolution gives the argument of necessity much of its force. The perception that rational men will indeed come to revolutionary conclusions strengthens the claim of necessity. However, the application of the doctrine of necessity to justify harsher and more restrictive measures against the slave only increases the theoretical justifications for revolutionary steps, leading, from the master's perspective to the justification of still harsher steps as necessary.

Now the claim of necessity was made to justify a great deal of the legislation and the body of decisions regulating Negroes in the slave states. However, as Story so ably pointed out, the claim of revolution is not likely to arise in legal contexts. Yet, because of agitational needs and advantages, it was useful to attempt to secure judicial declaration of or acquiescence in the right of revolution for slaves, if

only as an abstract principle. Two opportunities for such attempts
presented themselves, and though they stand apart from the main-
streams of judicial work in international law, they are nevertheless
important in reflecting the interaction of the antislavery movement
with the courtroom and the continued search for dramatic enactment
of the injustice of "law."

Moralists have often sought to strip ethical issues of the complicating layers of fact and competing interests that seem to always characterize choice in society. Indeed the common association of natural
right with a preexisting state of nature is itself an example of such an
attempt. The tendency remains strong today as it was thousands of
years ago. We have the relatively recent attempt of Professor Lon
Fuller to plumb the depths of the scope of responsibility for the taking of human life, the famous case of the speluncean explorers,[18]
which itself is but an elaboration of the hypothetical of Rabbi Akiva,
now two millennia old, of two men lost in the desert with only
enough water for one.[19] What is of interest to us is not only that phi-
losophers should create such hypotheticals, but that where life has
imitated art, where events have occurred that seem in part to mirror
the choices presented by these hypotheticals, jurists have seized on
the cases as presenting fundamental problems about the nature of
law. Thus, cases like *United States v. Holmes* and *Regina v. Dudley
and Stephens* have received extended attention from jurists.[20]

It is not surprising then, that when facts arose that appeared to
present the issue of the slave's natural right of revolution, stripped of
many of the usual societal complications, the case would be seized
upon as critical—revealing underlying truths. The shipboard mutiny
of slaves presented such an opportunity. The ship as a microcosm of
society was already a familiar literary device. It was used again and
again by Herman Melville. Indeed, in *Benito Cereno,* Melville even
used the device for purposes of dealing with the problem of slavery
and insurrection. In the case of shipboard mutiny of slaves, conditions were as close to ideal as possible in a concrete world, for isolat-
ing the "abstract" right of revolution. First, the complicating factor
of the safety of the white community was severely attenuated. Necessity no longer could claim so large a stake. The white men who ran
slave ships were thought of as a degraded class even by most slave-
owners. Thus, whatever claim to necessity the slaver could make for

himself, it was at least unlikely that he could arouse the degree of sympathetic extension of the claim to all white men, that the Virginia planter often successfully invoked. The evils of slavery were also exaggerated on board a slave ship. Men were constantly in chains; sanitation was nonexistent; mortality was terribly high. Indeed, the trade had always been the least sympathetic part of slavery and claimed opponents among firm defenders of the peculiar institution. Finally the high seas themselves had something of the law of nature about them. They were the shared province of all nations and the substance of the rules that were supposed to govern transactions upon the sea had always been associated with the law of nature. It was in international law that the great continental jurists had applied their speculations to natural law.

In 1839 and, again, in 1841 slave mutinies occurred that became the subject of public controversy in the United States. Both incidents had international consequences, both occasioned expression of congressional concern, and both ended with judicial or quasijudicial decisions. Both occasioned a burst of antislavery organization. The results of the two cases, taken together, reaffirmed the supremacy of positive law to natural right and extended that supremacy, in international contexts, to include the supremacy afforded the positive law of a foreign sovereign. Yet, the cases seemed to legitimate the appeal to nature as residual law, even when the natural right in question led to revolution.

In 1839, a Spanish sloop, the *Amistad,* was seized off Long Island by an American Navy vessel. Forty-nine Africans were found on board, in control of the ship. They had taken the ship while on the high seas and had tried to return to Africa. Barely two years later, an American ship, the *Creole,* limped into the British port of Nassau. While en route from Virginia to New Orleans, the ''cargo'' of slaves had risen and taken the ship. Under their direction the ship reached the free British Island. The British authorities took the position that they had no lawful authority to return the Negroes to the captain.[21]

The *Amistad* case began with the imprisonment of the Africans. Their confinement lasted throughout the two years of litigation that ensued, despite several challenges. Conflicting libels were filed in the case by two Americans for salvage, and by the Spanish owners of the cargo, which was alleged to include the forty-nine Africans. The United States government intervened, asserting the interest of the Spanish government, claimed by virtue of treaty, in the return of the slaves to the Spanish owners. The Africans, themselves, were represented and claimed their freedom.[22]

Roger Sherman Baldwin, a prominent Connecticut attorney, represented the Negroes. A defense committee was formed to finance the operation and to assist in preparation of the case. The work of the committee was directed by Lewis Tappan, long associated with the antislavery cause and with other benevolent activities in New York. Contributions were solicited throughout the North, and the story of the mutiny was billed as an heroic struggle for freedom. Care was taken to avoid identification of the *Amistad* case with the more controversial work of the American Antislavery Society. The defense committee did more than raise funds and distribute literature. When communication with the Africans, who spoke neither English nor Spanish, became imperative, a translator was found—no mean feat. Harassment of the Spanish claimants through lawsuits in New York may also fairly be attributed to the committee.[23]

In the courtroom the question of the Africans' freedom hinged on three issues. The first issue was whether the treaty between Spain and the United States applied to the case at hand. The treaty provided that merchandise rescued from the hands of pirates or robbers should be restored to the owners under the law of the treating countries. The second issue was whether the Negroes were slaves under the law of Spain. This question was relevant both to the question of the applicability of the treaty and to the question of whether international law should mandate rendition of the slaves even should the treaty not apply. The third issue was one of "pure" international law. Assuming the Negroes to have been unlawfully enslaved, could or should a foreign tribunal recognize an act of insurrection or mutiny by which freedom is reacquired? The district court, to the surprise of the antislavery forces, ruled that the court had power to look behind the ship's documentation to determine whether the enslavement of the Negroes had been lawful. This procedural ruling was critical. For upon such enquiry, it appeared plain that the enslavement of the Africans had been illegal even under Spanish law, the law of the ship's flag. Having taken this step, the court further ruled that the treaty with Spain did not require rendition since the Africans were not property under Spanish law. Finally, District Judge Judson ruled that mutiny by one wrongfully enslaved was not cognizable as a crime in an American court. Again, the shape of the argument is one that finds the absence of positive law controlling. It is because there is no law, Spanish or American that authorizes the slavery, that the Negroes are entitled to fall back on natural law even to the extent of revolution.[24]

The United States appealed from the judgment of the district court, arguing that the treaty with Spain applied. Before the Supreme Court John Quincy Adams joined Baldwin, representing the Africans. He was seventy-four years old, already notorious for the radical turn that his second political life had taken in the House of Representatives. To antislavery forces he was Old Man Eloquent. His two-day argument began with a direct assertion of the natural right to revolution. Pointing to the Declaration of Independence, he asserted:

> I know of no law . . . no code, no treaty, applicable to the proceedings of the executive or the judiciary, except that law, . . . that law. . . . I know of no other law that reaches the case of my clients, but the law of nature, and of Nature's God on which our fathers placed our own national existence.[25]

Adams's appeal to the right of revolution was not only rhetoric. He was asserting in extended form the technical argument that natural law had a place to determine rules of decision where there was no positive law. His assertion that he knew of no law save that of nature that applied was a *double-entendre*. He could be saying that nature's law applied because there was no other law or that there was no other valid law because nature's law applied. We know that Adams went on to rely on more conventional legal authority during the bulk of his oration. Yet one is tempted in the case of Adams, more than any other man of the time, to suspect that the ambiguity was purposeful and fully appreciated by its author. Justice Story, for one, found Adams's appearance extraordinary: "extraordinary, I say, for its power, for its bitter sarcasm, and its dealing with topics far beyond the record and points of discussion."[26]

Story wrote the opinion for the Supreme Court that largely upheld and followed the reasoning of the district court. The Africans were

illegally enslaved and the treaty therefore was inapplicable. With neither Spanish law nor the treaty to authorize enslavement,

> The conflict of rights between the parties under such circum-
> stances becomes positive and inevitable, and must be decided
> upon the eternal principles of justice and international law.[27]

Again, the absence of positive law renders "eternal principles of justice" controlling. The question is then presented squarely: May men
wrongfully enslaved, rebel against their captors, kill the captain of
the ship, and hold others captive to sail to Africa? Story firmly concedes the right of mutiny in such circumstances.

> We may lament the dreadful acts by which they asserted their
> liberty, and took possession of the Amistad, but they cannot be
> deemed pirates or robbers in the sense of the law of na-
> tions. . . .[28]

The case of the *Creole* provided a fact situation upon which the
doctrines of the *Amistad* might be elaborated to good effect. Yet at
first the international consequences of the event overshadowed matters of doctrine. In 1842, shortly after the British authorities on Nassau refused to restore the *Creole* Negroes to the captain, Secretary of
State Daniel Webster sent a strong dispatch to Edward Everett, the
American ambassador to Great Britain:

> In all your communications with Her Majesty's Government,
> you will seek to impress it with a full conviction of the danger-
> ous importance to the peace of the two countries of occurrences
> of this kind. . . .[29]

The dispatch, however, was a finely honed legal argument as well
as a war threat. Webster argued that the British were bound to apply
American law to determine the status of persons on board a vessel
sailing under the American flag. The application of American law
would find the Negroes lawfully enslaved. Then, principles of general international law would require the British to give help to a vessel in distress and to restore on board the ship the *status quo ante*.[30]

In the Senate of the United States, the *Creole* had given impetus to
shrill war cries from the South. In the House of Representatives,
however, the event coincided with the height of agitation by John

Quincy Adams and by the small band of the self-selected "select committee on slavery" to break the so-called "gag rule" by which all petitions on the subject of slavery were tabled without vote or reference. Joshua Giddings, a young congressman from Ohio, had already achieved a degree of notoriety as one of the leaders of the antislavery forces when (on March 21, 1842) he introduced a series of resolutions commending the mutiny of the *Creole* Negroes as both legally and morally justified. His legal theory was that the moment a ship leaves the territorial waters of a state by whose law slavery is created, the slave has passed into the jurisdiction where only nature's law is valid. Giddings was censured for his speech. He resigned and was reelected easily, whereupon he again put forward the *Creole* resolutions, effectively breaking the gag rule.[31]

Giddings's legal position was not idiosyncratic. It was characteristic of the thinking of the Ohio-centered wing of antislavery thought that tried to construct a viable legal sword against slavery out of the "municipal" character of the institution stressed in *Somerset's Case.* In the *American Jurist and Law Magazine,* based in Boston, a major article went as far as Giddings and farther. With no attempt to confine the argument to the high seas, the right of revolution for the slave was asserted:

> "as man has chosen to throw them exclusively upon the law of nature, to that law alone can they look for redress." [32]

The most important reply to the legal argument of the administration, however, was penned in a series of articles in the New York *Herald,* later published in pamphlet form. The articles were anonymous, though they have been attributed to William Jay. The work bears the signs of the thinking of either Jay or of Theodore Weld, two of the leading legal theorists of antislavery. Jay, himself, was steeped in the law: He was the son of John Jay, had been trained in law, held a minor judgeship for a while, and was the friend and correspondent of Chancellor Kent. The pamphlet, *The Creole Case and Mr. Webster's Dispatch,* was a point-by-point reply to the Secretary.[33]

Jay saw immediately that the most obvious precedent, the *Amistad,* was a two-edged sword. At first glance it appeared directly on point. If American courts would free slaves who had taken a Spanish flag ship, why shouldn't British authorities be entitled to free slaves who had taken a ship flying the American flag? Jay understood, however, that the reasoning of Story's decision rested upon the finding that the *Amistad* Negroes were not lawfully enslaved according to the law of Spain. The reference to the law of the ship's flag would ill suit the needs of the *Creole* mutineers. Jay applied the municipal theory of the law of slavery to break through that point:

> In this view the decision of our Supreme Court in the Amistad case was wrong—not wrong in its effect, but in the principle on which it was founded. That principle was, that by the law of Spain the Amistad Negroes were not properly slaves. But out of the jurisdiction of Spain the law of Spain had nothing to do with them. They were entitled to their liberty by the law of Nature. . . .[34]

Although Jay recognized that the ordinary rule in international law would afford extraterritorial effect to the domestic shipboard arrangements of a foreign nation, he argued that slavery's peculiar position in natural and international law constituted it as an exception to this rule. When slaves were shipped on the high seas, the protection afforded by the local law that creates slavery ceases. True, if the voyage is successful from the master's point of view, the security arrangements of the ship will suffice to prevent insurrection. But the issue is entirely one of superior force. If the slave should gain the upper hand, then no rule of law may be appealed to in the master's defense.

> . . . resistance of . . . force . . . even unto death, cannot be called mutiny or murder—because they are violating no law by such resistance, but on the contrary vindicating their natural freedom—the gift of God alike to all.[35]

The *Creole* affair was finally submitted by both Great Britain and the United States for arbitration. The decision of the umpire upheld in full the claims of Webster and the United States. An award of over $100,000 was made to the American claimants.[36] Following the reasoning of Webster, the decision did not adequately distinguish between the case at issue and that of an American ship landing voluntarily in Nassau. The *Amistad* seems to stand for the point that those wrongfully enslaved commit no breach of law when they take a ship.

And *Somerset's Case* stands for the proposition that the domestic arrangements of one nation need not be given extraterritorial effect. Why, then, must a rebellion against law which, because of its immorality, need not be and would not be given effect on the British Isles, be given lesser effect than rebellion against a lawless enslavement? The umpire's opinion does not directly answer the question, though two possibilities are suggested by it. First, the facts of the British part in the *Creole* incident are murky. There was a claim, apparently accepted by the umpire, that the British not only refused to help the captain restore the old order, but indeed, interfered after he had managed to regain a measure of control. This fact, however, would also be permissible under an extension of *Somerset's Case* to an instance of mutiny. Second, the umpire rests his decision heavily upon the obligation of one nation to give succor to the ships of another nation when they are in distress. Though why this obligation should not extend to a ship in the plight of the *Amistad* is not clear.

The attempt to reconcile the decision of the umpire in the *Creole* with that of the Supreme Court in the *Amistad* is not really necessary. The Supreme Court certainly intimated that its own decision would have been different had the case involved slavery legal under Spanish law. Moreover, it is by no means clear that the basis for that decision would have been the treaty alone. The clue to the dilemma lies in the character of natural law as subject to defeasance by the exercise of sovereign lawmaking powers. Though a court need not recognize the acts of sovereignty of another nation, it will often do so for reasons of state or of comity. Moreover, the fact that such acts of the sovereign provide a conclusive ousting of natural law in the domestic context makes reasonable the position that some effect should be given even to foreign positive law. Since ordinarily foreign positive law is given effect as to shipboard domestic status, it should be given effect also with regard to slavery.

For the abolitionist legal theory, much rode upon the attempt to make law end at the border of territorial waters. Thus, the cases of the *Creole* and the *Amistad* constituted a qualified victory only. True, the formal principle that when law did not create slavery, the slave retained the right of revolution, was conceded and even implemented in the case of the *Amistad*. But the principle was virtually confined to the facts of the *Amistad*—where the illegal slave trade was involved.

The right of revolution, which in classical eighteenth-century terms depended on the law's inadequacy—upon the failure of that consideration that society affords man in return for his consent and acquiescence to be governed—is turned on its head. The attempt to get a legal declaration of the right of revolution ends with a declaration that the right depends on legality. The more unjust the positive law of the state, the greater the extent to which it legalizes slavery and approves it, the more certain it is that the right to revolution will not be recognized by international law. The right of revolution becomes nothing more than a remedy of self-help authorized where the confinement is illegal. In short, the attempt to find a measure of legal recognition for what Story observed was necessarily an appeal beyond law, succeeded only through the unusual reference of revolutionary justification back to law itself. Since nineteenth-century American slavery was marked almost throughout by the stamp of legality, that fact in and of itself served to remove the possibility of a "legal right of revolution" even in international contexts.

The *Amistad* and *Creole* cases conclude this chapter with a strange and powerful reinforcement of the positivist approach to natural law and morality. The judiciary was superbly consistent in a wide variety of contexts in that positivist approach. Yet the *Amistad* also reinforces the conclusion that adherence to a natural right to freedom as a proposition that has its place, albeit limited, in the legal doctrinal order was a dangerous ideological remnant. For the *Amistad* more than any other case, was a disturbing ideological monument to both antislavery and proslavery forces. For the slaveholder it was a Supreme Court declaration that in the natural order of things—even though not in the legal order—his slave had a right to kill him. For antislavery forces, the *Amistad* and *Creole* together were a confession in open court of the depths of the difference between the order of right and the order of law.

PART II

RULES, ROLES, AND REBELS:
Nature's Place Disputed

And I beseech you,
Wrest once the law to your authority;
To do a great right, do a little wrong.

It must not be; there is no power in Venice
Can alter a decree established;
'T will be recorded for a precedent;
And many an error, by the same example,
Will rush into the state.

The Merchant of Venice

CHAPTER SEVEN

Some Paradigms
of Judicial Rhetoric

The Judicial "Can't"

The rhetorical function of a judicial opinion ordinarily relates to the law and not to the judge. The opinion is designed to persuade the parties and the world that the decision arrived at is just, that the evidence has been weighed, that the rules of law have been justly applied, that the rules of law themselves have been fairly determined. However, occasionally one finds the judicial opinion used to suggest the immorality of the law. Very often this suggestion is coupled with a statement that the judge is, nevertheless, bound to apply the law, immoral as it may be. In such cases, and in the law of slavery they abound, it is useful to ask whether we are not dealing with a different rhetorical purpose: not the justification of the result and of the underlying principles, but the justification of the judge. The judge may be telling us: I know the result reached is morally indefensible and I wish primarily that you understand the sense in which I have been compelled to reach it.

Consider Joseph Story. In 1842 he had been the target of antislavery attacks for his decisions in two important fugitive cases: *Prigg v. Pennsylvania* and the *Latimer* affair. He wrote to a friend, "You know full well that I have ever been opposed to slavery. But I take my standard of duty as a judge from the Constitution." [1] We have no problem recognizing the nature of this statement. It is part of a private letter. It is written in the first person. It appeals to what the correspondent already knows about the writer. Clearly, we are dealing with a justification of self. Story is justifying what he has done, though the nature of his actions and the premise providing the reason that they stand in need of justification are implicit.

Now consider the words of John McLean in three fugitive slave cases. McLean was associate justice of the Supreme Court sitting on circuit. In *Miller v. McQuerry,* he wrote:

With the abstract principles of slavery, courts called to administer the law have nothing to do. It is for the people, who are sov-

ereign, and their representatives, in making constitutions and in
the enactment of laws, to consider the laws of nature, and the
immutable principles of right. This is a field which judges cannot explore. . . . They look to the law, and to the law only. A
disregard of this by the judicial powers, would undermine and
overturn the social compact.[2]

In *Vaughn v. Williams,* the Justice stated,

It is argued that slavery had its origin in usurpation and injustice, and is continued in violation of man, . . . these are topics
which this court will not discuss. We look to the law, and only
the law.[3]

Finally, in *Norris v. Newton,* McLean asserted, "In these matters,
the law, and not conscience, constitutes the rule of action." [4]
Though the context of McLean's statements are judicial—though they
are not in form personal—might we not best understand them as justifications of the judge? Explicit in McLean's judicial statements is
the same moral condemnation of slavery that is in Story's letter. Both
judges are responding to the same question: Why are you, who stand
opposed to slavery, rendering a decision that sends a man to bondage
or that punishes a man for his part in helping the slave seek freedom?
Both judges respond: I would see slavery struck down if I could, but
I can't. The law prevents me.

I have chosen to emphasize the words of Story and McLean not
because they were the first or the most eloquent in resorting to this
form of self-justification, but because of their preeminent positions at
a critical point in time. The phenomenon itself was quite widespread.
In 1837 Judge Bissell of Connecticut, dissenting from a holding in
favor of the liberty of a black man, felt constrained to state:

As a citizen and as a man, I may admit the injustice and immorality of slavery; that its tendencies are all bad; that it is productive of evil, and of evil only. But as a jurist, I must look at that
standard of morality, which the law prescribes.[5]

Nor was McLean alone in the West. In 1845 Judge Read of Ohio
wrote:

Slavery is wrong, inflicted by force and supported alone by the
municipal power of the state or territory wherein it exists. It is

opposed to the principles of natural justice and right, and is the mere creature of positive law. Hence, it being my duty to declare the law, not to make it, the question is not, what conforms to the great principles of natural right and universal freedom— but what do the positive laws and institutions . . . command and direct.[6]

Similar utterances may be found in Massachusetts, Pennsylvania, Michigan, Kentucky, and North Carolina cases.[7]

It is no accident that such judicial pronouncements of helplessness before the law were so frequent in slave cases and especially in fugitive slave cases. For the fugitive slave case, after 1840, typically presented a pattern of intense, ideological advocacy coupled with a potential for civil disobedience and resistance. Moreover, as the two decades leading to civil war wore on, the fugitive slave issue appeared to present a case of divergence of legal norms from antislavery morality. The course of judicial decisions seemed to move in a direction less and less susceptible to ameliorist solutions. And the Fugitive Slave Act of 1850 evinced clear congressional policy favoring harsh and summary enforcement of the rendition policy over any solicitude for procedural or substantive rights of alleged fugitives. Thus, given the pervasive positivist orientation described in the preceding chapters, there was substantially less room for the outlet of principled preference for liberty, which operated in more amorphous doctrinal situations. Such a situation was the most troublesome of all to the antislavery judge.

When a judge, like McLean, asserted that he "cannot" explore or apply the purely moral norms relating to slavery, his statement had both logical and psychological connotations. In a certain limited sense, to say that one cannot perform an action is a definitive answer to the moral prescription that one ought to do it. As R. M. Hare, a leading British philosopher, put it: The impossibility or inevitability of an action keeps the question of whether to perform it (asked as a practical question) from arising. If a man is told that he ought run to get help, but answers that his leg is broken, we absolve him of moral responsibility because he "can't" perform the prescribed action. The physical impossibility of his running excludes the question of whether he ought to do so. But "cannot" may be used in many other senses than physical incapacity. "I can't" may be a way of saying "I don't want to,'' though certainly ''can't'' connotes something beyond lack of volition.[8]

The limits that ''cannot'' invokes may not be physical ones, but rather logical or conventional ones. Justice McLean's statement, quoted from *Miller v. McQuerry,* will serve as an example. As to the natural right of slavery, McLean stated, ''This is a field which judges can not explore.'' It is clear that McLean is not saying that the exploration of this area is impossible in the sense that it prevents the issue of whether or not to engage in the mental operation from arising. It is equally clear that McLean is trying to say something more than that he or others are disinclined to explore the area. For, he goes on, ''A disregard of this, by the judicial powers, would undermine and overturn the social compact.'' McLean's ''can't,'' then, may be translated into the following moral statement: A judge ought not explore the natural right of slavery unless he is prepared to destroy the social compact. This is an appeal to a limit that the audience will presumably agree upon.

Does this use of ''can't'' retain any of the significance as an excuse to a moral imperative, which ''can't'' in the physical sense seems to have? After all, McLean explicitly admits the possibility of ''disregard'' of the limitation on power. Is he not simply asserting ''social compact'' as a competing moral value against ''natural rights?'' The ''can't'' in the physical sense eliminates moral dilemmas and absolves the actor from choice. Competing, inconsistent, moral demands, by contrast, do not resolve but define moral choices. The ethical man still must choose and choose well.

It is interesting, therefore, to find that McLean keeps harping upon his lack of power and that he seems to think of this supposed lack of power as an answer to the demand that he apply natural law. To remedy oppressive law, he states, ''is a power which the judiciary *cannot* reach.'' The law ''has been enacted by the highest *power,*'' and, therefore, he *''cannot* turn aside from the sacred duties of . . . office to regard ought but the law.'' All this is put forward as a dispositive answer to the arguments of counsel, James Birney and John Jolliffe, that natural law condemned the Fugitive Slave Act.[9]

The fact that McLean thought he was giving a responsive and dispositive answer to a moral demand does not mean that he was correct. However, the fact that not only this Justice, but so much of the antislavery bench, gave similar responses to similar moral demands at least suggests that a search be made for senses, if any, in which their use of the language of power assumes the moral significance of "can't" in the sense of a justification. The position assumed in the following pages is that the context of moral discourse may create such a strong sense depending entirely on the assumptions with which the participants in the discourse confront each other.

Analogic Interludes

Rules of the Game [10]

Suppose one analogizes the professional, conventional, and constitutional limits on the judicial function to rules of a game limiting the movements of a piece upon a board.* By this admittedly simplistic analogy, the limits on the judge function in the same manner as the rule limiting the movement of a bishop in chess to the diagonals; though the rules of judgeship are more complicated than those regarding a bishop. Such rules not only limit, they define. It is not the physical piece that is a bishop in chess. Indeed, the only way to define a bishop is as that piece that is permitted to move the length of a diagonal, but only diagonally. Similarly, one may claim that within any given legal system (game), a judge is that man who————(here read the professional, conventional, legal and constitutional parameters of function).

If the game analogy is accepted—if the disputants agree that they wish "to play" the game—what kinds of argument about the judicial

* By invoking the "rules" of the game, I do not intend to enter the debate over whether such a rules-model is a defensible one for the legal order. I certainly intimate no belief that either a rules-model or a game-model can serve as a useful analogy to a legal system for more than very limited purposes. On the problem of "rules," see R. Dworkin, "Is the Law a System of Rules," in Robert Summer, ed., *Essays in Legal Philosophy* (Berkeley and Los Angeles: University of California Press, 1961). The obvious distinctions between law and games have often been made. See, e.g., the recent statement in John Rawls, *A Theory of Justice* (Cambridge: Harvard Univ. Press, 1971), p. 236. A recent and very useful analysis of the different senses of rules appears in D. N. MacCormick, "Legal Obligation and the Imperative Fallacy" in A. W. B. Simpson, ed., *Oxford Essays in Jurisprudence, Second Series* (Oxford: Clarendon Press, 1973), pp. 100 ff. MacCormick is quite aware of the senses in which the statement "You, the judge, ought to apply natural law" may have truth value depending upon the circumstances of the utterance; chiefly, whether there is an understanding between the speakers of a common system of conventions and rules. See especially p. 114. See also, H. Wellington, "Common Law Rules and Constitutional Double Standards: Some Notes on Adjudication," 83 *Yale Law Journal* 221 (1973).

function may arise? Three kinds of debates might ensue about a proposal to move a bishop along a rank or file instead of a diagonal. One
argument, among novices, might be whether or not the move is a permissible one; another argument is whether or not cheating is justified
in some given context; a third argument is whether such a move
would not make the game a better or more enjoyable one. The first of
these arguments involves an implicit agreement among the parties
that they wish to play chess. It is necessary that the conclusion of the
argument will be the statement "I can't make that move." This
"can't" is a dispositive answer to the prescription, "you ought to
move along that file," so long as both speakers accept the formal
framework of playing chess. For it is, in fact, logically impossible to
move the piece in such a manner and still remain within the formal
structure *agreed on* as defining "chess." The "can't" holds because
there is an agreed on reference for a limit.

If the prescription, "you ought to move along the file," is intended
to be a suggestion to cheat, the rules of chess will be wholly irrelevant to the argument. Both parties begin with the assumption that the
rules forbid the action. The terms of this argument must entail the
proposition that some value (furthered by ostensible victory) is preferred to playing "chess." Finally, if the argument is over whether or
not such a move ought to be incorporated into chess, the discussion
will be in terms of the effect of the change on the game. Moreover, if
one wishes the game to have certain consequences (to count in determination of whether one of the players should be afforded the status
of Grand Master), one would have to secure acceptance of the change
through a given legislative structure.

Judges are commonly addressed in law suits with an acceptance of
the formal framework. That is, the parties accept the fact that there
are certain rules defining the office and that, whatever those rules
may be, the judge should obey them. McLean's statement of "can't"
may be viewed in this light. He may be assuming an argument of
type one—the prescription "you ought to look to natural right with
respect to slavery"—is addressed to "You, as a judge, as defined by
rules and principles that we both accept." If the justice is correct in
assuming a type one argument, then his "can't" is a justification of
the strongest kind for denying the force of the moral prescription.
The only issue between the Justice and counsel for the fugitive is an

issue over the content of the law—Is it, or is it not the law that the judge is limited in such a way as to prohibit resort to natural law on this subject?

Because law, including the rules limiting the judicial function, evolves in part through judicial decision, it is also possible that counsel were engaging in a type three argument, stating in effect, that the judge ought to create a new judicial role in which he has the power to resort to natural law. Here, the issue is not what the law is, with respect to the place of natural law, but what it ought to be. Consequently, the appeal to what the law ought to be brings into play a different level of rule-generating rules—those determining whether and how the judge is empowered to create a different role for himself. Argument is not in terms of the rules of limitation themselves, but the principles· and rules governing the creation of such limitations. Nevertheless, at least those generative rules are agreed on as defining the scope of power.

As the last chapter has demonstrated, the judge had a tradition of half a century before him in which the application of a "natural law" in favor of liberty was, indeed, a recognized phenomenon. It was hardly ludicrous to appeal to nature. But that application was in practice narrowly circumscribed, confined to residual and interstitial situations. No single hard and fast rule could differentiate the appropriate from the inappropriate use of the idiom. Thus, an endeavor to procure judicial enlargement of the sphere of natural law was an almost inevitable step for men who recognized the role of judge as lawmaker.

Finally, the argument addressed to McLean might have meant, "You, John McLean, should disregard all rules concerning judicial behavior and free this man regardless of the definition of judicial activity." A "can't" response to this statement is not morally significant as an excuse, but represents disagreement. It may mean simply that McLean does not want to transgress the limits; or that McLean finds the competing value of the ordered formal structure more weighty; or that McLean misunderstands the nature of the argument of counsel. The argument that there are moral reasons to transgress the judicial limits cannot logically be met by simply reasserting the limits themselves. It must be met by justifying those limits in terms of external values.

The Language Analogy *

The comparison of the judicial function to the movement of a piece in a board game has obvious defects. The analogy is most clearly deficient in dealing with the lawmaking powers of a judge: with the conscious process of changing the rules of the game by the piece, subject to the rules, and with the less conscious process of growth of the law through the exercise of discretion over time. While the game analogy may be extended to meet this problem, as it was, by the hypothesis of a piece, subject to rules, which determine how it may itself change the rules governing its movements, that extension by no means solves the problem. First, as an analogy it has the singular defect of being less clear than the reference that it is supposed to illuminate. Pieces of the sort hypothesized would be very unusual—certainly not part of the ordinary game experience. Indeed, if one were explaining such an unusual game to a novice, it would be desirable to analogize the function of this piece to a judge. For the process of judging is, if anything, closer to common experience than the sort of game constructed for the analogy.

If one wishes to illuminate the lawmaking characteristic of the judicial function, recourse to a more accessible comparison is desirable. One might choose to analogize the judge to the speaker or writer of a language—law language. The speaker of a language is subject to rules, though of a different kind. The rules are arrived at primarily by examining the way in which the language has been spoken in the past. They are determined deductively from the practice of the language on the part of persons just like the speaker in question. Breaking a rule does not usually mean that the speaker is no longer speaking the language. It means only that he has made a mistake, or is speaking incorrectly. In the case of a chess player who

---

* The discussion in this section focuses upon two related elements of language: its generative capacity, and the mechanisms by which we consciously or unconsciously participate in the growth process. I concede abysmal ignorance on both scores and admit to having mashed together a bit of Noam Chomsky, primarily the introductory chapter of *Aspects of the Theory of Syntax* (Cambridge, Mass.: M. I. T. Press, 1965), with much more of Michael Polanyi, *Personal Knowledge* (Chicago: University of Chicago Press, 1958). I pretend to have used the latter responsibly. My ignorance of the field of linguistics precludes a similar statement as to Chomsky.

moves his bishop along a rank or file, it is by no means wrong to say
"he is not really playing chess." However, even serious mistakes in
grammar or syntax ordinarily call only for the conclusion that "he is
speaking incorrectly." We recognize a statement of the sort "he is
not really speaking English" to be either hyperbole or a description
of a vast number of mistakes rendering the communication as a whole
unintelligible to other speaker-listeners.

More important, language grows and the rules change as the
speakers of the language do things not covered by the rules or even
against the rules. A great speaker or writer of the language ordinarily
acts according to the rules but knows when and how to ignore them
as well. Often as not, when the articulate user of language consciously departs from the rules, he creates changes in the rules themselves. Since the rules are derived from the speaking and writer of
users of the language, they must reflect protracted good usage.

What determines whether a departure from the rules of language is
simply a "mistake," or ignorance—in short, poor usage—or an example of the process of changing the rule itself? The question admits
of no easy answer. Part of the answer involves the degree to which
the departure becomes normal among a significant portion of the language users. If the departure becomes sufficiently widespread, the
rule may change despite the protestations of the acknowledged masters of the language. Sometimes, however, the change may be
wrought in far less democratic a manner. For the usage of the masters
counts for more than the usage of the masses. A departure may ring a
bell. Readers or listeners may feel, "Hey, that's good!" despite its
character as a departure from a rule. No sure sign marks the departures of this sort. We depend on the judgment both of the enlightened
critic and of the mass of users.

The process of change described above is not only tolerated in language, it is an integral part of the language. A language that does not
grow in this way is a language continually in the process of becoming
obsolete. As Michael Polanyi has written:

> Thus to speak a language is to commit ourselves to the double
> indeterminacy due to our reliance both on its formalism and on
> our own continued reconsideration of this formalism in its bear-
> ing on experience.[11]

So with the judge. There are those who speak law-language poorly—whose departures from the rules will not live; who reflect neither the wave of the future to be washed into prophecy by the acceptance of the masses nor the compelling idiosyncratic departure of the master, which will pull the masses after it. Others—the vast majority—speak according to the rules, for the rules are largely derived from such as these. They depart occasionally, usually inadvertently. Then there are prophets and masters who move the law more than their democratic, *per-capite* share. Either they evoke the response: "This is what we've known or wanted all along, but never before so articulated." Or they strike the chord: "we've rejected or never thought of this before, but your argument compels attention, even conviction."

The process of change is the "reconsideration of the formalism" to which the judge is normally subject. For most departures are, like most departures in language, simply ignorance, mistake, or unsuccessful efforts at eloquence. The formal rule structure normally suffices. When there is a departure from the rules, however, that which determines whether the rules have been changed is not so much another rule determining changes in rules as it is the acceptance of the change by others over time. In this respect the language analogy is far better than the extended game analogy.

If we apply the language analogy to McLean's statements at the beginning of this chapter, his protestations take on a somewhat different hue. One cannot talk "law" that way, he is saying. But such a statement remains ambiguous. At the least, it means that to talk law in such a way defies ordinary usage. It is a departure from the practices and rules. But, the question of whether the departure would be simply bad law—incorrect usage—or eloquence is necessarily left open. To approach the problem with the model of a game is to assume that located somewhere is a rule that will determine whether the unusual exercise of power by the piece to change the rules is itself against the rules. But by analogy to language, the answer is not so simple. A departure from ordinary usage or even from the rules of the language, cannot easily be characterized as a valid change in the language. McLean, as a speaker, exercises judgment, concerning the utility, the elegance, or the symmetry of the proposed change. His judgment is not simply a declaration of the rules, but also a vindication of them. For he tells us that a man who would speak law as proposed would be a poor speaker of the law.

We might sum up the three possible dialectical contexts for McLean's words with their moral significance as follows: (1) The demand to apply natural law may be nothing more than counsel arguing that the content of the appropriate substantive rule of law is "x," where x is the natural law condemnation of slavery. Counsel may be right or wrong. As we have seen in Part One, there were perfectly acceptable spheres for application of "natural law." McLean might be assuming that the argument is that this is one such area. His response that he "cannot" resort to natural justice is intended as a justification of the strongest sort in that he assumes that the attorney shares the formal assumptions of the Justice. (2) McLean may be assuming that a demand is being made that he take the leap of creating a new sphere for natural law by incorporating it where it had not yet been established. His response that he "cannot" is ambiguous. It may presuppose some relatively solid principles and rules concerning "judging" that forbid or militate against such a result, or he may be making a point closer to the realm of aesthetics—that such an act is inelegant. Insofar as McLean feels rule-bounded to avoid such a creation and insofar as he assumes that counsel accepts such rules, the "cannot" is again used as the strong sense of a justification. The point at issue is only whether counsel or McLean are correct as to the content of the rules limiting judicial creativity. But, as we have seen, the process of judicial lawmaking is not easily described as rule-bound. Consequently, it is entirely possible that Justice and counsel are using inconsistent, conflicting standards of elegance in the law language. If that is the case, McLean must justify his standard, not designate his rule. His "cannot," alone, is not significant. (3) Finally, McLean may be addressed as a potential rebel against his role. As I have stated, above, the "cannot" is not a significant response. The formal restraints are under challenge and cannot be justified by mere reiteration.

It is true, however, that McLean did not simply respond "I cannot." He offered a somewhat enigmatic justification. To violate the role strictures is to destroy the "social compact." In the next four chapters I shall examine first the conventional judicial notions of the limits on the judge's role; second, the various antislavery positions on the nature of the judicial role. I shall then examine the interaction of movement advocacy and judicial decision in the crucible of fugitive slave litigation. Finally, I shall return to a consideration of the justifications for adherence to formal constraints on the judge in the context of fugitive slave laws.

CHAPTER EIGHT: Formal Assumptions of the Judiciary

So far I have spoken of the formal limits on the judicial role abstractly. It is time to specify. The antebellum judge's concept of his role was largely determined by three phenomena external to the slavery question: "constitutionalism" and judicial review, codification's challenge to the common law, and the selection and tenure of judges controversy. These three battles were different dimensions of a single, more general problem: the tension between independence and accountability of the undemocratic branch of representative government. The problem of selection and tenure of judges put the issue directly. Should the judge be accountable to the people directly through popular elections; indirectly through election by state legislatures? Should the role be completely insulated through a tenure of "good behavior," or should there be a term of years? [1] But the selection and tenure issue could not have arisen without recognition of the lawmaking input of the judiciary. There was impetus to subject the judiciary to democratic processes because the creative side of the judge had come to be appreciated more than ever before. That appreciation included the common law function (evolution of doctrine through case-by-case adjudication) and the interpretive function—the creation of doctrine through application of an instrument to particular facts.[2]

While the mere fact of recognition of judicial lawmaking gave rise to pressure to democratize the judge, the methods of and occasions for judicial lawmaking produced more specific critiques. Common law jurisprudence was under attack for a variety of reasons. A Benthamite approach contended that the common law process provided no check upon the idiosyncratic judicial will and only chaotic, unsystematic guidance for the good faith judge. American nationalists contended further that insofar as the common law tradition did provide guidance, it was based on the archaic, undemocratic, monarchic principles of the English judiciary. Codification and legislation were preferred systems because they were more systematic and precise, but also because they put law-generating initiative and authority where they belonged, with the democratically elected legislature.[3]

The power of judicial review was under attack in part for analogous reasons. The generalities of constitutions provide little enough strict guidance for the judge. More important, the assertion of judicial review implied not only judicial lawmaking without legislative control (as does common law jurisprudence), but even judicial supremacy over the legislative branch.

To all of these attacks, the defenders of judicial faith presented a relatively coherent picture of the judge's role. Interpretation and case-by-case lawmaking was both inevitable and desirable, they asserted: inevitable because no instrument or group of instruments could be sufficiently detailed or complex to adequately mirror all future reality; desirable because growth required the flexibility that only case-by-case adjudication could provide. The dangers of nonresponsible lawmaking were conceded, but role principles were asserted as providing guidance and limits for the good faith judge. The principal limiting factor is the abnegation of all sovereign qualities. A sovereign power, in nineteenth-century terms (whether delegated or not; whether limited or not) was the power to enact one's will (personal or collective) into law. While the judiciary conceded that law grew through their work, they never conceded that it grew because of the application of their own will. Responsible fulfillment of the role meant application of the will of others. Not that this application was always easy. Indeed, the sovereign will was often hypothetical or imagined. However, in no event was it proper to substitute the personal will of the judge.

Constitutionalism—Supreme Law and Supreme Court

Despite the vigor of the battle over ratification of the Constitution, by the turn of the century the anti-Federalist position had all but disappeared from respectable legal writing. The leading Jeffersonian jurists were no more opponents to the growing sanctity of the Constitution than were their Federalist opponents. For most Americans, and, certainly for the legal profession, the Constitution was supreme law but had a moral authority beyond its supremacy as positive law. This moral authority arose both from the supposed origins of the Constitution and from its utility. For many, the Constitution embodied, or was the concrete manifestation of, the first "real" social contract in the history of mankind.[4] While British philosophy had, by the time of the American Revolution, decidedly rejected the doctrine of the social compact as the origin of the state, Americans were not convinced. Blackstone had denied the historic reality of a state of nature and, consequently, considered the social contract as nothing more than a metaphor to express the interdependence of men and their helplessness apart from society.* St. George Tucker, with some condescension, acknowledged that Blackstone's doctrine was probably correct when it was written:

> But the American Revolution has formed a new epoch in the history of civil institutions, by reducing to practice, what, before, had been supposed to exist only in the visionary speculations of theoretical writers. . . . The world, for the first time since the annals of its inhabitants began, saw an original written compact formed by the free and deliberate voices of individuals disposed to unite in the same social bonds. . . .[5]

Tucker's enthusiastic vision of the Constitution as the social contract brought to life was by no means universally shared by antebellum commentators. Nevertheless, it was a common enough way of approaching the Constitution to require even its most fervent opponents to devote a great deal of effort to refuting it.†

The moral power of the compact vision of the Constitution is derived from the integrated notions of voluntariness, promise, and

---

* 1. *Blackstone* 47: "But, though society had not its formal beginning from any convention of individuals, actuated by their wants and their fears; yet it is the *sense* of their weakness and imperfection that *keeps* mankind together. . . . And this is what we mean by the original contract of society; which, though perhaps in no instance has ever been formally expressed at the first institution of a state. . . ." Bentham was furious at even the limited recognition that Blackstone was willing to afford the idea of a social contract, accusing him of ignorance of the basic refutation that Hume had made of the idea. See Jeremy Bentham, *Fragment on Government,* 2nd ed. (London, 1823), Chap. 1, Part 36.

† Joseph Story was easily the most persuasive and fervent of the commentators opposed to the compact theory. See his chapter entitled "Nature of the Constitution—Whether a Compact," in Story, *Commentaries on the Constitution,* 3rd ed. (Boston: Little, Brown & Co., 1858), Book 3, Chap. 3. There, he states Tucker's characterization at length (vol. 1, pp. 206–12) and refutes it. His most telling point is that the notion of contract, which provides such a nice flavor of consent to be bound by the processes of the state, is precisely in the particular of consent wholly false to the historic reality. Story argues that the opponents of the Constitution never consented to be bound, and many of them never would have consented to abide by the results of the Constitution-making had anybody asked them. The critical point is that nobody should believe that authority in any way depends on consent. See § 327–30.

mutuality. One of the best reasons for adherence to rules is that they have been agreed on without coercion and that men have come to mutually depend on that agreement.[6] Tucker saw only one essential difficulty with this vision of the Constitution. He recognized that it was a document designed to govern posterity—men who had no part in the agreement. Borrowing from Paine and Locke, Tucker solved the dilemma by erecting a structure of constructive consent through the twin elements of a fair and available process for amendment and the failure so to act.[7]

Even Story, the strongest of the opponents to a compact theory of the Constitution, recognized that moral power for the Constitution was derived from its character as a system of mutual promises freely entered into. He was primarily concerned with demonstrating that the character of the Constitution as supreme law did not depend on whatever happy coincidence there might have been of these elements in the origin. Story was more thorough than Tucker in pointing out the historic evidence contradicting the vision of a free acquiescence by the "people": a very limited social base from which the ratifiers were drawn and the very small percentage of the total population that had in fact voted affirmatively with respect to the Constitution.[8] But, for Story, whatever its origins, the Constitution was acknowledged as a superlative system that could stand on its own merits. It was "the only solid basis, on which to rest the private rights, the public liberties and the substantial prosperity of the people composing the American Republic." [9]

Whether its force were traced to utility or consent, the Constitution was supreme law. Story's eagerness to destroy the social compact theory of the Constitution stemmed from no impulse to debunk a myth. Rather, he was concerned lest the contractual theory of origins give rise to a contractual approach to breach. Such an approach would make continued obedience dependent on satisfactory performance of the whole series of interrelated material conditions of the system of government. For Story such a tendency was wholly unsatisfactory, as it made the "supreme law" too conditional.

Starting with *Marbury v. Madison* in 1803,[10] the power of judicial review was also justified by virtue of the supremacy of the Constitution as a source of law. Because a written Constitution forms "the fundamental and paramount law of the nation," Marshall wrote, "an act of the legislature repugnant to the Constitution is void.'' The Constitution, therefore, requires judicial review. For

> those . . . who controvert the principle that the Constitution is to be considered, in court, as paramount law, are reduced to the necessity of maintaining that courts must close their eyes on the Constitution.[11]

But that conclusion is unacceptable because ''courts, as well as other departments, are bound by the instrument.'' *Marbury* thus becomes a superior example of the institutional elevation of the judiciary by virtue of the theoretical subordination of the judge to ''law''—in this instance, the Constitution.

The Jeffersonians understood this model of constitutionalism. But they also understood that one can never wholly distinguish the dancer from the dance. The act of construction must be performed by judges ''as honest as other men, and not more so. They have, with others, the same passions for party, for power, and the privilege of their corps.'' [12] Marshall, of course, could hardly dispute the personal input of the construing judge. Indeed, in *Cohens v. Virginia,* the Chief Justice's argument for the appellate power of the Supreme Court over state court decisions rested in large part on recognition of the power of construction.[13] The only alternative to a single ultimate authority for constitutional construction would be ''that the Constitution, laws, and treaties may receive as many constructions as there are states. . . .'' [14] This was obviously unthinkable to Marshall. And, even in *Marbury,* where Marshall sometimes appears to take a disingenuous approach to construction as if the contradiction of texts were self-evident, there is yet a passage that reads: ''Those who apply the rule to particular cases, must of necessity expound and interpret that rule.'' [15]

The defense of the power of construction and interpretation of constitutional provisions necessitated refutation of the proposition that judges were unconstrained in their work: that whim, caprice, party or passion were operative. This refutation proceeded by affirming canons and principles of interpretation and construction to which judges must adhere, by divorcing those canons as much as possible from the ''will'' of the judge, and by tying them to the ''will'' of others or to purely impersonal considerations. Thus, the judge may be the final instrument of construction, but it is not his personal "will" that ever governs. There is, then, a simultaneous acknowledgment of the potential vagaries and varieties of constitutional construction—indeed that very potential justifies the supreme arbitral authority of the Supreme Court—and an attempt to divorce the construction process from the independent will of the construer.

In his great treatise on the Constitution, Story laments the perversion of rules of interpretation to "the passions and prejudices of the day, or the favor and odium of a particular measure," and declares his purpose to be the search for "true rules of interpretation . . . so that we may have some fixed standard by which to measure its powers and limit its prohibitions. . . ." [16] No fair assessment of the chapter on interpretation in the *Commentaries* could conclude that Story was successful in his search for more or less judge-proof neutral principles. But the first two of his principles show the attempt to extract the will of the construer from the construction:

> The first and fundamental rule in the interpretation of all instruments is, to construe them according to the sense of the terms and the intention of the parties. [17]

Story is aware of the complexities of constitutional "intent," and in a later section states "that contemporary interpretation must be resorted to with much qualification and reserve." But "in proportion to the uniformity and universality of that construction," the intention and interpretation of contemporaries is persuasive. [18] Ultimately, however, "the safest rule of interpretation" is "to look to the nature and objects of the particular powers, duties and rights . . . and to give to the words of each just such operation and force, consistent with their legitimate meaning, as may fairly secure and attain the ends proposed." [19] The latter half of the chapter trails off into a polemic against the Jeffersonian-Jacksonian doctrine of strict construction. But Story's lapse should not obscure his objective.

The problem of the institutionally unchecked power of construction of the Constitution by the Supreme Court, inherent in judicial review, was not satisfactorily resolved by asserting the Court's subordination to the "instrument" itself. Nor was it resolved by asserting canons of construction that denied the autonomous will of the construer any place in the process. But the ultimate authority of the Supreme Court, while an institutional problem on its own, helped resolve the more general dilemma of idiosyncratic judicial caprice in the lawmaking process. The supremacy of a single tribunal meant "uniformity in the interpretation and operation of those powers and of the laws enacted in pursuance of them." [20] A large measure of certainty is achieved by the appellate jurisdiction of the Supreme Court and by the *stare decisis* effect of its prior rulings.

It remained for Francis Lieber, a German immigrant of catholic intellect and interests, to write the definitive defense of interpretation and construction.* Lieber's thought was a synthesis of the political ideology of American Whiggery. Much of what is most interesting in his work is simply a reworking of the legal-constitutional ideas of Story, of Kent, and through them, of Marshall. In *Main Currents in American Thought,* Parrington went so far as to credit Lieber with marking the beginning of a swing from the ideology of natural rights toward the "engrossing political state." [21] While such a characterization is an absurd exaggeration, it is indeed true that Lieber was preoccupied with the embodiment of political thought in institutional forms. He was no innovator; the ideas were present in the constitutional theory of the Federalists (characteristically slighted by Parrington). However, as an immigrant, Lieber realized, valued, and expressed what was institutionally distinct and conservative in America. He was concerned with the fragility of libertarian institutions. His experiences in the Greek war of liberation and in prison in his native Germany did not radicalize him but made him a conservative watchdog of what he considered the distinctively American "liberal" tradition. In his writings on political theory, Lieber turned to the Ameri-

---

* Francis Lieber's career was a remarkable one. He arrived in America in 1826, after a political and intellectual odyssey in Europe. He embraced the ideology of Kent and Story. The *Encyclopedia Americana* was his work. He authored three original works of note: *Civil Liberty and Self-Government,* 2 vols. (Philadelphia: Lippincott, Grambo and Co., 1853); *Manual of Political Ethics* (Boston: C. C. Little and J. Brown, 1838–39); *Legal and Political Hermeneutics* (Boston: C. C. Little and J. Brown, 1839). For further details of Lieber's life and work, see Lewis R. Harley, *Francis Lieber: His Life and Political Philosophy* (New York: Columbia University Press, 1899); Chester S. Phinney, *Francis Lieber's Influence on American Thought* (Philadelphia: International Printing Co., 1918); Frank Freidel, *Francis Lieber, Nineteenth Century Liberal* (Gloucester, Mass.: P. Smith, 1968).

can bench for inspiration. He dedicated one of his books to Kent, another to Story. In editing the first *Encyclopedia Americana,* Lieber leaned heavily on Story for articles on legal subjects.[22]

Most of Lieber's personal intellectual product was broad political theory: the *Manual of Political Ethics* and *Civil Liberty and Self Government.* Given his predilection for the legal perspective, it is not surprising, however, that he would also turn his mind to a consideration of the implications of technical legal tasks. In 1839 he published a small book, *Legal and Political Hermeneutics,* which was the first American work devoted to the study of interpretation and construction of instruments. The book was well received by Story, Kent, and Choate—the sort of men from whom it drew its inspiration.[23]

Lieber related that one of the first articles he read upon reaching America in 1827 was a Jacksonian polemic against the principles of construction of the Adams administration. He declared himself intrigued by the fact that canons of construction served "as a distinction of political men and measures" and thought this a peculiarly American phenomenon.[24] I am inclined to view the *Hermeneutics,* the result of Lieber's inquiry, as the most coherent single exposition of the legal establishment's view of the interpretive process to be found in the antebellum period. It is a synthetic work and does not in any important respects contradict the more random and incomplete statements of Kent, Story, Duer, or Rawles in their respective works.[25]

Lieber first distinguished interpretation—"finding out the true sense of any form of words; that is, the sense which their author intended to convey"—from construction—"the drawing of conclusions respecting subjects, that lie beyond the direct expression of the text, from elements known from and given in the text." Lieber considered both interpretation and construction inevitable processes. Interpretation was inevitable because language is not mathematically precise. Ambiguity and imprecision are unavoidable. Even if words are "distinct as to the central point they cover, [they] become less so the further we remove from that centre." Construction is inevitable because no text, even assuming precision, can foresee and provide for all future eventuality. The lack of prescience would doom even the hypothetically perfectly precise text to the fate of construction as the future outruns the ambit of its clarity.[26]

Construction is the more "dangerous" of the two processes because its purpose is "to arrive at conclusions beyond the absolute sense of the text." But it is no less unavoidable for all its danger. As a result, "we must strive the more anxiously to find out safe rules, to guide us on the dangerous path." Lieber's safe rules of construction, especially as applied to constitutions, turn out to be nothing less than a political philosophy. He is totally unsuccessful in resolving the dilemma of judicial lawmaking by precise rules for the manipulation of texts.

In constitutional construction, Lieber asserts, we start with good faith, common sense, a determination not to let great matters hinge upon trifling accidents of "casual position of a word." But, if the Constitution "contains only the great principles and general outlines of the state, faithless interpretation has free play." The only solution is to recognize that it is not the text that "makes liberty," but a free people's handling of it. The great principle *salus populi suprema lex* must be grudgingly accepted. But the people's welfare is to be properly understood as encompassing their liberties as well as their material benefit.[27]

There are two checks on the construing judge. The first is internal:

> We must guard ourselves against mistaking our private views and interests, our passions and appetites, for public wishes and demands; in short, against confounding our individuality with public welfare.[28]

The second rule is that of preference for consistency. Security, peace, stability, and certainty of legal and political rights depend on a level of reasoned generality that is susceptible to repeated and consistent usage. For these reasons, "rules which relate to precedent demand particular attention in the construction of constitutions." "Unsteady construction," such as that prevailing in post-Napoleonic France, means that every important matter can only be debated on "the very first principles of government which lie beyond the constitution, we would almost say, to political metaphysics." [29] Lieber's rules of construction, then, are not so much rules as a state of mind. The abnegation of the construer's personal preferences is an important part of the mental state; so, at the same time, is his own view of the public weal and the scope of liberty. However, that political philosophy should be mitigated with time, as precedent and consistency loom larger as result-determining factors. There may be reasons, growing out of necessity for the moment, for departing from adherence to precedent, but Lieber warned, most strongly, of the direful consequences of too casual a recourse to such departures.

Common Law and Codes

The battle over constitutional construction and judicial review was closely paralleled in the controversy over codification. Both were reactions to judicial lawmaking in a democratic state. However, until the second decade of the nineteenth century, the "common law," though not immune from attack, was subjected to scrutiny for very different reasons. Some critics were hostile to the continued intellectual dependence on Great Britain, which a common law jurisprudence implied.[30] And a battle royal had already emerged on the issue of federal court jurisdiction over common law crimes.[31] The common law character of the federal court was an issue, however, not so much out of hostility to judicial lawmaking as out of hostility to aggrandizement of the national government at the expense of the states.[32] Although they did not focus on the issue of judge-made law, these two early disputes demonstrated at least implicit recognition of two difficulties in common law jurisprudence.

A common law system is dependent on the inherited corpus of past decisions by judges. It is a viable system only insofar as the traditions, circumstances, and principles of those prior decisions are adequately variegated; sufficiently analogous to current problems; and founded upon a tradition of common fundamental values. Without a broad spectrum of past decisions, rules and legal concepts are not well-defined on the anvil of specific circumstances. For principles emerge only through their repeated application, or if broadly stated from the outset, become limited through such application. In early nineteenth-century America, without reference to the British corpus, the richness of experience desirable for common law jurisprudence would be lacking. But resort to the English decisions meant potential adoption of rules and principles from highly suspect Englishmen and an admission of national inadequacy. The very attack on the "Englishness" of the common law implied a recognition of the past's hold on present common law judging.

The controversy over federal court application of common law jurisprudence implied recognition of the other important common law input: the deciding judge. The Jeffersonians attacked common law jurisdiction in the federal courts not only because of the Alien and Sedition Acts, but more importantly because they understood that common law jurisdiction is a form of legislative power: that there is no principled distinction between common law jurisdiction for the national courts and legislative power for the national Congress. Both Congress and the common law judge are lawmaking agencies, and the basic distinction between them is the occasions and processes of their lawmaking. Without full recognition of the judge as lawmaker, the Jeffersonian would not have so thoroughly opposed federal common law jurisprudence.

By the 1820's the common law was under attack directly both for its slavish adherence to precedent and for its broad judicial powers.[33] William Sampson campaigned vigorously for codification. Only a code could insure: "The law will govern the decisions of judges, and not the decisions the law." [34] But Sampson was even more concerned that common law meant dependence on the past. Admitting that there is much of good in those old decisions, Sampson attacked the doctrine that that which is valuable stands on any other ground than its intrinsic worth. The present must choose the content of its law, not inherit it. Moreover, if the job of weeding out the evil from the good and eventually reforming the law is left to judges, it will happen incoherently and take centuries, while if done by digesting the good and enacting it by legislative authority, the present generation will enjoy the fruits of the endeavor.[35]

Sampson's works were reprinted and his doctrines echoed by Livingston in Louisiana, by Grimké in South Carolina, by Field some years later in New York, by Rantoul in Massachusetts.[36] Rantoul and Grimké began to emphasize somewhat more the issue of the nondemocratic character of judicial lawmaking. They stressed that common law jurisprudence put the future of the law at the mercy of the caprice, whim, class, and party passions of the men who sit on the bench.* The 1830's saw attacks of this sort mount in frequency with less attention paid to the inherent undesirability and chaotic organization of the common law.

The common law did not go undefended. Story, Kent, DuPonceau, and Lieber were its greatest champions, though they were all qualified critics, as well, conceding much for both tactical and ideological reasons to the attackers. The defenders' first concern was to rebut the assertion that the common law was dominated by the dead hand of the past. When Joseph Story spoke to the Boston bar in 1821, he praised the achievement of the legal profession in America since the Revolution.[37] He placed the law of the United States in the grand tradition of common law growth exemplified by the work of Holt, and most important, Mansfield. The achievement of the common law could be summed up as a progressive one, involving not the conservation of old rules, but the discovery and creation of new. He praised Mansfield as a great judge for his innovative work in commercial law.[38]

Story's emphasis in sketching the history of common law judgeship is reinforced by the prevailing American doctrine of precedent that became canonized and was justified by Kent and Lieber. Precedent did not itself constitute the common law, Kent wrote, but was only evidence of what the common law is.[39] The distinction is important, for it justified selectivity in the holding to the past.

The values of consistency and certainty are, of course, recognized. Lieber quotes Montesquieu: "it is with a trembling hand that we ought to change law." Some adherence to precedence is necessary, therefore, so that the law may "approximate certainty in cases of doubt." Nevertheless, slavish adherence to precedent is condemned:

---

* Consider the following extracts from Rantoul's "Oration at Scituate," reprinted in Luther Hamilton, ed., *Memoires, Speeches and Writings of Robert Rantoul* (Boston: J. P. Jewett & Co., 1854), pp. 278–79:

"It is because judge-made law is indefinitely and vaguely settled . . . that it possesses the capacity of adapting itself to new cases, or, in other words, admits of *judicial legislation*" [italics in original].

"The law *should be* a positive and unbending text, otherwise the judge has an arbitrary power, or *discretion:* and the discretion of a good man is often nothing better than caprice, as Lord Camden has very justly remarked, while the discretion of a bad man is an odious and irresponsible tyranny. . . ." "Judge-made law is special legislation. The judge is human, and feels the binds which the coloring of the particular case gives."

If we should consider all future cases of a similar nature as prejudged by our [past] decision, stagnation would be the consequence, instead of an expansion and development of the law.[40]

The rejection of the ultimate authority of precedent was necessary if the defenders of the common law faith were to hold off the attacks of Sampson and the codifiers. However, by the end of the 1820's this very emphasis on the absence of rigid guide lines opened the common law to the more dangerous criticism that judges were wholly unrestrained. Kent insisted that this was not the case. The common law, of which precedent was evidence, and which included the practices and maxims by which precedent is either followed or discarded, is itself the limitation on the judge. Without the common law, Kent wrote, "the courts would be left to a dangerous discretion to roam at large in the trackless field of their own imagination." [41] Lieber went into somewhat greater detail as to the ways in which precedent and principles differed from a "trackless field of . . . imagination." In the first place, precedent had a "natural" power of its own. As a form of reasoned consistency, it has an attraction that is universal. Second, even the doctrine of precedent, which embraces change, requires a reason for departure from the old rule. And the necessity of giving a reason permits an analysis of the "soundness" of prior judicial decisions. Thus, there is a basis for distinguishing or denying as well as following precedent. Adherence to precedent even has a "moral" dimension:

By citing a precedent, we at once become followers. . . . our responsibility, therefore, seems to be divided, or at any rate it is shared by someone else. . . . On doubtful points of high importance . . . we may be a precedent, leave the high seas of theory, and cast anchor in the solid ground of practical life.[42]

The common law process, however, was much more than the past body of doctrine. And ultimately, its adherents stressed its generative qualities. Joseph Story chaired a commission of five jurists to report to the Massachusetts legislature on the "practicability and expediency of reducing to a written and systematic code. the Common Law of Massachusetts." [43] Story drew a line between process and doctrine. The commissioners were eager to have order brought to a hodge-

podge of cases. The doctrines of past cases could be digested, codi-
fied, and reused with good effect especially in commercial, criminal,
and adjective law. In that sense the report strongly favored codification. But Story forcibly rejected the possibility or desirability of a
code so all-encompassing that it could be the primary basis for future
adjudications. The flexible case by case approach to new problems
and transactions, to "modifications, limitations and enlargements of
old rules and doctrines," must be left to the judiciary:

> It seems to them [the Commissioners] that private convenience
> as well as public policy requires, that the common law should be
> left in its prospective operations in future . . . to be improved,
> and expanded, and modified, to meet the exigencies of society
> by the gradual application of its principles in courts of justice to
> new cases. . . .[44]

The conclusion of the commissioners was hardly a victory for the
codification forces. It was a concession, indeed, as to the desirability
for greater system and order. Story compared the object of the code
to that of a treatise, like Fearne's *Perpetuities.* And Story's own treatises did much to render the code of his vision less necessary. But on
the nub of the codification controversy for the Jacksonians the answer
of the commission was a resounding NO! The place of the judge as
the primary mover of the law, as the organ for the modernization and
reform of doctrine, was defended. The code would be simply a
cleanup operation that would help him do his work efficiently.

Judicial Independence

Joseph Story's homage to common law creativity in his 1821 address
apportioned a great part of the credit for this process to the Settlement
Act of 1701, by which the tenure of English judges was changed
from "the King's pleasure" to "good behavior." * A vigorous judi-

---

* Joseph Story, "Address to the Suffolk County Bar," 1 *American Jurist* 10 (1821). The literature on the independence of the judiciary is so vast as to render even a limited bibliography
difficult. The *Federalist,* No. 78, is as good a place to start as any. The movement to more limited tenure and more "political" selection processes has not been adequately explained. A fair
chronology is provided by Evan Haynes, *The Selection and Tenure of Judges* (Newark: National Conference of Judicial Councils, 1944). Haynes, Aumann, Friedman, Hurst, Miller, and
Boudin share a common, conventional wisdom on this movement. See note 1 to this chapter. It

ciary required independence, and the independence of the federal judiciary was almost universally acknowledged as desirable in the ratification controversies. Many spoke against the scope of the federal judicial power, but few against the judges' tenure.[45]

Yet, starting with the attempt to impeach Chase (or, perhaps, starting with Adams's twelfth-hour appointments), the tenure of the judiciary came to be an important political issue in America. Jefferson called for reconsideration of life tenure.[46] Moreover, after the Supreme Court's holdings in *Sturgis v. Crowninshield, McCulloch v. Maryland,* and *Cohens v. Virginia* the problem of judicial tenure became more forcibly associated with democratic control over lawmaking.[47] After 1820 a number of states began to experiment with a judicial tenure of a term of years. Mississippi even provided for popular election of judges in 1821, but that great step was not followed by another state until New York took the leap in 1846.[48] The attack on judicial tenure has often been characterized as a part of "Jacksonian democracy." Louis Boudin has gone so far as to see it as the wellspring of Jacksonian democracy.[49]

However, the attack on the life tenure of the judiciary was not simply a random offshoot of a larger democratic impulse. It proceeded from a very realistic and, often, cautious appraisal of the judge's role in American society. The most thoughtful of the attackers of judicial independence was Frederick Grimké. Grimké's great work, *The Nature and Tendency of Free Institutions,* was not a rallying point.[50] It did not precipitate change, but gave intellectual coherence and respectability to movement that had almost run its course.

Grimké conceded that independence for the American judiciary had not been as harmful as it might have been. He attributed this to two checks on the judge's will. The first was the law's character as

---

is attributed to "Jacksonian Democracy" and to resentment of the undemocratic lawmakers, the judges. A more sophisticated history of this phenomenon must be written and must be grounded more closely in the specifics of particular states and times. The fact that in all the histories of this phenomenon mentioned above there is but a single sentence—a casual remark of Miller— that attests the ties between the movement for a more "responsible" judiciary and antislavery, suggests that further explorations of particular issues and states will yield still more data on the complexity of the movement. My narrative will treat a couple of instances of interrelation of antislavery and judicial independence at some length.

A starting point for exploring my hunch as to the significance of unmined data for the movement against the independent judiciary would be a monograph on the roots of the New York constitution of 1846 and its changes with respect to the judiciary.

"an intellectual pursuit." The judge confronted both a tradition and an expectation of rationality in the "application of . . . morality to . . . life." This experience has a decidedly "favorable influence" on the judge, himself, even though "the investigation of legal questions may not contribute to open and invigorate the understanding so much as some others of the mental occupations." [51] The second check is the "system of judicial precedents." While this check is not absolute, it "prevents any marked or habitual dereliction of duty." This check is not simply a doctrinal one but also has a sociological side as: "The profession are apt to be keenly attentive to both the motives and the reasons of the bench when it undertakes to overthrow a decision which has grown to be a principle." [52]

Despite these checks, Grimké thought a limited tenure desirable because of the "character and functions of a court of justice" in mid-nineteenth-century America. He realized that the justification for independence rested on a characterization of the judicial task as one of "applying," "expounding," or "declaring" law in the most neutral manner as between two parties. Grimké presented the familiar arguments of the defenders of the common law, themselves, that new realities were constantly overtaking the legislative process, so that a measure of creation through application was inevitable. He would not blame the judiciary for this lawmaking, nor attempt to obviate it through a code or a prohibition. Instead, he argued, the quasilegislative aspect of the judge's role necessitates the possibility of recurrent appraisal of the direction and quality of his work. [53]

Grimké's book was published only a year after New York embarked on its "experiment" in a popularly elected judiciary. Grimké was hopeful but not Pollyanna-like about this new development. For Grimké never forgot that the court was only quasilegislative. He was fully aware of the need for professional skill and respect in a judge and well aware that the popular election could distort the choice process. He was hopeful, however, that the people of New York would "persevere in the immense exertions which they have hitherto made to educate themselves." With such perseverance, the author concluded, "I cannot doubt that the experiment will succeed." [54]

The rallying cry of the faithful to judicial independence was that independence from other men is the best guarantor of total and scrupulous servitude to the law. Francis Lieber, as we have seen, was by no means unaware of the complexity and importance of interpretation and construction. Yet he could assert that, precisely because of the area of ambiguity or uncertainty in application, independence was necessary:

> Those who fix and link the generality of the law to the individual case, ought to be placed in the best possible manner which human wisdom can devise for the unbiased application of the abstract rule to the practical instance.[55]

Lieber went on to link the institutional independence of the judge to his sense of impersonality in his work. He should have no doubt that his "moral weight" is impaired by mixing in the "excitement" that goes into lawmaking:

> His moral weight . . . is derived . . . from the fact that he can say, "Not I, directly or indirectly . . . but the law, which is given to me and is my master says thus." [56]

Self-Abnegation

The inclination to conceive of the judicial role as one of will-less, self-abnegating application of law was not, then, a product of a naive distinction between *ius dicere* and *ius dare*. It was the result neither of a failure to appreciate the creative input of the judiciary, nor of a failure to understand the limitless bounds of discretion and of its exercise. Rather, the self-abnegation was the very product of the realization that judicial input was inevitable, substantial, and controversial. If the rhetoric of impersonality served as a response to critics of the judiciary, it also operated, among serious and conscientious men, as a limit upon self. For the attacks on judicial review, on common law jurisprudence, and on judicial independence were not only threats from outside the law's inner sanctum, but were also articulations of a lag in descriptive jurisprudence. The judge knew he made law, he knew that neither instruments nor precedents constrained him absolutely, and by 1820, if not earlier, he had come to articulate this in his admiration for the creative common law process.[57] Yet he felt, and rightly so, that he was more constrained than free; that he made law differently than did legislators, and that the difference was a qualitative one. The denial of the judicial *will* as a legitimate basis for lawmaking was the device for expressing this complex of limits. As Horace Binney proclaimed in his eulogy for William Tilghman,

> His first inquiry in every case was of the oracles of the law for their response; and when he obtained it, notwithstanding his clear perception of the justice of the cause, and his intense desire to reach it, if it were not the justice of the law, he dare not to administer it.[58]

This act of transcending "will" despite—indeed, because of—the absence of constraint has been well articulated by Michael Polanyi:

> While compulsion by force or by neurotic obsession excludes responsibility, compulsion by universal intent [to exclude subjectivity] establishes responsibility. The strain of this responsibility is the greater—other things being equal—the wider the range of alternatives left open to choice and the more conscientious the person responsible for the decision. While the choices in question are open to arbitrary egocentric decisions, a craving for the universal sustains a constructive effort and narrows down this discretion to the point where the agent making the decision finds that he cannot do otherwise. *The freedom of the subjective person to do as he pleases is overruled by the freedom of the responsible person to act as he must* [italics in original].[59]

CHAPTER NINE: Formal Assumptions of the Antislavery Forces

After 1840 a significant part of all antislavery writing was devoted to analysis of the legal system of the United States and to its bearing on problems of slavery.* There were lawyers of note among the abolitionists, and the works of William Jay, James Birney, Charles Sumner, Salmon Chase, Robert Rantoul, or Richard Dana bear witness to the professional skill with which arguments were shaped.[1] However, the story of abolitionist legal theory by no means stops in the courtroom or with the speculations of established lawyers. Richard Hildreth's book *Despotism in America*, Harriet Beecher Stowe's *Key to Uncle Tom's Cabin*, Thoreau's essays "Civil Disobedience," and "Slavery in Massachusetts," Frederick Douglass' "Speech on the Meaning of the Fourth of July for the Negro," Theodore Weld's *Slavery as it Is* and *The Power of Congress over the District of Columbia*, to mention but a few, bespeak the pervasive concerns of the leaders of the antislavery movement with the legal structures of slavery.

* The legal literature of antislavery is of several sorts. One category, not discussed here in any detail, is that of descriptions of slave codes and their administration. The purpose of these works was to use slave law as data, credible data, as to the realities of slavery. The first, and in many ways the best, of these works was George Stroud, *A Sketch of the Laws Relating to Slavery*, first published in 1827 (Philadelphia: Kimber and Sharpless) and reissued in 1856 (Philadelphia: H. Longstreth). The best known of this category of work was William Goodell, *The American Slave Code in Theory and Practise* (New York: American and Foreign Antislavery Society, 1853). Two works that did not concern themselves exclusively with the law of slavery, have long sections using legal materials as data for depicting slavery. Theodore Dwight Weld, *American Slavery As It Is* (New York: American Antislavery Society, 1839), a powerful and very influential work, and Harriet Beecher Stowe, *The Key to Uncle Tom's Cabin* (Boston: J. P. Jewett, 1853), an attempt to document the general picture of slavery in the novel published the year before. A second category of antislavery legal work was that of legal arguments on relatively circumscribed issues. These position papers or briefs abound, and range in size, from newspaper columns to books. A few notable examples are: Theodore Dwight Weld, *The Powers of Congress Over Slavery in the District of Columbia* (New York: American Antislavery Society, 1838); [William Jay], *The Creole Case and Mr. Webster's Despatch* (New York: New York American, 1842); Samuel May, *The Fugitive Slave Law and Its Victims* (New York: American Antislavery Society, 1856); American Antislavery Society, *Fugitive Slave Bill, Its History and Unconstitutionality* (New York: W. Harned, 1850). This last is but one of a number of pamphlets discussing the Fugitive Slave Act with regard to a particular case, in this instance that of James Hamlet. See also Robert Rantoul, "The Fugitive Slave Law," in Luther

Antislavery was never a unified movement. It is no wonder therefore to find a sharp split among different factions of the movement over an issue of such pervasive concern. In its approach to law, the antislavery movement split primarily because of differences over the sorts of formal problems that have been discussed hitherto in their relation to the legal establishment. The split was between the Garrisonians and a variety of opponents. On the one hand, the Garrisonians steadfastly preached and advocated scrupulous respect for the formalism of the legal system, and understood that formalism largely in the same terms as the leading judges and lawyers of the day. Their opponents, on the other hand, either urged disregard for the formalism of the law or advocated an unorthodox understanding of the nature of the law's formalism. These generalities must be spelled out in detail.[2]

The Garrisonians: Formalism Conceded

The Garrisonians, with Wendell Phillips their chief spokesman, stressed the dichotomy between natural and positive law. They ac-

Hamilton, ed., *Memoires, Speeches, and Writings of Robert Rantoul* (Boston: J. P. Jewett & Co., 1854). A third category of works on legal issues is the "Constitution and slavery" problem. This literature is discussed below.

A fourth category, often connected to the third, is the literature on legal obligation and civil disobedience. I have discussed in the text only certain examples of that literature that (a) treat the issue of obligations of magistrates or jurors; (b) were reasonably widely read. Notable examples of works on disobedience that fail to meet the first condition are Henry David Thoreau, "Essay on Civil Disobedience" and "Slavery in Massachusetts," both in *Thoreau's Complete Works* (Boston and New York: Houghton, Mifflin, 1929). There was also a rich harvest of sermons on obedience and disobedience, many of which are discussed or noted in Stanley Campbell, *The Slave Catchers* (Chapel Hill: University of North Carolina Press, 1970), in his discussions of public opinion. Relatively neglected have been the academic, philosophical religious works on obligations by such notables as Francis Wayland. See Edward Madden, *Civil Disobedience and Moral Law in Nineteenth Century American Philosophy* (Seattle: University of Washington Press, 1968), for an account of these men and their works.

Still another category was that of diatribes against legal institutions or judges for their evil, class-ridden oppression of the downtrodden. These works might use any of the sorts of arguments found in other categories as grist for their mill. Richard Hildreth is my favorite of these authors. Richard Hildreth, *Despotism in America* (Boston: J. P. Jewett & Co., 1854), and, by the same author, *Atrocious Judges: Lives of Judges Infamous As Tools of Tyrants and Instruments of Oppression* (New York: Auburn, Miller, Orton and Mulligan, 1856). See my review of this last work in 68 *Columbia Law Review* 1003 (1968). Also in this category is the delightful Theodore Parker, *The Trial of Theodore Parker* (Boston, 1855). A final category of literature is that of reports and accounts of trials or arguments in particular cases. The category is too large for cataloguing here. Many such titles have appeared or will appear in notes in this work.

cepted the orthodox position that the law as it is and the law as it ought to be present two distinct spheres. Moreover, they agreed that the function of a judge, according to constitutional principles, is the application of positive law—the law as it is. Finally, this group of theorists also accepted as right the obligation of the judge to apply only positive law and to disregard natural law when in conflict with the law as it is. This obligation of judicial obedience was, itself, derived from natural law justifications of the state—social contract in various forms.

Since William Lloyd Garrison and his followers were, above all, moralists, it is not surprising to find them among the first to appreciate the consequences of the Constitution for moral choices. That is, they understood the moral weight of presumptive consent attendant on a largely democratic, constitutional compact. It was precisely because they appreciated the inference of moral obligation from constructive consent that they reached their radical prescriptions for action: disobedience, abstention from voting or office holding, and disunion. Their line of analysis of law was ironically similar to that of the most troubled of our federal judiciary: McLean and Story. Wendell Phillips was the most articulate spokesman for the Garrisonian position on these issues, and it is to his work that reference will be made.* First, Phillips, like most of the judiciary, perceived the Constitution as, in critical part, a compromise over slavery, a compromise that could, in operation, lead to servitude for millions of human beings. Phillips pointed to five provisions as evidence of this view of the Constitution: The three-fifths clauses that provided that for both

---

* The Garrisonian position was well developed in the pages of the *Liberator* before the publication of the three Phillips works discussed here. But Phillips's treatment is much better and more systematic than the give and take of the columns. Phillips's position is proclaimed in three excellent works: *The Constitution: A Pro-Slavery Compact* (Boston, 1844), which was a masterpiece of compilation of all then available data on the intentions and opportunities of the framers of the United States Constitution with respect to slavery. The work makes use of the then recent publication of Madison's *Notes* and of *Elliot's Debates*. The compilation is persuasive as to the intent of the framers and ratifiers to afford slavery a measure of legitimacy and protection. A year later Phillips published *Can Abolitionists Vote or Take Office Under the United States Constitution?* (New York: American Antislavery Society, 1845), which purported to derive the general abstentionist position from the nature of the Constitution and the obligation to refuse complicity with oppression. Still one year later, Phillips published *A Review of Lysander Spooner's Unconstitutionality of Slavery* (Boston: Andrews and Prentiss, 1847) [hereafter cited as *Review*], which not only destroyed Spooner's position, but argued persuasively for resignation by antislavery judges.

representation and direct taxation a slave would count as three-fifths of a person; the limitation on the power of Congress to prohibit the "migration or importation" of slaves until 1808; the Fugitive Slave clause; the clause affording Congress the power to suppress insurrection; the clause insuring, upon application from a state, federal assistance in the suppression of domestic violence. Despite the fact that the word slave is circumlocuted everywhere in the Constitution, Garrison and Phillips, no less than Story, argued forcefully that the purpose of these provisions was to effectuate a bargain, the terms of which conferred legitimacy and a measure of protection for slavery. Story called the Fugitive Slave clause, "a fundamental article, without the adoption of which the Union could not have been formed." And Phillips wholeheartedly agreed, denoting the five proslavery clauses as "the articles of the 'Compromise,' so much talked of between the North and South." [3] Indeed, Wendell Phillips's book *The Constitution: A Pro-Slavery Compact* consisted of extracts from the then recently published *Madison Papers* and from Elliot's reports of various state ratifying conventions demonstrating that the unabashed intent of the framers was to recognize and protect slavery.

A second point of basic agreement between the Garrisonians and the judiciary concerned the proper limits of the judicial function. Phillips argued that the law as it stood did not permit the judge to apply his own vision of natural law with respect to slavery. More important still, Phillips agreed that the law *should* not permit the judge to apply his own perception of natural law. For authority on the proposition that judges do not have the power, under existing law, to apply their own natural law, Phillips quotes at length Blackstone, Kent, Locke, Chitty, Mansfield, Coke, Scott, Marshall, Iredell, and Baldwin. Story, himself, could not have done better. As to the wisdom of this constraint, Phillips is eloquent. He fully recognized that the natural law of South Carolina was likely to prove different from his own. Because "nature" no longer spoke with a single voice, only the judge's conscience ultimately determined the source of right. He concluded by quoting Lord Camden:

> The discretion of a Judge is the law of tyrants; . . . In the best it is often times caprice—in the worst, it is every vice, folly and passion, to which human nature is liable. [4]

Finally, the Garrisonians would have agreed wholly with the judiciary that, by external moral criteria, it would be improper for a judge to use judicial power in a manner contrary to agreed rules. The external moral values that Phillips brings to bear are those of good faith and trust. Phillips states that the officeholder, at least in a government in which there is some measure of participation, stands in a contractual relationship to those who confer on him his power. To accept power on certain conditions and then fail to live up to the conditions is to deceive those to whom one stands as a sort of fiduciary and to subvert the values that are supposedly served by participatory government—a measure of responsibility to the people on the part of their representatives.[5]

At this point it should be clear that the premises and reasoning of the radical Garrisonians compel a full measure of acquiescence in the judicial refusal to apply natural law concerning slavery. It would, indeed, be impossible for McLean or anyone else to effectuate natural law with respect to slavery while still playing by the rules that Phillips acknowledged were and ought to be in force. Moreover, Phillips also agreed that the Constitution, which by those limits had to be enforced, was in conflict with natural law on the issue of slavery. Phillips did not shrink from the conclusion: "Their only 'paramount obligation', as judges, is to do what they agreed to do when they were made judges, or quit the bench." [6]

Since the logic of moral discourse leads to an unacceptable result if the choice point is to be between applying natural law and the Constitution, it was necessary to relocate the point of moral choice. If choice is made at the point of participation or abstention, there are no considerations of a formal character or of role limitation that inhibit a "pure" choice on the basis of which alternative more nearly conforms to moral desiderata.

In the second edition of his book *The Constitution: A Pro-Slavery Compact,* Phillips included a letter of resignation from an obscure Massachusetts Justice of the Peace, to drive home the logic of resignation. This Justice, Francis Jackson, wrote,

> The oath to support the Constitution of the United States is a solemn promise to do that which is a violation of the natural rights of man, and a sin in the sight of God. . . . I withdraw all pro-

fession of allegiance to it [the Constitution], and all my voluntary efforts to sustain it.[7]

The Phillips-Garrison view of judicial obligation was not a disinterested one. The struggle for dominance in the antislavery movement was in part between those, like Garrison, who refused to participate in the processes of government and those who wanted a political, even electoral, movement. The jurisprudence of Wendell Phillips served the end of justifying his own faction's position and of impugning the opposition as both morally and legally obtuse. But, of course, the very fact that Phillips found himself on the abstentionist side was in part the result of an intellectual and temperamental preference for the clean logic of a pure moral choice. Such a choice is obscured by confusing the law as it is with the law as it ought to be:

> But alas, the ostrich does not get rid of her enemy by hiding her head in the sand. Slavery is not abolished, although we have persuaded ourselves that it has no right to exist. . . . The Constitution will never be amended by persuading men that it does not need amendment. National evils are only cured by holding men's eyes open, and forcing them to gaze on the hideous reality.[8]

Constitutional Utopians

While the legal theories of the Garrison-Phillips wing of abolitionism have attracted little attention except insofar as they confirmed the diagnosis of acute antiinstitutionalism, their opponents in this internal antislavery debate have been seized upon by one dissenting wing of American constitutional law scholarship as prophets of the Fourteenth Amendment and as evidence of that Amendment's thrust toward racial equality. Reacting to the apologists for *Plessy v. Ferguson*, these dissenting scholars—men like Jacobus tenBroek and Howard Graham—discovered roots for their own constitutional aspirations in the visions of William Goodell, Lysander Spooner, Joel Tiffany and Alvan Stewart.[9] Just as these scholars in the 1940's and early 1950's appealed to what the Constitution could become, to the highest of the principles that went into it, so their "discovered" progenitors had appealed beyond case law and history to a grand vision of society that they found *in potentia* in many of the phrases of the Constitution.

The argument of tenBroek and of Graham is that the Fourteenth Amendment and its language—"due process," "equal protection," and "privileges and immunities"—cannot be understood except in the context of three decades of abolitionist legal theory aspiring to an antislavery vision of the Constitution and using precisely these phrases in their theories. The "due process" language of the Fifth Amendment and the "privileges and immunities" language of Article IV were viewed by these abolitionists as potential sources of an antislavery constitution. Their reincorporation into the Fourteenth Amendment might therefore be best understood as an embodiment of the abolitionist understanding of the words.

Whatever the merit of this Fourteenth Amendment argument, the ulterior motives of the tenBroek-Graham hypothesis distort somewhat the image of the antislavery constitutional utopians. For this handful of relatively unimportant antislavery thinkers had some meaning for their legal madness. And the meaning related more to theories of obligation than to the substance of the law.

By "constitutional utopians," I am not referring to the many lawyers and writers who appealed to a not yet accepted antislavery version of some constitutional issue. The utopians were reacting against such theorists. When Theodore Dwight Weld wrote that Congress had authority and a moral duty to end slavery in the District of Columbia, he appealed to a notion of congressional authority (if not of congressional morality) that was well within the accepted limits of the day.[10] When William Jay castigated the federal government's complicity in the crime of slavery, he did so by contrasting actual federal involvement in slavery with the constitutionally required minimal involvement. He also contrasted the gratuitous complicity with slavery with a vision of what the national government might permissibly do against slavery. Most of Jay's positions on congressional or executive power were well within the mainstream of legal thought of the day. Those few issues on which Jay advanced an unorthodox position were either unimportant or not related to the fundamental problems of distribution of power. On the critical issue of the states' rights to determine their own domestic institutions, Jay and his followers were orthodox in their understanding of the Constitution.[11] To

accept William Jay's understanding of the Constitution was to confront the dilemma of conscience posed by Garrison and Phillips. How
can one swear fidelity and undertake, by some affirmative act, the
obligation of obeisance to a bargain condemning one's fellow men to
servitude? True, Jay emphasized how the Constitution holds out the
promise of dealing limited blows to slavery, through national legislative action against the trade and against slavery in all islands of national legislative competence. But the slave in Alabama was constitutionally forsaken.[12]

William Goodell, Alvan Stewart, Gerritt Smith, Joel Tiffany and,
most notable, Lysander Spooner, replied that the Constitution out-
laws slavery, even in Alabama.[13] The position that slavery, itself,
was unconstitutional was so extreme as to appear trivial. TenBroek
and Graham "rediscovered" these theorists because they used certain
phrases that presaged the Fourteenth Amendment. Yet their real significance in the antislavery movement was the answer they provided
to the formal problems. They searched, not for a legal theory, but for
a way out of the Garrisonian argument with regard to "obligation."
The purpose of the argument was not to prove slavery unconstitutional (whatever that means in a confessedly utopian context) but to
prove that antislavery men may become judges and may use their
power to free slaves.

Lysander Spooner's opus, *The Unconstitutionality of Slavery*, is
the most complete of the arguments for the utopians. Spooner makes
use of phrases like "due process" and "privileges and immunities"
as pegs on which to hang his theory. But the substance of his argument is natural law. That substance was largely ignored by ten-
Broek.[14] Spooner begins by forcefully asserting that no law in conflict with natural law is valid and that judges have no obligation to
enforce such naturally invalid law. This natural law operates quite
apart from incorporation by any human constituent process.* In form,
Spooner moves on to assume *arguendo* the validity of positive law in
conflict with natural law and to derive the unconstitutionality of such

---

* Lysander Spooner, *The Unconstitutionality of Slavery* (Boston: B. Marsh, 1845), p. 14:
". . . it follows . . . that no law inconsistent with men's natural rights, can arise out of any
contract or compact of government: that constitutional law, under any form of government,
consists only of those principles of the written constitution that are consistent with natural law,
and man's natural rights. . . ."

laws by reference to the United States Constitution and related sources alone; but, in substance, the argument remains infused by the natural law point, for he relies heavily on an interpretative mechanism that rejects any construction save one in harmony with natural law.*

There is ingenuity in Spooner's work, but it is the haphazard ingenuity of rule and phrase manipulation ignoring the "method" of the judge in any real sense. He rejects any argument based on the appeal to history and the purposes of the framers; he rejects all arguments based on the uninterrupted course of applications.[15] Spooner's constitution is amputated from any societal context. Garrison condemned it most succinctly: "The important thing is not the words of the bargain, but the bargain itself." [16]

Alvan Stewart used Spooner's arguments and a host of others in his challenge to the remnants of slavery in New Jersey.[17] But this New York maverick had his own unique legal theory that declared slavery to be a violation of the due process clause of the Fifth Amendment. He argued that no slavery was constitutional unless it had come about by due process—presentment by a grand jury of twenty-three and unanimous conviction by a petit jury of twelve. His reading of the constitutional bargain was that the North had agreed to the clauses that seemed to recognize slavery in return for the South's promise that any slavery be due-process slavery. Stewart's argument is remarkable because it does not depend on a single reference to natural law or to a principle affording preference to interpretations that favor natural law. It is an argument founded wholly on constitutional text and requires nothing more than a suspension of reason concerning the origin, intent, and past interpretation of the clause.[18]

The preoccupation of the utopians with a consistent theory of the Constitution outlawing slavery was only one prong of the attack on the judge's dilemma of conscience. Lysander Spooner was willing to treat the problem *arguendo* as one of a judge who had sworn to uphold an *unjust* constitution, even though he believed the Constitution to be properly interpreted as a just, antislavery instrument.

---

* "I shall not insist upon the principle of the preceding chapter, that there can be no law contrary to natural right. . . . I shall only claim that in the interpretation it be observed. The most important of these rules . . . is the one that all language must be construed strictly in favor of natural right" (ibid., pp. 15–18).

Spooner acknowledged that the dominant position seemed to be that such a judge should resign. But he thought the proper analogy was one of a man given a weapon on condition that he kill an innocent and helpless victim. In such a situation, Spooner argued, it is proper to make the promise, keep the weapon and use it, in violation of the condition, to defend rather than attack the victim. To give up the sword, to resign the judicial office, is "only a specimen of the honor that is said to prevail among thieves." [19] Spooner also argued that acceptance of the total invalidity of an oath of office to violate natural law would have a salutary effect on judges:

> Judges and other public officers habitually appeal to the pre-
> tended obligation of their oaths, when about to perform some act
> of iniquity, for which they can find no other apology, and for
> which they feel obliged to offer some apology. [20]

Spooner is acute in recognizing the appeal to the oath as an apology, but his prescription, though cutting against the notion of judicial fidelity to positive law, does not refute in any way the Phillips prescription of resignation. The only responsive point on the issue of whether a judge ought to resign is the intimation that it is a waste to refuse to use accessible power for a good purpose, whatever the basis of, or conditions upon, its acquisition.

On the level of theory, then, the issue had been joined by 1845. The solution to the moral-formal dilemma was resignation, according to one school. According to the other, it was the judicial enforcement of natural law, preferably through a forced reading of positive law instruments, but if need be, as an act of naked power. Neither of these solutions promised widespread acceptance by the men who sat on the bench. That practical obstacle had to be confronted by the attorneys who confronted these judges and sought relief from them.

CHAPTER TEN: Positivism Established:
The Fugitive Slave Law to 1850

The attorney's role within a system of law assumed to be immoral is
much easier to justify than that of the judge. The practical tasks of
freeing alleged slaves and defending those accused of harboring fugitives were not often thought of as inconsistent with antislavery.
While Henry Thoreau thought that the very argument of whether one
man was the property of another conceded too much to slavery and
was demeaning to a free man or free state, there is no evidence that
either he or the Garrisonian no-government theorists placed serious
moral blame on lawyers who consistently defended the slave within
the legal system. On the contrary, we know of Garrison's support and
affection for Samuel Sewall, a Massachusetts lawyer who did much
of the legal work for antislavery from 1831 on.[1]

Organized legal activity on behalf of Negroes claiming freedom
was not a creation of the militant abolitionist movement. For example, the New York Manumission Society—a respectable organization started by Quakers in 1785 and claiming governors, a vice president, and a chief justice of the United States Supreme Court among
its members—had a vigorous legal arm operating more or less contin-
uously from 1796 to 1822.* The Society represented Negroes claiming freedom, prosecuted actions to prevent export of Negroes from
the state, and tried to prevent importing of slaves. A standing com-

---

* The New York Manumission Society included among its members John Jay, Chief Justice
of the United States Supreme Court; Vice President of the United States, Daniel Tompkins;
New York mayor, Cadwallader Colden. For a description of some of its work, see, e.g., Edgar
McManus, *A History of Negro Slavery in New York* (Syracuse: Syracuse University Press,
1966); Arthur Zilversmit, *The First Emancipation* (Chicago: University of Chicago Press,
1967). The conclusions concerning the work of the Standing Committee of the Society are
drawn from the New York Manumission Society, Minutes of Standing Committee; unpublished
manuscript material in the collection of the New York Historical Society. I am indebted to
Mr. George Hritz, a student in my seminar on American Slavery and the Law offered Spring
Semester 1971 at Columbia Law School, for identifying, analyzing, and tabulating selected data
from these manuscript sources. Hritz, "Legislating and Litigating Social Change: Gradual
Emancipation in New York 1799–1827" (unpublished paper on file with the author at Yale Law
School). Hritz has tabulated almost two hundred case dispositions by the Standing Committee
of which 123 were "won" and 64 "lost." He discovered some gaps in the records, so the
tabulation is certainly incomplete.

159

mittee saw to these legal duties and provided periodic reports on the success of its actions. In Pennsylvania the Antislavery Society also provided encouragement and legal services for freedom-seeking Negroes.[2] Even in Virginia, it seems that Quakers encouraged freedom suits with substance as well as spirit.[3] Material is difficult to come by, but it seems likely that we may some day have a better notion of the contours of these early efforts at legal coordination. I do not pretend to know enough about these efforts to identify the personnel, their assumptions, and methods. What does seem clear, however, is that litigation was treated as a practical necessity, not as an ideological opportunity. A service was provided to those arguably entitled, under existing law, to claim freedom or some other right. Most cases depended on proof of facts, and legal arguments were almost always narrow.[4]

These limited aspirations for litigation were the product of the early antislavery movement itself. This movement stressed gradualism, consensus, and absence of dislocation (for whites).[5] Broad legal attacks on slavery as a whole or on its place in the Constitution could not but be antithetical to these goals. Such attacks would neither reflect nor produce consensus, and legislation was a far better tool for gradualism and for adjusting competing interests.

The shape of early litigation was also determined by the "local law" character of the issues. In the North the gradual emancipation statutes were the primary legal framework for most cases. In the South the manumission laws or the black codes governed. For every Negro affected by the Fugitive Slave Act, hundreds were affected by registration provisions and other technical enforcement details of gradual emancipation. By the 1840's this was no longer the case. In 1827, New York had ended slavery by freeing the few Negroes who had been born prior to the Act of 1799. The year 1840 was the last census in which Pennsylvania reported slaves. As indicated above, New Jersey had only 700 slaves in 1845. Connecticut ended slavery in 1848, but there were only fifty-four reported in the 1840 census. Gradual emancipation had worked, and the need for litigation on that front correspondingly disappeared.

The development of immediatism in the abolitionist movement, the demise of servitude in the gradual emancipation states, and the bitter sectarian divisions of the abolitionist movement produced an impulse to use litigation as a dramatic forum for ideology. The qualitative difference in antislavery advocacy may be dated, rather imprecisely at the mid-1830's. This development in legal strategy coincided with the rise of militant abolitionism. The reasons for the development of a militant form of antislavery at this time lie beyond the scope of this book. The reader is referred to the standard works on the movement—Dumond's *Antislavery,* Barnes's *The Antislavery Impulse,* and Filler's *The Crusade Against Slavery*—for various theories on this issue.[6]

From the 1830's on, the antislavery bar was largely ideological in character. It consisted of a fairly well-defined group of men who did the antislavery legal work without compensation. Most of these lawyers had strong connections with one or another of the groups within the antislavery movement. Thus, Salmon P. Chase was connected first with James Birney and the Liberty party and later with the Republican party;[7] Samuel Sewall was a Garrisonian;[8] Richard Henry Dana, Jr., was involved with the Free-Soil party.[9] Thaddeus Stevens, Charles Sumner, and William Seward all tied antislavery advocacy to antislavery politics. John Jolliffe was an intimate friend of Levi Coffin, "President of the Underground Railroad," and was a founder of the Liberty party in Ohio.[10]

Despite their different, often conflicting, sectarian affiliations, the antislavery bar had a common litigation experience: representation of the fugitive slave and of his friends. A few highly dramatic legal dramas were presented outside the fugitive arena—most notably the trial of Prudence Crandall in Connecticut and the *Amistad* affair.[11] The Somerset issue in conflict-of-laws cases also persisted. But by 1840 that problem was settled in most of the North. The great cases of the twenty years preceding the Civil War were almost all fugitive cases. That common litigation context determined a degree of uniformity in argument. The fugitive's advocate stood four-square for states' rights and against extensions of national power. However much the ultimate extension of national power owes to the slavery controversy, its debt does not arise from the courtroom experience or strategy of the antislavery lawyer. On the legislative front, many of the abolitionists' goals depended on a broad reading of the authority of the national government: abolition of slavery in the District of Columbia, elimination of slavery from the territories, the suppression of first the international and then the domestic slave trade, ultimately even the elimination of slavery from the states. But such goals seldom manifested themselves in lawsuits, while the fugitive rendition process was the single leading courtroom crucible for abolitionists after 1835.

The Fugitive Slave clause of the federal Constitution provided:

> No person held to service or labor in one state, under the laws thereof, escaping into another, shall, in consequence of any law or Regulation therein, be discharged from such service or labor, but shall be delivered up on claim of the party to whom such service or labor may be due.[12]

The Act of 1793 provided for enforcement of this clause by way of summary process before any federal judge or state magistrate.* Proof of the material elements of identity and of escape from an obligation of service could be made either orally or by affidavit. In form and substance the fugitive rendition requirement was a limitation on state power. It deprived the state of plenary legislative competence to determine the status of its residents. However, the Act of 1793 was quite vague and left unclear the extent of state power to supplement the skeletal processes of the act with its own procedural or substantive safeguards. Antislavery lawyers argued for the broadest possible view of state power. They sought a state forum with jury trial; a right of confrontation; a right to present evidence. They sought to compel the slave-catcher to use peaceable process and to refrain from forcible recaption as constitutionally authorized self-help.[13] None of these objectives were explicitly precluded by the clause or by its implementing legislation. Achievement of these objectives would be facilitated by a strong states rights approach to the Constitution. The argument was simple. The plenary legislative power of the states could be

---

* Act of February 12, 1793, Chap. 7, 1 Stat 302 (1793): ". . . the person to whom such labour or service may be due . . . is hereby empowered to seize or arrest such fugitive from labour, and to take him or her before any judge of the circuit or district courts of the United States, residing or being within the state, or before any magistrate of a county, city or town corporate . . . and upon proof to the satisfaction of such judge or magistrate, either by oral testimony or affidavit taken before and certified by a magistrate of such state or territory, that the person so seized or arrested doth, under the laws of the state or territory from which he or she fled, owe service or labor to the person claiming him or her, it shall be the duty of such judge or magistrate to give a certificate thereof to such claimant. . . ."

infringed on only by explicit limitation or by explicit grant of the power to Congress. There could be no "implied" powers of the national government, nor "implied" limits on the states. With respect to the fugitive, the Constitution was silent as to the mechanism and circumstances of rendition, leaving the states the power to decide such issues as they saw fit.

Not only was it argued that the states retained these powers, it was asserted that Congress lacked legislative power with regard to fugitives. The Fugitive Slave clause is found in Article IV of the Constitution and does not have a specific authorization for congressional implementation. The Full Faith and Credit clause, of the same article, does have an implementation clause. From that juxtaposition, antislavery lawyers argued that there was no authority for congressional implementation of the Fugitive Slave clause: *expressio unius, exclusio alterius*.[14] They limited the scope of the "Necessary and Proper" clause to the specific congressional powers of Article I. Furthermore, they conceived of Article IV as a directive to the states with regard to their comity obligations. The states had the obligation to determine their own institutional means to realize the constitutional objective of comity and reciprocity.

By the time militant antislavery began its courtroom campaign against the fugitive rendition process, almost a half-century of experience with the act had elapsed. Some case law had developed, largely unfavorable, though not conclusive.[15] In 1818, a federal court in Indiana upheld the constitutionality of the act against the lack-of-congressional-power argument.[16] And in 1819, Judge Tilghman had denied to Pennsylvania courts the power to interpose a state proceeding, including a jury trial, in the rendition process.[17] In 1823, a dictum in a Massachusetts case intimated agreement as to the act's constitutionality.[18] In 1834 and 1835 New York judges split as to the proper scope of congressional power to implement rendition.[19]

These early failures had preceded systematic development of the antislavery argument on the Fugitive Slave Act. That development began in 1836 and 1837 in the columns of the *Philanthropist,* an antislavery periodical controlled by James Birney. Trial by jury was one important strand of Birney's more general constitutional argument.[20] But it was an issue on which a basic value question would hinge— would the *presumptions* of the free states or of the slave states govern the rendition process? If the presumptions of the free state govern, then any man, even one allegedly a fugitive, is presumed free; and only proof to the contrary, in a proper forum with procedural safeguards, will overcome the presumption. If rendition is to take place without the benefit of procedural safeguards, then those safeguards and the presumption itself will be lost: In a slave state a black man would be presumed a slave, would lose the right to testify, and would lose the right to trial by jury on the issue of freedom.[21]

In 1837 a series of practical attempts was made to resurrect the right to jury trial for the fugitive. These attempts, from Massachusetts to Ohio, reflected the now national character of the movement. In 1835, the Massachusetts legislature abolished the writ *de homine replegiando* or "personal replevin." This old, common law writ was seen as out of date, replaced in large part by habeas corpus. But the writ of personal replevin, already obsolescent in Blackstone's day, was a common law writ and carried with it the right to trial by jury. In 1837, the report of a committee of the Massachusetts legislature recommended restoration of the writ. The report was also published in a leading law journal.[22] It is recognized that the only important factor favoring restoration was that it would provide an additional measure of protection for the alleged fugitive slave. The argument of the committee supporting the interposition of state process in fugitive cases was the classic one. First, the report noted that the argument that the constitutional protections such as trial by jury do not apply to slaves begs the question. For the process under attack is precisely for the purpose of determining whether the man is or is not a slave. As applied to a free man, the report argued, the Act of 1793 would surely be unconstitutional. In Massachusetts, moreover, every man is presumed free. Consequently, the only way to save the constitutionality of the Act of 1793 is to insure that there be some "due process" by which the question of slave or free may be determined. The writ *de homine replegiando*, affording a collateral form of relief that would include trial by jury, filled the hole.[23] The same year saw a similar attempt to secure a state right to trial by jury in Pennsylvania. There state senator Francis James introduced and supported a bill on familiar due-process jury trial grounds.[24] In Ohio the jury trial issue was raised prominently in the case of the slave Mathilda, an alleged fugitive. That case was Salmon Chase's antislavery debut. He argued that the black woman, in Ohio, was presumptively free and constitutionally entitled to a jury trial. This claim, though not the exclusive basis of Chase's remarkable argument, was an important part of it. Chase's argument was printed and widely circulated.[25] That same year a petition for a state statute affording alleged fugitives a jury trial was turned down, with a detailed report, by the Ohio legislature. The *Philanthropist* printed the Ohio report and a rejoinder by Birney.[26]

These developments in 1837 seem to be more directly related to the national revival of interest in constitutional theory among abolitionists than to local legal developments in the respective states. Indeed, in Massachusetts the interest in reviving the writ of personal replevin coincided with a series of startling victories through habeas corpus.[27] Chief Justice Shaw's opinions in conflicts cases could hardly have given rise to strong antijudicial feelings and to the felt need for a jury. Conversely, the Pennsylvania courts had only recently affirmed the holding of *Wright v. Deacon,* reaffirming the unconstitutionality of the writ of personal replevin in fugitive cases.[28] While these developments may have influenced state senator James, it seems likely that the speculations of the Birney-Weld wing of abolitionism were more directly involved.

For more than a year preceding the sudden interest in developing the right to trial by jury, James Birney and his followers had been stressing the values inherent in the Constitution that were antithetical to slavery, including, but by no means limited to, trial by jury. The columns of the *Philanthropist* were filled with theory, much of which could have no practical application in the courtroom. The lawyers in effect seized upon the only strand in the mélange that had some prospect for immediate practical utilization, the insistence on the presumption that the black man is free coupled with the "right" of a jury trial. Moreover, if the northern states were willing to set up both the presumption and the procedural guarantee as a matter of state law, then it would be unnecessary to argue like Spooner, that the United States Constitution guaranteed any rights of due process or jury trial. The 1833 decision of the United States Supreme Court in *Barron v. Baltimore* meant that such an argument was likely to fail. That case held that the Fifth Amendment's guarantee against the taking of property without just compensation was not a limitation on state power, but only on the federal government.[29]

So long as the practical ends of fugitive litigation seemed remotely attainable, the ideological differences of various antislavery factions were obscured by their common objective and by the common strategic outline determined by the characteristic of the Fugitive Slave clause as a limitation on state power. The decision of the United States Supreme Court in *Prigg v. Pennsylvania,** in 1842, was a serious blow to that strategy.

The defendant, Prigg, had been an agent for a Maryland slave owner. He sought to recapture alleged fugitives in Pennsylvania but was refused a certificate of removal by a state magistrate. He then recaptured the fugitives without aid of process and removed them to Maryland. He was convicted of violating the Pennsylvania kidnapping statute that forbade, in general terms, the forcible removal of a Negro or mulatto from the state. The Supreme Court reversed the conviction and held the Pennsylvania act unconstitutional, at least as applied to alleged fugitives.

Since seven of the justices wrote separate opinions, it is difficult to speak of the Court's reasoning. Joseph Story's opinion is often spoken of as that of the Court, though no five judges concurred in all of its

---

* *Prigg v. Pennsylvania*, 41 U.S. (16 Pet.) 539 (1842). Given *Prigg's* position as the earliest of the three most important Supreme Court decisions on slavery (along with *Scott v. Sanford* and *Ableman v. Booth*), there is a serious dearth of careful analysis of the opinion. I have suggested certain features of the opinions that are relevant to my inquiries here, but they certainly do not exhaust the case. Of particular interest is the question of consistency between judicial utterances in *Prigg* and the general constitutional and judicial standards of the three major actors: Story, Taney, and McLean. I treat Story and McLean at some length in Chapter 13. As to Taney, there is a case to be made that he permitted greater latitude for federal authority when supporting slavery than in other cases. Contrast his highly nationalistic proslavery decisions in *Prigg,* in *Dred Scott* 60 U.S. (19 How.) 707 and in *Ableman v. Booth* 62 U.S. (21 How.) 506 with his well-known opinions in the *License Cases,* 46 U.S. (5 How.) 504 (1847) and *Mayor City of New York v. Miln,* 36 U.S. (11 Pet.) 102 (1837).

Prigg has often been mishandled by commentators. Corwin, in "The Passing of Dual Federalism," 36 *Virginia Law Review* 1 (1950), cites *Prigg* as an example of a shift to state autonomy as the Marshall court gave way to Taney's. Actually, if there is a move to state autonomy in the case, it is presented by Story, while Taney takes a more nationalist position *consistent with* his nationalism in *Dred Scott* and *Booth.*

Prigg also raises (along with *Booth*) the issue of whether the modern lawyer and scholar must forsake all the slavery cases as too infused with a substantive issue to be of any use in understanding our federal system. Though the substantive issues they dealt with are, in a sense, gone, cases like *Martin v. Hunter's Lessee* are still a source for principles of federalism. It is interesting that *Tarble's Case,* 80 U.S. (13 Wall) 397 (1872), rather than *Ableman v. Booth,* is the "leading case" on the lack of state power to release one held under federal custody, though *Booth* is quite unambiguous about the matter and antedates *Tarble's Case* by a dozen years.

reasoning. He began by reaffirming the dogma of much of the northern judiciary; that the Fugitive Slave clause represented a necessary compromise by which a limited exception was carved out of the rule of *Somerset's Case.* Story assumed that the choice-of-law rule, operating outside of constitutional prescription, would have rendered the fugitive free. The Constitution, however, was more than a provision to limit state choice-of-law rules. He read Article IV as providing, independent of congressional action, a remedy of peaceable recaption for the slaveholder or his representative. The self-executing character of Article IV did not, however, imply any limit to congressional power to supplement the remedy of recaption. Story recognized that the aid of process was often necessary if the clause were not to be turned into a dead letter. If the aid of process was contemplated, then, "the natural inference . . . is that the national government is clothed with the appropriate authority and functions to enforce it." Story found the Act of 1793 entirely constitutional insofar as it provided a federal remedy. However, Story found that part of the act that conferred jurisdiction on state magistrates very troublesome. At two different points in the decision, he intimates doubt as to congressional power to compel state judges to act.[30]

The question of whether or not state judges could be compelled to exercise jurisdiction under the act was not involved in the decision in *Prigg.* Story found that the Pennsylvania statute under attack was unconstitutional because

> It purports to punish as a public offense against the state, the very act of seizing and removing a slave by his master, which the Constitution of the United States was designed to justify and uphold.[31]

Story strongly intimated that any state action with respect to the fugitive would be of doubtful constitutionality.

Chief Justice Taney concurred in the result but argued that states could certainly legislate to supplement the remedies provided by Congress. Thus, he would uphold state legislation that would afford the slaveholder the benefit of process for arrest of the alleged fugitive. While Taney is explicit in finding that the states have the power and the constitutional obligation to cooperate in the apprehension and rendition of fugitives, he never squarely confronts the question of whether Congress may empower—in the face of state law to the contrary—state magistrates to cooperate in the rendition process.[32]

Justice Thompson concurred, completely rejecting, however, Story's position of exclusivity of remedy. He considered legislative competence to be concurrent, subject, of course, to the limits imposed by the supremacy clause. Justice Baldwin also concurred, apparently reasoning that the Constitution provided, without the necessity for legislation, the full panoply of remedies that the slaveholder might need. Wayne and Daniel concurred as well. Wayne agreed with Story as to federal exclusivity of remedy, while Daniel disagreed on that point.[33]

Only John McLean dissented. He upheld a pervasive view of federal power, arguing that Congress could require state officials to take cognizance of proceedings under the act. McLean, however, reserved to the states a broad police power. He asserted that the states had the power to insist on peaceable process in the rendition procedure. McLean was the only justice of nine to interpret Article IV, Section 2, as not providing a remedy of self-help in the face of state law designed to insure legal process.[34] Despite McLean's dissent, *Prigg* was a unanimous reinforcement of the characterization of Fugitive Slave rendition as an article of compromise. The full weight of constitutional legitimacy was placed behind the clause. It was that element of the decision (from which there was no dissent) that split antislavery legal forces.

If insistence on the use of peaceable process was not within the state's police power, if the state could not even make the slave-catcher pause to get a certificate, then the prevailing strategy of securing a state interposition of jury trial was almost certain to fail. The antislavery bar did not simply forsake the jury-trial strategy, since the issue was not squarely decided in *Prigg*. However, whatever hopes there had been faded. One segment of the movement came to concede more and more that the Constitution was what the judges said it was and focused on the nature of moral obligation to such laws. The other part of the movement was forced to the anomalous position that the Constitution could not mean what the Justices were saying it meant.

In 1842, just after the decision of the Supreme Court in *Prigg*, many of the loose threads suggested by that case, by developments within abolitionist legal thought, and by the moralist-abstention position of the Garrisonians came together around the person of George Latimer.* Latimer, who had been living in Boston, was seized in 1842 as a fugitive and brought before the aging Justice Story. Story ordered him held while the slaveowner sent for further proof as to his identity. Samuel Sewall, one of William Lloyd Garrison's first converts from the bar, sought a writ of personal replevin from Chief Justice Shaw of the Massachusetts Supreme Judicial Court, arguing that the alleged fugitive should have the right to have his identity determined by a jury. Shaw denied the writ, apparently on the ground that even initiation of such a process would constitute an infringement upon an exclusive federal domain.[35] According to the *Liberator*'s account, Shaw said,

> that he probably felt as much sympathy for the person in custody as others, but this was a case in which an appeal to natural rights and to the paramount law of liberty was not pertinent! It was to be decided by the Constitution . . . and by the Law of Congress. . . . These were to be obeyed, however disagreeable to our natural sympathies or views of duty.[36]

Shaw went on to justify the obligation of obedience on the ground that without the clause the nation could not have been formed.

* Unlike certain fugitive cases that provoked a spate of contemporaneous accounts, the Latimer affair lacks a single comprehensive secondary treatment. There is a brief, but adequate account in Irving Bartlett, *Wendell Phillips* (Boston: Beacon Press, 1961), pp. 116–19. For valuable contemporaneous perspectives on the elements of Latimer analyzed below, see "The Latimer Case," 5 *Law Reporter* 481 (1843) and issues of the *Liberator* from Oct. 28, 1842, to early 1843. However, occasional pieces of relevance appeared thereafter. See, e.g., Wendell Phillips's remarks on Story's death, the *Liberator*, Sept. 11, 1846, pp. 2–3. The most comprehensive view of the case and of its impact on abolitionism can be had only by examining the *Latimer Journal and North Star*, an *ad hoc* newspaper published by abolitionists and edited largely by H. I. Bowditch. The issue of Wednesday, May 10, 1843, contains many "legal" articles. Bowditch did not accept the resignation logic, but felt that the very least that could be accepted was resignation. The *Latimer Journal* is hard to come by. I examined the copy in Bowditch's scrapbook in the Massachusetts Historical Society. There is a touching manuscript addition to the paper of May 10, 1843, dated February 15, 1885, and initialed H. I. B.: "I read this today as the work of another man and I feel refreshed at thinking that I was once capable of writing such a letter—But what tame times the young men have now. Where is there now any moral fight equal to the antislavery battle [?]"

Though disagreeing with Shaw's constitutional law, the *Liberator,* especially in light of *Prigg,* took his argument of helplessness before his legal obligation as a judge very seriously. Garrison replied to Shaw that his actions had proved his

> readiness to aid and abet . . . in kidnapping a guiltless and defenceless human being, and to act the part of Pilot [sic] on crucifixion of the Son of God; for rather than to have been made an instrument in sending Latimer back to prison and ultimately to slavery . . . he had it in his power, and as an honest and humane man was duty bound, to resign his office and to bear his testimony against all such legal diabolism. . . . Villainy is still villainy though it be pronounced equity in the statute book.[37]

Meanwhile, Wendell Phillips was busy at Faneuil Hall. He, like Shaw, was concerned with the Constitution: "There stands the bloody clause—you cannot fret the seal off the bond. The fault is in allowing such a constitution to live an hour." [38] The Latimer case, in the wake of *Prigg,* was powerful evidence that interpretation of the Constitution would not only fail to elevate the values antithetical to slavery, but would clearly subordinate them to the terms of the "bargain." The Faneuil Hall meeting voted for disunion and vowed resistance to every effort to turn Massachusetts into a slave-catcher. An important sidelight to the Faneuil Hall affair was the presence, in a prominent manner, of Latimer's counsel. Sewall chaired the meeting. At least one law journal construed such conduct as improper, in effect accusing Sewall of participating in an attempt to intimidate the judiciary.[39]

It was with respect to his role in Latimer that Justice Story pleaded his obligation to the Constitution quoted at the beginning of Chapter 7. His justification of himself by virtue of the limits on his role can now be more fully appreciated. Story, as we have seen, was a firm proponent of the impersonal approach to constitutional construction. In the Fugitive Slave clause, he had ample authority for a mandate to ignore natural law. Indeed, Story's view of conflicts forced him to read the Fugitive clause as a direct ousting of natural law from its normal sphere of operation. And Story had long been a consistent adherent of the view that an act of legislation determing a conflicts principle must be given effect by the courts.[40] While Story's earlier writing in the treatises on the Constitution and on conflicts would have led one to anticipate precisely this response to Latimer, the *Prigg* decision, less than one year earlier, reinforced the conclusion. For *Prigg* was not only the occasion for reiteration of the constitutional views of the *Treatise,* it was also a Supreme Court imprimatur for those views. Even had Story disagreed with the Court on the merits—by his own view of the Court as a necessary supreme arbitor—he would have been bound by its decision. As it was, he embraced it.

By contrast, Wendell Phillips was confronted with the proof of his thesis. Realistically, Story and Lemuel Shaw were as close to confirmed opponents of slavery as existed on the bench. Story was sitting, prepared to send Latimer back to slavery, inviting the slave-catcher to prepare his case thoroughly. Shaw was denying his own authority as a state court judge to interpose Massachusetts process between Latimer and slavery. Both Story and Shaw not only perceived their primary obligation, as judges, to the Constitution, but they also affirmed the general principles of impersonal, neutral construction; adherence to recent precedent in spirit as well as holding; and obligation to make a good faith effort to effectuate the instrument's purpose even in the face of their own moral beliefs. This practical demonstration of the power of the principles of self-denial in the public activity of the judge followed closely upon the authoritative, unanimous characterization of the Fugitive Slave Clause as a basic component of the national cement. It is precisely at this critical juncture that Phillips made his boldest attack on the Constitution itself; for at this point to tinker with interpretation would be too dangerous a tack. To enter into the interpretive framework would be to concede, implicitly, the obligation of the Constitution. Only by pointing out the "bloody clause," by conceding that, by God, it meant just what Story and the gang thought it meant, could one lay the ground work for dissolving the moral bond of obedience.

The Latimer case ended with the purchase of the fugitive from his master. But the Boston legal community was disturbed by the implications of the attacks on the judiciary. The *Law Reporter* published a lengthy defense of Story and Shaw with an attack on those who would have had them act otherwise.

The very object of the oath of office is to prevent the judge from exercising his discretion, in declaring or not declaring what the law is according to his opinion or feeling of its moral character. . . . It [society] placed him there to declare its will and apply it in every case before him.[41]

The *Law Reporter* made the concession that a right of revolution might follow from law contrary to natural law, but certainly not a violation of the proper role of the judiciary as subordinate to the "will of society." It is interesting that the profession did not yet apprehend the affinity of the Garrisonian position to their own.

In Ohio, response to the *Prigg* decision came with the ascendancy of the legal ideas of Salmon Chase and John Jolliffe. As far back as 1837, Chase had come to dominate the western antislavery bar. It was apparent that in Chase antislavery had a "comer," an ambitious, capable man who seemed destined for successful respectability. His first effort in the antislavery cause had been the *Mathilda* case. Mathilda had been working for James Birney and her arrest as a fugitive was an attack to the heart of the western movement. Birney contemplated appearing for Mathilda, himself, but decided she would be better served by the more respectable Chase. Chase was given a crash course in the Birney view of the Constitution.[42]

The argument on behalf of Mathilda, which was printed and widely circulated, was marked by a characteristic ambiguity as to the place of natural law propositions about slavery in constitutional law. Chase began by disclaiming that any but legal principles were relevant to the case. Yet thereafter he pursued his argument with the plea that

There is such a thing as natural rights, derived not from any constitution or civil code, but from the constitution of human nature and the code of heaven. . . .[43]

These rights, Chase maintained, should at least govern the construction of positive law. If there is a conceivable construction that will harmonize positive and natural law, it should be seized upon by the court.

Chase's exhortation was not for judicial disregard for positive law.

Indeed, in an 1843 meeting of the Liberty party, he refused to support a resolution urging judicial refusal to uphold the Fugitive Slave law regardless of its legality.[44] Yet, in 1843 and 1844 just after *Prigg*, in the famous *Van Zandt* litigation, Chase trod a fine line, attributable in part to his ideological position, between urging disregard of positive law and urging incorporation of natural law within it. The *Van Zandt* litigation was particularly important for Chase and the Ohio theorists. First, it was an opportunity to measure the shadow of *Prigg*. Second, it put Chase as counsel before his friend John McLean as circuit Justice.[45] Chase admired McLean and believed in his fundamental antislavery character. In arguing before him, Chase was not simply a lawyer trying to win a case, but a friend trying to win a convert.

Van Zandt was an action for civil damages for harboring a fugitive, brought under the Act of 1793. Chase sought reconsideration of the dictum in *Prigg* that the Act of 1793 was constitutional. One of Chase's pleas was that principles of natural law and the Declaration of Independence condemned slavery. Therefore, the Constitution must be interpreted most narrowly to avoid conflict with natural right. There being no specific authorization for an enforcement mechanism that punishes men for acting in a Christian and godly manner, such a remedy ought not be implied. Generous or implied-powers arguments are improper in derogation of natural right.[46]

McLean's response to this barrage was straightforward rejection of the argument. He charged the jury not to pay any heed to conscience except in that a proper view of conscience leads to obedience to positive law. He interpreted the Fugitive Slave clause as it had been viewed in *Prigg*.[47]

Before the Supreme Court, Chase had no better success. At times he seemed on the verge of a judicial disobedience argument: "No court is bound to enforce unjust law; but on the contrary every court is bound, by prior and superior obligations, to abstain from enforcing such law."[48] And he explicitly noted that "Multitudes, in all parts of the country, regard the act of the defendant . . . not merely as no crime, but as an act of humanity and mercy."[49]

There is no other point in Chase's life where he comes so close to the higher law theorists. Perhaps, having lost before his friend McLean, the only dissenter in *Prigg*, he felt the need for a different sort of plea. Perhaps he simply wanted more political capital in antislavery Ohio. In any event, the plea brought a sharp rejoinder from the Court. Rejecting squarely all of the legal points of the argument, Justice Woodbury, for the Court, concluded:

> . . . It may be expected by the defendant that some notice should be taken of the argument, urging on us a disregard of the constitution and the act of Congress in respect to this subject, on account of the supposed inexpediency and invalidity of all laws recognizing slavery. . . . But that is a political question, settled by each State; . . . and the federal power over it is limited . . . in the constitution itself, as one of its sacred compromises, and which we possess no authority as a judicial body to modify or overrule.[50]

Van Zandt, then, reaffirmed the three cardinal principles that had come to be established by 1847: an unqualified positivist approach to constitutional adjudication, the recognition of the Fugitive Slave clause as one of the "sacred compromises" of the Constitution, and the acceptance of a congressionally prescribed summary rendition process as a valid implementation of the compromise.

CHAPTER ELEVEN: Positivism and Crisis:
The Fugitive Slave Law, 1850–1859

The Garrisonians' emphasis on a positivist approach to the Constitution and their resulting conclusion that the compact was a bargain with hell produced a focus on the issue of participation in the system, rather than on novel theories of substantive law. Conversely, where the Chase-Birney theories held sway, the objective of incorporating natural law into positive law by some bootstrap or another continued unabated. The Fugitive Slave Act of 1850, with the concomitant public uproars of this last antebellum decade, produced new opportunities for both approaches to slave law and for the sober lawyers. In Massachusetts the logic of the Garrisonians culminated with the dramatic Burns affair and Loring removal in 1854 and 1855. In the West, in Ohio and Wisconsin, the Chase-Birney approach was relentlessly pursued, achieving its one great success in the *Booth* cases in 1854, and then failing miserably when, at the end of the decade, the Ohio courts rejected the approach and the United States Supreme Court reversed *Booth*.

The Fugitive Slave Act of 1850 was sufficiently different from the Act of 1793, which it amended, that a lawyer might find good ground for considering *Prigg, Jones v. Van Zandt,* and the supporting state court opinions as no longer dispositive as to the act's constitutionality. The heart of the new legislation was the commissioner's jurisdiction. It provided for the appointment of special federal commissioners who would hear the fugitive rendition proceedings and issue certificates of removal. The commissioner was to hear the slaveholder or his representative or examine their affidavits, ex parte, and issue certificates thereon. If a certificate were issued, the commissioner was to receive a ten-dollar fee. If it were denied, he would receive five dollars. Moreover, the act explicitly excluded the alleged fugitive's testimony from the proceeding.[1]

Although an opinion of the Attorney General proclaimed the act's constitutionality apparent on the basis of cases decided under the Act of 1793,[2] the antislavery bar was prepared to make new and coherent arguments against the act that had not already been rejected by the

Supreme Court. The first important legal test of the act came in Boston in the *Sims Case.* In 1851 Boston was seething. Webster had been repudiated for his part in the Great Compromise.[3] The Garrisonians redoubled the vigor of their attacks on constitutional obligation. On the other side, Benjamin Robbins Curtis, soon to sit on the Supreme Court, defended the act and upbraided those who would prefer the liberty of a mere black to the unity and security of a white man's country.[4] The first attempt to return a fugitive from Boston after the act—the *Shadrach* affair—was met with a dramatic rescue. Shadrach went free.[5] Consequently, when Thomas Sims was apprehended as a fugitive, the federal authorities saw the rendition as a test of strength. The courthouse was ringed with chains and troops. The *Liberator* proclaimed, "Justice in Chains." A vigilance committee tried, unsuccessfully, to plot another rescue.[6]

Samuel Sewall, Robert Rantoul, and Richard Henry Dana began the legal attack on the act. All three were competent lawyers who had imbibed the stern Massachusetts legal positivism of Story and Shaw. Sewall was a Garrisonian; Rantoul was a Jacksonian Benthamite of strong antislavery views; Dana was a former Whig Free-Soiler of generally conservative views. For very different reasons none of these three men would have been capable of the kind of argument that Birney or Chase or Jolliffe could make. They would have choked on the suggestion that the Constitution somehow has a necessary relationship to what is right.[7]

A writ of habeas corpus was sought on behalf of Sims from Chief Justice Shaw. Shaw finally conceded that the state court had jurisdiction to entertain the petition for the writ. This result was in keeping with the general antebellum view of state habeas corpus jurisdiction.* Rantoul delivered the principal argument against the constitutionality of the act before the Massachusetts court. Like a good craftsman, he steered away from the arguments that had already been rejected under

---

* There was an important technical distinction between issuance of the writ and discharge upon it. Shaw acknowledged jurisdiction to issue the writ, meaning that he considered that the Court had power *in appropriate circumstances* to try the issue of such a prisoner's detention. Prior to *Ableman v. Booth* (1859), such was the prevailing view of state habeas corpus jurisdiction. A leading treatise, Rollins Hurd, *Habeas Corpus* (Albany: W. C. Little & Co.), published in 1858, so proclaimed on p. 166. See also D. Oaks, "Habeas Corpus in the States—1776–1865," 32 *University of Chicago Law Review* 243 (1965). Shaw's upholding of jurisdiction meant that the constitutionality of the Act of 1850 could be argued as it was relevant to the question of whether the writ ought, as a matter of law, to issue.

the 1793 act. Instead, he argued first that the Act of 1850 purported to vest judicial power in an officer who was not a judge within the meaning of Article III. For the commissioner was not appointed for a tenure of good behavior and with no diminution in salary. Second, he argued that the fee differential denied due process to the alleged fugitive, as it made the commissioner an interested party in the outcome.[8]

Shaw's opinion in *Sims* was a telling blow to the legal strategy of antislavery. He did reach the merits of the suit, but declined, in an elaborate opinion, to even let the writ of habeas corpus issue. He asserted that no court should issue the writ if it appeared on the face of the petition that the prisoner would have to be remanded.[9] Since the petition of Sims showed his restraint for purpose of the rendition process under the Act of 1850, Shaw held that his remand would be immediately necessary should the writ issue. He reached that conclusion by holding the act free of all constitutional doubt. Moreover, he rested his conclusion on precedent decided with respect to the Act of 1793, holding the differences between the acts irrelevant for purposes of the constitutional questions presented.[10] Shaw's decision in effect closed the doors of the Massachusetts state courts to any collateral attacks on renditions. This consequence meant that the only remaining tribunal was the commissioner himself from whom no appeal was provided. In *Sims* the commissioner, in an elaborate opinion, upheld the act, his own authority, and the rendition of Sims.[11] By dint of military might, Sims was returned.

The furor over the *Sims* case had immediate and important consequences for the Massachusetts judiciary. In 1853 a constitutional convention was held. For the first time in Massachusetts, a serious proposal for an elected judiciary was put forward.[12] It was handily defeated. But a remarkable feature of both the defense of and attack on the independence of the judiciary was the use of *Sims's Case* and the fugitive problem as support for their assumed position. As defender of judicial independence, Dana argued, "Take the fugitive slave law. Suppose the court equally divided upon that subject. A new judge is to be elected. . . . The votes will be given for principles and not men." [13] But for Mr. French of New Bedford, supporting an elected judiciary, the loss of a good man for the bench was less important than the loss of justice caused by a too independent court:

We have been told that every citizen however humble, may come before our courts, and spread out his case and demand his rights.

I stand here and tell you, that a free citizen of Mass.—as free Mr. Pres., as either you or I—has failed to be protected by the judiciary. . . . but I do stand here to say that I heard the claim for a writ of habeas corpus in the case of Thomas Sims . . . and it failed to induce the supreme judges to issue the writ and thus secure to that citizen his inalienable rights.

Now Sir, I would like to have judges elected by the people that they may not be so independent of them, so that if another case upon the writ of habeas corpus similar to the one to which I have referred should come up before them, they will be dependent enough to listen favorably to argument. . . .[14]

Mr. French, however, was not as sensitive to the formal issue as he might have been. Richard Henry Dana, one of Sims's counsel, strongly supported the maintenance of an independent judiciary. He felt that the fugitive's interest lay with the system that would best preserve a courageous and intelligent judiciary. The coincidence of popular passion with moral right in the *Sims* Case was by no means clear and, in any event, not inevitable.[15]

The convention of 1853 implicitly rejected the notion that a judge ought to perform his tasks with an eye to the morality of the majority. But Dana's suggestion that an independent and high-minded judge was the fugitive's best refuge was simply whistling in the dark. The list of independent and high-minded judges who upheld the Act of 1850 began to lengthen: McLean in Ohio and Michigan; Kane in Pennsylvania; Grier in Pennsylvania; Miller in Wisconsin; Conkling in New York; Woodbury and Curtis in Massachusetts; and, of course, as always, Shaw. More and more, it appeared the question ought not to be put, ''How should a judge of integrity decide these cases?'' but rather ''how can a man of integrity judge these cases?'' Finally, in 1854 the ''Burns affair'' provided a forum for just this issue.*

---

* A detailed contemporaneous account of the Burns affair is provided by Charles Stevens, *Anthony Burns, A Narrative* (Boston: J. P. Jewett & Co., 1856). That work includes not only an account from which most subsequent work has borrowed heavily, but an appendix of some of the documents. The work is least good on the issue of Loring's removal. For a more up to

Anthony Burns, an alleged fugitive, was arrested in Boston in June, 1854. At first, the *Burns* case seemed to be but another in a long line of fugitive cases. The question was simply whether Burns would be purchased like Latimer, rescued like Shadrach, or returned to slavery like Sims. Dana went through the motions as counsel. The state courts and Shaw held firm to their line in *Sims*. Recourse to collateral attack before the federal district court by writ *de homine replegiando* was similarly to no avail. The commissioner, Edward G. Loring, issued the certificate of removal despite conflicting testimony on whether Burns was, in fact, the same man as the fugitive in question.[16]

Public opinion in Massachusetts was virtually unanimous in its sympathy with Burns. For the first time, if Dana's assessment of the matter is to be credited, the tide in Boston harbor had shifted clearly against the Act of 1850. Because of the strong public reaction and because Loring, the commissioner, also held the office of state probate judge, it was possible, in effect, to put the commissioner on trial for having consented to be a judge—or at least the sort of judge who might have to decide fugitive slave cases. Wendell Phillips and Richard Hildreth instigated a campaign to seek Loring's removal from his office of probate judge by means of "address" by the state legislature. In February 1855, hearings were held before the Committee on Federal Relations of the Massachusetts legislature. The Garrisonians had their forum. Edward G. Loring was on trial for having been a slave commissioner.[17]

The hearing before the House Committee pitted Wendell Phillips against Richard Henry Dana. Others appeared on both sides, and Loring defended himself, but the Phillips-Dana confrontation raised all of the issues and provided the drama. Phillips steadfastly refused to characterize the proceeding as an attempt to remove Loring for the content of his decision. He maintained, consistent with his past work, that it is acting as commissioner that is reprehensible, not deciding in

date and impartial account, see S. Shapiro, "The Rendition of Anthony Burns," *Journal of Negro History,* 44 (1959) : 34–51. The jurisprudential implications of the Loring removal have not been adequately explored. It is usually treated as evidence of the volatile antislavery atmosphere of Boston. Never is its connection with conflicting bases of role and personal responsibility analyzed. Yet, to some of the main actors, Dana and Phillips, its significance lay precisely there. The Shapiro article is a bit disappointing in this respect as is the same author's biography of Dana. See Samuel Shapiro, *Richard Henry Dana, Jr.* (East Lansing: Michigan State University Press, 1961).

accord with the law as it appears to be on a good faith reading. To participate in the re-enslavement of a humble, hard-working man, who at last secured a small measure of personal integrity under the "free stars" of Massachusetts was a morally reprehensible act. The perpetrator of this act should not sit to protect widows and orphans. Admitting the competing value of a judge's obligation to obey the law and apply and interpret it in good faith, Phillips stressed that a man need not embrace the opportunity to be a legalized kidnapper. The examples that Phillips would hold up to Loring were not the judges of Wisconsin who found the act unconstitutional, but an obscure United States commissioner who quit rather than enforce the act of 1850, a police officer who resigned rather than participate in a return, and another commissioner who recused himself in all fugitive cases. Even before the Act of 1850, Phillips had published and approved the letter of an obscure Massachusetts Justice of the Peace, resigning his commission because he could not morally swear to enforce the Constitution of the United States. Phillips would not have held Loring to so high a standard, but at least the commission designed specifically for fugitive slaves ought to be refused.[18]

Next, Dana addressed the committee. He was a particularly persuasive ally for Loring, since he had been the chief counsel for Burns before the commissioner. Dana, as an antislavery man whose sympathies were well-known, brought an air of impartial, institutional concern to the proceeding. Certainly, no one thought Dana spoke out of love for Loring or for his decision. He characterized the commissioner as weak, petty, unimaginative, a lackey to other and larger interests. But Dana opposed the removal of the man because he thought it would do violence to the value of an independent judiciary. Dana argued that only that principle made possible the Wisconsin Supreme Court's thunderbolt in the *Booth* cases (discussed within). He did not buy Phillips's careful distinction between retaliation for the content of a decision and retaliation for accepting the office. He cited Charles Sumner's standing offer to act as a slave commissioner. Antislavery opinion applauded this thinly veiled threat to find the act invalid. Surely, if Loring had been an antislavery man, determined to find the act invalid, or even likely to favorably stretch the evidence, the petition for removal would never have been presented—at least not by the present petitioners.

Dana closed by suggesting that the object of preventing state judges from serving as United States commissioners could best be served by prospective legislation that could not, in any sense, be construed as, or have the effect of, diminishing the independence of the judiciary.[19]

Dana and Phillips could respect each other, but they could not agree on the order of value and factual priorities. Nonparticipation seemed, to Dana, a fruitless strategy, in a sense, a cop-out. He recognized the severe integrity of Phillips's view and the personal integrity of its proponent who, himself, had given up a promising career at the bar and social prestige:

> All this he sacraficed, because he would not misconstrue the Constitution, and his sense of duty, growing, he will permit me to say, out of a wrong view of the relation of men to the state, or rather of the state itself to the Great Lawgiver, this sense of duty called upon him for the great sacrafice, and he made it.[20]

Dana would have substituted for this strategy, the objective of procuring a great freedom-loving decision in the manner of Holt. A giant of the law could do a gigantic act. To prepare the path for this giant, the antislavery bar should develop its arguments and preserve the process—especially the independence of the judiciary.

Phillips could not have agreed as to the tactical or moral soundness of this position. Tactically he had already expressed himself as certain that the continued veneration of Constitution and judge could only be self-defeating since the nature of the bargain, the nature of the instrument, and the nature of the office precluded results favorable to freedom. Morally, he was skeptical as to the possibility of a man acting with wisdom, compassion, and strength vis-à-vis the fugitive and remaining faithful to his duty as a judge. The independence of the judiciary was not a major value for Phillips, while the moral purity purchased through nonparticipation was not a critical value for Dana.

In the battle on the floor of the House, Phillips's objective and Dana's fears were both realized. The legislature voted to address the Governor for Loring's removal. But the speeches of the leading proponents for the measure failed to incorporate Phillips's careful distinctions. James Stone of Boston, chairman of the committee that reported out the measure, thought the main objective was to insure that no slave be removed from Massachusetts without a jury trial. He opposed making state office and the office of commissioner incompatible, since it would prevent men like Sumner from subverting the act. Loring's failing was "his defiance of the moral sentiments of Massachusetts." Stone concluded,

> But these incidental points should not control the case. Above and beyond them all, is the one great fact, that, by a dash of the Commissioner's pen, he transmuted a human being into property. Any law that you may pass to prevent this in the future, will be, at least, amenable to the objection of alleged unconstitutionality, maintained by a certain class. But you can adopt this address, while no one can complain that it is nullification, or that it is unconstitutional, and no state or individual can deny the power and the right to do it.[21]

John Swift of Boston also supported the measure. He met Dana's judicial independence point head on. Empirically the "independence" provided had been shielding men like Loring who, by Dana's own admission were weak, dependent, and without instincts of humanity. Swift accused Dana of regarding "the Priesthood and the judiciary as sacred institutions."

> . . . if to serve the phantom of an independent judge, which some men have, we must submit to injustice—if the only condition of safety to our own present judicial system is the subjugation of conscience—then it is time . . . that we have a judiciary dependent upon justice and rectitude.[22]

Whatever Phillips's careful qualifications might have been, Messrs. Swift and Stone simply wanted to beat some fellows into line.

The successful removal of Loring did not regain the Constitution for Massachusetts antislavery. Rather, insofar as it represented anything more than retaliation against a man for a particularly unpopular decision, it constituted acquiescence in the loss of the Constitution to slavery. It was an acceptance not only of Wendell Phillips's stern morality, but also of his constitutional positivism.

In the West the Act of 1850 also brought renewed hope of legal success by antislavery forces, though it by no means led to abandonment of the strategy of making natural law positive. Although Salmon Chase's political career took him out of the courtroom arena, the views he had so vigorously pursued continued to be asserted by John Jolliffe and James Birney. *Miller v. McQuerry* was the first of the important Ohio cases to consider the constitutionality of the act. Despite the differences between the Act of 1850 and that of 1793, the thrust of the argument against the statute continued to be its inconsistency with natural right and justice along with the presumption that the Constitution ought to be interpreted to be consistent with natural law. In *Miller v. McQuerry,* McLean announced his judgment that the Act of 1850, too, was constitutional, and he renewed his determination that all such cases be decided by positivist principles and with no recourse to "natural justice." It is in the *McQuerry* case, which was considered a critical sounding board by the antislavery movement, that McLean stressed most fervently an inability to do anything but uphold the act.[23]

John McLean's decision hardly came as a surprise. Chase wrote to Sumner that the course of the Justice's earlier work prepared him for it. But it should be noted that in *McQuerry* the earlier tendencies became a sharply focused argument. McLean had gone from constitutional bargain to social contract. He had escalated the basis for enforcement of the Fugitive Act from the terms upon which the Union was formed—itself a dubious proposition—to the consensual basis of ordered society. In *McQuerry,* McLean concerned himself not with a law, but with law as antithesis to anarchy. McLean's decisions with respect to the Act of 1850 brought renewed attempts to secure a state forum for the act's victims. In Ohio the battle for an alternative forum was fought out in the most prolonged and bitter series of confrontations between state and federal courts of the period. In 1855 free blacks in Cincinnati sought the release of a child, Rosetta Armstead, claiming that her master had voluntarily brought her into Ohio.[24] A probate court ordered a guardian appointed for her and subsequently ordered the discharge of the child on a writ of habeas corpus brought on her behalf.

The master then obtained a warrant for Rosetta as a fugitive from service. The guardian obtained another writ of habeas corpus from a state court, upon the return to which the child was again discharged. Upon the marshal's refusal to obey the order of the state court, the court held him in contempt and ordered his arrest. The marshal sought release through a federal writ of habeas corpus directed to the sheriff. Justice McLean, on circuit, issued the writ and released the marshal. The Justice made plain his belief that the state lacked constitutional authority to even compel a return to its process on the part of a federal officer: "A sense of duty compels me to say that the [state habeas] proceedings were not only without the authority of law, but against law, and that the proceedings are void. . . ." [25]

The conflict was finally resolved without the necessity of force when the United States commissioner refused a certificate of removal on the ground that there had been no escape—that Rosetta was not a fugitive within the meaning either of the act or the Constitution. The *Rosetta* case demonstrated dramatically the utility of securing a state forum even if the last word were to be that of the federal court or commissioner. The state court proceedings permitted the testimony of the alleged fugitive. They could then be used to establish certain facts by documents in the proceeding before the commissioner. Moreover, in the state court proceeding the alleged fugitive could obtain other protections—here, the benefit of a guardian *ad litem*. [26] The result in the Rosetta case also seemed to suggest that where there was evidence that would lead a state court, in a good faith adjudication, to find that the alleged fugitive was not in fact a fugitive from service, the commissioner would be less likely to grant the certificate as a matter of form. Finally, the state court proceedings could prolong the entire matter to the point where a rescue might be made, a purchase might be negotiated, or a witness might be found to help the fugitive's case.

The confrontation of state and federal process became something of a familiar scene in Ohio. A year after the *Rosetta* case, the same marshal arrested alleged fugitives on a commissioner's warrant. Again, a writ of habeas corpus was obtained from the state courts. This time the marshal refused to present the prisoners. Again the marshal was held in contempt; and, again, he was released on a federal writ of habeas corpus. [27]

Still a year later, the scenario was repeated with a considerable escalation in the level of conflict. A posse of nine men and a deputy federal marshal were in the process of bringing in four men accused of aiding and abetting in a rescue. The sheriff of Clark County, Ohio, tried to serve the marshal and posse with a writ of habeas corpus, but was "violently resisted and assaulted" in his attempt at service. Piqued, the sheriff gathered a substantial armed force that apprehended all ten in the federal posse, holding them in Clark County, while their four prisoners were brought before the probate judge of Champaign who had originally issued the writ. The four prisoners were discharged upon the default of the marshal who was, all the while, locked up in the adjoining county. In the annual federal habeas corpus proceeding, the district court saw the state process as something more than a simple legal battle over jurisdiction. He characterized the state habeas as "merely colorable, issued in fraud of the law, and . . . a part of a conspiracy by which to effect the rescue of the prisoners." [28]

With the use of state process to attempt to free aiders and abettors, a new element of legal strategy was introduced. The resort to the state courts on behalf of the alleged fugitive himself, we observed, was almost a matter of necessity. The proceedings before the commissioner admitted of no appeal and excluded the testimony of the fugitive. An aider and abettor, however, was simply one accused of a federal crime. He would have the right to a full trial by jury in a federal court. Yet while obstruction and the hope for rescue undoubtedly played some part in the decision to use the tactic, there is at least one other reason that was present in the decision to precipitate conflict. The Constitution was slipping away from the antislavery forces. The course of federal court decisions not only was decidedly adverse to the novel arguments proposed by antislavery lawyers, it also seemed to be actively furthering the congressional objective of plugging up loopholes in the scheme for rendition of fugitives. Indeed, before the federal courts it was difficult even to get an acknowledgment of such arguments as the right to a trial by jury. If nothing else, a sharply defined struggle between state and federal courts would reestablish the dialectic.

If the potential conflict inherent in federalism were to be used as a lever to secure a dialogue on constitutional principles, some state court more prestigious than the probate court of Champlain, Ohio, would have to endorse the antislavery theories. The endorsement came with the *Booth* cases in Wisconsin. In the *Sherman Booth* affair the long string of failures was finally broken with a single, crowning, if fleeting, achievement.[29] The elements were typical, the result unique. The slave Glover was apprehended in Racine by a federal marshal pursuant to a warrant. Upon Glover's arrest, the slaveowner, Garland, and the federal marshal were arrested by the sheriff for assault and battery upon Glover. While they went off to jail, Glover was rescued by a mob. The federal district court released the owner and marshal on a federal writ of habeas corpus.[30] Sherman Booth and John Rycraft were then apprehended for prosecution as aiders and abettors in the rescue of Glover. They sought discharge on a writ of habeas corpus from the Wisconsin state courts. After apprehension, and before indictment, Booth was ordered discharged on the writ by Judge A. D. Smith of the Wisconsin Supreme Court, sitting alone during vacation. Smith upheld virtually all of the arguments that had been made against the Fugitive Slave Acts for the past two decades. He held the Act of 1850 unconstitutional on the ground that Article IV conferred on Congress no power to legislate with respect to fugitives; on the ground that the Act of 1850 denied to the fugitive a right to a trial by jury; and on the ground that the act denied the alleged fugitive due process of law. Smith considered *Prigg* an incorrect decision, and felt that he was bound to hold the Act of 1850 void in spite of that decision, even assuming it to be applicable.[31]

Upon reconvening, the full bench of the Wisconsin Supreme Court affirmed Smith's decision. After indictment, Booth was rearrested. Upon his application for a writ of habeas corpus, the Wisconsin court denied the writ. It held that the state court should defer to the federal court during the pendency of the criminal matter.[32] However, after conviction both Booth and Rycraft again sought discharge from the Wisconsin court. This time, the State Supreme Court ordered their discharge, reaffirming their holding that the Act of 1850 was unconstitutional.[33] The United States sought review in the Supreme Court of the United States. Upon instructions from the state judges, the clerk of the Wisconsin court refused to make any return to the writ of error from the United States Supreme Court. The high Court then held that such a refusal could not prevent the exercise of its appellate jurisdiction, and issued a direct order to the clerk to make a return.[34] The return was never made. The Supreme Court proceeded to hear the case upon a certified copy of the record. The Supreme Court's decision was the last and greatest blow of the Taney court against antislavery.[35] *Dred Scott* had greater political implications, but *Ableman v. Booth* was the nail in the coffin of a legal strategy that had preoccupied the antislavery bar for almost the entire period of militant abolitionist activity.

The Supreme Court first denied the power of the state courts to reach the restraint of one held pursuant to federal process even through habeas corpus. Taken at its broadest, and there are no qualifications in the decision, the doctrine was a startling assertion of federal power. Only a year before, the leading treatise on habeas corpus had concluded that the state and federal courts had concurrent jurisdiction in habeas corpus with respect to prisoners held through federal process. Even the Massachusetts court in *Sims's Case* had declined to hold that the states had no power to issue the writ against a federal prisoner. The *Booth* decision was written by that champion of states' rights, Roger Taney.*

As an aside, the Court in *Ableman v. Booth* also upheld the constitutionality of the Act of 1850—the first and only such imprimatur that the act would have from the Supreme Court of the United States. Taney did not see fit ever to mention most of the grounds on which the Supreme Court of Wisconsin had found the act invalid. Taney seemed to think that the course of decisions upholding the Act of 1793 provided ample authority.[36]

For purposes of this section, the most important attributes of this case are in the opinions of the Wisconsin judges. Judge Smith rested his decidedly radical view of the Constitution, not upon precedent, not upon history, and not solely upon a view of the judicial function

---

* 62 U.S., pp. 507–26. It seems highly relevant to note that the broad assertion of federal power and state helplessness concerning habeas corpus jurisdiction in *Ableman v. Booth* (1859) had to be reasserted after the Civil War in *Tarble's Case*, 80 U.S. (13 Wall.) 397 (1872). It is as if the unambiguous language of *Booth* could not be trusted because of its intimate connection with slavery and with the court that had rendered *Dred Scott*. It is equally significant that the lone dissenter in *Tarble's Case* was Chief Justice Salmon P. Chase, ordinarily an advocate of a strong national position. But the man whose career, in a sense, began with *Mathilda's Case,* a state habeas proceeding concerning a fugitive, the man who struggled to create a viable forum for testing the odious Fugitive Acts, could not reconcile himself to the withering of the formal apparatus for realizing such a test. The formal apparatus had become intertwined with the very idea of liberty and would not be forsaken even after slavery had been abolished.

that would permit him, as an individual, to incorporate his own ideas of right into the law. Smith's doctrine was articulated largely in terms of states' rights. It was not A. D. Smith, but the state of Wisconsin, that had the authority to disavow particular decisions that infringed upon the right of the state with respect to fugitive rendition:

> At least such shall not become the degradation of Wisconsin, without meeting as stern remonstrance and resistance as I may be able to interpose, so long as her people impose upon me the duty of guarding their rights and liberties. . . .[37]

The chief justice, Crawford, was less inclined to assert authority to reexamine matters foreclosed by United States Supreme Court decisions. Consequently, Crawford took a most limited view of what prior cases had determined. He considered the right of trial by jury for the fugitive not yet decided. Moreover, the jurisdiction of the commissioners was especially vulnerable since it came in only with the Act of 1850. Crawford relied heavily on these points, holding them still open under applicable precedents.[38]

Wisconsin was to prove unique in its course of creating new constitutional law. In Ohio all the seed were present, but they never bore fruit. The lower state courts had often been used to inhibit the federal rendition process. The issue did not reach the state supreme court, however, until 1859—well after the Wisconsin decisions in *Booth,* and just after reversal of those decisions by the United States Supreme Court.[39] The dramatic events leading to *Ex Parte Bushnell* were not atypical. A forcible rescue of a captured fugitive, John, took place in Wellington, Ohio. The mob that rescued John was largely from nearby Oberlin, a hotbed of abolitionist sentiment. The remarkable feature of the Oberlin-Wellington rescue case was the determination of the federal authorities to try some forty participants in the rescue for criminal violations of the Act of 1850.[40]

The Oberlin-Wellington affair was a showcase for conflicting theories of obligation. Rufus Spalding, for the defendants, ventured to urge on the federal district court, a course of purposeful disobedience to the mandates of the Supreme Court. Noting *Prigg* and *Booth,* he concluded, nevertheless, that "so glaringly unjust a decision as the affirmation of the constitutionality of this act can bind no one." He went on to state that were he in the judge's place, he would, in violation of those decisions, declare the act unconstitutional,

> though in thus doing, I should risk an impeachment before the Senate of my Country; and, sir, should such an impeachment work my removal from office I should proudly embrace it as a greater honor than has yet fallen to the lot of any judicial officer of the United States.[41]

In response, the District Attorney derided higher-law theories and branded the defendants as St. Peck, St. Fitch, the Saints of Oberlin, etc. The court ignored much of the rhetoric of both sides but charged the jury that much of what has been said "would be entitled to great weight if addressed to Congress . . . or to an ecclesiastical tribunal. . . ."[42]

A verdict of guilty in the first of the cases tried led to vigorous attempts to secure state habeas corpus relief. The Ohio Supreme Court, however, in a very long opinion, refused to use the state writ of habeas corpus to release accused aiders and abettors. Two of the five justices dissented and would have held the act unconstitutional. The opinion of the court was written by Chief Justice Swan who had been elected to the bench as an antislavery man. He admitted that confronted with a helpless fugitive he might be disposed to help the man. However, as a judge, he hoped that he would have the courage to uphold his own legal convictions, since he could not but find the Act of 1850 constitutional.[43]

The Wisconsin Supreme Court and the Ohio dissenters asserted the power to reach independent conclusions on constitutional law and treated the precedents of the Supreme Court of the United States in such matters as no more conclusive than the opinions of a high court of coordinate level. They were able to establish the freedom to work new law by denying nothing beyond the hierarchy of authority within the legal structure.[44] The substance of the new law they would have made was not, itself, beyond the pale of progress by the judiciary.

Ableman v. Booth and the Anthony Burns affair mark the culmination of the two major threads of antislavery legal thought. The one was the most extensive and successful of the many attempts to make a new constitutional law that would at least emphasize the elements of the Constitution that were essentially antithetical to slavery; the other marked the only full-scale debate before a tribunal of sorts over the principle of nonparticipation as a "legal" strategy. The results revealed the inherent limitations of the two approaches. Because neutral principles of constitutional lines of authority had to be violated to effectuate the result in the *Booth* cases, they became not a showcase for the legal denouement of slavery, but a battle over the structure of federalism. Moreover, the federalism of the Wisconsin courts in *Booth* was by no means one uniformly in keeping with the needs of the antislavery movement. Such a federalism might have meant concession to the South on such bitterly fought issues as Negro Seamen's rights, and the right to send antislavery materials into Southern communities. Moreover, it would have been a step in the opposite direction from the assertions of national power to control slavery in the territories or the domestic slave trade. Finally, as the first half of the Supreme Court's opinion reversing the Wisconsin judgment made clear, it was possible to join issue in most relevant and conclusive terms with the Wisconsin court's decision without even mentioning slavery.

The difficulties with the tactic assumed in *Burns* were no less formidable. Most important, the tactic promised no help for the particular person affected, or likely soon to be affected, by the system attacked. Neither the removal of Loring nor the state prohibition against its officials assuming such tasks had any hope of putting a block on the rendition process. Here too, moreover, a "neutral" principle of importance was involved. Although not of constitutional dimension, the principle of an independent (state) judiciary was one that had become a major public issue by the mid-nineteenth century. The translation of the moral principle of voluntary abstention into the practical, political proposition to penalize for nonabstention created an inevitable conflict between these values, a conflict that even strong antislavery lawyers such as Dana could not lightly abide. Conflict between the values that create a viable and desirable system of law and the value of maximizing the pressure against slavery remained, then, even with Wendell Phillips's route.

I have noted that many of the cases under the Act of 1850 were not collateral proceedings directed to the captivity of the fugitive himself, but criminal or civil proceedings directed against the rescuer, aider, or abettor of the fugitive. *Jones v. Van Zandt,* under the old act, had been such a case, but criminal and civil proceedings against the fugitive's friends multiplied fearfully after the Act of 1850. The most important procedural consequence of this fact was that the jury, so long sought as a forum for the fugitive himself, was at last attained at least for his supporters. For the criminal and civil cases against aiders and abettors were simply ordinary criminal trials or actions at common law. The jury was available as of right. In practical terms, this forum was very important. In Massachusetts nine accused aiders and abettors went free largely because hung juries on the first two prosecutions indicated almost certain failure for the rest. In Pennsylvania, draconian attempts to convict resisters of treason, rather than simple "aiding a fugitive," ended with verdicts of not guilty. These instances, and many others, are documented in Stanley Campbell's excellent treatment, *The Slave Catchers*. But it should not be thought that federal judges either welcomed or easily tolerated jury proclivities to acquit. In Boston, Benjamin Curtis vigorously fought against any enlargement of the area of jury discretion. In *United States v. Morris*, a prosecution against a black attorney for his alleged part in a rescue attempt, Richard Dana and John Hale argued that the jury should be instructed that it could independently decide both law and fact. Curtis not only refused to give any such discretion to the jury, he explicitly charged them that their moral responsibility was to make every conscientious effort to apply the law as charged by the judge to the facts as found by themselves. He stressed that "power" is not "right;" and that the mere fact that there was no easy way to pierce a general verdict of acquittal, in no sense gave the jury a "right" to render such a verdict contrary to the law charged by the judge.[45] It is interesting to note that in Boston, Dana and Hale did not even attempt to appeal to natural law or to the conscience of the jury. They knew such an explicit appeal would be countered by the judiciary, though, of course, they hoped the indirect route would have the same impact. In Ohio, McLean instructed juries a half-dozen times to ignore conscience and decide according to the artificial morality of law; Judge Grier gave similar instructions in Pennsylvania.[46]

Given the background to those jury cases, any other result would have been surprising. However, it should be made explicit that responsibility to positive law was conceived and articulated as the duty of the juror every bit as much as of the judge.

The narrative of fugitive slave cases in this chapter makes clear that the interplay of antislavery demand and judicial "cannot" was seldom on the simple level of "what is the law?" The antislavery bar sought doctrinal growth, minimally. The utopians sought constitutional upheaval. Both practitioners and utopians seemed to tread the line of demanding conscious disregard of role limits. The judicial responses to these demands, insofar as they went beyond refusal, appealed to one or more of four justifications for role fidelity.

The most extreme justification asserted that ordered society itself depended on judicial adherence to positive law, constitutional limits. Thus, McLean's assertion that disregard of these limits "would undermine and overturn the social compact." The terms of ordered society embrace fidelity to the limits and conditions on which power is conferred.

A second, somewhat more common, justification for "cannot" is that of "separation of powers": "It is for the people . . . and their representatives . . . to consider the laws of nature." Now, the "social compact" justification may be used (as it was by McLean) in conjunction with the separation of powers. But the judge may appeal to separation of powers as a self-evident, presumably acceptable, argument, without in turn justifying it with the social compact. He may consider the principle of distribution of sovereignty a desirable end, in itself, regardless of whether sanctioned as one of the terms of the original agreement.

A third justification of judicial role fidelity—in particular with regard to the Fugitive Slave Law—was "union." I have already noted the common view of the Fugitive Slave clause as a basic part of the constitutional bargain. I think it fair to say that not a little of this vision was a reading of the problems of the present backward into history. As the fugitive issue was one of the critical issues for compromise or adjustment in 1850, it was seen as one of the great issues of 1787.

Finally, a few judges justified their adherence to role limits by stressing their oath to support the Constitution. The oath was entitled to respect because it was a solemn, consensual undertaking on their part, and because it was a legitimate requirement for the exercise of delegated power.

When Story pointed to the Constitution as the only legitimate source of his judicial obligation, he evoked all four of these justifications. The Constitution derived its moral authority from its character as a substantially democratic and consensual arrangement of a polity. In its wisdom, it preserved limited spheres for the various branches of government. And, it embraced the agreed upon terms for cementing the Union. Story, like all other judges, was sworn to uphold it. Thus, the word "constitution" was a remarkably powerful shorthand—a symbol that evoked all of the relevant values on the side of judicial fidelity to law.

PART III

THE MORAL-FORMAL DILEMMA

He who clings to a law does not fear the judgment
that reinstates him in an order he believes in. But the
keenest of human torments is to be judged without a
law. Yet we are in that torment. Deprived of their
natural curb, the judges, loosed at random, are rac-
ing through their job. Hence we have to try to go
faster than they, don't we?

Camus, *The Fall*

The preceding chapters have described a variety of contexts in which antislavery judges decided cases amidst claims that the morality of slavery be considered as a major factor in the decision. Usually these claims were put forward directly by the parties or their representatives. Few of the men who made such claims and none of the judges who heard them, however, thought that consideration of the morality of slavery alone would suffice to reach a decision. Most of the actors assumed that in many cases an antislavery result could be achieved only with some stretching or reconstruction of formal principles. By formal principles I mean: (1) those governing the role of the judge, his place vis-à-vis other lawmaking bodies, his subordination to precedent, statute, Constitution; (2) the hierarchical character of the judicial system and the respect due to both the decrees and the precedents of higher tribunals and especially the Supreme Court; (3) the standards of professional responsibility, articulated more often in schools, treatises, and controversy literature than in decisions and statutes; (4) the sense of the judicial craft.

Both the judges and the men who addressed them understood that these formal constraints were independently justifiable in terms of interests they served. Therefore, the judge's problem in any case where some impact on the formal apparatus could be expected, was never a single-dimensioned moral question—is slavery or enslavement, or rendition to slavery, morally justified or reprehensible? rather, the issue was whether the moral values served by antislavery (the substantive moral dimension) outweighed interests and values served by fidelity to the formal system when such values seemed to block direct application of the moral or natural law proposition.

I shall designate choices between these two sets of values as "moral-formal decisions." By this designation I do not mean to imply that there is no moral dimension to fidelity to formal principles or to the content of the principles themselves. In a sense the moral-formal decision was a moral-moral' decision—a decision between the substantive moral propositions relating to slavery and liberty and the moral ends served by the formal structure as a whole, by fidelity to it, or by some relevant particular element of it. Thus, the legal actor did not choose between liberty and slavery. He had to choose between liberty and ordered federalism; between liberty and consistent limits on the judicial function; between liberty and fidelity to public trust; between liberty and adherence to the public corporate undertakings of nationhood; or, as some of the judges would have it, between liberty and the viability of the social compact. Moreover individual cases seldom presented the choice between universal liberty and total destruction of the competing values underlying the formal restraints. Rather, they presented choices between incremental furtherance of liberty and marginal vitiation of these values.

Because of the difficulties inherent in making the sorts of choices outlined above, many antislavery advocates either argued that the relevant choice point be shifted to the decision of entering or remaining within the formal structures, or that moral imperatives be translated into legal ones. By deciding to act as insurgent rather than judge, a man could avoid confronting many of the formal issues involved in the judicial choice. He need not have worried about considerations of constitutional limits on judicial lawmaking, whether deemed to have emerged out of considerations of federalism or of separation of powers. Moreover, even his obligations of fidelity to decisions and processes of the majority were of a different and lesser character as citizen than as magistrate. To act as insurgent was to assume a role the ethic of which was compatible with an antislavery stance amidst a proslavery legal system. This decision thus eliminated the tension of moral-formal conflict.

The alternative course of working within the formal system to translate moral imperatives into legal ones led to a constant battle over the formal principles. Instead of arguing about slavery, the antislavery man found himself arguing about state court habeas corpus jurisdiction; the appellate authority of the United States Supreme Court over state court decisions; the proper bounds of judicial interpretation; and the deference due to imperfectly articulated legislative policy. Such sidetracks could be avoided only by asserting an alternative formal (legal) principle that either maintained the identity of moral and legal imperatives through requiring the law to conform to some "natural law," or presumed the identity of law and morality subject only to explicit defeasance by express legislative action. As I have shown, such natural law constructs bore little relation to the uses to which "nature" had been put in slave law for more than a half-century and conflicted directly with the dominant jurisprudential and constitutional assumptions of the profession.

In Part II I explored the ramifications of these two antislavery strategies. The practical limitations of each of them in terms of antislavery objectives became clear. In this section I want first to identify those characteristics of the doctrinal and adversary contexts in which cases were decided that seemed to produce the most pointed articulations of the moral-formal problem. Second, I wish to produce some very tentative conclusions about judicial behavior when subjected to such pressures.

Whenever judges confronted the moral-formal dilemma, they almost uniformly applied the legal rules. Moreover, they seemed very reluctant to resort to, and thus legitimate, substantial doctrinal innovations that might have made certain cases less a choice between law and morality and more a choice between alternative legal formulations. Furthermore, even as they opted for role fidelity and noninnovative behavior, these judges accompanied their decisions with striking manifestations of at least one of three related responsibility-mitigation mechanisms: (1) Elevation of the formal stakes (sometimes combined with minimization of the moral stakes). (2) Retreat to a mechanistic formalism. (3) Ascription of responsibility elsewhere.* While all three of these are related and, indeed, may be viewed as different perspectives on a single phenomenon, it is useful to treat them separately. The more aggravated the conflict between moral and formal demands on the judge, the more pronounced these

---

* By "elevation of formal stakes," I mean the tendency to choose the highest of possible justifications for the principle of formalism relied upon. By minimization of moral stakes I mean the failure to raise the moral issue to the same level of principle as the formal practice.

I use the term *"retreat* to formalism" intentionally rather than the more neutral *"appeal* to formalism." Obviously, "retreat" implies a somewhat unwarranted "appeal"—an "appeal" to formalism with the purpose or function of avoiding unpleasant decisions. The question of whether this label can be maintained depends on evaluation of rather inexact evidence. Some analysis is provided within, on pages 232–36. Further evidence is provided in the Appendix.

By "ascription of responsibility elsewhere," I mean something beyond a statement that legal authority lodges decisional power elsewhere, for I would argue that certain statements that purport to be statements concerning the locus of decisional power are, indeed, the functional equivalent of an expression of helplessness. This is especially the case where the denial of decisional power in the judge is accompanied by no precise statement of alternative locus of power or when a very vague locus ("the people") is put forward.

effects seem to be. For that reason, it is desirable to first identify the context variables that affected response and only, thereafter, to examine the behavioral products of the judicial dilemma.

It should be noted, parenthetically, that the hypothesis that follows is suggestive of an alternative approach to judicial "styles" from that set forward in the standard works. In *The Common Law Tradition,* Llewellyn contrasted a "grand style" of American judicial creativity, prevalent at mid-nineteenth century, with the "formal style" of the 1890's.[1] Horwitz, in his article on the "Instrumental Conception of Law," also was concerned to date the emergence of a utility-policy orientation in judicial lawmaking.[2] The following chapter and the data in the preceding chapters suggest that style, and especially appeals to formalism, may be not only the product of an "age" or a "jurisprudence," but of various external and internal pressures on the judge of which moral beliefs is one. I would suggest here that any fully descriptive jurisprudence must have complementary components for noting both the generative and the restraining elements of a formal legal system. Which of the components is stressed will be more issue-related than time-bound. Thus, in slavery, as we shall see, the 1840's and 1850's were not a golden age of free-wheeling policy jurisprudence, but an age of the retreat to formalism. Conversely, the first twenty-five years of the nation were far less formal. What follows is, in part, an attempt to account for the striking changes in slave case styles, but the hypothesis might profitably be expanded to test whether and how judicial styles vary with respect to issues and pressures.

CHAPTER TWELVE: Context for Conscience

The judicial conscience is an artful dodger and rightfully so. Before it will concede that a case is one that presents a moral dilemma, it will hide in the nooks and crannies of the professional ethics, run to the caves of role limits, seek the shelter of separation of powers. And, indeed, it is right and fitting that such insulation exists. As Professor Herbert Wechsler has written:

> . . . one of the ways in which a rich society avoids what might otherwise prove to be insoluble dilemmas of choice is to recognize a separation of functions, a distribution of responsibilities, with respect to problems of that kind, and this is particularly recurrent in the legal profession.[1]

But with all its resources for avoiding definition of judicial problems as moral ones, it is yet possible to trap the elusive creature. There must be a doctrinal situation that leaves the judge sufficiently little room for maneuver and a dialectical situation that forces the judge to move beyond the pat and normally sufficient answer of reiteration of role expectations. In this chapter I shall examine first the doctrinal patterns within which antislavery judges operated and then the dialectical ones. Finally, I shall examine the interaction of these two elements as they shaped the context for judicial response.

Doctrinal Direction and Weight

A judicial decision seldom simply states the law. It assesses the extant sources of law; measures them for appropriateness to the particular situation, for soundness, for the degree of deference due their author or proclaimer. The judge seeks a pattern to the possible sources of authority except in the plainest cases (where the pattern is apprehended without much discussion or thought). It is commonplace for a result to be justified, not on the basis of the force of square precedent, but on the basis of the direction in which the law is moving.

For a judge to be confronted with a moral-formal dilemma

required, by definition, some relevant disparity between the force of legal and moral norms. However, the judge intuitively dealt with the legal norms as a system of rules in flux. In any dynamic system the factors that relate to change are as important as those that describe position in the system at a given point in time. The antislavery judge, therefore, was aware not only of a disparity between the legal rules he enforced and his moral position, but also of the likely shape and effect of those rules in the future. To the extent that he saw law "moving" in a direction that would converge with his moral beliefs, the conflict generated by the gap at a particular point in time was lessened. Conversely, as legal doctrine grew apart from antislavery morality, the conflict was accentuated. (Divergence of law and morality suggested a sense of loss, and with loss frustration.) In the face of "divergence," the individual judge may have felt that any course of action entailed unpleasant risks. To strike out against the tide raised the specter of futility; to swim with the tide raised that of complicity.

Convergence or divergence of law and morality need not be total. On a systemic level, a judge might perceive the law in its entirety as tending toward either elimination or legitimation of slavery. Alternatively, and more commonly, he could see a particular issue or set of issues as moving toward a result harmonious with or divergent from the result consistent with antislavery morality. The multiplicity of ends served by law will more often than not produce a pattern that is not entirely consistent when measured by a single moral variable.

Systemic Convergence

Judges were, at times, required to act within a system that had already committed itself (or appeared about to do so) to the abolition of slavery. Acting during a transition period, they yet faced distasteful conflicts between law and morality in particular cases. Yet the perception that the "gap" was only a temporary phenomenon reduced any incipient degree of moral anguish and the motivation to "solve" the problem. Every case decided in the context of a working gradual emancipation scheme exemplified this phenomenon. In such cases, judges never seemed terribly torn between right and law. They did not speak of conscience and the need to steel oneself to duty. Where controversy existed, as between the Tilghman and Gibson approaches to defects in registration, the tone of the opinions was restrained and relatively impersonal.[2] Of the cases discussed in the previous chapters, none articulated the special character of convergence better than *State v. Post*.[3] The New Jersey Supreme Court confronted a demand by radical antislavery lawyers that either natural law be applied to free those Negroes remaining in bondage in New Jersey, or that the new state constitution's preamble he read to free them. The court responded to these demands with a description of the march of gradual emancipation in New Jersey. The denial of liberty to the plaintiffs and to others like them was part of a scheme the overall purpose of which was benevolent. Because of their perspective on the general convergence of the system with antislavery, the judges appeared almost bemused by the fervor of the abolitionist demands. In such a case, endangering formal values seemed to have the least possible justification.

While *State v. Post* presented an extraordinarily explicit use of systemic convergence to justify a result of nonconvergence in a particular case, the factor was discernable in almost all cases in the administration of gradual emancipation schemes: A commitment had been made to eliminate the evil; a balance had been struck as to the costs of the process; one ought not get too upset about the unfortunate few who were caught in the last rattles of the chains. While little of this was explicit in most cases, it was clear that judges did not get very upset about the cases in gradual emancipation schemes. There opinions present few, if any, signs of personal involvement, of anguish, or of guilt. The question of role fidelity simply did not arise. For counsel could argue, as did John Gibson, from the direction and purposes of the law. And even where this proved unavailing, they could hardly argue that the interim situation justified rebellion.

Issue Convergence

In the case of gradual emancipation, the law of slavery as a whole was moving in the direction of antislavery morality. However, even where there was no such general convergence there could be a perceptible movement of a particular legal issue toward conformity with libertarian values. Examples abound: Virginia's manumission policy from 1782 to 1806; the issue of the *Slave Grace* case, as treated by the courts of Kentucky, Louisiana, or Missouri prior to 1840;[4] interpre-

tation of laws against the importation of slaves in Virginia and Maryland from 1800 to 1815; [5] the *Somerset Case* issue in Massachusetts
or Connecticut in the late 1830's; [6] even the early Fugitive Slave Act
cases by Justice Bushrod Washington in the first quarter of the nineteenth century. [7]

In many of these issue-convergence situations there was ambiguity
as to the extent to which the convergence was the product of acceptance of the antislavery moral premise. For example, the Virginia
Manumission Act of 1782 was certainly reflective of public recep-
tivity to private emancipation of slaves. [8] But it was the master's
freedom to do what he wished with his "property" as well as the
Negro's potential liberty that was at stake. Thus, manumission could
be subsumed within the general category of "gratuitous transfers"—wills, trusts, and gifts. The same principles that warranted a
broad area of private transactional freedom, in ordinary "gratuitous
transfer" situations, would warrant a similar liberty for manumission.
Courts commonly look to the intent of the testator, settlor, or donor
in such situations. Consequently, the antislavery content of manumission could be derived wholly from examining the private wishes of
Quaker and other antislavery testators and settlors without need for a
decision as to the place of the antislavery natural law tradition within
the law of the state. The coincidence on a given issue of antislavery
morality with some other, more neutral, value made it unnecessary to
resolve many potential conflicts.

Just as it was usually unnecessary to decide whether freedom to
manumit was primarily intended to enlarge the liberty of masters or
of slaves, so it was unnecessary to decide whether anti-importation
laws were intended to weaken the institution of slavery, to reduce the
likelihood of insurrection, or to maintain slave prices at a high level.
All three purposes had potential adherents and were plausible.* In

---

* Two of the Supreme Court's first experiences with slavery involved these statutes and their
interpretations. The District of Columbia was then governed by Maryland law for portions
carved out of Maryland (Washington) and by Virginia law for portions ceded by Virginia
(Arlington) unless otherwise provided by Congress. Thus, issues of interpretation of the Maryland and Virginia statutes reached the Supreme Court by virtue of their having been incorporated into the law of the District of Columbia. In *Scott v. London,* 7 U.S. (3 Cranch) 324
(1806), a case arose under Virginia law. The federal circuit court, per Chief Judge Cranch, held
that even a technical failure by the master to follow the prescribed procedures of the Virginia
statute would operate to free the imported slave. (Slaves could be imported upon bona fide taking up of residence in Virginia, but only by following prescribed registration provisions.) The

such situations, convergence of antislavery moral ends with those of other significant values or objectives in the society gave the judge the valuable perception that his result, though it was determined in part by a moral sense, was also supported by a variety of alternative policies and principles that would, as they converged on a particular case, command the consensus of the community.

Such examples of issue convergence produced a low level of moral-formal tension for the judge. He did not often have to confront the choice as to how he would view the place of the libertarian component in the convergence taken by itself. For, as in *Pleasants,* several principles usually bespoke the same result. Counsel, in these cases, could also facilitate such avoidance of the moral-formal dilemma. Insofar as the potential for successful strategies was much greater where antislavery morality was but one of the ends served by a particular result, counsel would be likely to invite the judge to consider a less controversial device to achieve the libertarian end.

However, there were always borderline situations where the "neutral" and the "antislavery" components of the rule's purpose diverged. For example, the ambit of private transactional freedom for gratuitous transfers had always been limited by the rights of those with a nongratuitous claim against the donor, settlor, or estate. In confronting a creditor's claim against manumitted slaves, the courts of Virginia had to determine whether the power to manumit was nothing more than a corollary of the power to settle a trust or to leave property by will, or whether it was an attempt to enlarge the area of freedom in the polity, albeit in a limited fashion. In *Patty v. Colin* [9] the antislavery duo of Tucker and Roane struggled to reconcile their

---

Supreme Court reversed. There is, however, a fascinating footnote on p. 326 of the Supreme Court Report—a note to the arguments of counsel, apparently written by the reporter Cranch and purporting to explain the basis of the opinion of the circuit court (rendered by the same Cranch). This footnote explains the opinion of the circuit court as having been rendered upon the conclusion that the purpose of the Virginia statute was, along with other laws, to contribute to the process of gradual emancipation. On pp. 326–27: "The opinion of the court below seems to have been misunderstood by the counsel. . . . The right to freedom which the slave acquires is not a mere penalty to the owner, but an independent right, not to be controlled by its consequences. The object of the act was to discourage, and gradually to abolish, slavery. . . . To make slaves free, therefore, was as direct an accomplishment of their object, as to prevent their importation."

For Virginia's own interpretation, see *Murray v. McCarty,* 16 Va. (2 Munf.) 401, 406; see also *Scott v. Ben.,* 10 U.S. (6 Cranch) 3 (1810), for a parallel case arising under Maryland law applied in the District of Columbia.

perception that something more than ordinary property issues was at stake in manumission, with the clear logic of creditors' rights against a gratuitous beneficiary. Their resolution of "hiring out" slaves managed to salvage the convergence, while yet maintaining a special, albeit limited, sphere for the operation of antislavery morality. Because the antislavery element in Virginia's manumission policy was tangible, plausible, though certainly not exclusive, the court could, without infidelity to its role as servant to "the law," further that element subject only to the limits of the other "neutral" components of the relevant act. Such a dynamic of extension and reconciliation had its limits. When Roane and the Virginia court effectuated the statutory premise of ultimate preference for the rights of creditors, Roane was moved to write of his personal discomfort in such situations and of his helplessness in the face of his duty.[10] At this point he confronted the potential divergence of law and morality that was implicit in the very limited character of issue convergence. Unlike the judge in the gradual emancipation situation, Spencer Roane and St. George Tucker could not point to the coming day when the problem would not arise. The obstacles to convergence could well be eternal. The debt-ridden plantation owner was a common figure, and so long as he existed the clash between creditor and manumitted slave would persist.

Despite this troublesome border area, the interaction between antislavery principles and these other purposes in such cases provided the judge with the best opportunities for ameliorative solutions, gradually broadening the one objective, reconciling alternative principles, salvaging the "right" result even while denying ultimate preference for libertarian ends. So long as this broad field of quite legitimate and necessary judicial work remained open, the choice between moral and formal obligation did not often arise. Counsel would almost certainly choose a more traditional route of argument, and even the most self-scrutinizing of antislavery judges could have justified their work and their role in terms of the measurable gains achieved in extension of the domain of liberty on important matters.

Unlike the instances discussed above, the cases in the choice-of-law area were often quite explicit acknowledgments of the principled preference for liberty. These cases did not, themselves, raise issues of moral-formal divergence. But as the single most important source for articulation of a legal, common law, general preference for liberty, they were one of the conditions for embarrassing the judge in the decision of other cases. The choice-of-law cases told the slave state judge that the system he furthered was odious and barely tolerated. It told the free state judge that the fugitive was, under common law and general legal principles, free; that his rendition to a slave state was an expedient act—an excision from the prior rule of *Somerset's Case*, acknowledged to be the "true" rule for most applications.[11] Thus, whatever comfort the courts attained in deciding choice-of-law cases in a milieu of doctrinal convergence was purchased at the cost of articulating broad principles favoring liberty that would be thrown back at them in more threatening circumstances. The judges reinforced the conditions of their own inconsistencies.

Issue Divergence

The antislavery judge might perceive that a particular rule or issue was growing less amenable to libertarian results. A series of cases might reinforce an antilibertarian rule and make it less likely to change. A single decision could become with time an established rule; or the cases might gradually foreclose a series of libertarian claims or defenses, leaving a conclusion of general proslavery policy broader than what had existed at the outset. Finally, cases or statutes might reflect an antilibertarian purpose that would enlighten future decisions within their ambit.

The course of decisions under the Fugitive Slave Acts demonstrated all three processes. The constitutionality of the acts was a matter of first impression in 1818. It was well-established by the 1850's. The Supreme Court addressed the issue twice in the 1840's and again in 1852 and 1859.[12] State decisions numbered in the scores, and all but one upheld the acts.[13] Thus, a rule became, over time, an "established" rule. As Chapters 10 and 11 demonstrated, the fugitive cases also involved the progressive shutting off of antislavery claims and defenses. State kidnapping statutes were struck down first in *In re Susan* (1818) and more authoritatively in *Prigg v. Pennsylvania* (1842).[14] The interposition of state jury trial was denied by the Pennsylvania Supreme Court first in 1821 and again in 1836.[15] Massachusetts courts denied the state such power in 1851.[16] Congressional power to implement the rendition policy was squarely

upheld by the Supreme Court in *Jones v. Van Zandt* (1846).[17] After
the amendments of 1850—which themselves moved the law farther
from libertarian morality—first the Massachusetts court and later the
courts of Pennsylvania, Ohio, and New York upheld once again congressional power. Federal circuit courts were unanimous in upholding
the new act.[18] State interposition of habeas corpus was a hot issue
that was not finally foreclosed until 1859. As time wore on, then, a
line of strategies and arguments for antislavery forces was "settled"
against the antislavery view. Finally, the fugitive slave issue came to
represent a general policy of accommodation to divergent systems
within the constitutional structure. As such, fugitive cases were to be
judged with an eye to perpetuating the accommodation process and
fulfilling the promise and goal of rendition. A larger and larger "policy" function was thus read into the rule. The Union itself was said
to depend on it.

As the pattern of divergence became more evident, explicit choices
between fidelity to legal or moral norms had to be confronted. This
confrontation was all the more difficult to avoid when advocates
expressly raised the issue of confrontation, a matter I shall return to
in the next section. Insofar as these judges continued to sit on the
bench (a significant choice) and continued to abide their role limits,
they were drawn into general acquiescence with the pattern of divergence. Straightforward application of their own formal principles
seemed to lead to the unfortunate conclusions. As a result, many not
only acquiesced but participated in the determination of the divergent
course. But this participation was often accompanied by protests that
responsibility lay elsewhere, by indications of distress, helplessness,
and, indirectly, guilt.*

Issue divergence was threatening, first, simply because it afforded
none of the comforts of convergence. The two are only opposite faces
of the same coin. But issue divergence was also particularly threatening insofar as it raised the specter of systemic divergence. The com-

---

* The evidence for a sense of guilt is admittedly indirect and uncertain. It is partly a feeling
of the "Lady doth protest too much." The evidence is somewhat ambiguous. On the one hand,
judges appealed far more often than usual to the duty to obey and apply the law. Without more,
one might assume that the constant repetition of the theme was an indirect indication that the
issue bothered them. However, it is equally clear that the rise of the rhetoric of justification co-
incides with the rise of a form of advocacy that raised judicial fidelity to law as an issue for the
first time. Thus, the appearance of judicial concern for fidelity may be at least equally attributable to the need to convince hostile antagonists.

mitted insurgent constantly pointed out this specter. For Wendell Phillips, the fugitive slave issue was only a part of a coherent, proslavery constitution and legal order. And Phillips's rhetoric resounded in judicial chambers.

Systemic Divergence

Developments with respect to the fugitive slave issue were consistent either with a view of the Constitution as a whole as a proslavery document or with a view of it as a wobbly coupling for diverging societies. Issue divergence for the sake of coupling was distasteful, but many antislavery men could live with it. Issue divergence that was simply evidence of a general proslavery commitment in the fundamental law or of a trend in that direction was more threatening. A judge like John McLean respected the formal structure of his role because of a faith in the ultimate necessity and utility of a legal system with integrity.[19] But that respect was founded in large part on a firm conviction that the Constitution—the ultimate source of formalism—was not itself committed to slavery. It was that conviction that was the heart of his dissent in *Dred Scott*.[20] Other judges expressed even more directly their sense that *Dred Scott* was proof of a basic systemic proslavery bias.[21]

If an antislavery man became a judge in a legal system already committed to slavery, the continued perception of that commitment didn't need to be particularly troublesome. He could become reconciled to the "necessity," if not the desirability, of the slave code. Or he could become an ameliorist like O'Neall of South Carolina or Gaston of North Carolina—standing for reform of the crueler and more distasteful elements of slave control.[22] He could seek "issue convergence" where possible—appealing to rules of law not themselves designed to further liberty, but having that effect in particular slave cases.

These judges did not, however, have the sense of loss experienced by a Story, Shaw, Swan, or McLean. The accommodation, if any, to an ongoing gap between law and morality was built into the initial entry into their role. This was not the case for Northern judges confronting the specter of a proslavery Constitution. That the fugitive problem would be a thorny one could be expected. However, it remained for Wendell Phillips in the 1840's to transform this issue into a vision of the entire Constitution as bent to serve the cause of slavery. And not until the judicial claims and successes of proslavery forces between 1840 and 1860—the gag rule, the *Amistad* and the *Creole,* the Mexican War, the new Fugitive Act of 1850, *Kansas-Nebraska,* and finally *Dred Scott*—was this vision given a degree of credibility. Taken one at a time, these developments need not be given the interpretation of a proslavery Constitution. But Phillips and the Garrisonians would not permit the events to be viewed seriatim.

There are few instances of an antislavery Northern judge articulating a conviction that the legal system as a whole had come to diverge fundamentally from libertarian potential. As a result, we cannot point to particular cases and say, ''Here the judge saw systemic divergence and acted in such and such a way.'' However, one can identify the cases where the judge acted amidst pervasive claims of systemic divergence and heightened rhetoric eschewing legal obligation on that ground. In cases like *Jones v. Van Zandt* and *Miller v. McQuerry,* McLean faced appeals by counsel to save the Constitution from such a fate.[23] In *Latimer,* Story could not have been unaware that the lawyer, Samuel Sewall, who argued before him by day, chaired the anti-Union rallies by night.[24] Confronting the specter of systemic divergence, although unconvinced that the Constitution had to be so viewed, the antislavery judge's conflict was maximized. His behavior tended to extreme protestations of powerlessness or helplessness; to excessive reliance on mechanistic formalism, or to an exaggerated notion of the formal stakes. These attributes of the product of antislavery judges in the most trying of circumstances can be explained in part by their particular personal plight—the subject of Chapter 13. In fairness, however, it must be conceded that the protestation *dura lex, sed lex* was more and more plausible, the closer the doctrinal situation approached what some hypothetically ''neutral'' observer might declare to be ''systemic divergence.'' As most of the traditional signposts of the law pointed away from antislavery morality, it became harder to justify an antislavery result except through action that most of the profession would have viewed as violative of professional and constitutional role strictures. In such a case, the question of role fidelity could not but arise, especially when the advocates and resisters explicitly put it forward. It is to this element of context that I now proceed.

The Dialectical Environment

The judges' world was not one of books alone. Doctrine was only one element of the judging process. The judge acted amidst a dialectical process in two senses: in the sense of the adversary proceeding before him; and in the sense of the larger struggle of ideological movements to which the proceeding often seemed related. Of the literally limitless number of factors that made up the "dialectical environment," I would specify three as particularly influential on the judge: the ideological basis of advocacy; the presence of, or potential for, extralegal action (civil disobedience or resistance); the sympathetic qualities of the potential victims of injustice.

Ideological Basis of Advocacy

The strong relationship of antislavery to the substance and style of religious movements has long been noted.[25] Antislavery styles ranged from the "personal pietistic" attitudes of official Quakerdom, on the one hand, to the evangelism of the Lane Seminary 70, on the other. These different styles led to very different demands on the legal system. The objective of North Carolina Quakers in the first thirty years of the nineteenth century was to free themselves of sin. The objectives of James Birney in Ohio or Theodore Parker and Phillips in Massachusetts in the 1850's was to realize a free state. For the North Carolina Quaker, the judge was only a representative of the larger community addressed as the proper organ of decision. For the Massachusetts or Ohio abolitionist, the judge was a soul, a man of moral capacity and responsibility entrusted with the salvation of the Commonwealth. His action to support slavery was a particularly visible attribute of the polity's moral blight. It is strange to note the resurrection in Massachusetts abolitionism of a seventeenth-century motif of magistrate as moral trustee for the community.

To a large extent, the judge could control what was said in his courtroom. But, he could not control the public meetings, the demonstrations, and the ideological press. Nor could he easily ignore them when they were the principal news of the day. The fugitive slave cases of the 1840's and 1850's led to organized, militant representation, which in the West included direct appeal to the judge as responsible to a morality above the law. Even when such an appeal was not present—and in Massachusetts, as I have indicated, there was seldom such a direct appeal in the courtroom—the identification of counsel with the militant appeal in the street could not but charge the more tempered appearance in court. This was especially the case where the counsel appeared primarily as representatives of a movement.

Moreover, the presence of a jury in the criminal and civil actions brought under the Fugitive Slave Act's enforcement provisions precipitated direct appeals to conscience and to the responsibility of the jurors to God's law. These appeals required explicit consideration of the place of morality in the jury's deliberations.

The movement to extralegal arguments before judges, before juries, and before the masses was not the only characteristic of the later militant advocacy. Tone as much as content was important. Insofar as earlier issues of manumission or gradual emancipation precipitated the request for invocation of extralegal principles, it was with an appeal to the generosity, the sympathetic, and the pitying impulse of the law's minions (and presumably of the *law*). It is one thing to be begged to act in a particular way by appeal to the presumed magnanimity of the man and the institution, quite another to be threatened with scorn and damnation for being a gutless sycophant. In the charged atmosphere of a Boston fugitive case, even a less militant advocate like Dana noted caustically in his diary the "unmanly" submission of Lemuel Shaw to federal power; while Theodore Parker characterized Benjamin Robbins Curtis as a pimp for Daniel Webster's whoresome politics.[26]

Even the tempered appearance of the ideological bar before the court was threatening. They raised any and all arguments including some that seemed designed for the public rather than for the court. They pursued cases that seemed legally hopeless with the same fervor as matters of first impression. Sometimes their pursuit of the client's rights seemed to have no basis except the hope of a stroke of the lawless mob effecting a rescue.[27] In sum, the suspicion, well-founded in some instances, was always present that the attorneys were more than advocates; that they cynically used the courtroom for delay, obstruction, or publicity regardless of the legal merits.

The effect of the heightened moral intensity of advocacy on the antislavery judge was not simple. By and large, the intensity aggravated the sense of conflict. But ad hominem castigation and excess of rhetoric often permitted a kind of righteous dismissal of the abolitionist demands as extremist. To some extent, the political milieu could influence the response to heightened intensity. The Mexican War, the Act of 1850, and the Kansas-Nebraska Act each marked a watershed for antislavery opinion; in the wake of such events, the ideological advocate appeared to touch popular bases not ordinarily accessible to the abolitionist.

Finally, ideological representation often affected the environment indirectly by precluding compromise and settlement to avoid conflict. In general, in civil law suits, it is to everyone's advantage to work out a settlement. The costs and risk of litigation are usually not as acceptable as some attainable compromise. But the ideologically committed attorney may eschew settlement. Indeed, in contemporary test litigation, the term ''washout'' is used to denigrate a settlement that avoids resolving the basic legal-ideological issue. The slavery cases had their analogues to modern washouts. For example, in fugitive cases, one way out was always to purchase the runaway. It is indeed very interesting to note, in passing, that a statute that might have given the fugitive a right of self-purchase would have been a very real step in accommodation to diverging moral beliefs and interests. However, the law never gave a right of self-purchase. Nevertheless, slaveholders were sometimes willing to negotiate a sale of the runaway so that freedom might be maintained. Such a sale was often more advantageous to the owner than retention of a potentially rebellious Negro. The *Latimer* case ended with such a purchase, but many abolitionists condemned the purchase of a runaway as a concession on the basic issue that there may rightly be property in man. The most famous struggle over this principle occurred with regard to the question of whether the great Frederick Douglass, the nation's most famous fugitive, might rightly negotiate a self-purchase so as not to face the threat of eventual recaption. Douglass split with Garrison and Phillips on this matter and ultimately purchased himself.[28]

In the *Anthony Burns* affair it was proslavery ideology and the federal government as well as one wing of abolitionism that balked at settling the matter for money. Despite a rumor that a purchase would be negotiated, the owner insisted on his remedy of rendition. In this insistence, he was encouraged by the United States Attorney for Boston.[29] Indeed, this insistence is rather strong evidence that the forces of order in Boston saw a matter of principle—of moral principle—at stake in these fugitive cases, just as did the abolitionists. Some abolitionists seemed to reject the obligation of fidelity to even the minimum-order functions of law. For United States Attorney Benjamin Hallett, the death of a deputy in the attempt to rescue Burns dramatized the moral burden of those who would take law and life into their own hands. To demonstrate that the law would be enforced, rather than compromised, was a principled objective, not only a practical one. Consequently, both ideological poles had a distaste for settling the fugitive case, preferring to see it as symbolic of the struggle between inconsistent moral demands rather than as a simple matter of pecuniary interest. Readiness to let fugitive cases "wash" would have removed the single most troublesome category of cases from judicial view. Even assuming persistent difficulties in raising funds for such purchases, the judge's conflict would have been lessened. For fund raising would prove difficult in precisely those cases of public apathy that would have been least fraught with tension in any event.

Presence or Potential for Resistance and Disobedience

The presence or threat of resistance and disobedience intensified the environment in three ways. First, it operated to bar a formal resolution as ultimately determinative. The refusal to abide the results of the formal apparatus was a threat to the viability of that structure and a direct assertion that the moral values of antislavery were of higher priority than those underlying fidelity to legal process. On a more personal level, the readiness of others to go beyond the formal set of obligations was an invitation to the judge to consider his own priorities. The judge, in confronting the resister, had to be prepared not only to enunciate the law, but also to justify it. In the process of so doing, he confronted his own doubts and hesitations.

The level of intensity was also raised by a chain reaction of legal incidents. The resister in case "x" is a potential defendant in case "y"—often a popular and eminently respectable defendant. Strong resistance may lead to escalation in suppression and a further round of asking whether the formal system is indeed worth the cost. Certainly, the most dramatic instance of escalation of repression—with a concomitant boon to antislavery propaganda—was the Christiana affair.[30] There, the shooting and killing of a slave-catcher in Lancaster, Pennsylvania, by a community of armed blacks led to the return of forty-one treason indictments. The claim that armed resistance to the Fugitive Slave Act constituted treason was as good proof as Wendell Phillips could have hoped for that the very essence of the national Constitution was proslavery.*

The third way in which resistance intensified the moral environment was by generating a literature exploring the bases for obligation to law. Early antislavery efforts at legal treatises focused primarily on slave codes—the content of slave law as cruel, unjust, or simply barbaric. Later writings, while by no means forsaking that focus, also assumed the burden of impugning the legitimacy of any obligations a man might be said to have with regard to slave law or unjust law in general.[31] This third input of resistance had a discernible, direct impact on judges. While I know of no instance of a judge referring to or citing the antinomian literature of abolitionism, there are dozens of refutations of "theories of abstract right" or of "extremists." These works thus had substantial effect on the general atmosphere in which cases were decided.[32]

Moreover, this literature directly engaged and challenged the protective "professional role" justification for complicity in slavery.†By taking seriously the explicit judicial excuse of role fidelity, the Garrisonians came up with a widespread demand for resignation. Thus, they pushed the judge beyond the stage of reiteration of role definition.

---

* Although indictments were returned, largely at the behest of District Judge Kane, the jury in the first two cases returned verdicts of not guilty after Justice Grier delivered very strong charges that the law of treason required something beyond armed resistance to enforcement of some particular statute. See charge of Grier in *U.S. v. Hanway,* 26 F. Cas. 105 (No. 15,299), (C.C.E.D. Pa., 1851), pp. 121 ff. Kane also jailed Passmore Williamson and was the primary target for Richard Hildreth's *Atrocious Judges: Lives of Judges Infamous as Tools of Tyrants and Instruments of Oppression* (New York: Auburn, Miller, Orton and Mulligan, 1865). See my book review, "Atrocious Judges," 68 *Columbia Law Review* 1003 (1968).

† From time to time these challenges descended from the general to the very personal. See, e.g., Hildreth, *Atrocious Judges,* directed at Kane; Theodore Parker, *The Trial of Theodore Parker* (Boston, 1855), directed at B. R. Curtis; the *Liberator* of Nov. 6, 1842, which contains a strong attack on Shaw.

The Sympathetic Character of the Victims

In the 1859 Ohio case *Ex Parte Bushnell*, Chief Judge Swan delivered the final blow to the hope that Ohio would join Wisconsin in legitimating resistance to the Fugitive Slave Acts. In upholding the constitutionality of the act, remanding resisters to their federal law fate, Swan declared his empathy with the aider and abettor of the fugitive. He allowed that confronting the haggard fugitive at his door, he might well succor him, regardless of duty to law (though he concluded by hoping that should he so offend the laws, he would concede the justice of being punished).[33] What is significant here is Swan's explicit recognition of the pitiful character of the fugitive and of the natural impulse to aid him. Because he can envision this victim, he comes to understand, though not justify, the act of resistance.

Playing upon the potential for empathy, the abolitionists always tried to personify the victims; to stress the personal, dire consequences of an impersonal rule; to relate the victim's life story; to introduce the familial and vocational context from which he was torn. In a certain sense, almost every slave is a sympathetic victim to a man morally opposed to the institution. That fact provided one of the general and pervasive elements of conflict. However, some victims were more sympathetic than others. Victims of the international slave trade constituted one such category. Not born to slavery, they had lost liberty and family. In addition, they had suffered the cruelties of the passage. In the *Amistad* affair the special sympathy afforded victims of the trade must have been important in countering the peculiar antipathy ordinarily afforded insurrectionists.[34] Fugitives were also a generally sympathetic group. Among those quick to accept and even honor political refugees, the refugee from servitude had a place, albeit an illegal one. The underground railroad, even as discounted by contemporary scholarship, involved thousands of upstanding citizens in acts of disobedience. A good many of these came to their commitment by being confronted with the hapless refugee. So confronted, they acted as Judge Swan intimated he might himself act. The sympathetic victim also triggered the "hard-nosed" reaction: determination not to let tough cases make bad law; renewed determination to do one's duty in the face of temptation. But even these hard-nosed reactions are purchased at a cost if the judge empathizes with the victim.

Interaction of Doctrine and Dialectics

Mutual Reinforcement

Neither divergent doctrinal patterns nor intense dialectical environments played upon the legal actors in isolation. These two factors tended to appear together. Moreover, their conjoint presence was the starting point for a process of interaction that accentuated divergence and, by and large, further intensified the environment. A case that was highly visible and important in terms of the direction of the law, would attract, for that very reason, ideological representation and resistance. Certain preconditions had to be met: the presence of an ideological bar, the public consciousness of a moral fervor, some lack of willingness to trust the formal apparatus. But those factors could be present, yet not be ignited by a routine case or by one that promised continued convergence. Similarly, the preconditions for an intense dialectical environment were themselves likely to create divergence. For the committed moralist would describe and assert implications of magnitude where others might see matters in less glaring light. The ideologue was more likely to ascribe systemic implications to a doctrinal pattern. The divergent pattern was also used by resisters to justify their actions—both on the ground that encroachment upon libertarian values was progressing at a greater rate and because the increasing distance between legal and moral norms justified less respect for legal obligation. This pattern of action and its rationale by resisters in turn gave greater credibility to the proposition that, if the moral ends of antislavery were to be served, they would have to be served at the expense of, or in preference to, the formal obligations of law.

Consider Boston in the early 1850's.[35] The Fugitive Slave Act of 1850 may be taken as an "objective" and sharp instance of divergence. Not only were practical aids to enforcement added to the slaveholder's arsenal, but the act also stood as a symbol of national commitment to rendition. Great names of the Boston legal profession—Webster, Benjamin Robbins Curtis, Rufus Choate—defended the act and made it the test of constitutional fidelity.

At the same time, all the preconditions of an intense dialectical environment were present. In Dana, John P. Hale, Samuel Sewall, Rantoul and other less well-known attorneys, Boston had a dedicated, ideological bar organized to provide legal assistance at a moment's notice. Moreover, these lawyers were known to be committed to various elements of the movement.[36] Resistance could be expected in the streets as well as in the courtroom. Wendell Phillips, Garrison, Thomas Higginson and a host of others, including a relatively militant black community, were potential demonstrators, rescuers, or resisters. The abolitionist community, moreover, had already created a substantial literature justifying disobedience and resistance. The *Liberator* constantly applied the theory to the events of the day. Such was the setting for two dramatic confrontations within months of each other: the Shadrach rescue in February 1851 and the Sims rendition in April of the same year.

Shadrach was apprehended on February 15, 1851. Within hours Richard Henry Dana thrust both a writ of *habeas corpus* and a *writ de homine replegiando* under the nose of Lemuel Shaw as he stood in the courthouse lobby. Shaw temporized with equivocal, technical objections. Within a few hours, while Dana was revising the writs, Shadrach was rescued. Dana had not been the only lawyer on the scene. Indeed, Charles Davis, a moderate abolitionist lawyer, and Robert Morris, a black attorney, were ultimately charged and tried for their alleged part in the rescue.[37] The *Sims Case* followed two months later. The use of federal power and the failure of both resistance and law to abort the rendition process have been described in the preceding chapter.

These events, in stark form, exemplify the escalation hypothesized above. The abolitionists, convinced that the law of 1850 was an aggressive act of the slave power to make Massachusetts a man-stealer, made the most of the statute as a symbol not only of further issue divergence, but as a portent of the systemic commitment to slavery. Their readiness to resist was proven by *Shadrach*. As proclaimed in their own rhetoric, the resistance involved denial of the basic premise of fidelity to constitutional authority. The divergent pattern of the Act of 1850 was the occasion for application of this ideology. That ideology in action was, in its own terms, a challenge to underlying principles of obligation and was responded to as such by federal authorities. The massive use of federal force was, from the perspective of the "authorities," a response to lawlessness not antislavery. From the perspective of the resisters, however, the troops were further proof of the extent of the involvement of the legal system in legitimating slavery on a systemic level. As such, it reinforced their commitment to resist and fueled their propaganda efforts. Nothing Phillips ever dreamed up could compare with the effect of Lemuel Shaw bowing beneath federally imposed chains surrounding a Massachusetts courthouse. In sum, the readiness of men to act on moral beliefs on the assumptions of divergent law and morality led to a situation in which the divergence came to appear still more fundamental and irreconcilable.

The reciprocal reinforcement of doctrinal pattern and of ideological advocacy can be seen on a different level in the microcosm of the legal profession. The ideological bar was a subgroup in the profession. And the Boston bar in 1851 was badly split over the Fugitive Slave Act. Shortly after the Shadrach rescue, Rufus Choate delivered an attack on abolitionist teachings. He chose as his forum a meeting of the Story Association. It was a calculated slap at the abolitionist bar. Dana records that Choate actually told him before the speech: ''I shall have to offend you.'' Two days later Josiah Quincy delivered a slap back at Choate, implicitly accusing him of manipulating the memory of Story to partisan purposes.[38]

Dana may have been uncommonly sensitive, but he, at least, thought that his standing in the profession was under attack because of his role in fugitive cases. He thought that business was being diverted from his firm. Moreover, he seemed particularly anxious about his image in the eyes of the judiciary. After *Shadrach,* he confided to his journal that Shaw's ''insulting manner to me ha[s] troubled me more than any other manifestation.'' [39] Later, after the acquittal of several of the accused aiders and abettors of Shadrach, Dana noted with pleasure a third-hand report that United States District Judge Sprague felt that Dana had acted in a manner wholly consistent with the duty of an advocate.[40]

It is plausible to assume that Dana was suffering the fallout of suspicion directed at the ideological bar. He, himself, was rigidly cautious of the bounds of duty as an officer of the court. But Sewall, Morris, Davis, and others were at least accused of implication in resistance. Dana, himself, steadfastly refused to justify resistance, but he ''rejoice[d] in the escape of a victim of an unjust law.'' [41]

Given the superheated atmosphere in Boston, the role of the ideological bar was important. It forced judicial confrontation of unpleasant issues. It tried every possible route to victory, thus effectuating two unwanted results from the perspective of the judge. First, by trying every tribunal, these lawyers put every possible judge "on the spot." It seems Shaw's "insulting manner" to Dana may have been the product of great antipathy to being drawn into what could have been left as a wholly federal matter. By insisting on an answer from every oracle, however, the antislavery bar reinforced the divergent character of the doctrinal pattern. A Lemuel Shaw who had not yet spoken was better than the Shaw who added his great authority in favor of the act in *Sims's Case*. Moreover, the maneuverings of the bar could be viewed, plausibly, as attempts to buy time. The main reason that buying time could be worth the price was the potential for a rescue or for purchase. Purchase, moreover, often went hand-in-hand with intimidation of the slave-catcher.

Insofar as the ideological lawyers were characterized as a part of the movement rather than a part of the profession, they were taken less seriously in terms of their legal positions and more seriously as a threat to order. Judicial opinions came to be less responsive in terms of the specific attacks on the act or in terms of the facts of the case and more responsive to what they considered to be the "real" underlying problem—justifications of the rendition scheme and the obligation to obey the law and to enforce the law. Shaw's opinion in *Sims's Case* barely acknowledged the limited and very specific arguments of Rantoul. But it picked up and elaborated at great length the question of the role of rendition in creating and preserving union and the general obligation of judges and citizens to the United States Constitution.[42]

As the response to ideological advocacy and to the ideological bar produced doctrinal divergence and professional suspicion, the avenues for traditional representational forms and the prerequisites for traditional respect for the institutional structures gave way. After *Sims,* there seemed still less possibility of winning a fugitive case before any conceivable tribunal. The arguments of the antislavery bar appeared more tenuous, and its persistence, therefore, more suspect. From the perspective of these abolitionist lawyers, however, the prosecutions of Morris and of Davis, and Shaw's short temper confronting Dana were still further evidence that slavery had poisoned the wells of justice and that the Act of 1850 was only a small part of the total divergent pattern. It further reinforced their feeling that divergence could not be corrected in the context of a biased legal structure. The stage had thus been set for the Burns affair.

Countervailing Considerations

The pattern of escalation described above carried with it the potential for a break in the vicious cycle. For not all antislavery men would rank slavery as the ultimate concern of a moral man. In a sense, this is only an elaboration of the Hobbesian bargain. If men can be convinced that the alternative to mutual adherence to the obligations of a formal system is indeed a "life . . . poor, nasty, brutish and short," then virtually all will choose obedience.[43] As the escalation of moral-formal conflict occurs, the threat of serious damage to the fabric of civilized interaction grows more credible and produces a tendency to question whether the moral values of liberty for an oppressed group are indeed worth the price. Thus, certain potential resisters and supporters of resistance may be deterred from acting as the resistance appears to require more far-reaching threats to law, itself. Different individuals and groups will be deterred at different critical levels. Ordinarily, one may assume that, as the attack on the formal system becomes more total and more strident, fewer and fewer persons will weigh the moral-formal trade-off in favor of antislavery. Pushed to its limits, this process might culminate with the progressive "isolation" of extremist groups, which can then be suppressed. While the mutual reinforcement described in the preceding section tends to drive the level of intensity up, that very increase may have the effect of convincing potential resisters of the dangers in insurgency.

This potential for dampening of conflict depends on two factors. First, there must be some common denominator of agreement as to important values preserved or served by the formal structure, however imperfect. Second, there must be a way in which the marginal actors on the legal-moral scene at any given time become convinced that these common-denominator values of formalism are indeed threatened.

When antislavery men acted in different ways with regard to the legal system and its diverging components (some acquiescing, some "dissenting," some "lawyering," and some "resisting"), those differences may have been partly attributable to different priorities, i.e., different levels at which the formal costs were taken to be too great. They may have been partly attributable to different information, that is, to different ideas about what the formal costs were at a particular level of insurgent activity. Such information is necessarily incomplete and speculative, but important. An enormous range of behavior from men with identical priorities may be attributable to different "information" or beliefs. For example, Benjamin Robbins Curtis, before his ascension to the high court, argued, in support of the Act of 1850, that the failure to live up to the constitutional obligation of rendition of fugitives would lead to disunion—perhaps civil war.[44] Curtis's assertion of the danger of disunion, his strong support for the Webster position, was the product of his information and became a component part of the information available to others.

Richard Henry Dana was one antislavery figure who would have acquiesced in the priorities of Curtis. He too felt that the Union and the Constitution represented values more important than the freedom of the fugitive. But he was not easily convinced that such values were, indeed, threatened by the pattern of antislavery activity in Boston. It was only after the election of Lincoln, as civil war appeared imminent, that he took a public stand for good faith, even generous, implementation of the Fugitive Slave Acts. It took "information" of a most concrete form—secession—to satisfy Dana.[45] Needless to say, readiness to "believe" a prediction of this sort may well be related to one's priorities or to the strength of one's convictions.

For some, like Wendell Phillips and other Garrisonians, disunion was a promise not a threat. They had already expressed their willingness to rank the moral values of antislavery higher than the Union. Negative feedback mechanisms that could work for them would have to identify societal interests, other than the Union, as threatened. But even these committed abolitionists could be deterred from certain forms of activity through appeal to universalizable values underlying some elements of the law's formalism: adherence to undertakings; good faith; responsibility to abide by conditions placed on delegated power. Phillips and Garrison would have gladly seen the Union destroyed, but steadfastly fought against expedient betrayal of the public servant's trust.

Lawmakers as well as insurgents were concerned lest a vicious cycle of escalation continue. The insistence on the logic of a rule of law, or of a policy, may fade before a conviction that the costs of enforcement to the formal apparatus is too high.* Thus, insurrection scares brought in their wake simultaneous demands for extraordinarily harsh repressive measures and renewed calls for general emancipation. For, while the insurrection called for harshness, the sudden perception of what was necessary to insure safety demonstrated full well the costs of the enterprise in damage to principles of justified obedience.†

Even with respect to the Fugitive Slave law there were instances of judicial efforts to halt or mitigate the flow of events. While a reversal of the general doctrinal trend on the fugitive issue was precluded on the national political scene by the countervailing presence of a very different moral ideology, state adjustments were not precluded. The Wisconsin *Booth* cases were justified in large part by the sense that only such a stroke could possibly break the cycle of escalating resistance and renewed repression and divergence.[46]

The interposition of state authority in Ohio also persisted through the 1850's. And, while I have heretofore noted primarily the majority opinions in *Ex Parte Bushnell,* which refused to bring Ohio into the Wisconsin camp, it should be noted that two of five Ohio Supreme Court judges voted to go the *Booth* road. Thus, the outlines of the negative feedback system in which consequences to the formal system as a whole were appreciated by the judiciary, did, indeed, begin to operate. It seems likely, however, that the Supreme Court's opinion in *Ableman v. Booth* would have started another round of escalation had not the Civil War intervened.

The Judicial Office

The judicial office was an important part of the process outlined above. The judge confronted the ideological advocate or resister and

---

* Such, indeed, was Chase's plea before the Supreme Court in *Van Zandt*. And such may have been the rationale of the Boston juries that acquitted (or failed to convict), in turn, Robert Morris, Elizur Wright, and Charles Davis after the Shadrach affair.

† The most renowned instance of this phenomenon is the aftermath of Nat Turner's revolt, which brought a wave of repression along with the most serious of attempts to institute gradual emancipation in any state of the future Confederacy during the antebellum period. See Joseph Robert, *The Road from Monticello* (New York: AMS Press, 1970).

was a potential spokesman for the values underlying fidelity to law. He also was in a position to change the law or, if the formal costs seemed too high, to alleviate its harsh application by manipulating procedural components; by encouraging consensual settlements or washouts; by nondecision techniques to avoid further doctrinal divergence. Such are among the "passive virtues," and their very real place in the posited system was often critical.

The success of the judge in avoiding harsh moral-formal conflicts would depend on a variety of factors external to this system, including the demands to fulfill other policy functions that may be incompatible with this regulating mechanism (either in that they affirmatively demanded a doctrinal line that would aggravate the tension or because they demanded the preservation of procedural and role structures that were threatened by pursuing certain otherwise favorable conflict avoidance strategies). The success of the judge as regulator would also depend on his ability to communicate with ideological resisters. Information is not only factual, but also rhetorical. In this sense the eloquence of the judge was a factor to be considered. He had not only to state the values underlying the formal system that were threatened, but he had to convince. (There is also a question of who his audience was. The judge's function of regulator was served so long as he convinced enough people of the intolerable costs to formal values to isolate a relatively helpless, suppressible elite.)

There are reasons that a judge will act as such a regulator whether or not he so understands or articulates his role. He, himself, is educated to think in terms of the values underlying legality and ordered processes. His education, his colleagueship with others of similar training, his day-to-day experience with those processes lead him to be more alert than most to the potential dangers to law. Moreover, because so much of his own life integrates those values, he is, himself, threatened by threats to them. He is quite likely to react when they are under attack or when he feels slippage.

The prominent, antislavery judge thus found himself in a particularly critical role in the posited system. His prominence as a judge or jurist meant that he could have a greater than average say in the direction that the law might take. A great jurist-justice like Story had more leverage over doctrinal direction than almost any other single figure. If the doctrinal component of the system were to change, such a man would be in the best of positions to change it.

At the same time, a known, committed antislavery judge was in the best position to set an example of role fidelity and to convincingly articulate the rationale for law-abiding behavior. Why should an antislavery man be moved by a call for obedience to the Fugitive Act by men whom he distrusted as servants of the slave power? If anybody could reach and convince antislavery men of the real competing values underlying obedience, it would be a Story, Shaw, McLean, or Swan—all known to oppose the institution of slavery, all of unquestioned integrity. Before addressing their experiences, however, it is necessary to add one more element. Caught in the cockpit of the moral-formal battle, these men seemed subject to intense psychological forces. Had they not been deeply and personally involved, they could not have occupied so critical a position. But their very involvement suggests that forces might have been at work that could significantly affect the performance of their tasks.

The antislavery judge experienced a pervasive, but more or less latent, conflict between two potentially inconsistent prescriptive systems: law and (antislavery) morality. Neither system had a wholly satisfactory accommodation mechanism for the potentially inconsistent principles or rules of the other. That was true in the age of Aquinas, it is true today, and it certainly was true of the antebellum world of the antislavery judge. Where the doctrinal and the dialectical patterns permitted, the judge could salvage a degree of consistency and keep the potential direct clash of principles from arising in many cases. Even where a conflict arose, he could mitigate its effects by viewing it as an exception or as an unfortunate, but necessary, price for progress in related areas.

Where doctrinal divergence from libertarian values was most acute, however; and where advocates and resisters played upon and argued from that pattern to undermine fidelity to presumed obligations to law, the long-standing and latent conflicts came to the fore. All the points of potential inconsistency became relevant as the legal actors either argued or denied that the particular divergence exemplified more far-reaching inroads upon liberty. In such instances, the judges had to make decisions that slighted, rejected, or compromised at least one of the inconsistent moral and formal structures. In such a "context for conscience," an "either-or" situation was created. Whatever action the judge took would seem inconsistent with the "road not taken," yet highly valued. Moreover, insofar as the judge's personal world was populated by some people who valued the formal obligations very highly, and by others who were more strongly concerned with libertarian morality, whatever action he took would inevitably disappoint the hopes and expectations of one group. Such situations were uncomfortable ones.

The Dissonance Hypothesis

The analysis that follows proceeds on twin assumptions: (1) that we have relatively reliable information on the conscious, articulated basis for the action of the antislavery judges; (2) that it is useful, though in a limited way, to explore whether conflict among principles on that level might not have affected their judicial work.* To this end, the "theory" of cognitive dissonance will be employed as a heuristic device. It would be too much to claim that the dissonance hypothesis generates a rigorously testable prediction as to behavior in social situations as complex as those confronting our antislavery judges. However, the hypothesis does identify a range of behavior as consistent with the thesis and provides a reason for concluding that certain observed behavior is significant. The application of the hypothesis to the antislavery judges provides, I believe, a prism through which the judicial work of conflicted men may be refracted with suggestive, though not conclusive, results. Needless to say, our prism is not the only possible one.

The relevant elements of dissonance theory for this work may be briefly stated: [1] First, "dissonance" (a term for a sort of loose inconsistency) among cognitions "gives rise to pressures to reduce or eliminate the dissonance"; [2] second, the pressure to reduce dissonance will be greater, the greater the personal involvement in the inconsistent "cognitions"; [3] third, the greater the commitment to one "cognition," the less likely that the avenue of dissonance reduction will involve change in that cognitive framework; [4] fourth, in choice situations, dissonance is always present because of the knowledge that any choice made is dissonant with the positive attributes of the choice foregone; [5] and, therefore, fifth, dissonance is "highest" in situations where one must choose among closely balanced, inconsistent alternatives. [6] In such situations, according to the first premise, the tendency to pursue dissonance reducing behavior will be maximized.

---

* The second assumption needs further comment. Underlying much of what follows is the notion that inconsistency among consciously held and articulated principles will generate some tension and a tendency to try to reduce the area of inconsistency. This assumption lies at the bottom of much work in the consistency theories in social psychology. It is not unchallenged. Moreover, even if it is correct, it may isolate only relatively superficial elements of motivation in many cases. Thus, to take one scenario, it may have been the case that "deep" urges to hurt, to exercise power, to cause suffering existed in some antislavery judges; that their antislavery ideology represented a defense against their own threatening urges; and that the compulsion to obey role norms where they led to enslavement was at once a gratifying opportunity to hurt a victim with ostensible justification, and a threat to the defense structure of antislavery ideology. Such a scenario is entirely speculative, fictional really, given the data we have for these judges. Yet, were such the case, for a given judge, it might well overshadow in significance the problem of cognitive inconsistency explored within.

The antislavery judge confronting doctrinal divergence and an intense dialectical environment provides a classic instance of cognitive dissonance. In one sense there was a general, pervasive disparity between the individual's image of himself as a moral human being, opposed to human slavery as part of his moral code, and his image of himself as a faithful judge, applying legal rules impersonally—which rules required in many instances recognition, facilitation, or legitimation of slavery. That general, latent inconsistency was ordinarily not a very difficult one to handle. For commonly accepted and supported notions of professional responsibility either isolated such inconsistency from scrutiny or justified, by ipse dixit, the choice of role fidelity. However, in the circumstances described in the preceding chapter, those notions began to break down. The judge was confronted with the claim that the divergent character of the doctrinal pattern justified reexamination of the role assumptions. And this claim for reexamination was no abstraction. The ideological advocate and resister made and reiterated the demand in dramatic and personal circumstances. The normal appeal to a professional role would no longer be sufficient, for it was just that role that had been put at issue.

Each slave case potentially generated a more particular dissonance between antipathy to a result that would condemn a man, fundamentally innocent, to undeserved slavery and the knowledge or belief that such an action was required by fidelity to role expectations and rules.* Whenever a judge had decided in accord with the role expectations, the knowledge of his having sent a man back to slavery or having refused to emancipate a man, was dissonant with his image of himself as someone morally opposed to slavery. If a judge were to decide in favor of the Negro in violation of the role strictures, however, his decision would be dissonant with his image of himself as a man faithful to his judicial obligations. There would be a disturbing inconsistency whenever expectations arising from one or the other of

---

* It is entirely consistent with the experimental work done to date to posit that there is a good deal more tolerance for the sort of pervasive and often latent conflict between fidelity to law and antislavery than there is for the more specific conflict of a particular case. This is so in part because the value of fidelity to law is far more general than its specific application to slave law, while antislavery is also more general than opposition to slave law obligation. Thus, one could play out a law-fidelity role and an antislavery role with no immediate felt presence of inconsistency. The specific case, however, would trigger not only its particular conflict of values, but much of the latent conflict as well. This is all the more true if there are men who make it their business to demonstrate the sense in which the particular is but exemplary of the pervasive inconsistency of values.

those self-images was violated in the course of the decision.* The antislavery bar and movement could be expected to dramatize and publicize such dilemmas of conscience, thus making the problem all the more painful and all the more personal.

The dissonance hypothesis predicts that the judges who were most troubled by a result that favored slavery, but who nevertheless decided to be faithful to the judicial role where it seemed to require such a result, would be most likely to exhibit some form of behavior that reduced the dissonance that was a consequence of such a difficult choice. In the case of the four prominent judges to be considered in this chapter, striking instances of such behavior is apparent. These judges exhibited three patterns in their judicial and extrajudicial reflections on fugitive slave cases: (1) elevation of the formal stakes, (2) retreat to a mechanical formalism, and (3) ascription of responsibility elsewhere.

The claim put forth in the next section is not that such behavior constituted the creation of a special formal system for slavery cases, but that from among the many formulations that were within the juristic competence of the age, the antislavery judges consistently gravitated to the formulations most conducive to a denial of personal responsibility and most persuasive as to the importance of the formalism of the institutional structure for which they had opted.

Judicial Response Patterns

Elevation of the Formal Stakes

For a judge who believed himself to have chosen fidelity to law over a personal, moral impulse to set a man free or undermine slavery, the choice became an easier one as the underlying justification for adherence to formal obligation was raised to the highest possible level. Assuming the initial decision to have been a hard one, the judge might, therefore, begin to perceive the chosen formal values as more important than before or the not-chosen moral values as less important. Thus, we will expect that either in the course of making his

---

* In the remainder of this chapter, I have concentrated entirely on the antislavery judge who makes the law-fidelity choice. However, the reverse choice situation produced dissonance and some of the same fallout effects as predicted. For example, Judge Brinkerhoff of Ohio, dissenting in *Bushnell* and urging express disregard of applicable and recent Supreme Court precedent, chose to elevate the "moral (antislavery) stakes" and to see the escalation as attributable to the Supreme Court's own reversion to first principles in *Dred Scott*.

decision or as an immediate consequence of it, the judge will come to
enlarge the initially small gap between the desirability of the moral
and formal choices. The more strongly he feels about slavery, the
more likely that the cognitive avenue of least resistance will be upward revaluation of the importance of the formal restraints. It is this
upward revaluation that I shall label the "elevation of formal
stakes." In summary form, then, a close balance (barely weighed in
favor of formalism) between the moral and formal values is difficult
to live with and gives rise to a tendency to perceive the justification
for the original choice in the most persuasive of possible formulations.

The characteristics of the law's formal values contribute to easy
and less than conscious manipulation. It is a "soft" cognition, malleable in a way that experimental devices are not. For example, the
proposition that the judge ought to be impersonally faithful to the
"law" and the "law" alone is susceptible to justification on many
levels. (And the nature of the justification may influence the construction given the phrase.) One sort of justification is constitutional and
purely instrumental. The judge is to be faithful to "law" so that he
will not be unduly partial to some men. It is a device for securing impartiality. A second justification is that it serves to caution the judge
not to create law with broad strokes, but to presumptively tie himself
to extant sources of law. It is clear from the writings of Grimké,
Lieber, Kent, and Story discussed in Chapter 8, that the profession
had moved beyond any mechanistic reiteration of phrases in this
regard. In the reflective prose of treatises, these men were quite capable of moving to very precise analysis of the ends served by the proposition that the judge is bound by law.[7] This is to be contrasted with
John McLean's rhetoric in *Miller v. McQuerry* where a disregard of
the proposition, "by the judicial powers, would undermine and overturn the social compact." [8] Other examples are tabulated in the Appendix. Thus, the end served by fidelity to "law" is escalated to the
basis of society itself.

I do not mean to imply that there is no sense in which McLean's
statement may reflect real insight. For one may, indeed, justify the
principle of judicial obeisance to law in social contract terms. It is
precisely the amenability of these principles to a range of justifications at different levels that facilitates dissonance reduction through

the tendency to elevate the justification as far as possible. One has not chosen to participate in enslaving a man because of a mere device for controlling official behavior. No, one has been compelled to participate in enslaving a man because of fidelity to the consensual principles underlying ordered society itself.

At this point, it is necessary to both qualify and justify terminology. The data presented in the Appendix demonstrate how frequently the antislavery judges considered herein tended to express what was at stake to the formal structure in the gravest and highest of terms. I think it clear that no other single category of case in antebellum America called forth such a pattern of justification for role fidelity either by these judges, or by any judges of that time. Moreover, in common sense terms as well as in terms of dissonance theory, it seems right that a tough choice is easier to live with the deeper and more serious the justification for having made it.

None of this, however, demonstrates that an *escalation* of the formal stakes took place—that the more serious characterization of the formal stakes was something other than what the situation demanded or would otherwise have called forth. A demonstration of "escalation" is not possible, but some evidence converges with dissonance theory on this point. First the tendency to speak in such terms was not confined to instances of heightened political tension: It is as apparent in *Miller v. McQuerry* (1853) as in *Ex Parte Bushnell* (1859); as evident in *Ohio v. Carneal* (1817) as in *Sims* (1851). Second, the objective "stakes" were as high for judges who were not strongly "antislavery" as for those who were. Yet judges like Grier and Curtis confined such statements to somewhat narrower bounds. There are a very few instances of "high" justification by these two men, but it is not as dominant as with McLean. Moreover, in the cases of Grier and Curtis, the rhetoric is confined to situations of jury instruction or political harangue.* The escalation thesis, then, must rest

---

* In *Van Metre v. Mitchell*, 28 F. Cas. 1036 (No. 16,865) (C.C. Pa., 1853). Justice Grier instructed a jury very much along the lines of McLean's then recent *McQuerry* decision, ". . . the law of the land as stated to you by the court, . . . constitute the only elements of such a [true] verdict. No theories or opinions which you or we may entertain with regard to liberty and human rights, or the policy or justice of a system of domestic slavery, can have place on the bench or in the jury box. We dare not substitute our convictions or opinions, however honestly entertained, for the law of the land" (p. 1039).

Grier also quotes from McLean and from Tilghman on the necessity to follow an impersonal standard in slave cases. *Van Metre* marks the closest approximation by a judge not himself con-

upon a tentative position consistent with all our evidence, but by no means proven by it.

The fact of frequent justification for role fidelity in highest terms is, however, clear. And there were probably multiple determinants for that form of justification: the gravity of the actual threat to law; the rhetoric and presumed needs of the audience; the tendency to define one's own choice to oneself and to others in the most compelling manner possible. Moreover, as the dialectical context demanded a reason for, not a reiteration of, role limits and fidelity to them, the social compact or high reason of state justification came to sound almost inevitable. Any other answer seemed weak by contrast. To escalate the formal stakes when the moment demanded might have, from one perspective, reduced the dissonance of role fidelity and made the judge's decision easier. That does not mean, however, that it wasn't an act of statesmanship at the same time.

Retreat to a Mechanistic Formalism

Dissonance is reduced not only by the tendency to escalate the formal stakes, but also through a tendency to mechanize the formal requirements. The sorts of principles articulated as "fidelity to law,"

---

sidered to be an opponent of slavery to the formulations of McLean-Shaw-Swan. Grier's words, however, were part of a charge to the jury and may, though they need not, be viewed in terms of the purpose of convincing a jury to ignore conscience. Some of McLean's opinions tabulated in the Appendix are jury charges, but some are not. This variable is noted as to each case. Shaw's opinions in *Sims* and *Latimer* were not jury charges, nor, of course, was Story's opinion in *Prigg*.

Curtis most closely approximated the McLean epitome of rhetoric in his speech in defense of the Act of 1850—made in November 1850 at Faneuil Hall in Boston. There he spoke of the high ends served by fidelity to law, but he also let loose with the sort of explicit value preference that would have been unthinkable for McLean: "Whatever natural rights they [Negroes] have, and I admit those natural rights to their fullest extent, *this* is not the *soil* on which to vindicate them. This is *our* soil, sacred to *our* peace, on which we intend to perform *our* promises, and work out . . . the destiny which our creator has assigned to us." [Benjamin R. Curtis, *A Memoir of Benjamin Robbins Curtis* . . . (Boston: Little, Brown & Co., 1879), 1 : 135–36]. In a private letter of about the same period he phrased the issue in a manner more nearly resembling that of McLean: "I want to see someone come manfully up to the point, and attempt to show that the moral duty which we owe to the fugitive slave, when in conflict with the moral duty we owe to our country and its laws, is so plainly superior thereto, that we ought to engage in a revolution on account of it" (ibid., 1 : 122). It must be noted that Curtis, like many others of the day, would not concede the middle ground of civil disobedience. To assert conscience against law implied revolution. He was prepared to face the conflict and make an explicit value choice of order against freedom. For him the answer was an easy one, as the Faneuil Hall speech showed. For those who would not so willingly waive others' natural rights on racist grounds, it was a much harder choice.

adherence to "authority," to "precedent," or to legislative or constitutional "intent" seldom mechanistically compel a particular result in a given case. The fugitive slave controversy certainly illustrates this point. For a half-century the area of permissible state involvement in rendition was unclear. There was a series of constitutional issues of first impression: Are state magistrates under an obligation to enforce the federal rendition mechanism? May a state compel the slave-catcher to enforce his rights through court process? May detention of an alleged fugitive pursuant to federal process be challenged by state collateral proceedings? Is there congressional power to legislate with regard to the Fugitive Slave Provision of the Constitution? May Congress enforce the Provision through use of non-Article III judicial officers (commissioners)? May their fee be set higher for one result than for another? Does the alleged fugitive have any procedural rights in light of the probability that the rendering state considers him presumptively free? Even as more and more of these constitutional questions came to be foreclosed by Supreme Court decisions or by extrapolation from those opinions, there remained a broad area of adjective law that could have result-determining impact. What constitutes satisfactory proof of the identity of the alleged fugitive? Can a certificate from the slave state be challenged on any ground? On the basis of fraudulent procurement? In the trials of resisters and disobedients, how shall the jury be instructed? Will the courts invite or tolerate introduction of a local morality through that avenue?

Given these legal questions and the always present factor of determination of facts and establishment of presumptions and burdens where facts are disputed, it is clear that this issue, like all legal issues of complexity, was amenable to a broad range of solutions with a concomitant broad area for potential introduction of morality. However, the prevailing course of action of the antislavery judge was to speak in conclusary terms of the obligation to apply "the law and the law alone"; of the obligation to refrain from considering conscience, natural right, or justice. These statements often accompany rulings against the alleged slave on the basis of unclear and sometimes contradictory authority. The impression given is one of bowing, out of duty to law, to the inexorable force of crystal clear demands from Constitution, Congress, and Supreme Court.

The mechanistic view of judicial obligation and of doctrine has often been put to disingenuous use by judges. From Marshall's opinion in *Marbury v. Madison* through Pierce Butler to Hugo Black there have been Justices who believe or assert that "laying 'em side by side" decides cases.[9] That this is not a tenable description of the judicial decision was well known in the eighteenth century, was well articulated by Marshall, Story, Lieber, Kent, Grimké, and a host of others in the nineteenth century, and is but a truism for thoughtful constitutional commentary in the twentieth century.

But an impersonal mechanistic view of the judicial process has important dissonance reducing characteristics. Having chosen to be role faithful, the judge still had to keep the faith. If the law is clear and its application mechanical, then once the proposition of judicial subordination to law is accepted, keeping the faith seems easy. A less mechanical model would constantly raise the moral-formal question at each juncture: Am I pursuing a libertarian, innovative course because I want to, or because it is the "law?" The prevailing jurisprudence of excision of the personal will of the judge from judicial lawmaking made such a question a constant and difficult one.

The more mechanical the judge's view of the process, the more he externalized responsibility for the result. This phenomenon I label the retreat to formalism. It by no means characterized all judicial work around the fugitive cases. But Chief Justice Lemuel Shaw's opinion in *Sims* is an instance of such a retreat. It purported to view issues as foreclosed by precedents that, upon any fair view of the matter, were hardly on point.[10] Joseph Swan's opinion in *Bushnell* also purports to be forced by the inexorable march of precedent. In that case, however, the doctrinal pattern was, in fact, one that permitted, if it did not coerce, a rather mechanical result.[11] Both of these opinions, though they discuss policy matters, intimate that a different result would be forthcoming were it not for the "clear-cut" application of doctrines incumbent upon the judge.

Similarly, Joseph Story, in *Prigg v. Pennsylvania,* applied standards of interpretation that echoed the then recent *Commentaries on the Constitution.* Just as he sought in the *Commentaries* a judge-proof standard, so, here, he purported to be giving "to the words of each just such operation and force consistent with their legitimate meaning, as may fairly secure and attain the ends proposed."[12] Whatever input the judge has, according to Story, ought to be of an impersonal character. Story did not come to this formalism because of slavery. If there be a single cause, it is more likely a reaction to the pervasive distrust of the judiciary as unrestrained legislators. But, having responded to one threat in such a way, the response also served to make the slave cases seem easier.

In fugitive cases, John McLean most clearly revealed the "retreat to formalism." McLean vigorously asserted the compulsion to ignore morality from any source other than the purely legal ones in deciding these cases. He so instructed juries. Moreover, he considered *Prigg* to be a self-evident and unimpeachable source that required a proslavery result in a wide variety of fact situations involving state and private interposition in fugitive matters. At one point he noted his dissent in *Prigg* but concluded that he remained as bound by it as if he had concurred.[13]

The "retreat to formalism" was not dramatic. Had it been so, it would have been less effective for dissonance reduction. It involved, first, the choice from among formulations of interpretive principles that already existed. In part, the mechanistic model of decision making is so prevalent because of its service in dissonance reduction, in part, for its utility in masking allocation of decision making power. For Shaw, McLean, and Story, it was important that they hide the extent of their decisional power from themselves.

Thus, a second, complementary process that relieved the moral-formal dilemma is the following: The discomfort incidental to a difficult choice will be heightened insofar as the judge views himself as having had personal responsibility for a choice from among many alternatives before him. The discomfort will be reduced insofar as he can view himself as a mechanical instrument of the will of others. Therefore, he will choose from among available models of the judicial process that model that will most closely approximate the mechanical-impersonal formalism.

Two caveats are necessary. First, the judicial opinion is a public document. One can never be certain whether the rhetoric of formalism is dissimulation or honest self-reflection. I have no firm answer to such doubts, though private letters of Story and of McLean mirror the rhetoric of the opinions.[14] In both cases, however, the letters are not to intimates but to quasipublic correspondents. Second, the mechanistic view of the judicial process had a viability wholly independent of the slavery controversy. Thus, the claim here is not that the model was created by or for these cases, but that it was there to be chosen and that the tendency to choose it was reinforced by its utility in the service of dissonance reduction.

Ascription of Responsibility Elsewhere

Still a third device for reducing dissonance was the attribution of responsibility to some other person or group: Of the many attributes of the formal structure that were accentuated through the cognitive process described above, none was more important for this third process than the "separation of powers." * The doctrine of separation of powers not only reinforced the view of judicial power as limited, it also ascribed the power not enjoyed by the judge to some other branch of government. It further provided political and moral justifications for the helplessness of the judge to affect certain situations. To say that the "separation of powers" principle dovetailed neatly with the need of the antislavery judge to reduce dissonance is not, in any way, to impugn the political wisdom of the doctrine nor its utility. It is simply to perceive that an integral effect of the separation of powers is the facilitation of externalizing responsibility for unwanted consequences. Whether this effect is to be viewed as desirable or not may depend on the occasions of its appearance. In the fugitive slave cases, the denial of judicial responsibility or capacity for consideration of natural right and justice went hand-in-hand with the pronouncement that "it is for the people, who are soverign, and their representatives, to consider the laws of nature. . . ."

It was comforting (dissonance reducing) to be able to couple denial of personal responsibility for an unwanted result with the ascription of that responsibility to another. In the case of the Fugitive Slave Act, this phenomenon manifested itself in the broad and almost universal judicial acquiescence to congressional power to enforce the Fugitive Clause of Article IV and to enforce it wholly as it pleased.

It ought to be apparent by now that dissonance reduction by the antislavery judge, who had rendered a "proslavery" decision, did not

---

* Ascription of responsibility elsewhere included other devices as well. For example, McLean's statement that he had earlier dissented in *Prigg* amounted to the proposition: "I am not responsible for the keystone to the doctrinal edifice that now compels my decision against the fugitive. The responsibility lies with my brethren."

need to do violence to formal assumptions of the profession. Rather, the judge selected, as norms, those articulations of the process and its limits that invoked the highest possible justifications for formalism; that described the process in the most mechanistic terms; and that emphasized the place of others in the decisional process. Alternative articulations were available—articulations that gave the formal structure more down-to-earth, instrumental justifications, that stressed the inevitable and desirable role of the judge and of policy input in decision making, and that gave the judiciary a more explicit role as conjoint legislator. But a vision of the judicial process so articulated would be ill-suited to a man who is already experiencing a pervasive tension between conflicting role demands and who has decided a heart-rending lawsuit against his highest hopes. Surely, in reaching such difficult decisions, doctrinal patterns and the hierarchy of sources of normative authority are very important. The judge may not do as he wishes under any then-accepted formal pattern. How natural, then, to stress and reiterate the rhetoric of limits and confinement and their justifications rather than that of facilitation, power, and responsibility.

The hypotheses in this section of this chapter relate to the behavior of judges whose decisions ran against their own private conscience and hopes for public policy. The assumptions presuppose a broad distribution of opinion and of intensity of concern among judges. Only those whose concern was most charged and pervasive would experience serious dissonance and the resulting effects. Despite the fact that this "specially troubled" group represented but a small percentage of American judiciary, their position was strategically important. Insofar as credible dialogue took place between insurgent advocates and resisters and the officialdom they addressed, it was with these judges. The defense of the law's formalism, and of the proslavery results it determined, was not likely to have much weight with insurgents when it came from Taney, Campbell, Catron, or Wayne. It was, after all, easy to defend a process whose results were in harmony with one's own wishes or interests. The same conclusions from known opponents of slavery had far more impact.

Moreover, the opinions of these judges had great impact on another audience. The antislavery views of this small group of men were well known to other judges. If men such as these would eschew ameliorist manipulation of formalisms; if they would raise rhetoric to articulate the very highest ends served by law and obligation to law, then men less committed to antislavery had ready models for their own compliant behavior.*

Because of their strategic position, the escalation of formal values and the retreat to formalism discernible in this handful of judges had great impact on the balance of the system described earlier. Certain patterns of achieving stability through the judge as control mechanism were blocked. The ameliorist's path was not taken by the critical handful and the articulation of the formal process was such as to deter others from following that road. (The fact that the Garrisonians shared this perception of the formal process reinforced this deterrence.) The route of Wisconsin; the dramatic search for new doctrine based on a radical and outright rejection of a cardinal formal proposition (there, the obligation to follow Supreme Court precedent) was even more assiduously avoided. No antislavery doctrinal change of any importance had a hope of success unless the collaboration of this handful of prestigious antislavery judges was elicited. So, in effect, insofar as their own work tended to produce a response of helplessness and exaggerated formalism, one very important potential control on moral-formal crisis was destroyed. The pivotal character of these men warrants a brief excursion into biography.

Biographies

Joseph Story [15]

That Joseph Story would be faithful to his judicial role was a foregone conclusion. No man ever was more steeped in the law, intellectually and interpersonally. Professional study, the common element for bench and bar, attained new levels with Story. He wrote nine important treatises, taught at—virtually created—the Harvard Law School, and endured the sequestration of a Justice's life in an-

---

* For example, McLean's decision upholding the constitutionality of the Act of 1850 in *Miller v. McQuerry* was a very important signal to the South. Not only was he the first Justice of the Supreme Court to pass upon the act on circuit, but he was viewed as the most antislavery member of that Court. Therefore, his decision was the litmus test for fidelity to the law. See clipping in McLean Manuscripts, Library of Congress. The parallels between McLean's *McQuerry* decision and Grier's jury charge in *Van Metre v. Mitchell* might also reflect the "model" hypothesis put forward in the text. The district judge in *Van Metre* made even more use of the McLean model. *Van Metre v. Mitchell*, 28 F. Cas. 1042 (No. 16,865a) (D.C.D. Pa., 1853).

tebellum Washington. In term time, his waking hours were in the almost exclusive company of the other Justices—until 1832, dominated by Marshall. The respite from the court brought circuit duty and respite from circuit, the Harvard Law School. Moments begged from these institutional responsibilities were filled with the productive effort of the treatises—a one-man American Law Institute. Correspondence filled some time and was very much devoted to communications with other legal luminaries.[16] Purposeful infidelity to such a pervasive life-role would be unthinkable. This conclusion was further buttressed by the fact that it was only in the last five years of his life that Story came up against the slavery issue in high-intensity circumstances. By that time, alternative life-roles were not readily available.

Story's commitment to antislavery was of a different kind. Around the time of the Missouri Compromise, he seemed publicly committed to a strong antislavery stance. In 1819 he presented his passionate charges to the grand juries in Boston and Rhode Island concerning the slave trade. In 1819, he publicly declared for the complete eradication of slavery from the territories—one of his only public stands on a political issue—and in 1821, he rendered his opinion in *La Jeune Eugenie,* noted in Chapter 6. We may speculate that Story's ardor was cooled a bit by his idol, John Marshall, in the next few years. Marshall wrote to Story lamenting Justice Johnson's plunge into the mare's nest of the South Carolina Negro Seamen's Act while riding circuit. Perhaps the lament was a gentle caution against Story's exuberance in *La Jeune Eugenie.* Story concurred in *The Antelope* though this may well be attributable to the changed political circumstances described in Chapter 6.[17]

Nevertheless, Story's disapproval of slavery remained evident. His *Conflicts* accepted Mansfield's characterization of slave law with its explicit moral judgment upon slavery. *The Commentaries on the Constitution* treated the provisions recognizing slavery as necessary matters of compromise, justifiable only in terms of their making union possible. Story's relationship to antislavery was not simply academic. Here, too, the expectations of significant "others" reinforced personal belief. Wendell Phillips and Charles Sumner had been two of Story's most prized students at Harvard Law School. If Phillips's later career could not have pleased Story, Sumner was for a

long time conceived of as Story's likely successor to the Dane Profes-
sorship.[18] Moreover, Story's son, William, was militantly antislavery
by the late 1840's. It seems likely that his commitment was already
well formulated before his father's death. Indeed, William Wetmore
Story, in his filiopietistic *Life and Letters of Joseph Story* was at great
pains to justify the Justice's rulings on slavery matters.[19]

When the last few years of Story's career brought, in rapid succes-
sion, the *Amistad* case, *Prigg v. Pennsylvania,* and the *Latimer* affair, we might expect the elder statesman of the bench to reach for
accommodation mechanisms—to play the role of adjuster of moral-
formal conflict better than any other judge could. For, on the one
hand, Story as a true giant—a thirty-year man on the court—would
be as secure as anybody could be in his judicial life-role. On the
other hand, Story enjoyed the deep respect and affection of men like
Sumner and Dana and the grudging respect of Phillips. He, if anybody, could reach their ears and force attentive consideration to the
values threatened. In the *Amistad,* Story played the negative feedback
role superbly. His opinion gave the antislavery forces every bit of
relief requested while explicitly emphasizing the positivist elements
of reasoning, including the supremacy of any and all sources of sovereign expression to moral propositions deduced from nature or conscience.[20]

Story's role in *Prigg v. Pennsylvania* is more difficult to fathom.
For what appears to be a formidable example of a highly formalistic
abdication of the responsibility to weigh and consider policy and
moral implications of constitutional law, has been given a very different and plausible interpretation by the Justice's son. Story's opinion in *Prigg* was full of the very high purposes of the fugitive rendition clause. The clause was characterized as an indispensable element
of the formation of the Union. It was further a test of the good faith
of the participants in the national undertaking. Now, in a sense, all of
this talk of high purpose was not new in *Prigg*. Story so justified the
clause in his treatise on the Constitution. What was new in *Prigg* was
Story's very weak reasoning that the prohibition of the "discharge"
of a fugitive in Article IV must be interpreted to exclude any interposition of process that might operate to "delay" or "qualify" the
enjoyment of the right protected. Such word teasing was especially
unconvincing in light of McLean's dissent that included a forceful
policy attack against self-help.[21]

Story's *Prigg* opinion, then, was consistent with our prior characterization of him as one who was suddenly and in his last years confronted with the full force of role conflict. Confronted by the resulting dissonance, he was disabled from acting as a creative control and adjustment force to settle a moral-formal conflict. Instead, he retreated to formalism. However, William Wetmore Story has given us another view of *Prigg*, a view recounted far too uncritically by Story's most recent biographer. William Story characterized his father's *Prigg* opinion as not too subtle sabotage of the practical enforceability of the Fugitive Acts. For, Story, in upholding the broadest sweep of potential federal power in the premises, seemed to exclude the enlisting of state personnel for enforcement of the exclusively federal right. William Story pointed out that the natural result of this dictum was the passage of state personal liberty laws prohibiting state magistrates from aiding in enforcement and, thereby, leaving the slaveholder to his constitutional remedy of self-help or to recourse to the federal judges—too few and far between to be of practical value.* If William Story is correct, then we have a truly extraordinary ameliorist effort. Unfortunately, our records do not permit even a solid guess. In the *Latimer* case, which followed close on the heels of *Prigg,* Story handled the rendition process in a straightforward manner, affording the slaveholder all procedural amenities for proving his case. By that time, however, Story had painted himself into a doctrinal corner, even if his son's version of *Prigg* is correct. For, if Story fudged in *Prigg,* he did so through the ruse of asserting broad federal power that he, as a federal magistrate, could hardly refuse to exercise.

Story's impact on antislavery advocacy and resistance cannot, of course, be measured with any accuracy. His death came as the Mexican War gave new impetus to campaigns against "nationalizing" slavery and encouraged disunion sentiment among abolitionists. Texas was far more likely to be a direct factor than Story. Nevertheless, some tentative lines of influence can be traced.

---

* William Wetmore Story, *Life and Letters of Joseph Story* (Boston: C. C. Little and J. Brown, 1851), 2 : 381 ff. This proposition is reinforced by a somewhat similar though more moderate characterization of the Story opinion in the concurring opinions of Taney and Daniels. In opposition it must be noted that the federal exclusivity point did not command a majority of the Court, so that its efficacy as an instrument of sabotage was limited. This proved the case when *Moore v. Illinois* 55 U.S. (14 How.) 213 (1852) upheld state power to *enforce* the act's policy.

Richard Henry Dana said of Story, "He was our father in the law, our elder brother, the patriarch of a common family." [22] Dana's conviction as to Story's grandeur and integrity must have been at least partially responsible for the strong advocacy of respect for the values underlying the law's formalism that characterized Dana right up to the Civil War. Dana, in turn, as a highly visible antislavery lawyer, was a most effective advocate of respect for formal values. Of course, it would be ludicrous to attribute Dana's career wholly to Joseph Story. Yet there is certainly no other person to whom as much credit may be given. Not only was Story Dana's teacher, he was the single most impressive judicial and intellectual figure in a young lawyer's professional world. Dana, a most visible symbol of the attempted reconciliation of formal values and antislavery, alone, of the abolitionist bar, supported Loring in his defense of his judicial office.

Charles Sumner, too, was greatly influenced by Story. While still in law school, he was singled out by the Justice and made research assistant for the treatise on conflicts. Within a couple of years, Sumner became court reporter for Story on circuit and began to do some part-time teaching at Harvard Law School. For the next decade the two men remained in touch. Their correspondence transcended specific disagreements, especially over Sumner's pacifism in 1845, just before Story's death. There is no evidence that *Prigg* ever came to mitigate the enormous respect Story enjoyed in Sumner's eyes. In a eulogy shortly after Story's death, Sumner was at pains to note the late Justice's personal and private opposition to the acquisition of Texas.[23]

Finally, even Wendell Phillips gave grudging, though not complete, respect to Story. Upon the Justice's death, Phillips committed the sacrilege of stating that "even Story sullied at last the lustre of a long life by a decision [*Prigg*], the infamy of which even his large service cannot hide." It was because Phillips, a former student of Story, understood full well the power of the Justice's personality and integrity in the service of constitutional fidelity that he reluctantly criticized Story after his death, and later, still more vehemently, defended his criticisms. His rationale for fulfilling the unpleasant task of criticizing the honored dead was that

Mr. Justice Story has filled too large a space in the public eye, his decisions had too wide, and are destined to have too lustry, an influence on the courts of this country, to allow any man to surrender his right freely to canvass, and when wrong, earnestly to oppose and denounce them. . . .[24]

Story's leverage in the service of fidelity to law was not the product of his reputation as a jurist alone. Story, much like Felix Frankfurter, collected young men. His sincere interest in his students flattered them and bound them to him. His interest was aroused by talent and character not by ideological conformity. There is a tale, whose source I have not succeeded in verifying, that Story once said that of all his students, he was most interested in what would become of three: Wendell Phillips, Charles Sumner, and Benjamin R. Curtis.[25]

It is idle but tempting to speculate about the impact Story would have had upon the events of the 1850's had he lived another decade. Surely, he would not have joined the Wisconsin camp. Almost as surely, he would have come under increasingly hostile scrutiny by the antislavery bar and the resistance movements. However, his reservoir of good will was deeper than that of Shaw, McLean, or Swan. His general distaste for Taney and for the direction of his court might have moved him to a more idiosyncratic posture. Perhaps, however, it is *Prigg* that best presaged what the future would have brought: increasing insistence upon the rendition process as a keystone in the constitutional arch, increasing insistence upon union as the ultimate value, and still more rigid adherence to the excision of personal morality from the decisional process.

In sum, Joseph Story and his work may or may not exemplify the model constructed in this chapter. His life ended at a time when high intensity of conflict was just beginning. How much he was or could have been affected cannot be determined with any precision from the meager data. We may conclude without hesitation that Story and his explicit recourse to formalism had substantial impact as a model for others. But whether he, himself, might have used that formalism instrumentally to accomplish other ends or as a simple retreat from responsibility cannot now be finally determined.

John McLean [26]

John McLean's judicial career spanned the critical period of high-intensity moral-formal conflict. He was Justice of the United States Supreme Court from 1829 to 1861. During that period, he was circuit

Justice for the (seventh) circuit, which included Ohio, Michigan, Illinois, and Indiana—perhaps the area that most frequently presented cases of highly ideological advocacy, resistance, and quasirebellion. McLean was also a man of known antislavery views. In 1817, as a judge on the Ohio Supreme Court, he delivered an opinion in *Ohio v. Carneal* in which he stated that "slavery . . . is an infringement upon the sacred rights of man." [27] Perhaps more important than the brash utterance of a thirty-two-year-old up and coming judge-politician was McLean's involvement with antislavery Methodism, an involvement that was to continue as an important part of his adult life. McLean was "converted" in 1808 or 1809. The two most important religious figures for him were the Reverend John Collins, who converted him, and Philip Gatch. Both were characterized by a strong, religious antislavery stance, and both were sufficiently important to McLean to move him to write their biographies.[28]

Even in the *Carneal* decision, McLean perceived the potential conflict between conscience and judicial duty. Though he resolved that conflict-of-laws case against the slaveowner, he averred: "On this subject I confess it is difficult to deliberate without feeling—exertions to suppress every emotion would be in vain—to guard against any improper influence is all that can be expected." [29] McLean's model of responsible decision making on slavery at this point reflected a typical dualism. On the one hand, there was a kind of public morality running counter to slavery that could be expressed in natural law terms and that could properly be invoked, as it was in *Somerset's Case*, to create an antislavery rule of decision. On the other hand, the "improper influence" of merely personal moral beliefs was to be avoided.

McLean left the bench for Washington during much of the decade of the 1820's until his appointment by Jackson to the Supreme Court in 1829. It was not until the 1840's that he again faced the moral-formal conflict, this time in more acute form. The relatively important cases of *Groves v. Slaughter* and the *Amistad* were decided in 1841, not without agitation, yet not amidst the turmoil of total crisis.*

---

* McLean did not write in the *Amistad* case, joining in the opinion of Justice Story. In *Groves v. Slaughter,* 40 U.S. (15 Pet.) 448, McLean wrote a concurring opinion placing state power to exclude slaves upon a constitutional basis and rejecting the argument that the domestic slave trade constituted interstate commerce beyond the constitutional reach of the states, with

Prigg v. Pennsylvania followed in 1842 and was a far more difficult case. There, McLean felt constrained to dissent, as described in Chapter 10.[30] In much of his later judicial work on circuit, he either explicitly or implicitly referred to the formal obligation of the dissenter to accept the decision of the majority and to rule according to it. The call to accept the thrust of the majority in *Prigg* was almost immediate. For the following year McLean confronted the *Jones v. Van Zandt* case on circuit.[31] From his decisions in *Van Zandt* to his dissent in *Dred Scott,* McLean never wavered from his often eloquent calls to stand by the obligation to obey the law. He was particularly forceful in justifying the judge's obligations in social contract terms. The alternative to imperfect law was, he reiterated in each case, perfect anarchy. As the lone dissenter in *Prigg,* McLean's call was all the more forceful.

McLean's judicial positions are put in a more precise focus by describing something of his personal situation in the early 1840's. Always intrigued with politics, he had made an important choice to remain on the bench when he turned down Tyler's offer to become Secretary of War in 1841. McLean's biographer attributes the Justice's reluctance to a political move designed to shun an unpopular president.[32] However, Weisenburger belittles with a casual phrase the Justice's own statement about his reluctance to forsake the bench and his sense of commitment to the Court and to Story. That commitment was none the less strong for the obvious willingness and eagerness of McLean to entertain presidential ambitions. While he was prepared (with the support of men like Story) to leap for the presidency, he was constant in his reluctance to leave the Court for any lesser office, though the political advantages were high.[33] The maturing commitment to the role of Justice also coincided with the changes in McLean's personal life, which must have made the situation still more difficult.

---

the somewhat surprising phrase: "the right to exercise this power [of exclusion of new slaves], by a state, is higher and deeper than the Constitution. . . . Its power to guard against, or to remedy the evil, rests upon a law of self preservation." He also found the slave trade not interstate commerce because "the Constitution treats slaves as persons." McLean's rhetoric in *Groves* seemed designed not as a foundation for new constitutional law; for Taney and others easily reached similar results as to the scope of national power. Rather, he was concerned to demonstrate that it was not solicitude for slavery but a studied neutrality about it that underlay the failure of national competence. In this respect, McLean's views dovetailed with those of the Jay wing of antislavery jurisprudence.

A fifty-eight-year-old widower in 1843, McLean married Sarah Ludlow Garrard, a nationally prominent Methodist churchwoman of pronounced antislavery views. Indeed, her father, Colonel Israel Ludlow, had been involved with the Lane Seminary rebels, and her son, by a previous marriage, was an antislavery editor.[34] Thus, for McLean antislavery was not merely a political or moral position, it was a belief reinforced by others in close and perpetual proximity. This is not to say that there were not other significant interpersonal aspects to the Justice's dilemma. Salmon Chase, who by 1837 was a leader of the ideological antislavery bar in Ohio, was a friend of McLean's and a political supporter.[35] In 1846, the widower, Chase, would take his third wife, the niece of McLean's second wife. Chase remained a stalwart political supporter of McLean and praised him to others as a possible candidate for a Free-Soil or, later, Republican ticket.* Personal, indeed familial, contacts, some professional links, and political ambition might thus be seen as conspiring to determine a degree of reinforcement for religious and political opposition to slavery. Weighed in the balance was a moral concern for fidelity to law, a commitment to the enterprise of nationhood, and to the Court.

When matters came to a head in *Jones v. Van Zandt,* the actual case involved these very personal dimensions.[36] Chase, as I have noted earlier, was counsel for Van Zandt before McLean. Chase's arguments included appeal to the Christian duty of succoring the helpless fugitive and to the law of nature.[37] McLean both rejected the appeal to conscience and nature and elevated the justification for the rejection to the highest level. He instructed the jury:

> What have we to do with slavery in the abstract? It is admitted, by almost all who have examined the subject, to be founded in wrong, in oppression, in power against right. But in this case we have only to inquire whether the acts of the defendant, as proved under the law of Congress, subject him to a claim for indemnity by the plaintiff. . . .

---

* Weisenburger, McLean's biographer, became preoccupied with the presidential ambitions and, to a certain extent, machinations of McLean. He accordingly missed the significance of the fact that the Justice never suffered any lesser political ambition to lure him from the bench though there were plenty of opportunities. It might also be stressed that men like Story fed the Justice's ego by repeating that McLean, above all others, combined popularity with the sort of talent and integrity that an upstanding man could respect.

I have read to you the Constitution and the Act of Congress. These bear the impress of the nation. The principles which they lay down and enforce have been sanctioned in the most solemn form known to our government. We are bound to sustain them. They form the only guidelines in the administration of justice in this case.[38]

McLean's rhetoric cannot be explained solely as a concern for a potential runaway jury. Responding to Chase's subsequent motion for a new trial, the Justice stated:

I was not prepared to hear, in a Court of Justice, the broad ground assumed . . . that a man, in the exercise of what he conceives to be a conscientious duty, may violate the laws of the land. . . . The law is our only guide.

If convictions . . . are to be substituted as a rule of action in disregard of the law, we shall soon be without law and without protection. . . . What one man, or association of men, may assume as the basis of action, may be assumed by all others. And in this way society may be resolved into its original elements, and then the governing principle must be force. Every approximation to this state is at war with the social compact. . . . If the law be wrong in principle, or oppressive in its exactions, it should be changed in a constitutional mode. . . . But the law, until changed or abrogated, should be respected and obeyed. Any departure from this inflicts a deep wound on society, and is extremely demoralizing in its effects.[39]

Contemporaries who knew McLean well did not view such rhetoric as mere posturing or self-righteousness. Chase, his friend and losing lawyer, conceded, "I regret very much the decision of Judge McLean in the Van Zandt case and believe he fell into great error." Still, he thought McLean reasonably sound on slavery, politically and personally, if not judicially: "Add to this the constant and familiar association with antislavery folks in his family and among his friends, and his known aversion to slavery itself. . . ." [40] By the time of McLean's still more forceful reiteration of these principles in *Miller v. McQuerry*, Chase's assessment to the same correspondent was more despondent:

I mourn with you over the opinion of Judge McLean; but I expected nothing otherwise. His whole course of judicial action in reference to cases under the act of '93 had prepared me for it. With a kind heart and honest purposes he has suffered his reverence for imagined rights under the Constitution to lead him into conclusions from which you and I must ever shrink.[41]

In a sense, McLean's dilemma was all the more difficult because his antagonists were not in a stance of hostility toward him. That is, he was not only ideologically uncomfortable in ruling against the defendant resisters, he was also personally uncomfortable in denying Chase or, to a lesser extent, Jolliffe, relief.

Moreover, in McLean's personal papers, we have striking evidence supporting that of the public opinions. After the Indiana rescue case of 1849–1850 and, again, after the decision in 1853 in *Miller v. McQuerry,* McLean received and kept strongly condemnatory letters from clergymen. He sent carefully formulated responses, at pains to argue scripture as well as law. They argue a religious obligation to obedience as well as the normal Hobbesian parade of horribles.[42]

These letters reflect a strong policy objective in McLean's Fugitive Slave law position. An objective to preserve the Union and to be faithful to a provision so designed. Yet he, uniquely among prominent jurists, felt it necessary to answer the religious and moral argument in its own terms. He answered his correspondents not only, or even mainly, in terms of the law and its policy objective, but rather in terms of the lack of moral responsibility for slavery of the citizen or judge and his affirmative responsibility for obedience to law. He thus asserted, on the one hand, that "the institution of slavery is the work of a state for which no citizen of a free state is responsible morally or otherwise." And, on the other, he claimed that "formerly the enforcement of the 'higher law' caused more wars and bloodshed in the world, than all other causes united. . . . Conscience is not always a sure guide." [43]

The consensual basis for a constitution that, "[l]ike all other human productions . . . may be imperfect," requires a good faith effort to stand by the compact "until it shall be amended." The obligation to obey positive law thus stems both from the Hobbesian fear of anarchy, and from the undertaking of a constitution that was highly reminiscent of social compact.

Finally, the letters reflect in almost pathetic terms, the Justice's desire to convince himself and others of his personal antipathy to slavery and his lack of responsibility for it. He relates to the Reverend Wald:

> No one has held in greater abhorrence than myself the principles of slavery. With me this has not been a mere matter of theory. Some eight or ten colored persons are now free who were made so by my money, when I owed more debts than the value of my property. But I gave freedom to them. . . . I boast not of this. I have done nothing more than my duty, but I might ask how many of those have done more than I have to liberate individuals from bondage.[44]

The desire for personal absolution thus played as large a part as did political philosophy in this remarkable letter. Given McLean's dissent in *Prigg,* his religious and personal antislavery commitment, his antislavery family and friends, I assume that there was no single judge for whom the choice for the formal values was so difficult. And it was McLean whose opinions most forcefully demonstrated the phenomena suggested by our theory. He constantly appealed to a dichotomy between law and anarchy. He consistently attributed to others whatever power existed to ameliorate the situation, and he used the language of helplessness more than any other single judge.

Lemuel Shaw

Shaw's biographer, Leonard Levy, has provided us with a comprehensive and perceptive account of the Chief Justice's dilemma with respect to slavery and the Fugitive Slave Acts. Levy's chapters on those matters are judicial biography—indeed legal history—at its best: a rich portrait of the interaction of doctrinal, personal, and institutional histories.[45] Shaw's personal antipathy to slavery is demonstrated along with his pattern of conduct in conflict-of-law cases evincing a determination to take the logic of *Somerset's Case* to its very limits. Levy then provides us with a solid history of the Boston agitation surrounding the *Latimer, Shadrach,* and *Sims* affairs and of

Shaw's performance on each occasion. There is little to add to Levy's work except the theoretical framework provided by this chapter.

Shaw's antislavery reputation was as widespread and secure as that of any judicial figure before 1850. One has only to recall that the Supreme Court of New Jersey, in 1845, was concerned that Shaw's opinions on slavery might be unreliable authority because of his pronounced antislavery—indeed, abolitionist—sentiments.[46] Despite that reputation (a bit exaggerated to be sure), Shaw bore the brunt of abolitionist fury over the *Latimer, Shadrach,* and *Sims* affairs. To the *Liberator* he personified complicity with tyranny out of a sense of duty. As such, he was the bane of the Garrisonian ideologues.[47] *Latimer* provided the first intimation of Shaw's course of steadfast enforcement of the Fugitive Slave Act. Despite the Justice's prior work undermining slavery, it brought an immediate and very personal, biting attack on him by the abolitionist press. The comparison to Pontius Pilate, the emphasis on the alternate course of resignation, bespoke the opposition's sensitivity to the role limits and their effects on moral choice.[48] Curiously, Story, though directly involved in the *Latimer* case, was attacked with greater caution, perhaps because his great repute signaled the likely failure of a frontal blow.[49]

Shaw believed in fugitive rendition as a necessary evil.[50] In this respect he seems very like Joseph Story. His conception of policy as well as of duty pointed to compliance. But this in no sense may be taken as a retreat from the recognition of the injustice or cruelty done the victim of rendition, nor does it signal a lesser opposition to slavery per se. Just as Captain Vere acknowledged, indeed defended, the necessity of the Mutiny Act, yet understood the innocence of its victim, so Shaw approached the fugitive problem. I would tender a guess that Shaw's singular act that so captured the imagination of the abolitionists—the bowing beneath the federally imposed chains surrounding the courthouse for the *Sims* case—was also an act fraught with symbolic import for Shaw himself. The chains were not of his making. He would have preferred that they not be necessary; but they were there, and his only choice was between accepting the yoke of office or resigning it. The sense of overwhelming and external compulsion, the subjugation of deep personal instinct to social necessity, was symbolized by the Justice's acceptance of the chains.

If I am correct in the reading of *Billy Budd,* advanced in the introduction to this work, then we have at least an indirect reflection of the character of Shaw for which there is little direct evidence. Captain Vere never doubted that he acted righteously, though he was certainly troubled by the injustice worked through his righteous conduct. Lemuel Shaw, on the eve of the Civil War, reaffirmed his long-standing fidelity to the obligation of rendition. Sectional strife simply reinforced his belief in the necessity of a "Mutiny Act" for the fugitive.

Lemuel Shaw was one of the principal carriers of what Llewellyn called the grand style of common law jurisprudence. In his railroad cases, his labor cases, in torts, criminal law, and church-state relations, Shaw was one of those who tested precedent against Llewellyn's threefold criteria of person (of the judge who authored the precedent), principle, and policy.[51] While no one entirely forsakes his genius as he shifts from area to area, I believe that *Sims's Case*, in particular, and the slave cases, in general, evidenced a method that differed markedly from Shaw's accustomed vigor and surefootedness.

Indeed, Levy, in discussing *Sims's Case*, notes, without attribution of special significance, the salient characteristics that I have identified as prevalent in the decisions of all or most of the antislavery role-faithful judges. First, Levy noted Shaw's reluctance to get involved; next, he stated, "he was obsessed with the fiction that it [the Constitution] would never have come into being had it not provided for the return of runaways." Levy considered such "history" to be Shaw's projection in impersonal terms of a personal policy commitment to appeasement for the sake of union. Finally, Levy notes Shaw's unjustifiable reliance on a long string of authority decided with respect to the Act of 1793.[52]

The escalation of the policy objectives of rendition in *Sims* is not a technique wholly foreign to Shaw in other areas of decision making. But, the very questionable, yet dogmatic use of precedent is not to be found in so striking a manner in any other of Shaw's leading cases. This phenomenon is the more striking as Shaw simply ignored the "new" arguments of counsel. Thus, the retreat to formalism combined with some escalation of the formal stakes—here, union—appeared in uncharacteristic combination in *Sims's Case*. From what we know of the Justice's *Latimer* decision—that case too was accompanied by protestations of personal helplessness.[53]

It must be conceded, however, that Shaw's opinions, though troubled, do not give as clearly evidenced recognition of an either-or dichotomy as do those of McLean. Nor has he left us the amount of extrinsic evidence of his consciousness of the dilemma as has Joseph Story. I am inclined, in the last analysis, to resort to *Billy Budd* for a speculative, but nonetheless useful, stab at understanding the man.

As Captain Vere dies, he repeats the words, "Billy Budd, Billy Budd"; and the author goes on:

> That these were not the accents of remorse would seem clear from what the attendant said to the *Billipotent's* senior officer of marines, who, as the most reluctant to condemn of the members of the drumhead court, too well knew, though here he kept the knowledge to himself, who Billy Budd was.[54]

Budd is Christ, revealed ultimately to Captain Vere, not as accuser, but as comforter and salvation. We must remember, again, the accusations against Shaw as Pilate and the current idiom of the abolitionists in which the fugitive was Christ. But, according to Melville, for Vere the end brings not the sword of Christ, but the peace of Christ the Savior. Melville, in his last artistic act, may have been paying his respect to the soul of his departed father-in-law to whom he dedicated in more conventional fashion his first novel.[55] If so, Melville, at least, saw the soul of Shaw as intertwined with the complex interaction of crucifixion forgiveness and salvation. Such theological symbolism would be unlikely without the more earthly concomitant of guilt, remorse, and justification.

Joseph Swan [56]

The presence of Joseph Swan among my quartet of significant antislavery jurists may occasion surprise. Certainly, Swan, with a single six-year term as judge on the Ohio Supreme Court, does not belong in the company of Story, McLean, and Shaw, of whom the first two served more than thirty years on the United States Supreme Court, while the third dominated the nation's most prestigious state court for three decades. Yet Swan might have become a judge of precisely such stature had it not been for the very issue I have been discussing. Swan rose to the Ohio bench with extraordinary professional and political credentials. He was the author of three well-known and respected state law treatises.[57] Such useful but modest work in no sense ranks Swan with the Kents and Storys, but it does indicate a proclivity to publish and a craftsman's expertise, qualities in relatively short supply in the old West of the 1850's.

Swan had also been a founder of the state Republican party. His political antislavery was unquestioned, and he had the backing of what would become the state's dominant political powers.[58] He could look forward to a long career on the bench. He was only fifty-one at his election in 1854. Indeed, he lived to the age of eighty-two, and his active life might have afforded him something like a thirty-year tenure had he remained a judge.

All that might have been was destroyed by Swan's opinion in *Ex Parte Bushnell*. Before that case, Swan had had occasion to deal with the slavery issue in only one other instance. In *Anderson v. Poindexter,* the Justice concurred specially in a matter involving the effect to be given the rule of *Somerset's Case* in Ohio. Along with all but one of the other judges, Swan argued forcefully for a broad, antislavery, Massachusetts-type approach to the issue. There was, in Swan's opinion, an intimation that the only exception to the rule of *Somerset's Case* in Ohio would be the constitutionally prescribed fugitive rendition process.[59]

As I have indicated in Chapter 11, the 1859 case of *Ex Parte Bushnell* found Justice Swan casting the deciding vote and writing the court's opinion, denying the state's power to release accused aiders and abettors of the fugitive slave upon state habeas corpus.[60] In *Bushnell* the familiar phenomena of formalistic reliance on precedent and of an apocalyptic vision of the consequences of disobedience to judicial norms were present, but with a significant difference. In *Bushnell* the circumstances were such as to make the formalism of precedent seem overwhelming and the threat of anarchy credible. Shortly before *Bushnell* was decided, the United States Supreme Court reversed *Booth*. Although the full text of *Ableman v. Booth* might not yet have reached Ohio, the court in *Bushnell* knew of the decision and was well aware that the general line of *Sims* had been upheld and probably fortified by the high court.[61] In argument, the Ohio court confronted no attempt to distinguish *Booth* (and indeed it was as "square" a precedent as one could imagine), but rather an attempt to undermine the obligatory authority of the Supreme Court. *Booth* was so recent and seemed so squarely on point that the attack on the institution promised better results.*

Perhaps because the test of the *Booth* opinion had not arrived, Swan's opinion does not rest on *Booth* but, in fairness, it must be judged in light of that case. The treatment of the constitutionality of the act as foreclosed by precedent was not, in the context of 1859, a retreat from responsibility. Any other decision would have required extensive justification for ignoring so strong, recent, and direct authority from the Supreme Court.

Similarly, Swan's appeal to law as the only alternative to a precipitation of a major crisis—civil war or anarchy—though it had about it something of the escalation of formal values, was a more realistic panic than that of McLean or Shaw. Salmon Chase was governor of Ohio in 1859 and he had pledged to use the state militia if necessary to enforce an order of the state court to release federal prisoners. Widespread rallies and demonstrations openly considered and endorsed a course of action that was explicitly articulated as a potential precipitant of civil war.[62] The situation in Ohio before 1855 and in Boston throughout the 1850's, though sometimes tense, never approached such a level.

In short, dissonance reduction for Swan did not require recourse to a model of precedent or to a vision of the threatened formal values that would not command general adherence by some hypothetical, objective observer. No "escalation" was necessary, for the stakes were already high. No retreat to a mechanistic formalism was necessary, for the doctrinal lines were already drawn by *square,* unambiguous, recent Supreme Court precedent.

Despite all this, Swan's opinion is troubled and troublesome. The Justice was well aware that the critical choice was not legal but moral. He knew that the issue was whether to abide the role or break

---

* Jacob Shipherd, *History of the Oberlin-Wellington Rescue* (Boston: J. P. Jewett Co., 1859): "And now, when I am pressed with any decision of that court as concluding any right of the citizen, I reply simply and only,—'Dred Scott!' Shall that Court extort more respect for its decisions that itself yields to them? If so much usage and precedent may be overturned in the interest of slavery, surely, surely, an extra-judicial opinion may be well disregarded in the interest of constitutional liberty" (p. 219).

"Your Honors, then, are not bound to follow the rule on which Prigg, or the Booth, or any other case was decided, if on careful examination and reflection, that rule is, in your judgment, wrong" (p. 224).

out of it.* As a result of the unambiguous character of the doctrinal
situation, the alternative of choosing an acceptable formal model by
which doctrine would be changed or ameliorated was available only
through rejection of a principle as important and as established as the
appellate authority of the United States Supreme Court. The dissenters understood this and relied on—indeed, quoted at length—the
Virginia and Kentucky Resolutions of 1798.[63] Both dissenters also
undercut the Supreme Court's authority, in part, by treating *Dred
Scott* as a Supreme Court invitation to reexamine basic principles on
slavery. Judge Brinkerhoff put it most succinctly:

> Yet in the recent case of *Dred Scott v. Sandford* . . . all this
> [past practice and law as to slavery in the territories] is over-
> turned and disregarded, and the whole past theory and practice
> of the government in this respect attempted to be revolutionized
> by force of a judicial *ipse dixit*. We are thus invited by that court
> back to the consideration of first principles; and neither it nor
> those who rely on its authority have a right to complain if we ac-
> cept the invitation.[64]

That Swan also so understood what was at stake is clear from a single
attempt to draw the balance between order and rebellion: "I must refuse the experiment of initiating disorder and governmental collision,
to establish order and even-handed justice." [65]

And at the close of Swan's long opinion, he ends on a personal
note, which, for the first time, reveals how troubled he was by the
issue. Swan makes an attempt, most uncharacteristic of judges, to
project himself into the place of the petitioners before him. Acknowledging that he might, confronted by the weary fugitive, "protect him
from his pursuers," yet he continues,

> if I did it, and were prosecuted, condemned, and imprisoned and
> brought by my counsel before this tribunal on a habeas corpus,
> and were then permitted to pronounce judgment in my own case,
> I trust I should have the moral courage to say, before God and

---

* Swan's awareness of the nature of the choice is revealed in the following passage:
". . . does it become the official conservators of the public peace (judges) to break through
those judicial sanctions which guide and limit their personal discretion and are the only safe-
guard against their own arbitrary and capricious tyranny and be the first to initiate such a civil
commotion?" (9 Ohio St., p. 191) (1859).

the country, as I am now compelled to say, under the solemn duties of a judge bound by my official oath to sustain the supremacy of the Constitution and the law: "THE PRISONER MUST BE REMANDED." [66]

This curious passage is both Swan's attempt to project himself into the petitioner's shoes and a transparent petition for the prisoners to project themselves into his (the Judge's) shoes. He is saying, "I understand how you could have come to do what you've done, but wouldn't you feel compelled to do as I do in my place?" This revelation suggests an interpretation that recognizes the extraordinary level of internal tension generated by the moral-formal dilemma, even where the formal issues were clear and unchallenged. I would read the subsequent biography of Joseph Swan in that light.

Because of the *Bushnell* Case, Joseph Swan was not renominated for the Ohio Supreme Court in 1859. After the heat of these prewar years passed, he was offered the post several times but always declined.[67] When he died in 1884, Swan was eulogized for the great courage of his opinion in *Bushnell*. It is apparent that the bench and bar thought of Swan's failure of reelection in 1859 as a dramatic proof of the unsavory effect of the popular election of judges. To me, it is highly significant that Swan never sought office after 1860, indeed, that he turned it down. I cannot doubt that the discomfort of having been a target for abolitionists in 1859–1860 was partly responsible. But I also suspect that the difficulty of the moral choice itself was an experience that Swan would not have wanted to relive. Throughout his life he considered *Bushnell* his most important act.* But acting out a tragic part, for all its import, may not be a very comfortable role.

---

* J. W. Andrews, "Joseph Rockwell Swan," in *Treatise on the Law Relating to the Powers and Duties of Justices of the Peace in Ohio,* 27th ed. (Cincinnati: W. H. Anderson Co., 1930), p. xiv: "Later in life he was asked what he considered the most important event of his life. He replied: 'My decision in the Bushnell and Langstan case.' "

POSTSCRIPT TO PART III

I do not wish to engage in psychological reductionism with respect to the four judges studied in the preceding section. Their dilemma was a real enough one, not in any sense created by the pathology of the actors. My point is rather that the responses of these men and of others like them were characteristic and predictable patterns of judicial performance in such most difficult of circumstances. The circumstances were difficult in part because there are no formal substitutes for hard priority value choices in situations like those confronting Story, McLean, Shaw, and Swan. They were also difficult because these men shared a jurisprudence that fostered imprecise thinking about the nature of the choices available. The persistence of the natural law idiom in slavery situations—kept alive in conflict-of-law, international law, and some state constitutions—fostered the illusion that there was an honest, bootstrap operation by which the law might be made to achieve libertarian ends. That illusion was particularly attractive to certain insurgent forces that developed a technique for constantly confronting the judiciary with extensions and reformulations of their own natural law idiom. Although good judges didn't have any trouble rejecting the natural law course as a basis for action where positive law provided a contrary rule, they did have difficulty justifying their positivism to these insurgents. A later age, having rejected the natural law idiom even as a device for expressing commonly accepted ends of law, would not face the dilemma of how to justify limiting its effect.

The jurisprudence of mid-nineteenth-century America also fostered a degree of imprecision through the formulation of responsible judging as a "will-less" operation. Having rejected as simplistic and inaccurate the traditional characterization of judging as simply *ius dicere,* mid-nineteenth-century jurists had not yet formulated an acceptable alternative that would both describe and explain the senses in which judges make law while justifying and explaining the difference between judicial and legislative lawmaking. By stating that judges did make law but ought never consult their personal "will" in

257

so doing, the age was groping for a way to justify judicial independence, preserve judicial impartiality, yet acknowledge judicial discretion and innovation. Outright confession that the personal will of the judge could be a legitimate determinant of law was a difficult step to take. It would have played into the hands of those who urged democratic controls over judicial tenure and activity, and it would have placed a burden of responsibility on judges that they were rightfully unwilling to accept, in part because there had not yet been an adequate description of alternative restraining devices.

A third characteristic of the jurisprudence of mid-nineteenth-century America was a persistent search for mechanical models for decision. Having discovered and appreciated "discretion," they searched for "technique" to limit it. While Grimké and Lieber exhibit occasional glimpses of the inherent difficulties in a rule-bound model of interpretation or construction, Story and Kent often seem to yearn for and propose just such models.

The jurisprudential tools of an epoch, its "juristic competence," do not determine or generate specific answers to particular problems, but they do determine the universe of viable responses. Antebellum jurisprudence was positivist and preoccupied with refuting the Jacksonian myth of judicial lawmaking run amuck. As a result, the universe of responses available for the judge in the moral-formal dilemma posed by the Fugitive Slave law tended to include and stress formulations of self-denial and mechanical limits. Thus, the juristic competence of the age dovetailed with the needs of the antislavery judge to externalize responsibility for his decisions. (That need was the more acute where the actors and past decisions created an either-or pattern.)

Yet, for analytical purposes, it is useful to separate performance from competence. The "juristic competence" of the age may have created predispositions, but the universe of possible responses generated by it was not circumscribed by any hard and fast failure to understand discretion or to value it. The consistent recourse to the highest justifications for formalism, the most mechanical understanding of precedent, and the steadfast excision of self and appeal to separation of powers suggests that it was the performance of troubled men in troubled times as well as the juristic competence of their age that determined the almost uniform response of the antislavery bench to the call for liberty. Some performance characteristics are idiosyncratic or random. But the predictability of the performance characteristics outlined above suggests that given a particular juristic competence, there will be very specific consequences to and limits on the performance of judges caught in the moral-formal dilemma. If a man makes a good priest, we may be quite sure he will not be a great prophet.

APPENDIX

In this appendix I wish to present the interested reader with the full range of data supporting the conclusions I have drawn as to the three responsibility mitigation mechanisms. I shall proceed on a judge by judge basis, presenting three sorts of data: first, quotations and citations supporting the existence of the phenomena I have asserted; second, a conclusory comparison with the same judge's work in non-slave cases insofar as possible; third, an assessment as to the possibility of drawing contrary conclusions from the opinions.

John McLean

John McLean decided fugitive slave cases on circuit between 1842 and 1853. I shall not consider his opinions written either in dissent or for the Supreme Court since the ethics of the role in a corporate decisional situation at the apex of the pyramid is very different from that of the individual justice on circuit. I have also indicated whether the quoted words were spoken before a jury or not. If the words were addressed to a jury, then there is much greater reason to discount them as reflective of a personal problem and more reflective of a purpose of persuading others who have moral doubts.

Escalation of the Formal Stakes

(a) *Jones v. Van Zandt,* 13 Fed. Cas. 1047 (No. 7,502) (C.C.D. Ohio, 1843) *no jury*—on motion for a new trial.

> If convictions, honest convictions they may be, of what is right or wrong, are to be substituted as a rule of action in disregard of the law, we shall soon be without law and without protection. . . .
> What one man, or association of men, may assume as the basis of action, may be assumed by all others. And in this way society may be resolved into its original elements and then the governing principle must be force. Every approximation to this state is at war with the social compact. (p. 1048)

(b) *Vaughn v. Williams,* 28 F. Cas. 1115 (No. 16,903) (C.C.D. Ind., 1845) *before a jury.* No passage comparable to that in a above, but there is a passage justifying obedience to the Constitution in the following terms:

> . . . it was the best [instrument] that could be adopted under the circumstances. It has saved us from anarchy and ruin. . . . Whatever defects there may be in the instrument, no one can fail to see that its beneficial results exceed the power of human computation. (p. 1116)

(c) *Giltner v. Gorham,* 10 F. Cas. 424 (No. 5,453) (C.C.D. Mich., 1848) *before a jury.*

> If you wish to give permanency to our government, and preserve its great principles, we must stand by the Constitution and laws; . . . if the law is found the only safe rule by which controversies between man and man can be decided. (p. 432)

(d) *Ray v. Donnel,* 20 F. Cas. 325 (No. 11,590) (C.C.D. Ind., 1849) *before a jury.* "If the guaranties of this fundamental law be disregarded, all our hopes for the future . . . must perish" (p. 329).

(e) *Norris v. Newton,* 18 F. Cas. 322 (No. 10,307) (C.C.D. Ind., 1850) *before a jury.*

> General rules have been adopted in the form of laws for the protection of the rights of persons and things. These laws lie at the foundation of the social compact and their observance is essential to the maintenance of civilization. . . . [As to following "conscience"] this would overturn the basis of society. . . . The chief glory and excellence of our institutions consist in the supremacy of law. (p. 326)

(f) *Miller v. McQuerry,* 17 F. Cas. 335 (No. 9,583) (C.C.D. Ohio, 1853) *no jury.* "This is a field [natural law and right] which judges cannot explore. . . . They look to the law and to the law only. A disregard of this, by the judicial powers, would undermine and overturn the social compact" (p. 339).

(g) Letter of John McLean to Reverend Jona Wald, 10 November 1850, McLean Mss., Library of Congress. "Formerly the enforcement of the 'higher law' caused more wars and bloodshed in the world, than all other causes united. . . . Conscience is not always a sure guide."

Retreat to Formalism.

The overriding fact in McLean's formalism is the treatment of *Prigg,* from which he dissented, as conclusive authority on a variety of questions concerning both the Act of 1793 and that of 1850. There is also a very general appeal to "law" or the "Constitution" as the only guide or only "safe guide," though the issue is in part one of what the "law" or "Constitution" is to be read as saying.

(a) *Jones v. Van Zandt.* "The law is our only guide." *Jones,* however, does not involve a mechanistic use of *Prigg.* (p. 1048)

(b) *Norris v. Newton.* "I dissented from the opinion of the court [in *Prigg v. Pennsylvania*] and stated my objections with whatever force I was able. But I am fully bound by that decision as if I had assented to it" (p. 324). "But our duty is found in the constitution of the Union, as construed by the supreme court" (p. 327)

(c) *Miller v. McQuerry.*

It is contended that the law authorizing the reclamation of fugitives from labor is unconstitutional. That the constitution left the power with the states, and vested no power on the subject in the federal government. This argument has been sometimes advanced, and it may have been introduced into one or more political platforms. In regard to the soundness of this position, I will first refer to judicial decisions. In the case of *Prigg v. The State of Pennsylvania,* the judges of the supreme court of the United States, without a dissenting voice, affirmed the doctrine, that this power was in the federal government. A majority of them held that it was exclusively in the general government. Some of the judges thought that a state might legislate in aid of the act of congress, but it was held by no one of them, that the power could be exercised by a state, except in subordination of the federal power. Every state court which has decided the questions, has decided it in accordance with the view of the supreme court. No respectable court, it is believed, has sustained the view that the power is with the state. Such an array of authority can scarcely be found in favor of the construction of any part of the constitution, which has ever been doubted. But this construction, sanctioned as it is by the entire judicial power, state as well as federal, has also the sanction of the legislative power. (p. 337)

Although *Prigg* did speak of federal power, it did not uphold federal legislative power, but rather a personal, constitutional privilege of self-help by the master. The antislavery bar was, from a distant perspective, quite correct in terming the rest of *Prigg* dictum, though obviously on more questionable ground, in assuming that no extrapolation may properly proceed from such dictum.

Also in *Miller v. McQuerry* is a strange formalistic catch-22:

. . . If the decision on such an inquiry as this, should finally fix the seal of slavery on the fugitive, I should hesitate long, notwithstanding the weight of precedent, without the aid of a jury, to pronounce his fate. But the inquiry is preliminary, and not final. It is true, it may be said, that the power of the master may be so exercised as to defeat a trial for the freedom of the fugitive. This must be admitted, but the hardship and injustice supposed arises out of the institution of slavery, over which we have no control. Under such circumstances, we cannot be held answerable. (p. 340)

This way of formulating the relationship of the supposed ''preliminary'' character of a fugitive rendition proceeding to the actuality of life under slavery is very strange. For McLean seems to say that the inquiry is not in terms of whether the process taken as a whole is commensurate with due process or the right to a jury trial, but rather whether he can be held responsible for that part of the process that works the ultimate ''illegal'' injustice.

Ascription of Responsibility Elsewhere (Denial of Responsibility)

(a) *Jones v. Van Zandt.* ''If the organization of our government be essentially wrong . . . change it in the mode provided'' (p. 1049).

(b) *Vaughn v. Williams.* ''If an alteration in the instrument be desirable, let it be made, or attempted to be made, in the mode provided'' (p. 1116). Also ''With this subject [the impolicy of the provision on fugitive slaves] in the abstract, this court has nothing to do." (p. 1119)

(c) *Giltner v. Gorham.* "With the policy of the local laws of the states, we have nothing to do. However, unjust and impolitic slavery may be, yet the people of Kentucky, in their sovereign capacity, have adopted it" (p. 432).

(d) *Ray v. Donnell and Hamilton.* "Slavery is an exciting topic. . . . But it can only come before us judicially. Here great principles are discussed and acted upon only as they bear upon the rights of litigant parties." (p. 329)

(e) *Norris v. Newton.* "If the law be unwise or impolitic let it be changed in the mode prescribed." (p. 327)

(f) *Miller v. McQuerry.* "With the abstract principles of slavery, courts called to administer this law have nothing to do. It is for the people who are sovereign and their representatives . . . to consider the laws of nature and the immutable principles of right" (p. 339). and ". . . but the hardship and injustice supposed arises out of the institution of slavery, over which we have no control. Under such circumstance, we cannot be held answerable." (p. 340)

(g) Letter to Reverend Wald. "The institution of slavery is the work of a state for which no citizen of a free state is responsible morally or otherwise."

Similar Quotations in Other Cases

There is, among all of McLean's circuit court opinions, only one instance of phraseology that approximates the recurrent themes of the fugitive decisions. That single instance involved instructions to a jury in the case of *United Sates v. Cole,* 25 F. Cas. 493 (No. 14,832) (C.C.D. Ohio, 1853) "Even those sympathies so honorable to our natures, are not to influence us here. Nothing but the facts and the law, should govern you." (p. 527)
The *Cole* case was decided almost immediately after *Miller v. Mc-Querry.* In sum, therefore, it is easy to conclude for McLean that the rhetoric of the fugitive cases is related to a special difficulty experienced only with respect to slavery.

The Question of Contrary Evidence

Quotation is a dangerous game. It seems to me that the most rigorous examination of these cases could not but reach the conclusion that the patterns I set forth with respect to formal stakes and denial of responsibility or ascription of it elsewhere are not established out of context. The assessment of the evidence for a mechanistic formalism is more in exact and more problematic. It largely turns on how one believes *Prigg* ought to have been read by judges in McLean's position. McLean's reading in *Norris,* and more especially in *McQuerry,* is broad but not unlike broad readings often given precedents in other areas. What is interesting is that the broad reading seems to be set forth as a matter of compulsion, not a matter of choice.

Lemuel Shaw

There is only one reported decision by Shaw in a fugitive case, *Thomas Sims's Case* 61 Mass (7 Cush.) 285 (1851). That case, however, has the distinction of being the first instance of consideration of the constitutionality of the Act of 1850 by a major court. In addition to *Sims's Case,* there is the *Liberator's* account of Shaw's opinion in *Latimer.* Moreover, Shaw's opinions in these fugitive cases may be compared with a variety of related slavery cases or cases involving Negroes. In particular, there are a series of *Somerset* issue cases and the case of *Roberts v. City of Boston* involving school integration. Finally, we may search for similar forms in major cases in other areas of law. First the fugitive cases:

Escalation of Formal Stakes

Sims (no jury). "The Provision [Fugitive Slave Clause] . . . was the best adjustment which could could be made . . . and was absolutely necessary to effect the general pacification by which harmony and peace should take the place of violence and war." (p. 318)
"The principle of adhering to judicial precedent . . . is absolutely necessary to the peace, union and harmonious action of the state and general governments." (p. 310)
Latimer (no jury—third person report of the *Liberator*). "He

repeatedly said that on no other terms could a union have been formed between North and South, at the time of the adoption of the Constitution.''

Retreat to Formalism

Sims. ''But we are not entitled to consider this a new question; we must consider it settled and determined by authorities of official duty and a disregard of judicial responsibility to overlook.'' (This is preceded by an acknowledgment that the Article III courts issue is, on its face, a serious one.) (pp. 303–304)

''The question raised by the petitioner . . . is settled by a course of legal decisions which we are bound to respect, and which we regard as binding and conclusive upon this court.'' (p. 309)

Ascription of Responsibility Elsewhere

Latimer. He said in substance that he probably felt as much sympathy for the person in custody as others, but this was a case in which an appeal to natural rights and the paramount law of liberty was not pertinent! in [the Constitution] was to be obeyed, however disagreeable to our own natural sympathies or views of duty. (*Liberator*, November 4, 1842, p. 3)

Sims. Much of the appendix to Sims consists of an argument that slavery is not a creature of the Constitution, but that the Constitution, as enforced by judges, simply made a necessary adjustment to a system of slavery instituted by others.

Slavery was not created, established or perpetuated by the Constitution. It existed before; it would have existed if the Constitution had not been made. . . . The Constitution, therefore, is not responsible for the origin or continuance of slavery. (p. 318)

Other Cases Involving Slaves or Rights of Negroes

Levy's biography contains a complete account of Shaw's work in conflict-of-laws cases presenting the *Somerset* issue. Examination of *Aves*, the leading case, and of the several cases not officially reported, but appearing in law journals of the day, indicates no use of the responsibility avoidance techniques. This result is totally unsurprising since the result reached is always in favor of the alleged slave.

More important is the opinion of *Roberts v. City of Boston,* 59 Mass. (5 Cush.) 198 (1849), where Shaw denied relief to Negro petitioners for school integration. The opinion ultimately rests upon the rationale of administrative discretion within the school committee to determine whether "this maintenance of separate schools tends to deepen and perpetuate the odious distinction of caste . . . having in view the best interests of both classes of children . . ." (p. 209).

Thus, in a sense, Shaw attributes primary decisional power elsewhere. But he is quite straightforward in exercising a limited judicial review of the administrative action and in concluding: ". . . we cannot say, that their decision . . . is not founded on just grounds of reason and experience, and in the results of a discriminating and honest judgement" (pp. 209–10). There are no intimations that any mechanical manipulations of rules or precedents require the result. There is no parade of vast matters at stake in the judicial fulfillment of duty.

Non-race Cases

In none of a sampling of major cases is there a series of utterances approaching those in *Sims*.

While the data base for Shaw is quite small, it supports the conclusions of Chapter 13. *Sims* is a departure and a departure in a predictable direction. The unreliable report of *Latimer* also fits the model, though we have no assurance that it accurately represents Shaw's words.

NOTES

Prelude

1 All references to Antigone and Creon are to Sophocles' *Antigone*. The biographies referred to are Erik Erikson, *Young Man Luther* (New York: Norton, 1958) and *Gandhi's Truth* (New York: Norton, 1969).

2 Herman Melville, *Billy Budd,* ed. Hayford and Sealts (Chicago: University of Chicago Press, 1962). This novella was published posthumously. I have used the critical edition of *Billy Budd* edited by Hayford and Sealts. All references herein are to that edition. This edition differs in a few significant respects from the more common, earlier reading of the text. The most significant difference for the very limited purposes of this section is the reading of the name of Vere's ship. See note 10, infra.

3 Melville, *Billy Budd,* pp. 110, 111.

4 Ibid.

5 Ibid., pp. 61–63.

6 Ibid., p. 115.

7 The best biography of Chief Justice Shaw is Leonard Levy, *The Law of the Commonwealth and Chief Justice Shaw* (Cambridge: Harvard University Press, 1957). Levy gives extensive consideration to Shaw and slavery in that work, pp. 59–108.

8 See infra, Chapter 9.

9 For consideration of the Fugitive Slave Act, see Chapter 10, infra. I have taken Melville's characterization of the Mutiny Act uncritically, since what is important for the analysis here is the portrait of the Act in *Billy Budd,* not the historic reality.

10 Most editions of *Billy Budd* used the name *Indomitable* for Vere's ship. The Hayford-Sealts edition has argued for *Bellipotent*. In light of the traditional rationale for slavery related in Chapter 1 and the arguments for repressive slave codes from necessity, the name of *Bellipotent* is somewhat more suggestive. Naturally, I intimate by my use of that name no position on the textual issues among the Melville experts. Hayford and Sealts, in their introduction, p. 20, argue that the manuscript contains both names for the British ship, but that despite less frequency of use, *Bellipotent* was probably Melville's final choice as a name.

Chapter 1

1 Brief of Levi Lincoln, in "Letters and Documents Relating to Slavery in Massachusetts," *Collections of the Massachusetts Historical Society,* 5th Ser., 3

(1877) : 438–442. For a more thorough account of Quock Walker, see Chapter 3, infra.

2   This quotation is from the text established in Cushing, The Cushing Court and The Abolition of Slavery in Massachusetts," 5 *Am. J. Leg. Hist.* 1186 (1961), at 132.

3   T. R. R. Cobb, *The Law of Negro Slavery* (Philadelphia: T. & J. W. Johnson & Co., Savannah: W. T. Williams, 1858). Cobb's work, which was in many ways the *Summa* of the proslavery legal position, begins with an elaborate introduction. The introduction establishes a philosophical position that slavery is a "natural" relationship—a position derived principally from Aristotle's natural slave. It also argues for slavery's acceptance in natural law from the almost universal acceptance of the institution from antiquity through the nineteenth century. Finally, he uses biological and medical theories to assert that the Negro is the "natural slave."

4   J. C. Hurd, *The Law of Freedom and Bondage in the United States,* 2 vols. (Boston: Little, Brown & Co., 1858–62). Hurd begins his work with a long jurisprudential essay on slavery in natural law, international law, and conflicts of laws. He borrows heavily from Austin in attacking natural law as a source for "jurisprudence." Indeed, I have never come across another American law book of this period that demonstrates as great direct reliance upon Austin. *The Province of Jurisprudence Determined* came to exert more influence only after the posthumous 1863 edition prepared by Austin's widow. The first edition was published in 1832.

5   For Smith's course of study, see P. Hamlin, *Legal Education in Colonial New York* (New York: New York University and Law Quarterly Review, 1939), pp. 62, 197–200. For Adams see L. Wroth and H. Zobel, *Legal Papers of John Adams* (Cambridge, Mass.: Belknap Press of Harvard University Press, 1965), 1 : 1–25. For Adams' study of natural law and roman law, see Charles Francis Adams, ed., *The Life and Works of John Adams* (Boston: Little, Brown & Co., 1856), 1 : 46–47; for Jefferson, see Dumas Malone, *Jefferson the Virginian* (Boston: Little, Brown & Co., 1948) (Vol. 1 of *Jefferson and His Time*), pp. 65–74.

6   Justinian, *Institutes* 1. 3. 1–2.

7   William Buckland, *The Roman Law of Slavery* (Cambridge, England: The University Press, 1908), pp. 1–9, esp. p. 1.

8   Ibid. I do not mean to imply that there were no differences between ancient and nineteenth century natural law traditions. For two very different discussions of these differences, a matter that lies beyond the scope of this introductory material, see Leo Strauss, *Natural Right and History* (Chicago: University of Chicago Press, 1953); A. P. d'Entreves, *Natural Law* (New York: Harper & Row, 1965); Frederick Pollock, "The History of the Law of Nature" in Frederick Pollock, *Essays in the Law* (Oxford: Clarendon Press, 1922).

9   Edward Coke, *First Institute* (London, 1670), Cap. 11, § 172.

10   Fortescue, *De Laudibus Legum Angliae,* ed. and trans. S. B. Chrimes (Cambridge, England: The University Press, 1942), Chap. 42.

11 See Viner, *A General Abridgment of Law and Equity* (London: G. G. J. and J. Robinson, 1791–95), sub. "Negroes," 15 : 549.

12 In the following brief discussion of the continental theorists I am simply setting forth evidence for the currency of the natural law way of addressing slavery and for its presence in the colonial legal lexicon. However, the reader who wishes a more elaborate consideration of the history of the ideas of slavery that includes but goes far beyond these sources should consult David Davis, *The Problem of Slavery in Western Culture* (Ithaca, N.Y.: Cornell University Press, 1966).

13 Thomas Rutherforth, *Institutes of Natural Law* (Baltimore: W. & J. Neal, 1832), p. 240. Rutherforth, who simply popularizes Grotius, was popular in the colonies. For the contents of representative law libraries in eighteenth-century colonial America, see P. Hamlin, *Legal Education,* note 5, supra.

14 Pufendorf, *Of the Law of Nature and Nations* (London: R. Sare, 1717), Book 3, Chap. 2, ¶ viii and Book 6, Chap. 3.

15 Ibid., Book 6, Chap. 3, ¶ 4.

16 Ibid., Book 6, Chap. 3, 6 and Book 6, Chap. 3, 8.

17 The reader interested in a more thorough discussion of slavery in the work of Montesquieu should consult D. Davis's penetrating analysis in the *Problem of Slavery in Western Culture* and the very thorough work of P. Jameson, *Montesquieu et L'Esclavage* (Paris: Hachette, 1911).

18 Montesquieu, *The Spirit of the Laws,* trans. T. Nugent (New York: D. Appleton & Co., 1900), Book 15, Chap. 2.

19 Ibid., Book 15, Chap. 5.

20 See supra, Note 11, and see A. McDowall Bankton, *Institutes of the Laws of Scotland* (Edinburgh: A. Kincaid & A. Donaldson, 1751–53), sub. "Civil Rights," 1 : 66 ff., especially 76, for treatment of English law.

21 See, e.g., Jeremy Bentham, *A Fragment on Government* (London, 1823), which first appeared in 1776 and was reprinted in 1823. Bentham's more thorough critique of Blackstone, *A Commentary on the Commentaries* (Oxford: The Clarendon Press, 1928), was not published by Bentham and came to light only in 1928. For a brief comparison of Bentham and St. George Tucker as critics of Blackstone, see my "Review of St. George Tucker's Blackstone," 70 *Columbia Law Review* 1475 (1970).

22 Jefferson believed Blackstone to be a trap, teaching Toryism to the unwary. For general treatment of Blackstone's reception in the Colonies, see, e.g., C. Warren, *A History of the American Bar* (Boston: Little, Brown & Co., 1911), pp. 178–80; A. E. Dick Howard, *The Road From Runnymede: Magna Carta and Constitutionalism in America* (Charlottesville: University of Virginia Press, 1968), pp. 267–274; Elizabeth K. Bauer, *Commentaries on the Constitution 1790–1860* (New York: Russel & Russel, 1952), pp. 17–24. For a more specific treatment of one colony, see P. Hamlin, *Legal Education,* note 5, supra.

23 On the appeal to a sort of mixed up common and natural law, see Bernard Bailyn, *Ideological Origins of the American Revolution* (Cambridge, Mass.: Belknap Press of Harvard University Press, 1967). Nowhere is the mix-up more apparent than in the writing of James Otis. See notes 32–34, infra.

24 1. Blackstone, *Commentaries on the Laws of England,* 127. (Hereafter cited as *Blackstone.*) The general discussion of slavery is at pp. 422–425. Pagination in all editions of *Blackstone* is standard. Unless otherwise stated, the edition used is the 1803 Tucker edition: St. George Tucker, *Blackstone's Commentaries with Notes of Reference to the Constitution and Laws of the Federal Government of the United States and of the Commonwealth of Virginia,* 5 vols. (Philadelphia: William Young Birch and Abraham Small, 1803).

25 1. *Blackstone,* p. 423.

26 Ibid., p. 424.

27 See *Smith v. Brown & Cooper,* 2 Salk. 666, 91 Eng. Rep. 566, assumpsit for a Negro; and the related *Smith v. Gould,* 2 Salk. 667, 91 Eng. Rep. 467, holding that Trover will not lie for a Negro.

28 See sources in note 22, supra.

29 The report of *Somerset's Case* that reached the Colonies was that of Lofft, 1 Lofft's Rep. 1; 20 Howell's State Trials 1, 98 Eng. Rep. 499. One scholar has argued that that report is inaccurate, and that a more precise rendering of Mansfield's words is to be found in *Gentleman's Magazine,* Vol. 42, 1772. See J. Nadelhaft, "The Somerset Case and Slavery: Myth, Reality and Repercussions," *Journal of Negro History* 51 (1966) : 193. In a work to be published in late 1974, David Davis has convincingly established still another text, that reported in *The Scots Magazine* 34 (1772) : 298–99. Whichever text is most accurate, there can be no doubt as to which text reached America—that reported by Lofft. Since my concern is purely with transatlantic impact, I shall steer clear of the textual controversy and use only the standard Lofft text. The quotation is at 20 Howell's State Trials 82, 98 Eng. Rep. 510. See David Davis, *The Problem of Slavery in The Age of Revolution* (forthcoming) for a superb treatment of *Somerset.*

30 On the carryover of the multiform way of thinking, see M. de Wolfe Howe "The Sources and Nature of Law in Colonial Mass.," in George Billias, ed., *Law and Authority in Colonial America* (Barre, Mass.: Barre Publishers, 1965). Unquestionably, the legal system of mid-eighteenth century American colonies had already gone far along the road of integration. More than a century of institutional experience with court systems far less variegated and complex than the English model had had its impact in thought as well as process. Nevertheless, I think it clear that the broad institutional and doctrinal distinctions remained significant. Equity and admiralty jurisdiction were live points of contention in the decades leading to revolution. And John Adams as a law student was still, in the 1750's, assiduously copying out Coke's list of eleven kinds of law. Moreover, the early court systems of nationhood reflect both reaction against and persistence of the terminology of the English heritage.

31 *Robin v. Hardaway,* in *Jefferson's Reports of Cases Determined in the General Court of Virginia* (1772), p. 109.

32 J. Otis, "The Rights of the British Colonies Asserted and Proved," in Bernard Bailyn, ed., *Pamphlets of the American Revolution* (Cambridge, Mass.: Belknap Press of Harvard University Press, 1965). See also Bailyn's introduction on

Otis and the sections on Otis in his *Ideological Origins of the American Revolution* (see note 23, supra).

33   Otis, *Rights,* p. 439.
34   Bailyn, ''Introduction'' to *Pamphlets of the American Revolution,* pp. 74–75.
35   See Bailyn, *Ideological Origins,* pp. 232–246.
36   Carl Becker, *The Declaration of Independence* (New York: A. A. Knopf, 1942), pp. 212–213.
37   Robert Medde, *Patrick Henry, Patriot in the Making* (Philadelphia: Lippincott, 1957), 1 : 229.
38   See Philip Foner, ed., *Complete Writings of Thomas Paine* (New York: Citadel Press, 1945), 2 : 15. For the background of the Pennsylvania Act, see Arthur Zilversmit, *The First Emancipation* (Chicago: University of Chicago Press, 1967), Chap. 5, pp. 124–137.
39   Benjamin Quarles, *The Negro in the American Revolution* (Chapel Hill: University of North Carolina Press for the Institute of Early American History and Culture, 1961), p. 43. The text of the Massachusetts Blacks' petition is preserved in ''Letters and Documents Relating to Slavery,'' *Collections of the Massachusetts Historical Society,* 5th Ser., 3 (1877) : 432.
40   L. Wroth and H. Zobel, *Adams' Legal Papers* (1965), 2 : 48.
41   In Jefferson's *Commonplace Book* there are extensive excerpts from Hume. See G. Chinard, ed., *The Commonplace Book of Thomas Jefferson* (Baltimore: Johns Hopkins Press, 1926), pp. 374–376. For Bentham's late reception in America, see George W. Keeton, ed., *Jeremy Bentham* (London: Stevens & Sons, 1948). Burke was well-known to the Americans by virtue of his defense of their interest in Parliament. See, e.g., his famous ''Speech on Moving His Resolutions for Conciliation with the Colonies, March 22, 1773,'' *Works of Burke* (Boston, 1807), 2 : 17.
42   See the tribute paid Hume by Bentham in the *Fragment on Government,* pp. 33–35, notes (1823 ed.).
43   David Hume, *Enquiry Concerning the Principles of Morals,* ed. Charles W. Hendel (New York: Liberal Arts Press, 1957), pp. 15–21. For significance of this and other threads in Hume for late thinkers, see Elie Halevy, *The Growth of Philosophic Radicalism* trans. Mary Norris (London: Faber & Faber, 1949). A good, contemporary elaboration of this and related points is to be found in John Rawls, *A Theory of Justice* (Cambridge, Mass.: Belknap Press of Harvard University Press, 1971), pp. 126–130.
44   Hume, *Enquiry,* p. 150.
45   Jeremy Bentham, *Fragment* (1823 ed.), Chap. 4, p. 110, § 19.
46   See Charles Warren Everett, ed., *A Comment on the Commentaries* (Oxford: Clarendon Press, 1928), p. 17. This quotation was Bentham's comment on the French Declaration of Rights.
47   Edmund Burke, *Reflections on the Revolution in France,* ed. T. Mahoney (New York: Liberal Arts Press, 1955), p. 71. For treatments of Burke's thought see, e.g., P. Stanlis, *Edmund Burke and the Natural Law* (Ann Arbor: University of

Michigan Press, 1958); Leo Strauss, *Natural Right and History* (Chicago: University of Chicago Press, 1950).

48 On Blackstone's view of natural law, see John Gough, *Fundamental Law in English Constitutional Law* (Oxford: Clarendon Press, 1961), especially, Chap. 11. In the discussion of the origins and sources of obligation, 1. *Blackstone,* 43, the Commentator asserts: "Upon these two foundations, the law of nature and the law of revelation, depend all human laws; that is to say, no human laws should be suffered to contradict these." Later, in speaking specifically to the powers of Parliament, the passage quoted in the text appears (1. *Blackstone,* 91).

49 This appears to be Gough's conclusion as well.

50 See Granville Sharp, *A Declaration of the People's Natural Right to a Share in the Legislature, which is a Fundamental Principle of the British Constitution of State* (London, 1774). For Bentham, see note 45, supra.

51 David Hume, "Of the Original Contract," in *Political Essays,* ed. Charles W. Hendel (New York: Liberal Arts Press, 1953), p. 43.

52 1. *Blackstone,* 93. This "definition" of law has been a favorite leap-off point of jurisprudes. It makes an ideal straw man for the positivist attack on Blackstone, as it seems to, on the one hand, associate law with power—supreme power—while on the other hand it intertwines law by definition to right and wrong.

53 For an excellent general discussion of the jurisprudential and constitutional ideas of this period (1776–1787), see Gordon Wood, *The Creation of the American Republic* (Chapel Hill: University of North Carolina Press, 1969), especially pp. 259–305. Wood deals with the confusion of Otis on pp. 262–64 and 292–93. I heartily agree with Wood that the American constitutional jurisprudence of the 1780's is confused and consists of strands harkening back to fundamental, natural law thought of a medieval cast as well as of strands presaging Benthamite and Austinian positivism. However, I think the practice and theory was far more clear-eyed than does Wood. Wood seems at times to take the natural law foundations of constitutions or of the content of law as somehow inconsistent with the idea of judicial obligation to positive law alone. Actually, holding to natural law as a source or measure of positive law, while yet insisting that the latter alone is supreme in guiding the judge, reflects no "ambivalent attitude toward law" whatsoever. See G. Wood, p. 303.

54 For Adams, we may take as proof of his positivism, the "Novanglus" letters, where it is Adams who argues vehemently that the fact that it is natural justice that judges receive an appointment for life does not in any way have legal significance if their commission reads during the King's pleasure. For Jefferson, note the reliance on Beccaria and Montesquieu for the ideas about law. See, Chinard, ed., *The Commonplace Book of Thomas Jefferson,* pp. 298–316. For Jay, Madison, and Hamilton, the entire *Federalist Papers* (Middletown, Conn.: Wesleyan University Press, 1961) suffices to establish a tendency to see law in practical and nonspeculative terms. Wilson is somewhat more problematic. His *Lectures on Law* have a tendency to resort to "nature," but these references are

often simply flourishes. For Mason and Henry, see, e.g., Jonathan Elliott, *Debates on the Ratification of the Federal Constitution,* 2nd ed. (Philadelphia: J. B. Lippincott Co., 1836), 3 : 271 (Mason); 3 : 445 (Henry), where he states: "If you intend to reserve your unalienable rights, you must have the most express stipulation."

55 See C. Kenyon, "Men of Little Faith: The Anti-Federalists on the Nature of Representative Government," *William and Mary Quarterly,* 3rd Ser., 12 (1955) : 3. Kenyon concludes that a major thrust of anti-Federalist policy was the security of "additional safeguards of two kinds: more explicit limitations written into the Constitution, and more institutional checks to enforce these limitations" (p. 21).

56 *Federalist,* No. 78.

57 *Federalist,* No. 22.

58 See Chapter 8, infra, notes 16–19.

Chapter 2

1 Bernard Bailyn, *Ideological Origins of the American Revolution* (Cambridge, Mass.: Belknap Press of Harvard University Press, 1967), *passim;* Benjamin Fletcher Wright, *American Interpretations of Natural Law* (Cambridge, Mass.: Harvard University Press, 1931); Charles Haines, *Revival of Natural Law Concepts* (Cambridge, Mass.: Harvard University Press, 1930).

2 Edward Corwin, *The Higher Law Background of American Constitutional Law* (Ithaca, N.Y.: Great Seal Books, 1955), originally published in 42 *Harvard Law Review* 149, 365 (1929). John Gough, *Fundamental Law in English Constitutional History* (Oxford: Clarendon Press, 1955).

3 See, e.g., Haines, *Natural Law Concepts;* Benjamin Fletcher Wright, *The Contract Clause of the Constitution* (Cambridge, Mass.: Harvard University Press, 1938); Thomas Reed Powell, *Vagaries and Varieties of Constitutional Interpretation* (New York: Columbia University Press, 1956); Louis Boudin, *Government by the Judiciary* (New York: Russel & Russel, 1968). A more sophisticated approach, which also gives due prominence to the doctrinal impact of natural law is Arnold Paul, *Conservative Crisis and the Rule of Law* (New York: Harper & Row, 1969).

4 See, e.g., H. Commager, "Constitutional History and the Higher Law" in Conyers Read, ed., *The Constitution Reconsidered* (New York: Harper & Row, 1968), pp. 224, 228–31; K. Greenawalt, "A Contextual Approach to Disobedience," 70 *Columbia Law Review* 48 (1970).

5 See Wright, *American Interpretations;* Haines, *Natural Law.*

6 Bailyn, *American Revolution,* p. 232; Dwight Dumand, *Antislavery* (Ann Arbor: University of Michigan Press, 1961); Arthur Zilversmit, *The First Emancipation* (Chicago: University of Chicago Press, 1967); Winthrop Jordan, *White Over Black* (Chapel Hill: University of North Carolina Press, 1968).

7 Zilversmit, *First Emancipation;* Jordan, *White Over Black;* John Russell, *The Free Negro in Virginia* (New York: Dover, 1969); Dumond, *Antislavery;* Rob-

ert McColley, *Slavery in Jeffersonian Virginia* (Urbana, Ill.: University of Illinois Press, 1964).

8 John Austin, *The Province of Jurisprudence Determined* (London: J. Murray, 1832), pp. 33–34.

9 See my review article on Tucker, 70 *Columbia Law Review* 1475 (1970).

10 Ibid., pp. 1491–93. For Tucker's concern with slavery, the reader may consider 2. St. George Tucker, *Blackstone's Commentaries with Notes of Reference to the Constitution and Laws of the Federal Government of the United States and of the Commonwealth of Virginia*, Appendix H. (Hereafter cited as *Tucker's Blackstone*.) *Tucker's Blackstone* is in five volumes, the first two of which contain the text of Volume 1 of a standard Blackstone edition. The pagination of the Tucker edition conforms to standard pagination for all Blackstone texts. However, as is common in annotated Blackstone, a page of Blackstone may run on for six or eight pages because of the annotations. Tucker's appendices are appended at the end of appropriate volumes and are paginated separately. Citation to the Blackstone text herein will be in the form 2. *Blackstone,* 54. Citation to the appendices will be in the form 2. *Tucker's Blackstone,* App., p. 31. The essay on slavery is at 2. *Tucker's Blackstone,* App., p. 31.

11 2. *Tucker's Blackstone,* App., pp. 54–55.

12 "Letters and Documents Relating to Slavery in Massachusetts," in *Collections of the Massachusetts Historical Society,* 5th Ser., 3 (1877) : 375–431. (Hereafter cited as *Belknap, Letters and Documents*.) See also *Collections of the Massachusetts Historical Society,* 1st Ser., 4 (1795) : 191 for the initial queries of Tucker and Belknap's compiled response. (Hereafter cited as *Tucker's Queries*.)

13 Tucker to Belknap, June 29, 1795, *Belknap, Letters and Documents,* p. 409.

14 Adams to Belknap, Oct. 22, 1795, ibid., p. 416.

15 Sullivan to Belknap, July 30, 1795, ibid., pp. 412, 413.

16 2. *Tucker's Blackstone, App.;* pp. 31, 63.

17 Ibid., pp. 77, 79.

Chapter 3

1 *Federalist,* No. 78.

2 Zephania Swift, *A System of the Laws of the State of Connecticut* (Windam, Conn.: Printed by John Byrne for the author, 1795–96), 1 : 93–4: "Judges have no power to frame laws—they can only expound them."

3 Ibid., p. 39.

4 See Francis N. Thorpe, ed., *The Federal and State Constitutions* (Washington, D.C.: Government Printing Office, 1909), 7 : 3812–3813 (Virginia); 5 : 3081–82 (Pennsylvania); 6 : 3737 at 3739 (Vermont); 4 : 2453 (New Hampshire); 3 : 1888–89 (Massachusetts); 1 : 536–37 (Connecticut); 5 : 2599 (New Jersey).

5 Vermont can claim primacy in ending slavery. The "free and equal" clause was followed by a specific prohibition against holding any person as "servant, slave

or apprentice" after age 21 for a male or 18 for a female. Vermont Constitution of 1777 in Thorpe, ed., *Federal and State Constitutions,* 6 : 3739. For judicial confirmation of this effect, see *Selectman v. Jacob,* 2 Vt. 200 (1804), which treats the Constitution as having ended slavery.

6   See, e.g., Robert Taylor, ed., *Massachusetts Colony to Commonwealth: Documents on the Formation of the Constitution 1775–1780* (Chapel Hill: University of North Carolina Press, 1961).

7   Ibid., pp. 64–65.

8   Massachusetts Constitution of 1780, Article I, in vol. 3 Thorpe, ed., *Federal and State Constitutions,* 3 : 1889.

9   See, e.g., George Moore, *Notes on the History of Slavery in Massachusetts* (New York: D. Appleton & Co., 1866); W. O'Brien, "Did the Jennison Case Outlaw Slavery in Massachusetts?", *William and Mary Quarterly,* 3rd Ser., Vol. 18, 1960; J. D. Cushing, "The Cushing Court and the Abolition of Slavery in Mass.: More Notes on the Quock Walker Case," 5 *Am. J. Leg. Hist.* 118 (1961); R. Spector, "The Quock Walker Cases (1781–83)—Slavery, Its Abolition and Negro Citizenship in Early Massachusetts," *Journal of Negro History* 53 (1968) : 12; Arthur Zilversmit, "Quock Walker, Mumbet, and the Abolition of Slavery in Massachusetts," *William and Mary Quarterly,* 3rd Ser., 25 (1968) : 614; E. MacEacheren, "Emancipation of Slavery in Massachusetts: A Reexamination 1770–1790" *Journal of Negro Hitory,* 55 (1970) : 289.

10 Tucker's Questions and Belknap's replies are collected in *Collections of the Massachusetts Historical Society,* 1st Ser., 4 (1795) : 194–211. The quotation is on p. 201. (Hereafter cited as *Tucker's Queries.*)

11 Ibid.

12 Sullivan's letters and those of other correspondents are published in "Letters and Documents Relating to Slavery in Mass.," *Collections of the Massachusetts Historical Society,* 5th Ser., 3 (1877) : 402.

13 Ibid., p. 438.

14 See *Proceedings of the Massachusetts Historical Society,* 13 (1874) : 292 ff. Cushing, 5 *Am. J. Leg. Hist.,* 131–32 (1961).

15 "Letters and Documents," p. 442.

16 Cushing, 5 *Am. J. Leg. Hist.* 131–32 (1961).

17 *Tucker's Queries,* pp. 203–04.

18 This appraisal of the Massachusetts "Negro problem" is borne out by the conclusions of Belknap and of Sullivan in "Letters and Documents" and in *Tucker's Queries.* It is also the assessment of Moore in *Notes,* pp. 200–223.

19 Thomas Jefferson, *Notes on the State of Virginia* (New York: Harper & Row, 1964). Jefferson's famous ambivalent passages on slavery are contained, appropriately, in his chapter on the administration of justice. They are, moveover, a digression from the observation that the original plan of law revision was to contain a gradual emancipation provision. For a thoughtful essay on Jefferson and slavery, see Jordan, *White Over Black,* Chap. 12, "Thomas Jefferson, Self and Society."

20 In 1782 Virginia passed an Act that permitted private manumission subject only

to a provision of security by the master should the slave become a public charge: "An Act to Authorize the Manumission of Slaves," 11 *Hennings Virginia Statutes* 39–40. The 1792 Act was a rehash and compilation of earlier provisions. The Act of 1806 required freed blacks to leave the state within one year. It is a significant law discussed within. The debate over this measure is thoroughly discussed in Jordan, *White Over Black,* pp. 574–82. Jordan demonstrates that there was, indeed, a sense in those debates that the aspirations and principles of the Revolution were being betrayed.

21 *Hudgins v. Wright* 11 Va. (1 Hen. & M.) 133 (Va. 1806).
22 William Clarkin, *Serene Patriot: A Life of George Wythe* (Albany, N.Y.: Alan Publications, 1970).
23 11 Va. (1 Hen. & M.) 134.
24 Jordan, *White Over Black,* p. 574.
25 Jefferson to Burwell, Jan. 28, 1805, in Paul Ford, ed., *Works of Thomas Jefferson* (New York and London: G. P. Putnam's Sons, 1904–05), 10 : 126–27, cited in Jordan, *White Over Black,* p. 347.
26 Thomas Jefferson, *Notes,* p. 132.
27 For an account of this tragic case, see J. P. Boyd, "The Murder of George Wythe," *William & Mary Quarterly,* 3rd Ser., 4 (Oct. 1955) : 534; Clarkin, *George Wythe,* pp. 191 ff.
28 The reasoning of Wythe is rejected by Tucker, *Hudgins v. Wright,* 11 Va. (1 Hen. & M.) at 140–41. Wythe's reasoning is also expressly disapproved by President Lyons in the Court's decree:

"This Court, not approving of the Chancellor's principles and reasoning . . . except so far as the same relates to white persons and native American Indians, but entirely disapproving thereof, so far as the same relates to native Africans and their descendants. . . ."

29 11 Va. (1 Hen. & M.) 141.
30 Ibid., p. 139.
31 St. George Tucker (under the pseudonym of *Sylvestris*), *Reflections on the Cession of Louisiana to the United States* (Washington, D.C., 1803).
32 *State v. Post, State v. VanBeuren,* 20 N.J.L. 368 (1845). These remarkable cases have been too often ignored. The only serious attention paid them in the secondary literature is in Jacobus tenBroek, *Equal Under Law* (New York: Collier Books, 1965), pp. 78–9 (published originally as *Antislavery Origins of the Fourteenth Amendment*), and, in Arthur Zilversmit, *The First Emancipation,* pp. 218–221.
33 20 N.J.L. 368 (1845). See Alvan Stewart, *A Legal Argument Before the Supreme Court of the State of New Jersey . . . For the Deliverance of 4,000 Persons from Bondage* (New York: Finch & Weed, 1845). Stewart counted 4,000 persons in bondage by (reasonably) including servants for a term of years as well as servants for life.
34 Stewart, "A Constitutional Argument on the Subject of Slavery," reprinted in Appendix B of tenBroek, *Equal Under Law,* pp. 281 ff.

35   20 N.J.L. 369 (1845).

36   Ibid., pp. 374–75.

37   Ibid., p. 379.

38   This [gradual emancipation] has been the law since 1804, and under its benign
       influence slavery in this state has become almost extinct, without leading to
       poverty or crime . . . Without complaint on this subject a convention is called
       . . . a constitution . . . is adopted, containing certain general phrases of ab-
       stract natural right, no stronger than those in the Declaration of Independence.
       . . . *jus dicere et non jus dare* is the province of the judiciary. . . . . ibid., p.
       386.

Chapter 4

1   "An Act for the Gradual Abolition of Slavery," July 4, 1780, *Laws of the
       Commonwealth of Pennsylvania* (Philadelphia, 1810), 1 : 339. For the reader
       who is unfamiliar with the basic sources concerning slavery in America, the
       moving preamble sections of the 1780 Act, written by Tom Paine, deserve quo-
       tation:

       WHEN we contemplate our abhorrence of that condition, to which the arms
       and tyranny of Great-Britain were exerted to reduce us, when we look back
       on the variety of dangers to which we have been exposed, and how miracu-
       lously our wants in many instances have been supplied, and our deliverances
       wrought, when even hope and human fortitude have become unequal to the
       conflict, we are unavoidably led to a serious and grateful sense of the mani-
       fold blessings, which we have undeservedly received from the hand of that
       Being, from whom every good and perfect gift cometh. Impressed with these
       ideas, we conceive that it is our duty, and we rejoice that it is in our power,
       to extend a portion of that freedom to others, which hath been extended to us,
       and release them from that state of thraldrom, to which we ourselves were ty-
       rannically doomed, and from which we have now every prospect of being de-
       livered. It is not for us to enquire why, in the creation of mankind, the inhabi-
       tants of the several parts of the earth were distinguished by a difference in
       feature or complexion. It is sufficient to know, that all are the work of the Al-
       mighty Hand. We find, in the distribution of the human species, that the most
       fertile as well as the most barren parts of the earth are inhabited by men of
       complexions different from ours, and from each other; from whence we may
       reasonably, as well as religiously, infer, that He, who placed them in their
       various situations, hath extended equally his care and protection to all, and
       that it becometh not us to counteract his mercies. We esteem it a peculiar
       blessing granted to us, that we are enabled this day to add one more step to
       universal civilization, by removing, as much as possible, the sorrows of
       those, who have lived in undeserved bondage, and from which, by the as-
       sumed authority of the Kings of Great-Britain, no effectual, legal relief could
       be obtained. Weaned, by a long course of experience, from those narrow

prejudices and partialities we had imbibed, we find our hearts enlarged with kindness and benevolence towards men of all conditions and nations; and we conceive ourselves at this particular period extra-ordinarily called upon, by the blessings which we have received, to manifest the sincerity of our profession, and to give a substantial proof of our gratitude.

II. And whereas the condition of those persons, who have heretofore been denominated Negro and Mulatto slaves, has been attended with circumstances, which not only deprived them of the common blessings that they were by nature entitled to, but has cast them into the deepest afflictions, by an unnatural separation and sale of husband and wife from each other and from their children, an injury, the greatness of which can only be conceived by supposing that we were in the same unhappy case. In justice, therefore, to persons so unhappily circumstanced, and who, having no prospect before them whereon they may rest their sorrows and their hopes, have no reasonable inducement to render their services to society, which they otherwise might, and also in grateful commemoration of our own happy deliverance from that state of unconditional submission, to which we were doomed by the tyranny of Britain. . . .

2 Standard accounts of abolition in Pennsylvania may be found in Arthur Zilversmit, *The First Emancipation* (Chicago: University of Chicago Press, 1967), pp. 124–137, 202–208, and in Edward Turner, *The Negro in Pennsylvania* (Washington, D.C.: The American Historical Association, 1911). There is no adequate account of the cases discussed in this section. Registration was an important administrative device, and the attitudes of the courts toward it reflect their openness to this technique as well as their views on freedom.

3 *Respublica v. Negro Betsey,* 1 U.S. (1 Dallas) 469 (Sup. Ct. Pa., 1789). Counsel for the master argued that failure of registration should only place the Negro in the best possible situation that she could have legally been in under the act. That is, either she was born prior to the act and is a slave or was born after it and must serve twenty-eight years. The court decided that there is a penal element involved, not simply a remedy for the slave.

4 Ibid., pp. 469–470. Counsel for the Negro added that should there be doubt about legislative purpose or intent or about "the frame of the whole," that "the law favors liberty more than property." Thus, even the advocate confines liberty to a supplementary role.

5 Ibid., p. 474.

6 Ibid., p. 477.

7 William Tilghman is still another important American judicial figure who lacks a decent modern biographical treatment. The leading source is John Golder, *The Honorable William Tilghman* (Philadelphia, 1829), a memoir printed soon after the judge's death. Assorted Tilghman manuscripts exist at the Pennsylvania Historical Society. I am endebted to my former student Kirk Robbins, Columbia Law School 1970, for an excellent treatment of Tilghman in a paper prepared by him for my course in American Slavery and the Law. That unpublished paper is

in the author's possession and was of help in collecting material on Tilghman. A second important memoir on Tilghman is the eulogy delivered upon his death by Horace Binney. It is published in Law Association of Philadelphia, *Addresses and Papers to Commemorate the Centennial Celebration* (Philadelphia, 1902), pp. 164 ff.

8 *Marchand v. Negro Peggy,* 2 S & R 18 (Pa., 1815); *Wilson v. Belinda,* 3 S & R 396 (Pa., 1817).

9 *Wilson v. Belinda,* 3 S & R, pp. 397–98.

10 In addition to cases already noted, see, e.g., *Jack v. Eales,* 3 Binn. 100 (Pa., 1810); *Commonwealth ex rel. Jesse v. Craig,* 1 S & R 23 (Pa., 1814); *Commonwealth v. Greason,* 4 S & R 425 (Pa., 1818); *Commonwealth ex rel. Bell v. Greason,* 5 S & R 333 (Pa., 1819); *Stiles v. Nelly,* 10 S & R 365 (Pa., 1823); *Commonwealth v. Barker,* 11 S & R 360 (Pa., 1824); *Commonwealth v. Vance,* 15 S & R 36 (Pa., 1826).

11 *Miller v. Dwilling,* 14 S & R 442 (Pa., 1826), quotation at 443.

12 *Marchand v. Negro Peggy,* 2 S & R 18 (Pa., 1815), p. 19.

13 On manumission in Virginia, see, generally, J. Russell, *The Free Negro in Virginia* (New York: Dover, 1969), Chap. 3, an old, but still very good monographic treatment. Russell provides limited demographic data as well as a chronicle of legislative and attitudinal changes. See also Winthrop Jordan, *White over Black* (Chapel Hill: University of North Carolina Press, 1968), pp. 347 and 573 ff. For the role of the Quakers, see Stephen Weeks, *Southern Quakers and Slavery* (Baltimore: Johns Hopkins Press, 1896). See also McColley, *Slavery in Jeffersonian Virginia* (Urbana, Ill.: University of Illinois Press, 1964).

14 Act of 1782, "An Act to Authorize the Manumission of Slaves." *Hening's Statutes at Large* (Richmond, 1823) Vol. 11, Chap. 21, pp. 39–40.

15 Act of January 25, 1806, *Shepherd's Statutes at Large* (New York: AMS Press, 1970) Vol. 3, Chap. 63, pp. 251–52. The best description of the forces leading up to this act is in Jordan, *White Over Black,* note 77, pp. 573 ff.

16 No one actually thought that slavery would dry up and die. However, literally tens of thousands of slaves were manumitted under the Act of 1782. According to Russell, *The Free Negro in Virginia,* p. 61, note 77, the number of free blacks lept from less than 3,000 to 20,000 in 1800 and over 30,000 in 1810. There was some hope that the experience with a free Negro class and with fewer slaves would cut slavery to manageable proportions.

17 The act provided that slaves emancipated in fraud of creditors could be taken or sold by the creditor. However, the act continued in force the preferred position of slave property. Only when other property was insufficient would slave property be liable for execution.

18 *Pleasants v. Pleasants,* 6 Va. (2 Call) 319 (1799).

19 Nathan Dane, *General Abridgment and Digest of American Law* (Boston, 1824), Vol. 4, Chap. 114, Article 18, ¶ 2.

20 *Pleasants v. Pleasants,* 6 Va. (2 Call), p. 335. Wythe took the remarkable step of ordering an accounting of the slaves' profits for the period of their wrongful

detention. This unprecedented holding was reversed. See, e.g., *Pleasants,* p. 343.

21 Ibid., p. 340.
22 Ibid., *passim.*
23 Ibid., p. 340.
24 Ibid., p. 391.
25 *Charles v. Hunnicutt,* 9 Va. (5 Call) 311 (1804).
26 Ibid.
27 Ibid., p. 312.
28 Ibid., p. 318.
29 Ibid., p. 330.
30 Ibid., p. 323.
31 Ibid.
32 *Woodley v. Abby,* 9 Va. (5 Call) 336 (1805), p. 342.
33 For an analogue of this choosing from among alternative broad principles—opposing one to another, using one rather than another—see Karl Llewellyn, *The Common Law Tradition: Deciding Appeals,* (Boston: Little, Brown, & Co., 1960), pp. 520 ff.
34 See discussion of *Lewis v. Fullerton,* 22 Va. (1 Rand.) 15 (1821). infra. Chapter 5 at note 36.
35 *Maria v. Surbaugh,* 23 Va. (2 Rand.) 228 (1824).
36 Roane had stated in *Pleasants:*

> The condition of the mothers of such children, is, that of free persons, held to service, for a term of years: such children are not the children of slaves. . . . and they . . . can no more restrain their right to freedom, than they can that of other persons born free. The power of the testator in this respect has yielded to the great principle of natural law, which is also a principle of our municipal law, that the children of a free mother are free.

(2 Call), p. 339. The reasoning of *Maria v. Surbaugh* is that the mother is not to be characterized as a free person serving a term of years, but as a slave with an inchoate, not yet perfected, right of freedom.
37 *Maria v. Surbaugh,* 23 Va. (2 Rand.), p. 287.
38 *Gregory v. Baugh,* 29 Va. (2 Leigh) 665 (1831), p. 680.
39 For a detailed consideration of the North Carolina court and slavery, see B. R. Holt, *The Supreme Court of North Carolina and Slavery* (1926), Ser. 17, *Historical Papers of the Trinity College Historical Society.* Holt does an admirable job of collecting and categorizing the cases, though he is short on analysis. Some more interesting work, especially on the application of the criminal law to slaves, has been done by A. E. K. Nash in "A More Equitable Past? Southern Supreme Courts and the Protection of the Antebellum Negro," 48 *North Carolina Law Review* 197 (1970), and in "Fairness and Formalism in Trials of Blacks in the Supreme Courts of the Old South," 56 *Virginia Law Review* (1970). For a general description of the role of the Quakers in the matters discussed below, see Weeks, *Southern Quakers and Slavery.* See also J. Basset,

Anti-Slavery Leaders of North Carolina (Baltimore: Johns Hopkins Press, (1896).

40   See Weeks, *Southern Quakers,* pp. 217 ff.

41   Ibid., p. 217.

42   "An Act to Vest in the Superior Courts of the State, the Exclusive Power of Emancipating Slaves," *Laws of the State of North Carolina,* 1818 (Raleigh, 1819), Chap. 13.

43   Weeks, *Southern Quakers,* pp. 224 ff. The pervasiveness of this scheme is also evident from the reported opinions. See, e.g., *Trustees v. Dickenson,* 12 N.C. (1 Dev.) 189 (1827).

44   Weeks, *Southern Quakers,* pp. 225–226. For a biographical study of William Gaston, see Joseph H. Schauinger, *William Gaston, Carolinian* (Milwaukee: Bruce Publishing Co., 1949), but the only treatment of Gaston's role in the Quaker trusteeship scheme is in Weeks. Gaston was a southern liberal opponent of slavery. In 1832 he spoke to the University of North Carolina graduating class as follows:

> On you too, will devolve the duty . . . of providing for the mitigation, and . . . for the ultimate extirpation of the worst evil that afflicts the southern part of our confederacy. . . . Disguise the truth as we may, and throw the blame where we will, it is slavery which, more than any other cause, keeps us back in the career of improvement. It stifles industry and represses enterprise—it is fatal to economy and providence, it discourages skill, impairs our strength as a community, and poisons morals at the fountainhead.

William Peele, ed., *Lives of Distinguished North Carolinians* (Raleigh: The North Carolina Publishing Society, 1898), pp. 176–77.

45   *Trustees of the Quaker Society of Contentnea v. Dickenson,* 12 N.C. (1 Dev.) 189 (1827). Gaston argued the case on behalf of the Friends and in defense of the instrument he had created.

46   Ibid., p. 202.

47   Ibid., p. 207.

48   Ibid.

49   Gaston was a Catholic, and faced difficulty in confirmation by virtue of a North Carolina constitutional provision forbidding office to anyone who "shall deny . . . the truths of the Protestant religion." He was nonetheless confirmed. Later he led a fight to remove the provision, and won a limited victory when "Protestant" was changed to "Christian." See Schauinger, *William Gaston, Carolinian,* p. 60. Examples of Gaston's more liberal opinions include: *State v. Will,* 18 N.C. (1 Dev. & Bat.) 121 (1834); *State v. Jarrott* 23 N.C. (1 Ired.) 76 (1840). The *Will* case has been much noted by commentators, often juxtaposed as antithetical to *State v. Mann.* Actually, Ruffin joined in the majority in *State v. Will.* The two cases are in no way inconsistent in holding. It is the tone of the two opinions that seems irreconcilable. See Holt, *Supreme Court of North Carolina and Slavery,* pp. 19–21. See also Battle, "The State of North Carolina v. Negro Will, A Slave of James Battle; a Cause-Célèbre of Ante-Bellum Times." 6 *Virginia Law Review* 915 (1919).

50 *Will and Jarrott* were both criminal prosecutions against slaves.

51 *Redmond v. Coffin,* 17 N.C. (2 Dev. Eq.) 437 (1833), pp. 440–41.

52 *Cresswell v. Emberson,* 41 N.C. (6 Ired. Eq.) 151 (1848), "The latest case on the subject, and we hope it will be the last," p. 154.

53 *Stevens v. Ely,* 16 N.C. (1 Dev. Eq.) 493 (1830). Hall's dissent is on p. 498.

54 *Cameron v. Commissioners,* 36 N.C. (1 Ired. Eq.) 436 (1841), "it is the declared policy of this state to . . . encourage their emancipation, so that they be but removed without the state," pp. 440–41. An interesting variant of the basic pattern is seen in Tennessee; see, e.g., *Harris v. Clarisson,* 14 Tenn. 525 (1834) and *Fisher's Negroes v. Dabbs,* 14 Tenn. 119 (1834).

Chapter 5

1 There have been two articles written on slavery and the conflict of laws. One, Horowitz, "Choice of Law Decisions Involving Slavery: 'Interest Analysis' in the Early Nineteenth Century," 17 *UCLA Law Review* 587 (1970) is an attempt to read nineteenth-century slave cases as precursors of contemporary choice-of-law theory. The article suffers from the refusal to read the cases with the conceptual apparatus of the men who wrote them. A second article, Note, "American Slavery and the Conflict of Laws," 71 *Columbia Law Review* 74 (1971) does a far more sophisticated job of trying to place the cases in the context of nineteenth-century conflicts theory. For the reader unfamiliar with the now voluminous literature of choice-of-law, some modern sources should be mentioned: D. Cavers, *The Choice of Law Process* (Ann Arbor: University of Michigan Press, 1965); A. L. I., *Restatement Second, Conflict of Laws;* Brainerd Currie, *Selected Essays on the Conflict of Laws* (Durham, N.C.: Duke University Press, 1963).

2 J. Kent, *Commentaries on American Law* (New York: O. Halsted, 1826–30), 2 : 457.

3 Joseph Story, *Commentaries on the Conflict of Laws* (Boston: Hilliard, Gray, and Co., 1834). (Hereafter cited as Story, *Conflicts.*) Story's treatise was the second American book on conflicts. The first, Samuel Livermore, *A Dissertation on the Questions Which Arise From the Contrariety of the Positive Laws of Different States and Nations* (New Orleans), was published in 1828. Livermore's work is occasionally noted simply because of its primacy, but Story's book eclipsed Livermore immediately. See Nadelmann, "Joseph Story's Contribution to American Conflicts Law: A Comment," 5 *Am. J. Leg. Hist.* 230 (1961); Lorenzen, "Story's Commentaries on the Conflict of Laws—One Hundred Years After," 48 *Harvard Law Review* 15 (1934). Lorenzen notes especially Story's adoption of the positivist view of conflicts and his reliance upon Huber.

4 Story, *Conflicts,* p. 24, § 23 (all references are to the first edition, 1834, unless otherwise noted).

5 Ibid., p. 33, § 33.

6 Ibid., p. 97, § 104.

7   William Burge, *Colonial and Foreign Laws,* (London: Saunders and Benning, 1838), 1 : 739–741.

8   *Somerset v. Stewart,* 98 Eng. Rep. 499 (K.B., 1772), p. 510.

9   Ibid., p. 510.

10 *Constitution of the Confederate States of America,* Article 4, § 2, # 1, "The citizens of each state . . . shall have the right of transit and sojurn in any state of this Confederacy with their slaves. . . ."

11 "An Act for the Gradual Abolition of Slavery," July 4, 1780, Pennsylvania Laws (Philadelphia, 1810), Vol. 1, p. 339, § 10.

12 *Mahoney v. Ashton,* 4 Harris & McHenry 295 (Md., 1799), p. 299.

13 Ibid., p. 325.

14 *Denison v. Tucker; Pattinson v. Whitaker;* William Blume, ed., *Transactions of the Supreme Court of Michigan 1805–1814* (Ann Arbor: University of Michigan Press, 1935), 1 : 385 ff. (Hereafter cited as *Blume.*)

15 *Blume,* 1 : 387.

16 Ibid., p. 388.

17 Ibid., p. 388.

18 *Pattinson v. Whitaker, Blume,* 1 : 414, 415–16.

19 Ibid., p. 416.

20 Ibid., p. 417.

21 Ibid., p. 416.

22 *Greenwood v. Curtis,* 6 Mass. 358 (1810).

23 Ibid., pp. 361 ff., below the line.

24 Story, *Conflicts,* § 259, p. 215, note 2.

25 *Commonwealth v. Aves,* 35 Mass. (18 Pick) 193 (1836). *Aves,* also known as the *Slave Med Case,* quickly became the leading American statement on the subject. In the second, and all succeeding editions of Story's *Conflicts,* Aves was reprinted in large part or in its entirety "below the line" (as a footnote to the original Story text). Despite a host of other decisions on the same or related points, *Aves* maintained its position as the leading American case on the subject.

26 *The Slave Grace,* 166 Eng. Rep. 179 (High Court of Admiralty, 1827).

27 *Rankin v. Lydia* 9 Ky. (2 A. K. Marsh.) 467 (1820). The *Lydia* case has a fascinating side to it, as yet unnoticed by commentators. Despite the fact that the case echoes the rhetoric of *Somerset's Case* throughout, the decision of Lord Mansfield is never actually cited. Kentucky in 1820 was in throes of an anticommon law antilawyer reaction. Citation of English cases by judges or attorneys had been forbidden by statute. In *Rankin v. Lydia* the court seems almost tongue-in-cheek in its use of motifs and idioms from the English cases.

28 Ibid., p. 475.

29 Helen T. Catterall, *Judicial Cases Concerning American Slavery* (Washington, D.C.: Carnegie Institution, 1926–37), 3 : 389–391.

30 *Lunsford v. Coquillion,* 4 La. (2 Martin, N.S.) 401 (1824).

31 *Marie Louise v. Marot,* 8 La. 475, aff'd on remand, 9 La. 473 (1835).

32 La. Acts of 1846, p. 163. And see *Eugenie v. Preval,* 2 La. Ann. 180 (1847); *Arsene v. Pignegny* 2 La. Ann. 620 (1847).

33   See, e.g., *Marie Louise v. Marot,* 8 La. 478. The court used the *in favorem libertatis* principle to notice sojourn in France that had not been part of the record.

34   The best description of the changeover and its rationale is in note, 71 *Columia Law Review* 74 at 92–98 (1971).

35   *Griffith v. Fanny,* 21 Va. Rep. (Gilm.) 143 (1820).

36   *Lewis v. Fullerton,* 22 Va. Rep. (1 Rand.) 15 (1821).

Chapter 6

1   *Respublica v. De Longchamps,* 1 U.S. (1 Dall.) 111 (Pa., 1784), pp. 114–16.

2   26 F. Cas. (No. 15, 551) 832 (C.C.D. Mass., 1822). The opinion of Story was separately published by William Mason, the reporter, in 1822. Story's attitudes on slavery are examined in Dowd, "Justice Story and the Slavery Conflict," 52 *Massachusetts Law Quarterly* 239 (1967); in Leslie, "The Influence of Joseph Story's Theory of the Conflict of Laws on Constitutional Nationalism," 35 *Mississippi Valley Historical Review* 203 (1948). And in Dunne, "Joseph Story, The Gathering Storm," 13 *Am. J. Leg. Hist.* 1 (1969). See also Gerald Dunne, *Justice Joseph Story* (New York: Simon & Schuster, 1970), pp. 241–46, 393–402.

3   26 F. Cas. (No. 15, 551), p. 845. See also Story's charge to the grand jury concerning the slave trade: "The existence of slavery under any shape is so repugnant to the natural rights of man . . . that it seems difficult to find for it any justification." William Wetmore Story, *Life and Letters of Joseph Story* (Boston: C. C. Little and J. Brown, 1851), p. 336. (Hereafter cited as Story, *Life and Letters.*) Story's charge to grand juries was repeated both in Boston and in Providence. His plea for vigorous prosecution of the traders raises somewhat different issues since the law clearly rendered the trade criminal for Americans.

4   26 F. Cas., p. 846.

5   *The Antelope,* 23 U.S. (10 Wheat.) 66 (1825).

6   Ibid., p. 120.

7   Ibid., p. 121. "Whatever might be the answer of a moralist to this question, a jurist must search for its legal solution. . . ."

8   On the general issue of visitation and search with regard to the slave trade, see John Basset Moore, *A Digest of International Law* (Washington, D.C.: Government Printing Office, 1906), 2 : 914 ff., § 310. For much greater detail on the Anglo-American relations than is provided in Moore, see Hugh G. Soulsby, *The Right of Search and the Slave Trade in Anglo-American Relations 1814–1862* (Baltimore: Johns Hopkins Press, 1933). For much of what follows, I am endebted to the work of Nicholas Kourides, Columbia Law School, 1971, an unpublished paper, "The Efforts of Great Britain and the U. S. to Suppress the Slave Trade 1810–1825," prepared under my supervision for a seminar on Slavery in American Law, Columbia Law School, fall 1969.

    The more recent literature on Great Britain and the slave trade is of major interest, but adds nothing to *Soulsby* on the particulars of the Anglo-American relationship in the 1810's and 1820's. See, e.g., Leslie Bethell, *The Abolition of the Brazilian Slave Trade* (Cambridge, England: The University Press, 1970), pp. 24–26. See also Arthur Corwin, *Spain and the Abolition of Slavery in Cuba* (Austin: University of Texas Press, 1967). For the domestic dimension of the slave-trade problem at a later period, see William Howard, *American Slavers and the Federal Law, 1837–1862* (Berkeley: University of California Press, 1963), a confused but richly detailed account.

9   *Le Louis,* 1 Dodson 260, 165 Eng. Rep. 1464 (High Court of Admiralty, 1817).

10   A table of British bilateral agreements is to be found in W. E. B. Dubois, *The Suppression of the African Slave Trade to the United States of America 1658–1870* (New York: Dover Publishing Co., 1970), p. 144. A true mine of detail on the workings of these agreements is the *British Parliamentary Papers, The Slave Trade* (Shannon: Irish University Press, 1968). See also Elizabeth Donnan, ed., *Documents Relating to the Slave Trade* (Washington, D.C., Carnegie Institution, 1930–35).

11   Letter from Secretary of State, J. Q. Adams to Messrs. Gallatin and Rush (special emissaries to the Hague), *American State Papers, Foreign Relations,* (Washington, D.C.: Gales & Senton, 1832–61), 5 : 72.

12   Ibid. See also Soulsby, *Slave Trade,* pp. 13–27, for a detailed discussion of these negotiations.

13   Story was simply seeking a return to the earlier British admirality doctrines as enunciated in *The Amedie,* 1 Acton 240, 12 Eng. Rep. 92 (1810); *The Fortana,* 1 Dodson 81, 165 Eng. Rep. 1240 (1811).

14   On these negotiations and their failure, see J. B. Moore, 2 *Digest of International Law,* (Washington, D.C.: G.P.O., 1906) 923–927; Soulsby, *Slave Trade,* pp. 27–38; *British and Foreign State Papers, 1822–23* (London: H.M. Stationery Office, 1829), pp. 94–110; *American State Papers, Foreign Relations,* (Washington, D.C., Gales & Seaton, 1832–61), 5 : 330–337.

15   Joseph Story, *Commentaries on the Constitution* (Boston: Hilliard, Gray & Co.; Cambridge, Mass.: Brown, Shattuck & Paul, 1833), 1 : 276. (Hereafter cited as Story, *Constitution.*)

16   For secondary literature on this changeover in Southern thinking, see, e.g., John Hope Franklin, *The Militant South, 1800–1861* (Cambridge, Mass.: Belknap Press of Harvard University Press, 1956); Clement Eaton, *The Freedom of Thought Struggle in the Old South* (Durham, N.C.: Duke University Press, 1940); William Jenkins, *Pro-Slavery Thought in the Old South* (Chapel Hill: University of North Carolina Press, 1935); Eric McKitrick, ed., *Slavery Defended: The Views of the Old South* (Englewood Cliffs, N.J.: Prentice-Hall, 1963). In terms of legal apologetics, nothing surpasses T. R. R. Cobb, *The Law of Negro Slavery* (Philadelphia: T. and J. W. Johnson and Co.; Savannah: W. T. Williams, 1858).

17   2. *Tucker's Blackstone,* App., p. 71.

18   L. Fuller, "The Case of the Speluncean Explorers," 62 *Harvard Law Review* 616 (1949).

19 *Babylonian Talmud, Tractate Baba Mezia,* 62a. And see D. Daube, *Collaboration with Tyranny in Rabbinic Law* (London, New York: Oxford University Press, 1965).

20 *Regina v. Dudley and Stephens,* 14 Q. B. D. 273 (1884)—involved the killing of a boy by ship-wrecked sailors in the good-faith belief that without cannibalism all would die. The boy was not consulted. In *U.S. v. Holmes,* 26 F. Cas. 360 (No. 15, 383) (C.C.D. Pa., 1842), a mate directed seamen to throw passengers overboard from a lifeboat after shipwreck. It was reasonable to believe that should all aboard stay aboard the boat would have gone down.

21 For a description of the *Amistad* case, see *Gedney v. L'Amistad,* 10 F. Cas. 141 (No. 5, 294a) (D.C.D., Conn., 1840), aff'd in part, revs'd in part sub nom. *United States v. Amistad,* 40 U.S. (15 Pet.) 518 (1841). An historical novel that is very faithful to the historical event has been written on the *Amistad.* See William Owens, *Black Mutiny* (Philadelphia: Pilgrim Press, 1968). For other accounts of the event, see Christopher Martin, *The Amistad Affair* (London and New York: Abelard-Schuman, 1970); Mary Cable, *Black Odyssey* (New York: Viking Press, 1971). For data on the *Creole* incident, see "Message from the President to the Senate Communicating the Proceedings Adopted by the Executive in Reference to the Case of the Brig *Creole.*" Senate Doc. No. 137, 27th Cong., 2d Sess.; John Basset Moore, *International Arbitrations* (New York: The Crane Press, 1914), 4 : 4,375; *McCargo v. New Orleans Ins. Co.,* 19 La. (10 Robinson) 202 (1845) and cases following; W. Jay, *The Creole Case and Mr. Webster's Despatch* (New York: New York American, 1842); "Case of the *Creole,*" 27 *Am. Jur. and Law Mag.* 79 (1842).

22 *United States v. L'Amistad,* 40 U.S. (15 Pet.) 518 (1841).

23 See Bernard Wyatt-Brown, *Lewis Tappan and the Evangelical War Against Slavery* (Cleveland: Case Western Reserve University Press, 1969), Chap. 11, for a discussion of the Tappan-directed defense fund.

24 *Gedney v. L'Amistad,* 10 F. Cas., pp. 146–50.

25 Adams's argument was not printed in the report of the case. It was published separately in pamphlet form. J. Q. Adams, *Argument of John Quincy Adams before the Supreme Court of the United States, In the case of the U.S. v. Cinque and others, Africans* (New York: 1841).

26 W. W. Story, *Life and Letters,* 2 : 348–49.

27 40 U.S., p. 593. The treaty alluded to is the Treaty of 1795, Article 9, continued in force by the Treaty of 1819.

28 Ibid., p. 595.

29 "D. Webster, Sec'y of State to E. Everett Ambassador to Great Britain," in *Message from the President.* . . . See note 21, supra.

30 Ibid., pp. 2–5.

31 See James Stewart, *Joshua Giddings and the Tactics of Radical Politics* (Cleveland: Case Western Reserve University Press, 1970), Chap. 4.

32 "Case of the *Creole,*" 27 *Am. Jur. and Law Mag.* 83 (1842).

33 [William Jay], *The Creole Case and Mr. Webster's Despatch* (1843).

34 Ibid., p. 22.

35 Ibid., p. 30.
36 J. B. Moore, *International Arbitrations,* 4 : 4,375.

Chapter 7

1 Joseph Story to Ezekial Bacon, William Wetmore Story, ed., *Life and Letters of Joseph Story,* (Boston: C. C. Little and J. Brown, 1851), 2 : 431. For the *Latimer* affair and *Prigg v. Pa.,* see Chapter 10, infra.
2 *Miller v. McQuerry,* 17 F. Cas. 332 (No. 9,583) (C.C.D. Ohio, 1853), p. 339.
3 *Vaughn v. Williams,* 28 F. Cas. 1115 (No. 16,903) (C.C.D. Ind., 1845), p. 1116.
4 *Norris v. Newton,* 18 F. Cas. 322 (No. 10,307) (C.C.D. Ind., 1850), p. 326. Similar language by McLean may be found in other cases: See, e.g., *Giltner v. Gorham,* 10 F. Cas. 424 (No. 5,453) (C.C.D. Mich., 1848), p. 432: "However unjust and impolite slavery may be, yet the people of Kentucky . . . have adopted it. And you are sworn to decide this according to the law."
    Jones v. Van Zandt, 13 F. Cas. 1047 (No. 7,502) (C.C.D. Ohio, 1843), pp. 1048:

I was not prepared to hear, in a court of justice, the broad ground assumed, as was assumed in this case before the jury, that a man, in the exercise of what he conceives to be a conscientious duty, may violate the laws of land. . . . We cannot theorize upon the principles of our government, or of slavery. The law is our only guide. If convictions, . . . of what is right or wrong, are to be substituted . . . in disregard of law, we shall soon be without law and without protection.

The above excerpt is from McLean's opinion on a motion for new trial and in arrest of judgment. For other declarations in the same affair, see *Jones v. Van Zandt,* 13 F. Cas. 1040 (No. 7,501) (C.C.D. Ohio, 1843); 13 F. Cas. 1054 (No. 7,503) (C.C.D. Ohio, 1849); 13 F. Cas. 1056 (No. 7,504) (C.C.D. Ohio, 1849); 13 F. Cas. 1057 (No. 7,505) (C.C.D. Ohio, 1851).
5 *Jackson v. Bullock,* 12 Conn. 39 (1837).
6 *State v. Hoppess,* in 2 Western L.J. (Ohio, 1845).
7 For Massachusetts, see the account of Chief Justice Lemuel Shaw's opinion in the *Latimer* affair in the *Liberator,* quoted on p. 169, infra. See also, *Sims's Case,* 61 Mass. (7 Cush.) 285 (1851), p. 304: "But we are not entitled to consider this a new question: we must consider it settled and determined by authorities, which it would be a derilection of official duty, and a disregard of judicial responsibility to overlook."
    For Pennsylvania, see, e.g., *Commonwealth v. Taylor,* 10 *American Law Journal* 258 (Ct. of Quarter Sess., Dauphin Co., 1851), p. 264: "The morality or immorality of slavery as an institution you have no right to consider. It is sanctioned by the laws and Constitution of the country, which are alike obligatory on all."
    And see *Johnson v. Tompkins,* 13 F. Cas. 840 (No. 7,416) (C.C.D. Pa., 1837), p. 843 (per Baldwin, Cir. J.):

It is not permitted to you or us to indulge our feelings of abstract right on these subjects; the law of the land recognizes the right of one man to hold another in bondage and that right must be protected from violation, although its existence is abhorrent to all our ideas of natural right and justice.

For Kentucky, see *Rankin v. Lydia*, 9 Ky. (2 A. K. Marsh) 467 (1820), p. 470: "In deciding this question we disclaim the influence of the general principles of liberty, which we all admire, and conceive it ought to be decided by the law as it is, and not as it ought to be."

For Michigan, see *Denison v. Tucker;* William Blume, ed., *Transactions of the Supreme Court of Michigan 1805–1814* (Ann Arbor: University of Michigan Press, 1935), 1 : 385, at 388:

So magistrates and public officers are the creatures of civilized society . . . Deriving their powers from this Source, they must necessarily be regulated by the obvious Condition of the trust, an implicit obedience to the known will of the nation or Society delegating it.

For North Carolina see *State v. Mann,* 13 N.C. (2 Dev.) 263 (1829), p. 267:

Merely in the abstract, it may well be asked, which power of the master accords with right. The answer will probably sweep away all of them, but we cannot look at the matter in that light. The truth is, that we are forbidden to enter upon a train of general reasoning on the subject.

And see *State v. Will,* 18 N.C. (1 Dev. and Bat.) 121 (1831), at 165–166:

The general rule is that which has been before declared. There is no legal limitation to the master's power of punishment, except that it shall not reach the life of his offending slave. It is for the legislature to remove this reproach from amongst us. . . . We must administer the law such as it is confided to our keeping.

8   In the above paragraph and within, I borrow heavily from two works of analytic philosophy. See R. M. Hare, *Freedom and Reason* (Oxford: Clarendon Press, 1963), Chaps. 4 and 5; and Stuart Hampshire, *Freedom of the Individual* (New York: Harper & Row, 1965). Hampshire's book treats distinctions between meanings of "can't" and their relation to volition that are not the same as those treated here.

9   For a contemporaneous account of the *McQuerry* case, see Levi Coffin, *Reminiscences* (Cincinnati: Western Tract Society, 1876). For a modern account, see Stanley Campbell, *The Slave Catchers* (Chapel Hill: University of North Carolina Press, 1970), pp. 121–23.

10   What follows is a very unphilosophical reworking of ideas suggested in John Searle, *Speech Acts* (London: Cambridge University Press, 1969). Searle, in turn, owes a great debt to Mabbot's famous article on *Promises* and to the theory of the utility of practices. I am well aware that the very sketchy notions in the brief account are but a skimming of the surface of deep waters, though I believe the skim is sufficient for the purposes for which it is used.

11   Michael Polanyi, *Personal Knowledge* (Chicago: University of Chicago Press, 1958), p. 95.

Chapter 8

1   For a general chronology of the various changes in selection and tenure of judges for this period, see Evan Haynes, *Selection and Tenure of Judges* (Newark, N.J.: National Conference of Judicial Councils, 1944). See also the comments of James Hurst, *Growth of American Law, The Law Makers* (Boston: Little, Brown & Co., 1950); Francis Aumann, *The Changing American Legal System* (Columbus: Ohio State University Press, 1940); and Lawrence Friedman, *A History of American Law* (New York: Simon & Schuster, 1973).

2   The assertions of cognizance of lawmaking power is demonstrated within. A good recent treatment of the problem is M. Horwitz, "Toward an Instrumental Concept of Law," in Donald Fleming and Bernard Bailyn, eds., *Law in American History* (Boston: Little, Brown & Co., 1971). Further authorities are cited within.

3   On codification and common law jurisprudence, see, e.g., Perry Miller, *The Life of the Mind in America* (New York: Harcourt, Brace & World, 1965), pp. 239–65; Friedman, *American Law,* pp. 90–98; Aumann, *Changing American Legal System,* pp. 3–8.

4   Elizabeth K. Bauer, in her *Commentaries on the Constitution, 1790–1860* (New York: Columbia University Press, 1952), has thoroughly documented the varied attitudes that the important commentators assumed toward the Constitution as a social contract or as the result of such a contract. The principal reason for the importance of the issue was that some commentators rested their defense of the right of secession on the nature of the Constitution as a compact. Needless to say, the most important sense in which the Constitution was viewed as a contract was as an agreement among corporate entities, the states. Nevertheless, the "We the people" language of the preamble also created a vision of the document as a compact among the people. See Bauer, pp. 253–308.

5   1. *Tucker's Blackstone,* App., p. 4. See also App., p. 140, where Tucker states: "The Constitution of the United States of America then, is an original, written, federal, and social compact, freely, voluntarily, and solely entered into by the several states of North America, and ratified by the people thereof. . . ."

6   See M. MacDonald, "The Language of Political Theory," in Antony Flew, ed., *Logic and Language* (New York: Anchor Books, 1965), pp. 174, 180–86.

7   1. *Tucker's Blackstone,* App., pp. 172–73.

8   See note on p. 133.

9   Joseph Story, *Commentaries on the Constitution* (Boston: Hilliard Gray & Co.; Cambridge, Mass.: Brown, Shattuck and Paul, 1833), 1 : 2. (Hereafter cited as J. Story, *Constitution.*)

10   *Marbury v. Madison,* 5 U.S. (1 Cranch) 137 (1803).

11   Ibid., p. 178.

12 Jefferson to William Jarvis, Sept. 28, 1820, Paul Ford, ed., *Writings of Thomas Jefferson* (New York and London: G. P. Putnam's Sons, 1904–05), 10 : 160. This and other quotations by Jefferson are collected by Haynes, *Selection and Tenure of Judges*, pp. 93–95.

13 *Cohens v. Virginia*, 19 U.S. (6 Wheat.) 264 (1821).

14 Ibid., p. 377.

15 *Marbury v. Madison*, p. 177.

16 J. Story, *Constitution*, Vol. 1, §§ 398, 399, p. 383. Book 3, Chap. 5 deals with "Rules of Interpretation." It, together with the preceding chapter, entitled "Who is Final Judge or Interpreter in Constitutional Controversies?", is the source for what follows.

17 Ibid., § 400.

18 Ibid., § 406, 407.

19 Ibid., (3rd ed., 1858), § 405a. This section was added after the first edition, normally cited in these notes.

20 Ibid.

21 Vernon Parrington, *Main Currents in American Thought* (New York: Harcourt, Brace & Co., 1927–30), Book 1, Chap. 2, Part 4.

22 See Hogan, "Story's Anonymous Law Articles," 52 *Michigan Law Review* 869 (1954); "Three Essays on the Law by Joseph Story," 28 *Southern California Law Review* 19 (1954).

23 See, e.g., Story to Lieber, letter of Nov. 11, 1839, congratulating Lieber on the *Hermeneutics* and remarking that he was "exceedingly pleased with it." William Wetmore Story, ed., *Life and Letters of Joseph Story* (Boston: C. C. Little and J. Brown, 1851), 2 : 279; see also Story's favorable comments on Lieber's other works, ibid., pp. 278, 329. See also F. Freidel, "Francis Lieber, Charles Sumner and Slavery," *Journal of Southern History* 9 (1943) : 75, for a discussion of Lieber's Boston circle, including Choate and Sumner, and of correspondence with Kent.

24 Francis Lieber, *Legal and Political Hermeneutics* (St. Louis: Filt. Thomas & Co., 1880), preface to 2nd ed., reprinted in 3rd ed. on p. vii.

25 See, discussions of interpretation and construction in J. Kent, *Commentaries on American Law*, 1 : 421–24. 1st ed. (New York: O. Halsted, 1826); Duer, *Constitutional Jurisprudence* (New York: Harper & Bros., 1843), pp. 318, 319; William Rawle, *A View of the Constitution of the United States* (Philadelphia: P. H. Nicklin, 1829), pp. 199 ff.; J. Story, *Constitution*, Book 3, Chap. 5; Bauer's *Commentaries on the Constitution, 1790–1860* provides a good introduction to all of the commentaries of the antebellum period. By and large, she ignores "interpretation" as an issue.

26 Lieber, *Legal and Political Hermeneutics*, pp. 14–15, 43–44. Page citation is to the third edition. The text is identical to the earlier two editions except for commentary "below the line."

27 Ibid., pp. 169–73.

28 Ibid., pp. 173.

29 Ibid., pp. 179.

30 For the reaction against the Englishness of the common law, note the statutes of
Kentucky and of Pennsylvania forbidding citation or use of English authorities.
Friedman, *American Law*, pp. 97–98. The case of Kentucky is interesting for its
probable impact on the case of *Rankin v. Lydia* discussed in Chapter 5. *Rankin
v. Lydia* contains a dozen allusions to the language of *Somerset's Case*, yet the
precise language of the case is never used, nor is it once mentioned.

31 On the federal common law and reactions against it, see William W. Crosskey,
Politics and the Constitution (Chicago: University of Chicago Press, 1953), *passim*. Of the major contemporaneous sources discussing the issue, the most lucid
(and important) are St. George Tucker, 1. *Tucker's Blackstone*, App. pp.
378 ff.; Peter DuPonceau, *Dissertation on the Nature and Extent of the Jurisdiction of the Courts of the United States* (Philadelphia: A. Small, 1824); the issue
of the "federal common law" in diversity cases, though fully appreciated and
commented upon by DuPonceau and by Tucker, was not as hot an issue of controversy as was "common law crimes" in the first decade or two of the nineteenth century. This issue of common law in diversity cases has, of course, an
enormous literature. The best single bibliographic aid to all the contemporaneous discussions remains Crosskey, *Politics and the Constitution*. Of course,
Crosskey's conclusions are not generally accepted. See, e.g., J. Goebel, "Book
Review of Crosskey, *Politics and the Constitution*," 54 *Columia Law Review*
450 (1954). On *Swift v. Tyson*, 41 U.S. (16 Pet.) 1 (1842), see note, "Swift v.
Tyson Exhumed," 79 *Yale Law Journal* 284 (1969).

32 This was certainly Tucker's perception of the problem. See, 1. *Tucker's Blackstone*, App., p. 378.

33 Despite more orderly and systematic treatments, Perry Miller's chapter on
"codification" in *The Life of the Mind in America* remains the richest amalgam
of the strands that went into what was a sort of motif rather than a movement
(prior to the Civil War). Other treatments are to be found in Friedman, *American Law*, pp. 351–55; J. W. Hurst, *Growth of American Law, The Lawmakers*,
pp. 70–85; Roscoe Pound, *The Formative Era of American Law* (Boston: Little,
Brown & Co., 1938).

34 William Sampson, *Discourse Upon the History of the Law* (Washington, D.C.:
Pishey Thompson, 1826), p. 63.

35 Ibid., pp. 57–68.

36 Livingston is one of several persons who has been acclaimed as the American
Bentham. See, e.g., Edward Livingston, *Report Made by Edward Livingston
. . . On the Plan of a Penal Code* (Philadelphia: J. Kay Jr. & Bro., 1833);
Thomas S. Grimké, *An Oration on the Practicability and Expediency of Reducing the Whole Body of the Law to the Simplicity and Order of a Code* (Charles-
ton, 1827); R. Rantoul, "Oration at Scituate" (1836), reprinted in Luther Hamilton, ed., *Memoirs, Speeches and Writings of Robert Rantoul* (Boston: J. P.
Jewett & Co., 1854), pp. 251 ff.; David Dudley Field's work in codification
spread from around 1840 to 1880. From the period under consideration here are
several letters, pamphlets, and reports directed to New York law and, in particular, New York practice from 1839 through the 1850's. These works are to be

found in Abram Sprague, ed., *Speeches, Arguments and Miscellaneous Papers of David Dudley Field,* (New York: D. Appleton & Co., 1884–90), 1 : 219–316.

37   J. Story, "Address to the Suffolk County Bar," 1 *American Jurist* 1 (1821).

38   Ibid., pp. 7–10.

39   Kent, *Commentaries,* 4th ed., Vol. 1, Lectures 21, 22, pp. 472, 498.

40   Lieber, *Hermeneutics,* p. 208.

41   Kent, *Commentaries,* 4th ed., Vol. 1, Lecture 16, p. 341.

42   Lieber, *Hermeneutics,* p. 185.

43   J. Story, "Report on the Practicability And Expediency of Reducing to a Written and Systematic Code the Common Law of Massachusetts," in Jeremy Bentham, *Codification of the Common Law* (New York, 1882).

44   Ibid., p. 14. The position of the commission, certainly penned by Story, is to be found in the Justice's other writings. See, e.g., his article on codification prepared for the Encyclopedia Americana, Hogan, "Story's Anonymous Law Articles"; Miller, *Life of the Mind,* p. 251.

45   See, e.g., the negative remarks of Pendleton and Mason in the Virginia Debates, which fail to attack the tenure of the judiciary, Jonathan Elliot, *Debates on the Federal Constitution* (Philadelphia: J. P. Lippincott Co., 1836), 3 : 517–30.

46   ". . . the original error of establishing a judiciary independent of the nation. . . ." "Jefferson to Eppes," May 28, 1807, X. Ford, *Works of Jefferson,* p. 412, quoted in Albert Beveridge, *Life of John Marshall* (Boston and New York: Houghton, Mifflin Co., 1916–19), 3 : 431.

47   For a brief account of the aftermath of *McCulloch,* see George Dangerfield, *The Era of Good Feelings* (New York: Harcourt, Brace, 1952), pp. 169 ff.; Beveridge, *John Marshall,* 4 : 310 ff.

48   See Haynes, *Selection and Tenure of Judges,* pp. 101–35, for a complete chronology.

49   ". . . the result of the decision in *Sturgis v. Crowninshield* was the impossibility of the enactment of any relief legislation, by the states . . . we have here the *economic situation* which resulted in the *political struggle* which was known locally in Kentucky as 'Old-Court—New Court' Controversy, and then, nationally, as the Rise of Jacksonian Democracy." Louis Boudin, *Government by Judiciary,* (New York: Russel & Russel, 1968), 1 : 334. Boudin's view is certainly simplistic, but the relationship he purports to trace between *Sturgis,* depression, Western debtor and the distrust for an independent Bench is persuasive so far as it goes. Analysis of economic conditions, voting patterns, and sources for antijudicial initiative would be necessary before a firm conclusion were assayed.

50   Frederick Grimké, *The Nature and Tendency of Free Institutions* (Cambridge, Mass.: Belknap Press of Harvard University Press, 1968).

51   Ibid., p. 446.

52   Ibid., p. 447.

53   Ibid., p. 448–52.

54   Ibid., p. 462. The New York Convention of 1846 was a forum for a series of
     speeches for and against the independent judiciary. See *Debates and Proceed-*
     ings of the New York Constitutional Convention of 1846 (Albany, N.Y.: Eve-
     ning Atlas, 1846), pp. 554–626.
55   Francis Lieber, *Political Ethics,* 2nd ed. (Philadelphia: J. B. Lippincott Co.,
     1875), 1 : 344.
56   Ibid., 2 : 404.
57   See, e.g., M. Horwitz, "Toward an Instrumental Concept of Law."
58   H. Binney, "An Eulogium Upon the Hon. William Tilghman," in Law Associ-
     ation of Philadelphia, *Addresses Delivered and Papers Prepared or Republished*
     to Commemorate the Centennial Celebration of the Law Association of Phila-
     delphia, 1802–1902 (Philadelphia, 1902), p. 154 at 164.
59   Michael Polanyi, *Personal Knowledge* (Chicago: University of Chicago Press,
     1958), p. 309.

Chapter 9

 1   See William Jay, *Miscellaneous Writings on Slavery* (Boston, 1853); Salmon
     Portland Chase, *Speech in the Case of the Colored Woman Mathilda . . .*
     March 11, 1837 (Cincinnati, 1837); Dwight Dumond, ed., *James Gillespie Bir-*
     ney Letters 1831–1857 (Gloucester: P. Smith, 1966), pp. 646 ff. See also the
     argument of Charles Sumner in *Roberts v. City of Boston,* 59 Mass. (5 Cush.)
     198 (1850); Argument of Robert Rantoul in *Sims's Case,* 61 Mass. (7 Cush.)
     285 (1851), and before the Commissioner in the same affair, see, J. Stone, re-
     porter, *Trial of Thomas Sims on an Issue of Personal Liberty, on the claim of*
     James Potter of Georgia, against Him, as an alleged Fugitive from service.
     Arguments of Robert Rantoul, Jr. and Charles G. Loring, with the Decision of
     George T. Curtis, Boston, April 7–11, 1851 (Boston: W. S. Damrell & Co.,
     1851). For Dana, see Dana, ed., *Speeches in Troubled Times;* see also, his
     speeches in *Sims's Case,* noted above with respect to Rantoul. Other notable ad-
     vocates included Samuel Sewall, Thaddeus Stevens, John Jolliffe, John Parker
     Hale, Charles Ellis, and T. C. Ware. Politicians whose forensic skills were evi-
     dent and used in the antislavery cause included Joshua Giddings, Benjamin
     Wade, and John Quincy Adams.
 2   Two works especially useful for understanding the split in antislavery are Gil-
     bert Barnes, *The Antislavery Impulse* (New York and London: D. Appleton-
     Century Co., 1933), and Aileen Kraditor, *Means and Ends in American Abo-*
     litionism (New York: Pantheon, 1969). Always useful is Dwight Dumond, *An-*
     tislavery (Ann Arbor: University of Michigan Press, 1961).
 3   W. Phillips, *The Constitution: A Pro-Slavery Compact* (Boston, 1844), pp.
     vi–vii.
 4   W. Phillips, *A Review of Lysander Spooner's Unconstitutionality of Slavery*
     (Boston: Andrews & Prentiss, 1847), p. 17. The avalanche of authorities is on
     pp. 18–25. (Hereafter cited as *Review*).
 5   "God does not require of any of his creatures to juggle their fellows out of the
     gift of power, and then use that power contrary to their promises, in order to

serve humanity. That were to ask 'robbery for burnt offering.' '' *Review,* p. 15.

6   Ibid.
7   Phillips, *The Constitution,* 3rd ed., pp. 171–181.
8   Phillips, *Review,* pp. 3–4.
9   Jacobus tenBroek, *Antislavery Origins of the Fourteenth Amendment,* republished as *Equal Under Law* (New York: Collier Books, 1965). H. Graham, "The Early Antislavery Background of the Fourteenth Amendment," 1950 *Wisconsin Law Review* 479 ff. and 610 ff. (1950). In a sense I proclaim the motives of tenBroek and Graham with little documentation though I believe they would embrace my description. TenBroek in his introduction to the new, enlarged edition of his work, praising *Brown v. Board of Education,* says:

> Equal protection is again emerging from its relative latency to strike down some of these vestiges. . . . The work in the name of equality is far from done, perhaps never will be done.
>
> . . . It was to explore the origins and nature of these goals . . . that this book was written *(Equal Under Law,* pp. 15, 26).

10 Theodore Dwight Weld, *The Power of Congress Over Slavery in the District of Columbia* (New York: American Antislavery Society, 1838).
11 William Jay, *Miscellaneous Writings on Slavery* (Boston, 1853). See Bayard Tuckerman, *William Jay and the Constitutional Movement for the Abolition of Slavery* (New York: Dodd, Mead & Co., 1893), which is less good on the *movement* than on Jay.
12 Jay, *Miscellaneous Writings,* pp. 207 ff.
13 William Goodell, *Views of American Constitutional Law in Its Bearing Upon American Slavery* (Utica, N.Y.: Jackson & Chapman, 1844); Alvan Stewart, "A Constitutional Argument on the Subject of Slavery," reprinted in Appendix B of tenBroek, *Equal Under Law;* Joel Tiffany, *The Unconstitutionality of Slavery* (Cleveland: 1849); Lysander Spooner, *The Unconstitutionality of Slavery* (Boston: B. Marsh, 1845). Some of this utopian thinking is mixed into the second and third editions of Richard Hildreth, *Despotism in America* (Boston: J. P. Jewett & Co., 1854). See also the argument of Gerritt Smith in *Trial of Henry Allen, U.S. Deputy Marshall, for Kidnapping with Arguments of Counsel and the Charge of* . . . (Syracuse, 1852).
14 TenBroek goes on at some length about the "imaginative" arguments of Goodell, Stewart, and Spooner. Actually, the manipulation of phrases was at all times justified because of the presumed necessity of harmonizing with natural law.
15 Spooner, *Unconstitutionality of Slavery,* pp. 54–123.
16 As quoted in Kraditor, *Abolitionism,* pp. 195–96.
17 See Chapter 3, supra.
18 Stewart, *Constitutional Argument.*
19 Spooner, *Unconstitutionality of Slavery,* p. 152.
20 Ibid.

Chapter 10

1   Nina Tiffany, *Samuel E. Sewall, A Memoire* (Boston & New York: Houghton, Mifflin & Co., 1898). The memoir is a poor one.

2   See E. Turner, *The Negro in Pennsylvania* (Washington, D.C., Am. Hist. Assoc., 1911) and especially, Arthur Zilversmit, *The First Emancipation* (Chicago: University of Chicago Press, 1967), pp. 203–207, for the work of the Pennsylvania Society. Zilversmit concentrates on legislative efforts and on the one "big case" of *Negro Flora v. Graisberry,* p. 205. Unquestionably, the Society was a resource in the registration cases as well.

3   The best evidence is indirect; the penal provisions of the Act of 1792 were designed to discourage aiders and abettors of unsuccessful freedom suits.

4   The failure of the *Flora* case in Pennsylvania in 1798, the failure of *Hudgins* in Virginia in 1806, and the inauspicious beginnings of Supreme Court litigation involving slavery in *Scott v. Ben,* 10 U.S. (6 Cranch) 3; *Scott v. London,* 7 U.S. (3 Cranch) 324; and *Mima Queen v. Hepburn,* 11 U.S. (7 Cranch) 290; may have conspired with the factors considered below in producing the narrow focus.

5   For descriptive works on the early antislavery movement, see Zilversmit, *First Emancipation;* Mary Locke, *Antislavery in America from the Introduction of African Slaves to the Prohibition of the Slave Trade* (Gloucester, Mass.: P. Smith, 1965); Stephen Weeks, *Southern Quakers and Slavery* (Baltimore: Johns Hopkins Press, 1896). More analytical and less useful as overviews are D. B. Davis, *Problem of Slavery in Western Culture;* and Winthrop Jordan, *White over Black* (Chapel Hill: University of North Carolina Press, 1968).

6   Dumond, *Antislavery,* is the most useful, comprehensive overview of the movement. Gilbert Barnes, *The Antislavery Impulse* (New York and London: D. Appleton-Century Co., 1933), provided, when it was written, a much needed corrective to identification of abolitionism with W. L. Garrison; Louis Filler, *The Crusade Against Slavery* (New York: Harper, 1960), emphasizes political antislavery. Kraditor, *Abolitionism,* is a corrective to Barnes. On the interaction of militant abolitionism with militant repression, see Richards, *Gentlemen of Property and Standing: Antiabolitionist Mobs in Jacksonian America* (New York: Oxford University Press, 1970). All of the above works have either explicit or important implicit theories to account for the emergence of a more militant antislavery movement in the early 1830's. Among these theories are: that abolitionism was a reaction to a more militantly proslavery South (conversely, the militant South is often attributed in part to abolitionism); that the militancy was a by-product of the militant evangelism of Charles Finney's religious movement of the 1820's; that it was a spillover of a strong utopian strain in American reformism.

7   See Robert Warden, *Salmon P. Chase* (Cincinnati: Wilstach, Baldwin & Co., 1874); Jacob Schuckers, *Salmon Portland Chase* (New York: D. Appleton & Co., 1874); and Eric Foner, *Free Soil, Free Labor, Free Men* (New York: Ox-

ford University Press, 1970), for information on Chase. The best sources for the Birney-Chase relationship are Warden and Betty Fladeland, *James Gillespie Birney: Slaveholder to Abolitionist* (Ithaca: Cornell University Press, 1955). The best source for Chase's role in the Republican party is Foner.

8   Nina Tiffany, *Samuel E. Sewall.* Tiffany attributes the following quotation to William Lloyd Garrison: "Had it not been for Samuel E. Sewall, I never should have been able to continue the paper [the *Liberator*]. He was the man who gave money again and again . . . ." (p. 38).

9   For Dana's flirtations with various parties and his ultimate involvement with Free Soil, see Robert F. Lucid, ed., *The Journal of Richard Henry Dana, Jr.,* 3 vols. (Cambridge, Mass.: Belknap Press of Harvard University Press, 1968), 1 : 347, 394. This new edition of Dana's *Journal* has rendered obsolete the C. F. Adams "biography" of Dana which is often cited. The Adams work is simply a series of excerpts from the Journals.

10 See Levi Coffin, *Reminiscences* (Cincinnati: Western Tract Society, 1876), p. 548, where Coffin claims for Jolliffe "an imperishable record of legal services for the slave."

11 For a brief account of the Prudence Cradall affairs, see Dumond, *Antislavery,* Chap. 25, and sources cited therein. For the *Amistad,* see Chap. 6 and sources cited therein.

12 U.S. Constitution, Article IV, Section 2.

13 For the jury trial issue, see *Comm. ex rel. Wright v. Deacon,* 5 S & R 63 (Pa., 1819); for the confrontation and presentation of evidence points, see arguments of Gerrit Smith in *Trial of Henry Allen, U.S. Dep'y Marshall for Kidnapping . . . in the Supreme Court of N.Y., 1852"* (Syracuse, N.Y.: Power Press, 1852). Smith refers to a case of Horace Preston in which the argument was made and rejected that ex parte evidence was not a constitutionally sufficient basis for extradition. The Preston case is mentioned by Smith, p. 19 of the *Allen* trial. The Preston rendition is listed as occurring on April 9, 1852, by Campbell, *The Slave Catchers,* Appendix, p. 201, without comment or discussion. For the peaceable process point, note the various state "kidnapping" statutes and *Prigg v. Pennsylvania,* discussed at notes 30 ff., infra.

14 *In re Susan* 23 F. Cas. 444, 445 (No. 13,362) (C.C. Ind., 1818). See also *Trial of Henry Allen, . . .* Argument of Gerrit Smith, pp. 29–30.

15 For a general and thorough review of the state legislation affecting the fugitive issue, of the politics involved in the most significant instances of such legislation, and of court cases construing these laws, see Thomas Morris, *Free Men All* (Baltimore: Johns Hopkins University Press, 1974), a study of the personal liberty laws.

16 *In re Susan,* 23 F. Cas. 444.

17 *Comm. ex rel. Wright v. Deacon,* 5 S & R 63 (Pa., 1819).

18 *Commonwealth v. Griffith,* 19 Mass. (2 Pick.) 11 (1823) reiterated in *Commonwealth v. Aves* 35 Mass. (18 Pick.) 193 (1836) (dictum).

19 *Jack v. Martin* 12 Wendell 311 (N.Y., Sup. Ct., 1834), mod., 14 Wendell 507 (N.Y., Ct. of Errors, 1836).

20   For a general view of Birney's theories, see H. Graham, "Early Antislavery Background of the Fourteenth Amendment," 1950 *Wisconsin Law Review* 479, 610 (1950); and Fladeland, *Birney*. A particularly important article on the jury trial issue appeared in the *Philanthropist* on February 24, 1837, when Birney refuted the Report of the Ohio legislature denying the jury trial.

21   In 1921 A. Johnson published an article, "The Constitutionality of the Fugitive Slave Acts," 31 *Yale Law Journal* 161 (1921), which, with no justification, totally ignores the abolitionist refutation of the preliminary character of the rendition process.

22   [Alvord] "Trial by Jury in Questions of Personal Freedom," 17 *Am. Jurist* 94 (1837). For this and other 1837 moves, see Morris, *Free Men All,* pp. 76–93.

23   17 *Am. Jurist* 97 (1837) 112: The proposed act was passed in 1837. Act of April 19, 1837, *Mass. Gen Laws 1836–53, Supp.,* Chap. 221, p. 44. (Note the date of the legislation to coincide with Battle of Concord and Lexington—the "shot heard 'round the world.")

24   As related by Jacobus tenBroek, *Equal Under Law* (New York: Collier Books, 1965), pp. 61–62.

25   S. P. Chase, *Speech in the Case of the Colored Woman Mathilda Who was Brought Before the Court of Common Pleas of Hamilton Co., Ohio, by writ of habeas corpus, March 11, 1837* (Cincinnati, 1837).

26   The *Philanthropist,* Feb. 24, 1837, p. 1, Columns 1–3. The only discussion in the legal literature of the writ *de homine replegiando* and of its role in the fight for a jury for the fugitive is to be found in D. H. Oaks, "Habeas Corpus in the States—1776–1865," 32 *University of Chicago Law Review* 243 (1965), pp. 281–88. Oaks discusses the Massachusetts Act of 1837 and the cases rejecting use of writ in fugitive situations, but he does not relate the other attempts in Ohio and Pennsylvania nor does he relate the timing of the development to issues in the antislavery movement. The very recent *Free Men All* goes beyond Oaks in all respects save that of placing the issue in the general legal context of state habeas corpus.

27   *Commonwealth v. Aves,* 35 Mass. (18 Pick.) 193 (1836).

28   *Morgan v. Reakirt,* 4 *Pennsylvania Law Journal* 6 (1835), denying relief on the basis of *Comm. ex rel. Wright v. Deacon.*

29   *Barron v. Baltimore,* 32 U.S. (7 Pet.) 243 (1833).

30   *Prigg v. Pennsylvania,* 41 U.S. 539 (1842), pp. 608–626. For a consideration of the proposition that Story intentionally laid a foundation for state obstruction, see Chapter 13, infra.

31   Ibid., p. 626.

32   Ibid., pp. 627–33.

33   Ibid., pp. 633–36.

34   Ibid., pp. 658–74.

35   See account of Shaw's action in Leonard Levy, *Law of the Commonwealth and Chief Justice Lemuel Shaw* (Cambridge, Mass.: Harvard University Press, 1957), pp. 78–84.

36   The *Liberator,* Nov. 4, 1842, p. 3.

37 Ibid.
38 Ibid.
39 "The Latimer Case," 5 *Law Reporter* 485 ff., (1842), where Sewall is not named but is alluded to as "one of Latimer's counsel." Abolitionist reaction to this article may be seen in the *Latimer Journal and North Star* of May 10, 1843.
40 For Story's attempts to construct an impersonal standard of interpretation, see Chapter 8, supra, at notes 16–20.
41 5 *Law Reporter* 493–94 (1842).
42 Fladeland, *Birney.*
43 S. P. Chase, *Speech in the Case of Mathilda,* . . . p. 37.
44 See Warden, *Salmon P. Chase,* pp. 299–300.
45 This was only the first of several such confrontations between Chase and McLean. See, e.g., *Driskell v. Parish,* 7 F. Cas. 1,093 (No. 4,087) (C.C.D. Ohio, 1847).
46 See *Jones v. Van Zandt,* 13 F. Cas. 1,047 (No. 7,502) (C.C.D. Ohio, 1843).
47 See ibid., Appendix.
48 S. P. Chase, *An Argument for the Defendant Submitted to the Supreme Court of the U.S.* . . . *in the Case of Jones v. Van Zandt* (Cincinnati, 1847), pp. 93–94.
49 Ibid., p. 54.
50 *Jones v. Van Zandt,* 46 U.S. (5 How.) 215 (1847), p. 230.

Chapter 11

1 "An act to Amend and Supplementary to, the act entitled 'An Act respecting fugitives from justice, and persons escaping from the service of their masters,' " 9 Stat. 462 (1850). For further information on the political background of the act, see the vast literature on the Compromise of 1850. The literature is far too large to review in a footnote. A starting point is Allan Nevins, *Ordeal of Union* (New York: Scribner's, 1947). See also Julius Yanuck, "The Fugitive Slave Law and the Constitution" (Ph.D. Dissertation, Columbia University, 1953).
2 5 *Op. Att'y Gen'l U.S. 254 (1850).*
3 For a taste of the bitterness toward Webster, see "Ichabod" by John Greenleaf Whittier:

> . . . .
> Let not the land once proud of him
>   Insult him now,
> Nor brand with deeper shame his dim,
>   Dishonored brow.
> But let its humbled sons, instead
>   From sea to lake
> A long lament, as for the dead,
>   In sadness make.

> Of all we loved and honored, naught
>   Save power remains;
> A fallen angel's pride of thought,
>   Still strong in chains.
> All else's gone; from those great eyes
>   The soul has fled:
> When faith is lost, when honor dies,
>   The man is dead!
>
> Then pay the reverence of old days
>   To his dead fame;
> Walk backward, with averted gaze,
>   And hide the shame!

4 Benjamin R. Curtis, Jr., *A Memoire of Benjamin Robbins Curtis* . . . (Boston: Little, Brown & Co., 1879), 1 : 136.

5 For more on Shadrach, see Chapter 13, infra.

6 There are several good accounts of the *Sims* affair. The account in Dana's *Journal* is an interesting one from a contemporaneous perspective. The events can be followed from the movement perspective in the *Liberator*. Of secondary treatments, that of Leonard Levy in *The Law of the Commonwealth and Chief Justice Shaw* is a most complete and perceptive account of the legal battles. Much of the material in the Shaw biography was published separately, L. Levy, "Sims' Case: The Fugitive Slave Law in Boston in 1851," *Journal of Negro History,* 35 (1950) : 39–74.

7 The Garrisonian objection to identification of law and right has already been explored. Rantoul was something of a Benthamite. He, too, would have objected to such an identification. Cf. his "Oration at Scituate" (1836), reprinted in Luther Hamilton, ed., *Memoirs, Speeches and Writings of Robert Rantoul* (Boston: J. P. Jewett & Co., 1854); Dana was cut very much in the Story mold.

8 The arguments of Rantoul and of Dana are printed in full in the official Massachusetts report of the case. *Thomas Sims's Case,* 61 Mass. (7 Cush.) 285 (1851).

9 The distinction here is not important in legal terms. Shaw's holding was that the writ need not issue because discharge could not be forthcoming so long as the relevant legal issue were the constitutionality of the Act of 1850.

10 61 Mass. (7 Cush.), pp. 294–319.

11 The proceedings before the Commissioner and the Commissioner's opinion were printed in pamphlet form: James Stone, reporter, *Trial of Thomas Sims on an Issue of Personal Liberty.* . . . See Chapter 9, note 1, supra.

12 *Official Report of the Debates and Proceedings in the Mass. State Constitu-*

tional Convention of 1853, 3 vols. (Boston, 1853), vol. 2, pp. 687–714, 756–832.

13   Ibid., 2 : 764.

14   Ibid., 2 : 786.

15   Ibid., 2 : 756–70. Much has been made of Rufus Choate's great speech favoring judicial independence. Ibid., 2 : 799–811. To my mind, Dana's is no less worthy and somewhat more interesting in that it confronts with specificity the issues of the day.

16   See Samuel Shapiro, *Richard Henry Dana, Jr.* (East Lansing: Michigan State University Press, 1961); C. Stevens, *Anthony Burns: A Narrative* (Boston: J. P. Jewett & Co., 1856), pp. 80–124. See also Robert Lucid, ed., *The Journal of Richard Henry Dana, Jr.,* 3 vols. (Cambridge, Mass.: Belknap Press of Harvard University Press, 1968), 2 : 625 ff., for some of the thoughts of one of the strategists for the legal affairs.

17   For accounts of the Loring removal, see, e.g., S. Shapiro, *Dana,* pp. 98–99; "Removal of Judge Loring," 8 *Monthly Law Reporter* (N.S.) 8 (1856); Stevens, *Anthony Burns,* pp. 218–44.

18   W. Phillips, *Argument of Wendell Phillips, Esq. Before the Committee on Federal Relations in Support of the Petition for the Removal of Edward Greely Loring* (Boston, 1855).

19   Richard H. Dana, Jr., *Remarks . . . Before the Committee on Federal Relations . . .* (Boston, 1855).

20   Ibid., p. 13.

21   *Remarks of James W. Stone in the Massachusetts House of Representatives, April 13, 1855* (Boston, 1855).

22   *Speech of John L. Swift, Esq. of Boston on the Removal of E. G. Loring, Esq., from the Office of Judge of Probate, for the County of Suffolk, delivered in the Massachusetts House of Representatives, Tuesday, April 10, 1855* (Boston, 1855), p. 25.

23   See *Miller v. McQuerry,* 17 F. Cas. 332 (No. 9,583) (C.C.D. Ohio, 1853). The *McQuerry Case* is extensively discussed by Levi Coffin in his autobiographical *Reminiscences,* 3rd ed. (Cincinnati: Western Tract Society, 1876), pp. 542–54. The instant case and most other important Ohio cases are discussed in their political contexts in W. Cochrane, "The Western Reserve and the Fugitive Slave Law," *Western Reserve Historical Society,* Publication No. 101 (1920).

24   A history of the Armstead case is to be found in L. Coffin, *Reminiscences,* pp. 554–57, and more concisely in Stanley Campbell, *The Slave Catchers* (Chapel Hill: University of North Carolina Press, 1969), pp. 141–42. The McLean opinion, which recites something of the earlier history of the case, is to be found in *Ex Parte Robinson* [Robinson I], 20 F. Cas. 969 (No. 11,835) (C.C.S.D. Ohio, 1855).

25   20 F. Cas., p. 972.

26   See Coffin, *Reminiscences,* pp. 555–56.

27 *Ex Parte Robinson* [Robinson II] 20 F. Cas. 965 (No. 11,834) (C.C.S.D. Ohio, 1856).

28 *Ex Parte Sifford,* 22 F. Cas. 105 (No. 12,848) (C.C.S.D. Ohio, 1857), p. 109.

29 The Booth affair is a standard "incident" related in all the histories of the Fugitive Slave Act or of the Underground Railroad. The main outline of the story is to be found in V. Mason, "The Fugitive Slave Law in Wisconsin," *Proceedings of the State Historical Society of Wisconsin* (1895), pp. 117 ff. The various judicial proceedings also relate the facts in detail and reveal much of the intensity of the issue.

30 Ibid., p. 124.

31 *In re Booth,* 3 Wis. 1, 7–49 (1854).

32 *Ex Parte Booth,* 3 Wis. 145 (1854).

33 *In re Booth and Rycraft,* 3 Wis. 157 (1854).

34 *U.S. v. Booth,* 59 U.S. (18 How.) 476 (1855).

35 *Ableman v. Booth,* 62 U.S. (21 How.) 506 (1859). The Wisconsin courts continued to resist the authority of the Supreme Court. In *Ableman v. Booth,* 11 Wis. 517 (1860), the state court split 1 to 1 as to whether the Supreme Court's appellate power would be acceded to. In *Arnold v. Booth,* 14 Wis. 195 (1861), a civil suit arising from the same transactions, the state court declined to interfere with the federal District Court's jurisdiction, but intimated continued resistance to the Supreme Court.

36 62 U.S. (21 How.), p. 509.

37 3 Wis., p. 144.

38 Ibid., pp. 70–87.

39 *Ex Parte Bushnell,* 9 Ohio St. 77 (1859).

40 A full account and partial transcript of the Oberlin-Wellington affair is provided in the contemporaneous Jacob Shipherd, *History of the Oberlin-Wellington Rescue* (Boston: J. P. Jewett & Co., 1859).

41 Ibid., pp. 81–82.

42 Ibid., p. 87.

43 *Ex Parte Bushnell,* 9 Ohio St. 198–99 (1859).

44 The Attorney General of the state of Ohio argued on behalf of the *Bushnell* petitioners. The argument was a confused and confusing one. We have become accustomed to arguing in the alternative. But Wolcott argued from alternative principles of obligation leaving the Court to choose from among the following:

1. Under the law as presently constituted the act is unconstitutional.
2. Under the Constitution, as it was properly read before 1840, the act is unconstitutional.
3. The true Constitution must be saved from the Supreme Court.

It is on the latter note that he concludes: "Go back I say to the text of the Constitution plant yourselves on its primal granite and follow the rule which you shall find so plainly and indelibly graven there." The Supreme Court that gave us *Dred Scott* need not be followed. It is characterized as a political, proslavery tribunal without legitimacy.

45   *United States v. Morris,* 26 F. Cas. 1,323 (No. 15,815) (C.C.D. Mass., 1851).

46   For McLean, see generally the Appendix where all fugitive cases before a jury are so marked and appropriate passages quoted. For Grier, see *Van Metre v. Mitchell,* 28 F. Cas. 1036 (Cas. 16,865) (C.C. Pa., 1853), p. 1039.

Part III Introduction Footnotes

1   Karl Llewellyn, *The Common Law Tradition: Deciding Appeals* (Boston: Little, Brown & Co., 1960). Llewellyn, of course, largely used cases from the area of commercial law.

2   M. Horwitz, "Toward an Instrumental Concept of Law," in Donald Fleming and Bernard Bailyn, eds., *Law in American History* (Boston: Little, Brown & Co., 1971).

Chapter 12

1   H. Wechsler, "Some Issues for the Lawyer," in Robert MacIver, ed., *Integrity and Compromise,* p. 124.

2   See Chapter 4, supra.

3   See Chapter 3, supra.

4   See Chapter 5, supra.

5   See, e.g., *Scott v. London,* 7 U.S. (3 Cranch) 324 (1806); *Murray v. McCarty,* 16 Va. (2 Munf.) 393 (1811), 406; *Scott v. Ben* 10 U.S. (6 Cranch) 3 (1810).

6   See Chapter 5, supra.

7   See, e.g., *Hill v. Low,* 12 F. Cas. 172 (No. 6,494) (C.C.E.D. Pa., 1822).

8   See Chapter 4, supra.

9   11 Va. (1 H. & M.) 519 (1807). And see text at p. 73, supra.

10   See Chapter 4, supra, notes 33 and 34. In *Patty v. Colin,* Roane characterized his *Woodly* decision as follows: "in . . . *Abby v. Woodly* . . . this court only determined against the paupers in the *last* resort and after every possible source of redemption should be found to have failed."

11   See Chapter 5, supra.

12   *Prigg v. Pennsylvania,* 41 U.S. (16 Pet.) 539 (1842); *Jones v. Van Zandt,* 46 U.S. (5 How.) 215 (1847); *Moore v. Illinois,* 55 U.S. (14 How. 213 (1852); *Ableman v. Booth,* 62 U.S. (21 How.) 506 (1859).

13   See Chapter 10, supra, notes 14–20.

14   See Chapter 10, supra, notes 30–34.

15   See Chapter 10, supra, notes 15 and 28.

16   See Chapter 11, supra, notes 9–15.

17   See Chapter 10, supra, notes 46–50.

18   See Chapter 11, supra, notes 16 ff. See, generally, Stanley Campbell, *The Slave Catchers* (Chapel Hill: University of North Carolina Press, 1969).

19   See Chapter 13, infra, for a sketch of McLean and of his values.

20   *Scott v. Sanford,* 60 U.S. (19 How.) 393 (1857).

21 See, e.g., the dissent of Brinkerhoff in *Ex Parte Bushnell,* 9 Ohio St. 77 (1859), p. 228.

22 For a good account of O'Neall, see A. E. K. Nash, "Negro Rights, Unionism and Greatness on the South Carolina Court of Appeals: The Extraordinary Chief Justice John Belton O'Neall," 21 *South Carolina Law Review* 141 (1969). For Gaston, see Chapter 4, supra, note 44 and sources cited therein.

23 See Chapter 10, supra, notes 46–50; and Chapter 11, note 24.

24 See Chapter 10, supra, notes 35–40.

25 The classic work playing upon this theme is Gilbert Barnes, *The Antislavery Impulse* (New York, London: D. Appleton-Century Co., 1933).

26 For Dana, see Robert Lucid, ed., *The Journal of Richard Henry Dana, Jr.,* 3 vols. (Cambridge, Mass.: Belknap Press of Harvard University Press, 1968), 2 : 420–21, 423–24; for Parker, see, Theodore Parker, *The Trial of Theodore Parker* (Boston, 1855).

27 Note, e.g., the extended maneuvers in the Burns affair, Chapter 11, supra, notes 16–22, despite the clear precedent of *Sims.*

28 See Benjamin Quarles, *Frederick Douglass* (Washington, D.C., 1948), pp. 51–52.

29 The basic story is recounted in C. Stevens, *Anthony Burns: A Narrative* (Boston: J. P. Jewett & Co., 1856), but much additional richness of detail, of hope and disappointment, is to be found by reviewing Theodore Parker's scrapbook of the Burns affair, which is located in Massachusetts in the Boston Public Library Theodore Parker Collection.

30 See William Still, *The Underground Railroad* (Philadelphia: Porter & Coates, 1872), pp. 148–68; William U. Hensel, *The Christiana Riot and the Treason Trials* (New York: Negro University Press, 1969); *U.S. v. Hanway,* 26 F. Cas. 105 (No. 15,299) (C.C.E.D. Pa., 1851).

31 For a detailed review of this literature, see Chapter 9, supra.

32 See, e.g., the very hostile remarks of Justice Grier in *Hanway,* supra, and of Kane in *Ex Parte Jenkins,* 13 F. Cas. 447 (No. 7,259) (C.C.E.D. Pa., 1853).

33 *Ex Parte Bushnell,* 9 Ohio St. Rep. 77 (1859), p. 198.

34 Chapter 6, supra, notes 21 ff.

35 See Chapter 11, supra, notes 2 ff. See also Levy, *Law of the Commonwealth and Chief Justice Shaw,* pp. 62 ff. For the "other" cotton Whig Bostonians, see, e.g., D. Van Tassel, "Gentlemen of Property and Standing: Compromise Sentiment in Boston in 1850," *New England Quarterly,* 23 (1950) : 307.

36 See Chapter 9, supra.

37 See Lucid, ed., *Dana,* 2 : 410–12, for Dana's action and Shaw's reaction. On the rescue and subsequent litigation, see *Dana,* 2 : 413–16. On the outcome of the cases, see *Dana,* 2 : 429, 466–69, 511–13, 531. See also the *Liberator,* Feb. 21, Feb. 28, March 7, and March 14 of 1851.

38 See Lucid, *Dana,* Chap. 2, pp. 438 ff., for these exchanges.

39 Ibid., p. 413.

40 Ibid., p. 472.

41 Ibid., p. 412.

42   See Chapter 13, infra, for a more detailed consideration of this "failure" by
     Shaw.
43   Hobbes, *Leviathan* (Morley, 1886 ed.), Book 1, Chap. 14, p. 64.
44   Benjamin R. Curtis, Jr., *A Memoir of Benjamin Robbins Curtis . . .* (Boston:
     Little, Brown & Co., 1879), 1 : 134–35.
45   Samuel Shapiro, *Richard Henry Dana, Jr.* (East Lansing: Michigan State Uni-
     versity Press, 1961), pp. 114–15.
46   See Chapter 11, supra, notes 29–38.

Chapter 13

1   The reader who is interested in a somewhat fuller description of the dissonance
    theory assumptions underlying the very brief textual enumeration of proposi-
    tions might find the following of use:
        In 1957 Leon Festinger outlined a theory of cognitive dissonance [Festinger,
    A Theory of Cognitive Dissonance (Evanston, Ill.: Row, Peterson, 1957)]. The
    basic units of the structure are "cognitions," defined as "any knowledge,
    opinion, or belief about the environment, about oneself, or about one's beha-
    viour." Cognitions are in a "dissonant" relationship when the obverse of one
    would follow from the other. The "follow from" relationship is not a logical
    entailment, but is loosely defined to include logical, cultural, or experiential ex-
    pectations. The basic premises of the theory are that cognitive dissonance
    "gives rise to pressures to reduce or eliminate the dissonance"; and that the
    "strength of the pressures to reduce the dissonance is a function of the magni-
    tude of the dissonance." Dissonance reduction takes place when either the na-
    ture or importance of one of the dissonant cognitions is changed. Reality and the
    psychological and cultural determinants of the individual create the barrier
    beyond which change in many cognitions cannot occur. In such circumstances,
    Festinger postulates that the individual either begins to value the least resistant
    cognition less, or to search out cognitions consonant with one or the other disso-
    nant poles. One of Festinger's primary examples of a situation that generically
    involves dissonance is that of the postdecision attitudes of the decider. When a
    decision has been made, then the cognition of the action taken is always disso-
    nant with the cognition of the positive attributes of "the road not taken."
        Later theorists have added several variations, important for us. First, they
    have postulated that intolerance for inconsistency increases with personal in-
    volvement: that there is a substantially greater stability to inconsistencies among
    cognitions about matters external to self. Second, they have postulated that
    commitment to one's cognitions is a key to prediction and certainty as to the ef-
    fect of other cognitions. This is so, first, because "commitment" may be taken
    as a personal involvement; second, because commitment establishes one pole as
    unlikely to change [Jack Brehm and Arthur Cohen, *Explorations in Cognitive
    Dissonance* (New York: Wiley, 1967)].
        The primary axiom remains that the individual seeks to reduce dissonance.
    There is less dissonance in a situation where the number or intensity of conso-

nant relations is increased. Festinger recognized in the first of the general formulations of the theory that this postulate had very clear implications for situations of duress or what he called "forced compliance." Countervolitional behavior always produces some dissonance. The knowledge that one is acting in a particular way is dissonant with the cognition of what one wants. Nevertheless, the reward or punishment that is associated with countervolitional behavior is consonant with so acting. For the actor has either gained something (presumably something more than what he lost) by complying or has avoided negative consequences. Festinger, in one of his most famous corollaries, thus postulates:

As the promised reward, or threatened punishment becomes smaller in importance, the dissonance resulting from compliance increases. The maximum possible dissonance would be created if the reward or punishment, was just barely enough to elicit the desired overt behavior or expression.

Festinger makes the obvious point that the converse also follows. That is, that reward or punishment which just *fails* to induce overt behavior change maximizes the dissonance incidental to noncompliance (Festinger, pp. 91–92). Since dissonance is maximized at low duress, compliant behavior, the motivation to further dissonance-reducing behavior will be more marked in such cases. Festinger postulated that internal, private opinion change will thus be more likely to take place in low duress, compliant behavior situations, than in high duress, compliant behavior situations. For in the latter instance the magnitude of the duress, itself, is sufficiently consonant with the cognition of counterattitudinal behavior. In nontechnical language, the greater duress is perceived as more than sufficient justification for complying with the demand for a particular behavior. Where duress is lower, the individual is "not sure" the duress justified the compliance and begins to justify his action is not really countervolitional. Subsequent work in dissonance theory has included a substantial number of experiments that tested the forced-compliance corollaries. For example, students were asked to write a counterattitudinal essay. Those given the larger reward experienced least dissonance and least attitudinal change. Those given markedly smaller rewards modified their previous attitudes to a much larger extent. There have been vigorous critiques of the compliant behavior experiments, but they do not destroy the larger principle of which it is a part; namely, that externalization of responsibility for an otherwise dissonant act, here duress, operates to reduce dissonance.

In these experimental situations the price of compliance was exact. The experimenter offered X dollars. The subject who retained any touch with reality could not reduce dissonance by perceiving $1.50 as $20. Dissonance reduction, if it were to take place at all, then, had to be through some other avenue such as attitudinal change. In more complex situations, however, sanctions may be vague, contingent, or uncertain. This area of haziness leaves open dissonance reduction through change in the perception of the sanctions. Thus, the common phenomenon of a man who gives in to force, exaggerating the extent of danger in order to better justify his having given in. For a review of the literature in dissonance theory through 1969, see Zajonc, "cognitive theories in social psychology" in Gardner Lindzay and Elliot Aronson, eds., *Handbook of Social Psychology,* 2d ed., (Reading, Mass.: Addison-Wesley Publishing Co., 1970), vol. 1, Chap. 5, pp. 359–411. See also E. Aronson, "The Theory of Cognitive Dissonance: A Current Perspective," in L. Berkowitz, ed., *Advances in Experimental Social Psychology* (New York: Academic Press, 1969), vol. 4, Chap. 1. I suspect that work currently underway by Professor Irving Janis will provide a far more subtle and useful theoretical framework in which to place the data assembled here, though I am not sure it will affect the hypotheses presented herein.

2   Festinger, *A Theory of Cognitive Dissonance,* p. 18.

3   Brehm and Cohen, *Explorations in Cognitive Dissonance.*

4   Ibid. See also Festinger's fromulation, *Theory of Cognitive Dissonance,* p. 266: "The maximum dissonance which can exist between two elements is equal to the resistance to change of the less resistant of the two elements."

5   Festinger, *Theory of Cognitive Dissonace,* pp. 32–47. Festinger also attempts a list of quantification variables: importance of decision, relative attractiveness of choices, degree of overlap of cognitive elements:

Once dissonance exists following a decision, the pressure to reduce it will manifest itself in attempts to increase the relative attractiveness of the chosen alternative, to decrease the relative attractiveness of the unchosen alternative to establish cognitive overlap. . . . (p. 47)

6   Ibid., pp. 37–38.

7   See Chapter 8, supra.

8   *Miller v. McQuerry,* 17 F. Cas. 332 (No. 9,583) (C.C. Ohio, 1853), p. 339.

9   A classic critique of this model of interpretation is Thomas Reed Powell's, *Vagaries and Varieties of Constitutional Interpretation* (New York: Columbia University Press, 1955).

10   See, pp. 249—52, infra.

11   See, pp. 252–56, infra.

12   Compare *Prigg v. Pennsylvania* 41 U.S., (16 Pet.) 539 (1841), pp. 610–11, with Story, *Commentaries on the Constitution,* 1833 ed. (Boston: Hilliard, Gray & Co.; Cambridge, Mass.: Brown, Shattuck & Paul, 1833), 1 : 383–86.

13   *Norris v. Newton,* 18 F. Cas. 322 (No. 10,307) (C.C.D. Ind., 1850), p. 324.

14   For Story, see letter to Ezekial Bacon, William Wetmore Story, *Life and Letters of Joseph Story* (Boston: C. C. Little and J. Brown, 1851), 2 : 430–31. For McLean, see portions of two letters reproduced from McLean Manuscript, Library of Congress, in Appendix.

15   For a modern biographical treatment of Story, see Gerald Dunne, *Joseph Story* (New York: Simon & Schuster, 1970). Still useful is W. W. Story, *Life and Letters of Joseph Story.* For Story's impact as a teacher, see Arthur Sutherland, *The Law at Harvard* (Cambridge, Mass.: Belknap Press of Harvard University Press, 1967).

16   See *Life and Letters.* See also the many unpublished letters of Story in the Mas-

sachusetts Historical Society Manuscripts. There are also letters between McLean and Story in the McLean Manuscripts, Library of Congress, that intimate a set of common professional problems with respect to the tenor of the Taney Court, though the letters show explicit caution about putting anything on paper. See, e.g., Story to McLean, April 17, 1843: "I have many, many things to talk over with you, not only respecting the court, but respecting public men and public measures, which it is impracticable for one to put on paper" (McLean Manuscripts, Library of Congress). On February 9, 1843, Story wrote to McLean that he had "seldom been more pained" than at the shabby treatment afforded Peters, the Court reporter. For this controversy, see Dunne, *Story,* pp. 422–23.

17 On Story and slavery, see Dunne, *Story,* pp. 393–402. See also M. Dowd, "Justice Joseph Story and the Slavery Conflict," 52 *Massachusetts Law Quarterly* 239 (1967), pp. 242–46.

18 For the Story-Sumner relationship, see Dunne, *Story, passim* pp. 317 to end. See also David Donald, *Charles Sumner and the Coming of the Civil War* (New York, Knopf & Co., 1960). For the Phillips relationship, see the interesting headnote in Van Vechlen Veeder, ed., *Great Legal Masterpieces* (St. Paul, Minn.: Keefe-Davidson Co., 1903), 2 : 777.

19 W. W. Story, *Life and Letters,* 2 : 381–98 and Dunne, *Story,* p. 402.

20 See Chapter 6, supra, notes 21 ff.

21 *Prigg v. Pennsylvania,* 41 U.S. (16 Pet.) 539 (1841), pp. 610–14, McLean dissent on p. 658.

22 W. W. Story, *Life and Letters,* 2 : 317, and see Samuel Shapiro, *Richard Henry Dana, Jr.,* (East Lansing: Michigan State University Press, 1961), p. 10.

23 Donald, *Charles Sumner,* p. 30.

24 The *Liberator,* Sept. 11, 1846, and Sept. 18, 1846.

25 Veeder, *Legal Masterpieces,* p. 777.

26 McLean deserves much better in the way of judicial biography. The one full-length treatment, Francis Weisenburger, *The Life of John McLean, A Politician on the Supreme Court of the United States* (Columbus, Ohio: Ohio State University Press, 1937), is mediocre. Though buttressed with much digging and usually reliable information, the work is unimaginative and reveals little of the intricacies of the judicial career. Chapter 13, "Slavery and Dred Scott," is useful as a beginning. Except where otherwise noted, biographical details rely on Weisenburger.

27 *Ohio v. Carneal,* Ervin H. Pollack, ed., *Ohio Unreported Decisions Prior to 1823* (Indianapolis: A. Smith Co., 1952), p. 133, at p. 139 [Hereafter cited as *Pollack.*]

28 Weisenburger, *John McLean,* p. 7. John McLean, *A Sketch of the Life of Rev. John Collins* (Cincinnati: Swormstedt & Power, 1849); John McLean, *A Sketch of Rev. Philip Gatch* (Cincinnati: Swormstedt & Poe, 1856).

29 *Ohio v. Carneal, Pollack,* p. 139.

30 See Chapter 10, supra, note 34, and authorities cited therein.

31 See notes 35 ff., infra.

32 Weisenburger, *John McLean,* pp. 101–103.

33   The McLean Manuscripts are full of correspondence about the Justice's decision
     whether to accept the cabinet post or remain on the bench. Daniel Webster,
     writing in part as advocate for the administration of which he was a part, ac-
     knowledged that the reasons for remaining on the Court were perhaps equally
     persuasive. He recognized loyalty to Story and to the kind of institution Story
     exemplified as a powerful force. See, e.g., "Webster to McLean," Sept. 11,
     1841, McLean Manuscripts, Library of Congress: "When I think of the Court—
     and Judge Story—my mind balances on one side—when I think of the success
     of President Tyler's administration, it gets a strong lean the other way."

34   Weisenburger, *John McLean,* p. 198.

35   For the McLean-Chase relationship, see Robert Warden, *Salmon P. Chase* (Cin-
     cinnati: Wilstach, Baldwin & Co., 1874), pp. 246, 294–308; Weisenburger,
     John McLean, pp. 122, 132–35.

36   *Jones v. Van Zandt,* 13 F. Cas. 1,040 (No. 7,501) (C.C.D. Ohio, 1843) [charge
     to jury]; 13 F. Cas. 1047 (No. 7,502) (C.C.D. Ohio, 1843) [motion for new
     trial]; 13 F. Cas. 1,054 (No. 7,503) (C.C.D. Ohio, 1849) [demurrer to *scire
     facias*]; 13 F. Cas. 1,057 (No. 7,505) (C.C.D. Ohio, 1851) [motion in arrest of
     judgment]. Aff'd. 46 U.S. (5 How.) 215 (1847).

37   Chase's argument may be deduced in part from the admonitions of McLean, in
     part from the nature of his argument before the Supreme Court; Salmon P.
     Chase, *Argument for the Defendant, Submitted to the Supreme Court of the
     United States in the Case of Wharton Jones v. John Van Zandt* (Cincinnati,
     1847), and in part from the very sketchy manuscript notes of Justice McLean,
     himself. See McLean Manuscripts, Library of Congress (Reel 14, Container
     21).

38   *Jones v. Van Zandt* (I) 13 F. Cas. 1,040 (No. 7,501), p. 1045.

39   *Jones v. Van Zandt* (II) 13 F. Cas. 1,047 (No. 7,502), p. 1,048.

40   Both quotations are from a letter from Chase to Charles Sumner, dated Feb. 19,
     1848, in *Assoc. Diary and Correspondence of Salmon P. Chase,* vol. 2 of the
     Annual Report of the American Historical Association, 1902 (Washington,
     1903), p. 131.

41   S. P. Chase to Charles Sumner, Sept. 3, 1853, ibid., p. 252.

42   Reverend Jona Wald to J. McLean 1850; John McLean to Rev. Jona Wald, 10
     November 1850; Joshua Blanchard to John McLean, 29 August 1953; E. H.
     Pilcher to John McLean, 9 September 1853; John McLean to E. H. Pilcher, 9
     September 1853. All in McLean Manuscripts, Library of Congress.

43   McLean to Wald, 10 November 1850, McLean Manuscripts, Library of Con-
     gress.

44   Ibid.

45   L. Levy, *The Law of the Commonwealth and Chief Justice Shaw,* pp. 59–108.

46   *Sate v. Post,* 20 N.J.L. 368 (1845), pp. 376–77.

47   See, e.g., the *Liberator,* Nov. 4, 1842. The most effusive attacks on the judi-
     ciary were printed in the *Latimer Journal and North Star,* which continued to
     publish for a time after the crisis. That "journal" is not readily available. The
     copy I consulted is in the Massachusetts Historical Society, Manuscripts collec-

tions. The *Latimer Journal,* published by nonlawyers, reflects only a hazy notion of what was and was not within the ambit of a creative judicial stroke. The *Liberator* is a more "pure" Garrisonian expression, as it is more than willing to concede, arguendo, all of Shaw's legal and factual premises, yet hold him to a moral standard that would then mandate resignation.

48 Ibid.

49 Levy suggests otherwise. I have not quantified adverse references, but it is my distinct impression that Story is more gently treated in the *Liberator* and the *Latimer Journal.* See Levy, *Law of the Commonwealth,* p. 85.

50 See Levy, *Law of the Commonwealth,* p. 91 and Shaw's opinion in *Sim's Case* 61 Mass. (7 Cush.) 285 (1851).

51 For railroads, see Levy, *Law of the Commonwealth,* pp. 118–165. Especially interesting is the famous case *Norway Plains Co. v. Boston and Maine R.R.,* 67 Mass. (1 Gray) 236 (1854). In terms of labor law, I have in mind *Commonwealth v. Hunt,* 45 Mass. (4 Metc.) 111 (1842), concerning which see W. Nelles, "Commonwealth v. Hunt," 32 *Columbia Law Review* 1128 (1932) and Levy, pp. 185–207. For torts, see *Brown v. Kendall,* 60 Mass. (6 Cush.) 292 (1850) and the discussion of it in Oliver Wendell Holmes, *The Common Law,* Howe ed. (Boston: Little, Brown, 1963), pp. 84–86; for criminal law, see, e.g., *Fisher v. McGirr* 67 Mass. (1 Gray) 1 (1854) discussed by Levy, pp. 283 ff.; for church-state relations see *Stebbins v. Jennings,* 27 Mass. (10 Pick.) 172 (1830), *Commonwealth v. Kneeland,* 37 Mass. (20 Pick.) 206 (1838). Both of these cases evoke from me little agreement as to substance. But they do exhibit the boldness of the Llewellyn model.

52 Levy, *Law of the Commonwealth,* pp. 98–101.

53 The *Liberator,* Nov. 4, 1842, contains a "report" of Shaw's opinion. It is not officially reported.

54 Herman Melville, *Billy Budd,* Hayford-Sealts ed., p. 129.

55 *Typee* (New York: Wiley & Putnam), Melville's first novel, was published in 1846. It is dedicated: "To Lemuel Shaw, Chief Justice of the Commonwealth of Massachusetts. This Little Work is Affectionately Inscribed by the Author."

56 There is no biography of Joseph Swan. Useful biographical sketches include: *DAB;* "In Memoriam," 42 Ohio State Reports, v–x; George Reed, *Bench and Bar of Ohio* (Chicago: Century Pub. & Engraving Co., 1897), 1 : 109–14; *Ohio State Bar Association Reports* (1885), Vol. 5; and, most useful, the biographical essay by J. W. Andrews, "Joseph Rockwell Swan," affixed as a prefatory statement in modern editions of Swan's *Treatise on the Law Relating to the Powers and Duties of Justices of the Peace in Ohio,* 27th ed. (Cincinnati: W. H. Anderson Co., 1930), pp. v–xvi. [Hereafter cited as *Treatise on the J.P..*] Also very useful concerning reaction to Swan's part in *Bushnell* is Eric Foner, *Free Soil, Free Labor, Free Men* (New York: Oxford University Press, 1970), p. 137.

57 The *Treatise on the J.P.,* note 56, was first published in 1837. In 1845 and 1850, he published two volumes on *The Practice in Civil Actions and Proceedings at Law in Ohio* (Columbus, Ohio: Whiting, 1845), and *Precedents in*

Pleading (Cincinnati: Whiting, 1850). In 1860, after leaving the bench, he published *Commentaries on Pleading Under the Ohio Code, with Precedents of Petitions* (Cincinnati: R. Clarke & Co., 1861). (He also served as revisor for Ohio Statutes in 1841, 1854, 1860, and 1868.) See *DAB*, p. 235.

58   See 42 Ohio State Reports, p. vi. See also Foner, *Free Soil*, p. 137.

59   *Anderson v. Poindexter*, 6 Ohio St. 622 (1856), pp. 639 ff.

60   Chapter 11, supra, notes 39–42.

61   *Booth* was decided by the Supreme Court of the United States on March 7, 1859. The decision of the Ohio Court in *Bushnell* was rendered on May 30, 1859, in outline form only. The syllabus of the opinion is reported in Jacob Shipherd's delightful *History of the Oberlin-Wellington Rescue* (Boston: J. P. Jewett & Co., 1859), pp. 225–26. And it does not mention *Booth* or seem to refer to it. Yet, according to Shipherd's report, the arguments of counsel on May 29 include several references to *Booth*, pp. 222, 223, 224. And see p. 217: "But I am reminded that the *Prigg* case has since been twice affirmed by this same Court [U.S. Sup. Ct.] in the Jones and VanZandt and the Booth case." The reported decision of Swan, 9 Ohio State Reports 77, p. 186, refers to *Booth* but without exact styles or page citation.

62   For a full description of the tenor of times in Ohio, see William Cochrane, *The Western Reserve and the Fugitive Slave Law*, Pub. No. 101, Western Reserve Historical Society, (Cleveland, 1920). See also Foner, *Free Soil*, p. 137.

63   9 Ohio St., pp. 308–310.

64   Ibid., p. 228.

65   Ibid., p. 198.

66   Ibid., pp. 198–99.

67   J. Andrews, "Joseph Rockwell Swan," in *Treatise on the J.P.*, p. xvi.

INDEX